AFFIXES

IN

THEIR ORIGIN AND APPLICATION,

EXHIBITING THE

ETYMOLOGIC STRUCTURE

OF

ENGLISH WORDS.

BY

S. S. HALDEMAN, A.M.

PHILADELPHIA:
PUBLISHED BY E. H. BUTLER & CO.
1865.

Electrotyped by L. Johnson & Co., Philadelphia.
Printed by Sherman & Co.

PREFATORY

THE number of English monosyllables is about 3200, and as many of these are not primitives, but have a prefix, a suffix, or both, it is evident that the affixes must be concerned in the formation of the greatest part of the vast vocabulary of English words; and that an accurate knowledge of these is to be acquired through a distinct appreciation of the modes used to vary them in form and meaning, according to the exigencies of thought and speech.

Some languages, as Greek and Welsh, have their etymologic material within themselves, and most of their words may be analysed independently of other languages; but if this is attempted with a composite language like English, the resulting knowledge will be imperfect, as in supposing aque to mean *water* in the word *aqueduct*, where *-e* is the genitive case sign of ĂQVĂ water, AQVAE *of* water, the A having been lost in aqueduct. (See § 7.) If therefore we ignore Latin forms in words derived from Latin, our analysis will be unreliable, and the force of the derivatives may be obscured rather than elucidated.

Unless we know, not only the affixes as they appear in English, but their etymology also, it will not be apparent that the *c* of the suffix -cy may be due to an *i*, a *t*, an *s*, or an original *c* (cay;) and we may mistake one form for another, as -y for -ly after -l, as in oil-y, and idl-y, or un- in un-loose for the negative un- in un-fix. For such reasons it was determined that this volume should be strictly etymologic, and that collateral forms should be cited where they might be useful, as in determining whether the supinal *to* in 'to live' is the ordinary preposition *to*. Languages not akin to English have been sparingly quoted, but more to exhibit accidental coincidences and occasional borrowed forms, than to claim them as indicating a closer relationship. (See Obs. 2, under **-n** adj., p. 141; and **-n** noun plural, p. 143.)

In the summer of 1861, F. J. Furnival, Esq., the obliging secretary of the Philological Society of London, examined the manuscript of this volume and made several suggestions, among them the addition of -m as a diminutive. Various illustrative passages have been added subsequently, a feature which would have been made more prominent and varied, had it not been for the difficulty of consulting genuine editions of standard authors like Shakspere and Milton, on the western side of the Atlantic. Supposing that an extract illustrating the word *battle* were required from Pope, we find it given as 'battle' in an American edition (book 7, line 292,) whilst in the London edition of 1716 the line stands—

And bear thick Battel on my founding Shield.

In like manner, a spurious edition of Young has the word 'sprightly' towards the end of Night 1, which, in "A NEW EDITION Corrected by the Author." 1776, is thus given in a more etymologic form—

The ſpritely *lark*'s ſhrill matin wakes the morn; . . .

Except in the Introduction, illustrative extracts from authors as late as the year 1800, are printed in old style type, to distinguish earlier writers from those of the present century, even when a modern edition like Wright's Chaucer, is quoted. A few extracts have been taken from the dictionary of Richardson, an author who is not always consistent, since he occasionally gives the same passage differently, as in quoting Beattie under DEDENTITION and FERIE,—"for falling teeth."—"for falling the teeth, &c." Under ALOES and BIAS he thus quotes Holland's Plinie—

"of the sea onion, but it is bigger, . . . gross and fat, chamfered and channelled"—
"of a sea onion but that it is bigger . . . grosse and fat chamfered and chanelled" . . .

As the etymology of a word is independent of the modes of spelling it, it has not been deemed proper to follow the practice of those who give orthographic rules in treatises on the subject. What is commonly called etymologic spelling would require the rejection of English *w*, *sh*, *gh*, *y*, *ck*, and in many cases of *th;* it would require *stable* as a noun to be spelt stabul, and as an adjective stabil; the letter *l* to have a place in writing *as*, to be rejected from *could*, and doubled in *idolatry* and *tranquil;* *n* to be placed in *mill* as it is in *kiln;* the *e* to be retained in *line* but not in *pine;* and *g* removed from *sovereign* to be placed in *noble.*

An etymologic orthography would require an indication of long and short *o* in words from the Greek. *Antíphŏny* would have to be given up for *antiphōny*, because the former would mean 'an avenging of (φονή) murder,' and the latter 'a replying,' from φωνή voice. By shortening the *i* of *liturgy* we virtually refer it to λιτȣργέω, 'to speak with malice,' instead of λειτȣργέω, 'to perform public service;' and *Calliŏpe* (*Καλλῐόπη*) 'she who has a fine voice,' with *o* lengthened would mean 'she who has a fine eye.'

As etymologic orthography is assumed to be the spelling of words as their cognates or cognate parts are spelt in other languages, examples would appear in bwgcllyedr for *buckler*, cllyedheamhor for *claymore*, czar (Russian *Царь*) for *tsar*, and in the following lines (Trevelyan Prize Essay, § 14,) of English, with the words as they stand in other languages—

Srdce moy szarcze ach hui deos sadnissa!
Kard man hiort ag cuige diz sathinassus?

The stereotyping of this work was commenced in February 1864, and it was expected to be before the public at latest in September, but in the meantime Webster's Dictionary appeared in the autumn of 1864, rendering, for example, the note on **-ness** (page 13) inapplicable, this suffix being correctly given by Dr. Mahn.

Although Dr. Mahn's etymologies differ from some of those here given, it will probably be found that neither author is right in all cases, and that a number of those here given will bear the test of investigation, as bullock page 196, charlock 182, croup 51, decoy 56, flannel 67, foray (maraud, porbeagle) 254, hanger 147, hoiden 143, Lestris 232. Dr. Mahn refers laudanum to *labdanum*, which we had abandoned as unsatisfactory. Raccoon is not derived from the French *raton*, but from an aboriginal basis, and we regard reamer and its verb as due to German *pfriem* (with the same meaning) rather than to *room*.

These remarks are not intended to detract from the great merit of this distinguished scholar, the etymology of a language being beyond the powers of a single inquirer, and the science one of those where a conclusion apparently well founded, may be disproved by a citation from an obscure or unwritten dialect. The affixes alone present many difficulties, and the present attempt to elucidate them is sent forth with the hope that the subject may receive the attention necessary to explain the points which still remain unsettled.

COLUMBIA, PENNSYLVANIA,
February 18, 1865.

INTRODUCTION

ENGLISH is not a language which teaches itself by mere unreflecting usage. It can only be mastered, in all its wealth, in all its power, by conscious, persistent labor; and, therefore, when all the world is awaking to the value of general philological science, it would ill become us to be slow in recognizing the special importance of our own tongue.—*Geo. P. Marsh,* Lectures on the English Language, 1860.

§ 1 In this work the Affixes, both Prefixes and Suffixes, are given in their etymologic connections. For example, the Latin CŎN or CO, and Greek SYN or SY are referred to the same original, the former having the *c* and the latter the *s* of ξὺν (csȳn) *with;* hence *con-st-*ant and *sy-st*(ematic) have essentially the same prefix and root. Depriving sy-stem of its prefix, it appears as s t e m, from the idea of standing, a *sy*-stem being a setting or standing *with* each other, of things which have qualities in common.

2 Affixes are here separated from words commonly treated as primitives, as the *p* in yel-p, cro-p, ras-p, which are primarily nouns, formed from the verbs *yell*, *grow*, and *raze*, but used as new verbs as the language instinct disappears.

Some do not consider words like per-me-ate, per-for-ate, per-egri-n-ate, con-tam-in-ate, met-em-psych-osis, cli-m-ate, de-mur, con-fer, re-fer, in-fer, be-gin, a-mong, gol-d, and thousands more, as derivative words, presuming that their affixes constitute an essential part of the primitive word, or that the root portion does not constitute a separate word in English. It is stated in the "16th edition revised and improved" of the English Grammar of Robert Sullivan, LL.D., T.C.D., that "A primitive word cannot be reduced or traced to any simpler word in the language; as *man, good, content.*" Hence con*tent,* de*tent,* re*ten*tive, *ten*able, con-, re-, sus-, abs-, ob-*tain,* are each to be considered a primitive, although TEN- of the Latin TĔNĔ-O (I hold) is precisely the English *tain.* Such views require *teacher* to be called a derivative, but not its more Latin form *doctor;* whilst *poem* and *poet* are not to be viewed as derivatives from a common root.

A schoolbook gives per-son, tur-n, and tal-k, as radical words. Another gives bitt-er, da-te, dee-d, fic-s (fix) and sigh-t as "*primitive* words or *roots*" and its author expects the uninstructed pupil to determine whether words like ru-n, tur-n, nigh-t, gloo-m-y, un-fi-t, under-sta-nd, gol-den, fore-hea-d, col-d-ness, are radical or derivative, evidently considering *night, gloom, cold,* and *fit,* as underived words. Another author states that *fame* and *sense* "are primitive words, because they can be reduced to no fewer *letters,*" (compare *fam*ous and *sens*ible) "and convey a distinct idea of each thing specified." According to this, *sensorial* and *defamatory* would be primitives, as they cannot be reduced without altering the "idea of each thing specified."

3 Many affixes commonly given as simple, are here resolved into their constituents, and additional means to understand the nature of derivatives are afforded by the large increase of the number of affixes, about five hundred being admitted—but not for the purpose of exceeding the lists usually given, nor to exhaust the subject, for the numeral prefixes (as tri-, hexa-, octo-,) and many parts of compounds (as manu–, pleni–, arch–,) have not been inserted. Several of the more doubtful forms, and some which furnish but one or two examples, are omitted also.

4 Welsh, the ancient language of Britain, has exercised an influence upon English, and is quoted to explain a few forms, and to give an idea of word-building in a living language with a living etymology.

5 The accent in Greek, and the length of the syllables in Latin are marked, that the pupil may have the means of avoiding the errors so common upon these points.

6 Observations will be found upon collateral points, and exceptions are cited to induce a proper caution in the application of the knowledge acquired. For example, under -et (as in lock-et, a small lock,) owl-et is given as an exception.

7 Those false forms are avoided in which Latin and

Greek are perverted to make them resemble the English derived from them, as in referring equal to ĔQVŬS a horse, instead of to ÆQVUS equal.

8 Certain common, but improbable or impossible derivations are rejected, such as syntax from the nonradical present tense τάσσω (I place,) which cannot account for the cay of syn-tac-s (present in the participle ταξάμενος etc.)—escape from the French échapper, instead of the Provensal *escapar*;—hide (a skin) from the German *haut*;—crept from *creep*;—gave from *give*;—and would from *will*—

Wolt thou wedde þis maide, if ich wolle affente.—'*Piers Plouhman.*' Written about 1362.

I wol no woman thirty yere of age.—*Chaucer.* Born 1382.

9 The relation of deluge to DĪLŬVĬŬM is not obvious to the beginner; the reference of city to CĪVĬS (citizen) does not account for the *t*; δέω (I bind) does not account for the *p* of despot, nor GRĀNŬM (grain) for the *g* in grange. Unexplained points like these, and vague statements in regard to them, are numerous in educational books, and as a result, the pupil gets a superficial knowledge, indefinite ideas, and loose habits of language and thought, which he is likely to retain through life.

10 As the etymology of numerous words cannot be understood without some knowledge of the grammatic inflections which they follow, those inflections are given which have the greatest influence on the forms of English words.

11 To diminish the number of heads and to prevent repetition, a system of notation has been adopted, as in placing a small reference letter after sol-ace[a] and gr-ace[c] to refer the former to the Latin suffix -ĀTĬŬM[a] and the latter to -ĀTĬĂ[c] for their original forms, in case they should be required.

12 As the form of most words depends upon the modifying portion, the extent of our knowledge of their structure and value will depend in a great degree upon *the number of distinct modifying elements* or affixes we may be able to

determine and appreciate. But as these affixes are applied to different classes of words, and assume various disguises, it becomes necessary not only to know, for example, that on-ce is *one* with -ce, and toward-s *toward* with -s suffixed, but to be able to decide that these, and the *s* in thu-s, in ma*s*ter, and in sati*s*fy, constitute but one etymologic element; whilst the *s* of amne*s*ty, alm*s*, the*s*is, and A*s*ia forms a different one.

13 Instead of allowing a little knowledge of derivation to be the accidental result of the study of Greek and Latin, principles should be mastered first, or be studied simultaneously, as the proper basis for the study of language in general.

14 The Latin and Greek cited in the etymology of the affixes, will form a useful introduction to these languages, and will facilitate the acquisition of foreign languages in a wonderful degree.

15 *It is a common error* to suppose that pupils who do not study Latin and Greek, can acquire the power of analysing words from a dictionary; and that those who learn these languages get at the same time a competent knowledge of etymology. But as a distinct science, it requires a special study, both by those who do, and those who do not learn Greek and Latin, and a book of this kind will be found almost as useful to the college graduate as to the pupil whose studies have not been extended beyond his own vernacular.

15a Those unaccustomed to the analysis and discrimination of words have a vagueness of idea which is exemplified in the following attempts at definition, given by the members of a class who had been studying Greek and Latin for several years, but without having their attention directed to the etymologic bearings of their studies.

Annihilate—break up, drive away, reduce, demolish. See AD.

Annul—abolish, drive off, cut off, demolish.

Exterminate—put out, put an end to, decrease.

Eradicate—kill, extinguish, shoot, radiate. See EX.

Anniversary—a celebration.

Anodyne—something to cause sleep, medicine. See AN-.
Desperate—furious, fierce, wild, savage, ferocious, mad, uncontrollable, not to be trifled with. See DE ¶ 2.
Ligament—sinew, tendon, muscle.
Prevail—coax, ask, beg, compel, attack.
Ruminating—roaming, carrying burdens, useful, domestic.
Immense—great, large, very large, vast. See IN- *not.*
Protect—defend, guard, take care of, keep from. See TEGO.
Elucidate—explain, describe minutely.
Explain—show.
Regulate—put in order, put in place.
Definite—particular, true.
Extasy—joy, delight, excitement
Docile—gentle. See -ILE.

16 The parsing of a word in its syntactic relations is very different from its analysis with a view to ascertain its origin, the value of its component parts, and the history of its meanings. Thus better is the grammatic but not the etymologic comparative of *good.* Whiter is both a grammatic and an etymologic comparative. A false orthography (like that which places '*gh*' in the derivative 'might' which is not represented in its primitive 'may,') and a word formed on false principles (like 'spasmodic' instead of *spastic,*) are offenses against etymology, but not against grammar.

17 A book of this kind has been a desideratum in the *Analysis of Words,* and as an *Introduction to English Lexicography,* definitional and etymologic—the meagre outlines given in dictionaries and grammars presenting nothing approaching to completeness.*

18 We are of the opinion that there are not 300 roots in any language, and if this view is correct, a knowledge of the affixes which give form and meaning to 100,000 English words must be of extreme value, greatly diminishing the

* See the dictionaries at -ness, or Richardson at un-, -en, and -ish. Grammar, instead of discussing the meaning and origin of words, should explain the parts of speech, grammatic inflection, and the relations and functions of words in speech; and it should be taught from the more condensed treatises.

time devoted to the dictionary, and giving the inquirer the means of consulting it understandingly.

19 *Most of the new words* which figure in the successive editions of English Dictionaries, are old forms with the commoner affixes, as un-, in-, -ly, and -ness, in un-forgetable *Prof. Geo. Wilson;* in-culpative *Sydney Smith* 1802; semicircular-ly *Bulwer* 1841; branched-ness *Boyle* 1675. Webster is said to have added 12,000 words to Todd's Johnson; Ogilvie added perhaps 20,000 more in his Imperial Dictionary, Glasgow 1850, and Supplement of 1855; and Worcester* claims about 104,000 for his quarto of 1860. Yet, a portion of the memoranda of words met with in our own reading furnishes under the prefix un-, the following one hundred omitted words from as many authorities, each authority being restricted to a single example.

unabundant Prof. Geo. Wilson
unacclimatized E. W. L. Davis
unaffinitive N. York Herald 1855
un-antique W. H. Leeds
unappealed Democratic Rev. 1838
unarduous W. H. Herbert
unartistic Ed. Rev.; Atl. Mnly; Home J.
unattractiveness Once a Wk
unaxical Penny Cyc. 1841
unblenchingly Dr Latham 1857
unblundering Ferrand Spence 1686
uncadenced Mrs E. B. Browning
uncall *v. t.* Roberts, Collectanea Cambrica 1811
uncarbonized Wm Scoresby 1839
uncarting Chambers' J.
uncatalogued Murray's Handb.
unchangability (sic) J. Asiat. Soc. 1854
vnchased 'Golden Boke'
unchemical Emerson's Mag. 1858
unchewable Dr Kitchiner
unconformedly Jn Phillips, Cab. Cyc. 1839
uncontemplative Bulwer
uncrackable Saml. Woodworth 1836
undefecated Nat. Rev. 1857
undefinedly Thos Aird
undetectable Charles Lever

---

* Worcester (pronounced *Woostr*) has *unplanned* (from Ash, but not *unplaned* the second word from it,) *unbelievefulness*, *undumpish*, *unrenavigable*, *unwerred*, which are not in Webster. Ash has *unbudgeted*, *unbundled*, *uncrinkled*, *undandled*, *undrubbed*, *uneffectuated*, *unelutriated*, *unencaved*, *uninterleaved*, and others, which Worcester, Webster, and Richardson have not admitted. Barclay in his Dictionary of 1772, contents himself with defining un-, without giving a single word under it. Richardson (Dict. 1837) omits *unfixedly* and *unrhyming*, altho the former is used by himself at DANGLE, and the latter occurs in a passage quoted from Byrom at COXCOMB.

undevotionality H. W. Bellows
undisfigured Brande's Dict. 1843
undistrest W. Wordsworth
unecclesiastical Sydney Smith 1831
unedible Hugh Miller
unembellishing Nsp. 1852
unescapable Lond. Econmst 1857
uneulogized Tr. of Duchess d'Abrantes 1854
unexceptionally O. W. Holmes
unexpansiveness Fr. W. Newman 1852
unfacetious Peacock, Crotchet Castle 1831
unfallacious A. B. Johnson 1854
unfine John Poole 1859
unfinish *n.* U. Kn. Gall. Portraits 1835; R. N. Wornum.
unforgivingness F. W. Faber 1853
ungaudy Moore, British Ferns 1849
ungenerosity Lond. Register 1860
ungenuineness Chrst. Examnr
ungravitating Rafinesque 1836
unhallowedly Wm. Howitt 1833
unharassing Ch. Lamb
unhartinesse John Cockburn 1735
unheralded Sthrn Q. R. 1857
unhesitatingness N. P. Willis
unhorsemanship Lond. News
unidead (sic) 'Warreniana'
unidealised Q. Rev.; **-ized** Mrs Ellet 1859
unimmediate Bentham 1826
unindoctrinated N. Br. Rev.
uninterfered H. T. Tuckerman
unissued Am. Railw. Rev.
unlichened Ruskin
unmathematical Phil. Mag.
unmercurialized J. W. Draper
unmisgivingly Laman Blanchard 1849
unmolesting Arnott's Physics 1829; Sharon Turner 1832
unmotived J. Am. Or. Soc.
unmummied Byron 1822
unnigger *v.* Sir Fr. Head 1851
unobsolete Leigh Hunt
unobstructable Knickrb. M. 1854
unorganizable Wstm. Rev. 1859
unpartaken 'Peter's Letters to his Kinsfolk' 1820
unpicturesqueness Home Jour. 1857
unpopularise Earl Ellsmere
unpraiseable Albert Smith
unproceeding Thos. Taylor 1824
unprotestant H. Harbaugh 1850
unpuritan Thos. Hancock 1859
unquakerly Chas. Mackay 1859
unquotable 'Punch'
unrefracting Gilfillan 1850
unscabbarded Sir W. Scott
unsensitive Atlnt. Mnthl. 1859
unsociality Wm. Hazlitt
unspellable Lond. Sport. M.
unstinting Jas. Sh. Knowles 1838
unstrap Miss Leslie 1853 **-ped** Nat. Misc. 1854
unstriped fibres Dr Jos. Leidy 1851
unstuccoed Ill. Guide to London
unsucceeding Boyle 1675
unsyllabled Motherwell
unsympathised Mnthl. Repos.
untactical Ill. Lond. News
untampered Aytoun 1856
unthoughtedly H. W. Beecher
untrophied Mrs. Sigourney 1834
ununiformd Th. S. Grimké 1834
unvaryingly Fraser's Mag.
unwardable 'Dow Jr.'
unwastable (sic) Literary Churchman 1859
unweighable Hsld. Wrds
unworsted Robert Walpole
unzoological Blkw. Mag. 1857

§ 20 The extent to which words are formed and modified by the aid of affixes is shown by the number of words belonging to the richest prefixes, suffixes, and roots, as in the following approximations:—

Prefixes.		*Roots.*		*Suffixes.*	
un-	5,600	**fact, face**	640†	**-ly**	2,000
co- con-*	2,400	**stand**	440	**-ion**	1,900
in- im-	2,900	**pos**ition	300	**-ness**	1,300
re-	2,200	**graph**ic	200	**-al**	1,000
di- dis-	1,800	**log**ic	200	**-er**	950
e- ex-	1,750	**ply**	200	**-ous**	900
ad-	1,600	**cap**able	190	**-ble**	800
de-	1,600	**drag**	190	**-ity**	650
sub-	700	de**tain**	180	**-ary** &c.	600
pre-	700	ad**mit**	175	**-$^{a}_{e}$nce**	600
pro-	600	**aspect**	175	**-$^{a}_{e}$nt**	500
per-	350	e**vid**ent	160	**-ive**	400
	22,200		3,050		11,600

21 Without special inquiry we can have but little idea of the comparative frequency of affixes, and in constructing this table we had at first included a-, ab-, abs-, which modify but 300 English words, and excluded di-, dis-, which enter into 1800.

22 The use of affixes in building up words is shown in the following examples based upon the root FAC (make)—

fac-t (-ion)	ef-**face**	ef-**fic**-aci-ous
fea-t (-ure)	pro-**fi**-t	in-de-**fea**-s-ibil-ity
fic-t-ion	counter-**fei**-t	of-**fic**-er
im-per-**fec**-t	de-**fec**-t-ive-ness	bene-**fic**-iall-y

To the Teacher.

23 *The Teacher will observe* that, besides the examples explained, others are added without explanation, some of which can be solved by inspection, as cord-age, whilst others, as badin-age, cannot be determined, even with the aid of a dictionary. These are given as examples of the affixes, rather than the stems to which they are affixed, and classes need not be required to study or enumerate them. But the originals of

* This includes com-; sub- includes suf- &c.

† An actual enumeration of the derivatives of *fac* (excluding *fac*-e) gave 604, but they were not counted from the more recent dictionaries.

many of these (as de-press, de-grade) will be found in the Vocabulary at the end of the Suffixes.

24 *The collateral forms* of the prefixes are often given to show that they are widely diffused; but whilst it is not necessary to learn, for example that un- is equally un- in Hindoostanee, and an- in Welsh and Irish, it is of importance to know that languages so dissimilar may have features in common, derived from a common ancestry in remote antiquity.

25 *Conventional Latin* is often pronounced in a mode which lessens its utility for etymologic purposes, because etymology, besides showing the *resemblance* between words, exhibits the degree of *variation* to which they have been subjected. Hence if Latin Cay in ĀCĔR or ĀCRĬS (keen, bold,) is pronounced like *s* in a "Latin" recitation, it should, in an *etymologic* recitation, have its *Latin* power, or its derivative *eager* will be an older word, a *gay* or *cay* sound being older than an *s* sound in cognate words; for *It is not the letters, but the sounds used in speech, which furnish the material for etymology.* The French *bagage* is different from the English *baggage* (or *bagage,*) but identic with the Polish *bagaż.*

26 As the ancient is beginning to replace the empiric pronunciation of Latin in our colleges, it is the more necessary that the pupils should be acquainted with it, whether they use it or not. Although as a *Latin* name CÆSĂR (*καῖσᾰρ*) has a genuine cay, an *s* (as in *sard*) and the diphthong in *aisle,* it need not be pronounced in this manner in *English* discourse; nor must words which accord with the laws of modern speech be perverted to accommodate the orthography, pronunciation, or meaning, of the cognate word in other languages:—*thin* must remain *thin,* although it is d ü n n in German and TĔNŬĬS in Latin.

27 As the Greek affixes are given in Roman typography, and as they are not numerous, a knowledge of the Greek letters is not essential; nevertheless, as an etymologic dictionary cannot be used without them, and as they are much used in mathematics and astronomy, the Greek alphabet should be acquired. This can be done in two or three lessons, or by using the alphabet as a key to learn the Greek words as they occur.

28 The alphabetic arrangement made it necessary to indicate affinities by references from one head to another, and when this is to later portions of the book, the pupil need not be required to follow the reference; nor need he search for the value of *-ic,* should he find a word like chimer-ic-al under the head -AL, until he passes through the book the second time.

29 *The teacher will determine* what parts are to be known thoroughly, and what may be merely read over, or omitted, whether in the Introduction, the Affixes, or the Vocabulary. In general, a knowledge of from *one* to *six* examples under each head will be sufficient. The words to be learned should be pointed out, and several additional examples asked for under heads like ab-, con-, de-, di-, sub-, re-, un, -ant, -er, -ful, -ile, -ing, -ous, -ness, -ive, -ly.

LATIN ALPHABET.

§ 30 The Latin Alphabet is composed of the following twenty letters—A B C D E F G H I L M N O P Q R S T V X; and of these, nine had the same power as in English, namely, B D F H N P Q T X.

C and G (named *cay* and *gay* by the Romans) were always pure, as in *car*, *celt*, *sceptic*, *scheme*, *get*, *give*; and never corrupt, as in *cent*, *gem*.

I when a vowel, as in f*i*eld; when a consonant, as in coll*i*er, or *y* in *year*, but the latter is distinguished in most modern books by having the base of the character turned to the left 'J.'

31 M as in English, except as a final, when it nasalises the preceding vowel, as in its derivatives in the Portuguese *bom* (good) or French *nom* (name.)

Hence in Latin poetry, as -UM &c. is U made nasal, it is treated like a pure vowel and elided in poetry before another vowel, as in BĔLLŪM ĪNGĒNS (a great war,) read BELL' INGENS, as FŌRTŪNĂ ĪNGĒNS (great fortune,) is read FORTUN' INGENS. In these pages nasal vowels are mostly printed as in BELLU^{m}. Those who cannot pronounce a nasal vowel may use a slight *m*, which is better than to confound the French nasality with English *ng*.

N has two powers, the first in *no*, the second in *angle*. The latter occurs in all cases before C, G, X, Q.

Q is a duplicate of C and indicates that the V (*oo*) which follows it has the consonant power of *w* in *well*, and not the vowel power in *ooze*.

R requires to be trilled.

S has its Spanish power, as in *hiss*, not as in *rose*, *miser*, *sure*, *mission*.

T always as in *tea*, NĀ-TĬ-O (nâ-tee-o, nation.)

32 V has a vowel power as in *rule*, and a consonant power as in *quart*.

U' is commonly (but not always) used for the former, and 'V' for the latter, as in Anglosaxon.

L is the only Latin letter about the power of which there is doubt, and to this the ancient grammarian Prisc^k^ian assigns three powers, the first being heard in ĬLLĔ (he,) the second in FLĀVŬS (yellow,) and the third in LE·CTŬS (a bed.)

33 Latin, like Italian, has consonants doubled, *nn* in CŌNNĔCTO being pronounced as in *one name*, *ll* in ĀLLĒGŎRĬĂ as in *all-loving*, *mm* in ĪMMŌRTĀLĬS as in *some man*, *drum-major*, and other English compounds.

34 The vowels have each a long (¯) a short (˘) or a common (≚ long or short) quantity, the last being often left unmarked. A long vowel (or syllable) is twice the length of a short one, and has the same quality, as in English *o*, which is long in *own*, *oh*, and short in *oath*, *obey*, without falling into the vowel of *moth*, *object*. A syllable is commonly "long by position" when a vowel is followed by two consonants. We often mark such a vowel with a dot. A vowel before another is commonly short. Diphthongs are long.

35 The *power* and *name* of the Latin vowels are as in the following English words—

A is *long* in	ārm,	*short* in	ărt,	never as in	ăt
E	"	thēy,	"	ĕight,	" ĕbb
I	"	fīeld,	"	deceĭt,	" ĭt
O	"	ōh,	"	ŏbey,	" ŏx
U	"	fōōl,	"	fŭll,	" ŭp

36 The diphthongs are combinations of two sounds each of which, according to Prisc^k^ian, must be pronounced. The first letter (as A in AE or Æ, and O in OE or Œ) has its ordinary Latin power, whilst the second must have such a modification as to allow the combination to form a single syllable. Thus *cloy* has, and *claw-y* has not a diphthong; and if *showy* and *clayey* were monosyllables, they would contain the Latin Œ and EI or EJ. Æ and Œ occur in the Portuguese p a e (a stick) and o e t o or o i t o (eight;) and

Shanghae (-high) is a Portuguese orthography. EI occurs in the Spanish l e y (law,) and AV in the Danish h a v n (a haven, rhyming with *town*,) and German b r a u n (brown,) h a u s (house,) m a u s (mouse.)

37 The following detached lines are from "Living Latin," London, 1847—

"The French, Italians, Spanish, Portuguese,
As did the Romans, sound their several Is. . .
"If its [M final] exact validity you seek,
You must with care observe a Frenchman speak,
Whose nasal sound without a question shows
Its power when any word with M did close. . .
"But who amongst us sounds the Latin V?
Echo the question only softens—Who? . . .
"The Latin diphthongs most in common use
Are Æ and Œ and AV; and to produce
Their proper sounds, you only have to turn,
And those of their component parts to learn.
Thus if you to the first this rule apply,
My rhyme will aid you to pronounce it Æ . . .
"And of the next I say the same, if you
Blend into one the Latin A and V,
(And this to be correct you must allow,)
You will not mispronounce the Latin AV."
To these we add, that English words like *showy*
Contain the Portuguese and Latin Œ.

38 The accent of Latin falls upon the second and third syllables from the end, in dissyllables always on the former, and in words of three or more syllables on the latter, unless the second from the end is long, when that takes the accent.

---

39 GREEK ALPHABET.

Figure.	Name.	Power.	As in	Figure.	Name.	Power.	As in
Α α	ἄλφα	a	*a*rm, *a*rt	Η η	ἦτα	ē	th*e*re
Β ϐ β	ϐῆτα	b	*b*ay	Θ θ ϑ	θῆτα	th	*th*in
Γ γ	γάμμα	g	*g*ivin*g*	Ι ι	ἰῶτα	i	f*i*eld
Δ δ	δέλτα	d	*d*ell	Κ κ	κάππα	k	*k*ing
Ε ε ϵ	ἒ ψῖλόν	ĕ	*e*psom	Λ λ	λάμϐδα	l	*l*amb
F '		h	*h*arm	Μ μ	μῦ	m	*m*oon
Ζ ζ	ζῆτα	zd	wis*d*om	Ν ν	νῦ	n	*n*oon

Figure.	Name.	Power.	As in	Figure.	Name.	Power.	As in
Ξ ξ	ξῖ	cs	*axis*	Υ Y υ	υ ψῖλὸν	y	[Danish.]
O ο	ὂ μικρὸν	ŏ	ŏ-bey	Φ φ φ	φῖ	ph	
Π π ϖ	πῖ	p	*p*ea	X χ	χῖ	ch	[German.]
P ρ ρ [ῥ]	ῥω	r	[*rh* Welsh.]	Ψ ψ	ψῖ	ps	ecli*ps*e
Σ σ ς	σίγμα	s	*s*eek	Ω ω	ὦ μέγα	ō	*o*wn
T τ 7	ταῦ	t	*t*ower				

40 ʽ SPĪRĬTŬS ĀSPĔR (rough breathing) is placed as in ὁ (read *ho*) *the*, οὗ (read *hō-w* or *hoo*) *where*. The ʼ SPĪRĬTŬS LĒNĬS (smooth breathing) indicates the absence of the initial rough breathing, as in the English *owe*. Some authors omit it. These and the accent marks are placed over the second letter of the diphthongs.

As *zd* has a single character ζ, so its cognate *st* is often written with ϛ, as in ἄϛρον or ἄστρον (astron) *a star*.

The character σ is initial and medial, and ς final, as in στάσις *firmness*.

The characters E, H, P, X, have not the same power in Greek and Latin.

Γ, γ, ɼ, before γ, κ, ξ, χ, has the power of ng in *sing*, as in ἄɼκυλος *curved*, Latin ĂNGŬLUS *angle*. In these pages this power will be represented by ɼ.

P, ρ, ρ, is the trilled Latin R; ῥ the whispered aspirate Welsh *rh*.

Φ, φ, phi is not F, being made by the contact of both lips, as in blowing.

Y, *Υ*, υ, is German *ü* and French *u*, a sound between Latin U and I. It was not thus pinched in the Aeolic dialect, nor as the last element of the diphthongs.

X, χ, is the German (Latin) Polish &c. *ch*.

41 Diphthongs—αι as in aisle; οι nearly like *oi* in *going*, *owe-ing*, ωι the same, but longer; ηι nearly as in *clayey*; ει like ηι but with the vowel of *get*, or as *e* and *y* in *get-ye*; αυ like *ow* in *brown*; ου, ȣ properly like *o-w* in *no-wonder*, but it was corrupted at an early day to Latin U, French *ou*, Eng-

lish *oo* in *too*, its power in Modern Greek. The former diphthongal power (for which the spelling was made) is the best, and it aids etymology, as in βοῦς *ox*, Latin genitive BŎV-ĬS *of an ox*, where υ corresponds with V (*oo*, English *w*,) as in ναῦ-ς, NĀV-ĬS *ship*.

42 Greek accent is of three kinds, the acute (′) which is the principal, the grave (‵) and the circumflex (ˆ ˜), the differences not being well understood. The marks show what syllable is to be accented—and that a final syllable may be accented, wherein it differs from Latin. Circumflexed vowels are always long.

GRAMMAR

43 *Conjugation* is the inflexion of verbs. Most Latin verbs end in -o (Greek -ω) in the first person singular number of the indicative mood present tense, as ĂMO *I love*, of which the root is ĂM. The infinitive mood *to love* adds -RĔ to the stem AMA, forming the infinitive ĂMĀRĔ *to love*. The infinitive sign of the 1st conjugation is -Ā-, of the 2d -Ē-, of the 3d -Ĕ-, and of the 4th -Ī-.

44 The Latin dictionaries give the present tense, as ĂMO *I love* (often loosely defined by *to love*,) and with it, either the infinitive, or a numeral, 1, 2, 3, or 4, to indicate the conjugation to which the verb belongs. To these are added the perfect tense, as ĂMĀVĪ *I have loved*, and the verbial noun called the first supine, as AMATUM *to love* (in order to love.) Other inflexions must be looked for in the grammar, as the second supine ĂMĀTŪ *to be loved;* the participles, present ĂMĀNS *loving*, future ĂMĂTŪRŬS *about to be loving;* ĂMĀTŬS *loved;* ĂMĀNDŬS *to be loved;* gerund (a kind of noun) ĂMĀNDŪM *loving*, ĂMĀNDĪ *of loving*, as—CŬPĬDŬS ĂMĀNDĪ *desirous of loving*.

§ 45 The four conjugations are thus distinguished—

Conjugations,	1	2	3	4
Infinitive,	-ĀRĔ	-ĒRĔ	-ĔRĔ	-ĪRĔ
Perfect,	-ĀVĪ	-ĒVĪ	-Ī	-ĪVĪ
Supine,	-ĀTŬm	-ĒTŬm	-ĬTŬm	-ĪTŪm
Part. passive,	-ĀTŬS	-ĒTŬS	-ĬTŬS	-ĪTŬS

PĂTĔR ĂMĀNS a *loving father;* PĂTĔR ĂMĂTŪRŬS a *father about to be loving;* SŪm AMATURUS *I am to love;* ĔRAm AMATURUS *I was to love.* DĬCĬT *he says,* MĒ *me,* ĂMĀRĔ *to love*—DICIT ME AMARE *he says (that) I love, he asserts me to love.* Here the verb DICIT governs the accusative (objective) case ME, and ĔGŎ *I* cannot be used as in English, where *I* is considered a nominative case to the verb *love.* The English sentence contains the assertion *I love* (which may not be true,) from which the Latin is free.

46 PŌSSŪm ĂMĀRĔ *I can* (am able *to*) *love;* VĔNĬO ĂMĀTŬm *I come to love* (in order to love.) In the expression "I can love," (German, ich kann lieb-en; Danish, jeg kan elsk-e,) *love* is an infinitive; in "I am able to love," *to love* is a supine. In the following examples (commencing with an interrogative adverb,) "can blind lead blind," both forms of "blind" (blind-person) are in the singular number, and *lead* is in the infinitive mood, in Gothic, Greek, and Latin—

ibai	mag	blinds	blindana	tiuhan.
μήτι	*δύναται*	*τυφλὸς*	*τυφλὸν*	*ὁδηγεῖν;*
NUNQVID	POTEST	CAECUS	CAECUm	DUCERE?
	can	*the-blind*	2 *the-blind*	1 *lead?* *Luc.* 6 ;39.

Forms like the following are due to grammatic inflexion—

immerge immerse	concur discourse	refund infuse	deface defeat infect
remit remiss	move promote	degrade digress	infringe infract
conduce conduct	draw trace tract	expend dispense	assail assault

47 Three cases are assigned to English, as exhibited in the pronouns—

Nominative	he	she	who	they
Possessive	his	hers	whose	theirs
Objective	him	her	whom	them

§ 48 The possessive corresponds with the Latin *genitive*, and the objective with the *accusative*. Latin has also a *dative* case, as SĔRMŌNĪ (to a speech;) and an ablative, as SĔRMŌNĔ (with a speech,) the nominative being SĔRMŌ a speech, and the accusative SĔRMŌNĔm.

A few nouns have a distinct *vócative* case, as DŎMĬNŬS a lord, DŎMĬNĔ *O lord; γίγᾱς* a giant, *γίγαν O giant.*

49 The cases which differ from the nominative are called oblique cases. The English *sermon* may be called an oblique case of SĔRMO, because it is not derived from the Latin nominative, nor from any single oblique case.

50 As the Latin cases vary considerably, they are divided into five declensions, distinguished by the termination of the genitive case singular number, as follows—

1	2	3	4	5
-AE	-Ī	-ĬS	ŪS	-ĔĪ

51 In English derivations from Latin nouns (adjectives, participles,) it is often necessary to know the "crude form," which is generally present in an oblique case, and the dictionary gives the nominative and genitive, as in CŎRPŬS, -ŎRĬS, *body*, whence *corporeal*, from the crude form CORPOR underlying the genitive case CŎRPŎR-ĬS (of the body,) which is implied by -ŎRĬS. The following are similarly derived—

itiner-ary, ĬT-ĔR, -ĬNĔR-ĬS, *a journey*
milit-ary, MĪL-ĔS, -ĬT-ĬS, *a soldier*
pulver-ise, PŬLV-ĬS, -ĔR-ĬS, *dust*
lapid-ary, LĂP-ĬS, ĬDĬS, *a stone*
fraud, FRĀV-S, -D-ĬS
front, FRŎN-S, -T-ĬS
sanguine, SĂNGV-ĬS, -ĬN-ĬS, *blood.*

Examples of case in Gothic, German, Anglish (Anglosaxon,) and Nordish (Islandic,) will be given under the suffix -mer.

As the *r, t, d, n,* of *pulver-ise, milit-ary, fraud, sanguine,* &c. occur in the declensions, they will be termed R declensional, &c. especially as they do not always form part of the base, or crude form.

52 As most English nouns borrowed from Latin happened to be of the second and third declensions, the *i* of their geni-

tive case has become the connecting vowel with nouns of the first declension, as in penniform (not pennaeform) from PĒNN-Ă, -AE (a feather.) Primigenous (first born) is formed from the adjective PRĪM-ŬS, -Ī (first,) and primogeniture from the adverb PRĪMŌ (at first.)

53 O, a common connective in words of Greek origin, may be due to the crude form, or to the noun and adjective termination -ος of the nominative case, with ς dropped, as in philo-sophy, auto-bio-graphy. O of a genitive case is present in phraseo-logy (φράσ-ις, -εως,) cȳnos-ure (κύων dog, gen. κυν-ὸς,) aer-o-naut, aer-o-lite, from ἀὴρ (air) genitive ἀέρος; but aer-ial is from the Latin form ĀĒR, gen. ĀĔRĬS.

54 Phos-phorus preserves the ς of the nominative φῶς (light,) whilst the genitive φωτὸς is used in photo-phorus, photo-graph.

55 Other connecting vowels appear in strata-gem, penta-gon, archi-tect, lexi-con, patri-arch, pan-e-gyric from πᾶν (all) ἀγορὰ (assembly;) where πᾶν is the neuter of πᾶς, as in pas-i-graphy, genitive πάντος, as in panto-graphy.

56 The *t* in ego-t-ism and *n* in tobacco-n-ist are connectives, and *g* has slipped into poly-g-archy, for poly-archy (rule of many) by the *induction* or influence of olig-archy, the rule of (ὀλίγος) few.

57 *A connecting element* may be no part either of the base-word or the affix, as *t* in ego-t-ism and *i* in penn-i-form; —it may belong to the base-word, as in gan-d-er (☞ -m,) asthma-t-ic; to the affix, as *a* of -ary in milit-ary, because (§ 51) MĪL-ĔS, gen. MĪLĬT-ĬS has no *a*;—or to both base-word and affix, as in making formul-a-ry from f o r m u l a and -ary; but as the *a* of f o r m u l-a was originally short, and that of -ary long, the suffix has the better claim to the *a* of f o r m u l a r y, s u b t e r r-a n e a n, and others.

58 The connecting element is often added to the suffix, as *a* in -ATe, -ĀTŬS, where the etymology, and forms like SĒLĒC-TŬS show that the participial portion is not -AT, but

-T, which may be preceded by any of the Latin vowels, the *a* of -AT being due to the first conjugation (§ 45) as in ĀDVŎ-CĀRĔ (to advocate,) ĀDVŎC-ĀTŬS. Nevertheless, as -ATUS occurs in words underived from verbs, as HĀM-ĀTUS (hamate, hooked,) the heading -ATe is given. Similarly, -AX, -EX, &c. might have been placed under -X; -ANT, -ENT, under -NT, &c.

59 In Greek there are three declensions and five cases, which bear some resemblance to the Latin cases. In the Latin LĀC and Greek *γάλα* (milk,) little resemblance is apparent until we take an oblique case, as the genitive *γdΛAKToς*, LACTIS. Compare—

πoὺς	PĒS	a foot,	whence	pace
πoδὸς	PĔDĬS	of a foot,	"	tri-pod, ped-al
oδoὺς	DĒNS	a tooth,	"	tine, tooth
oδόντoς	DĒNTĬS	of a tooth,	"	dent-al, mon-odon
χάρῐς grace,	*χάριτoς*	of grace,	"	charity
ϐoῦς BŌS an ox,	*ϐoὸς* BŎVĬS	of an ox,	"	beef, bov-ine.

60 *Inflectional* elements are such as are used in grammatic inflexions, as the participial -t in -tous. *Mutational* elements are such as interchange, as *d*, *t*, in spelle*d*, spel*t*. *Declensional* elements occur in declensions, as *n* in sermon, which is the crude form (§ 51) of SĔRMO a speech. *Formative* elements are used in making forms of words, as *p* in forming the noun ras-p from the verb raze.

61 The characteristic part of a derivative word is often to be looked for in the inflexions of the verb. Thus the Greek *Φρd·Zω*, in the Doric dialect *ΦράΣδω* (I speak) gives phrase, and the perfect tense *πέΦραKα* (I have spoken) is akin to the Latin PRĔCŎR (to pray,) German fragen (to ask,) and English prec-atory, pray.

62 Latin inflexions are much used in the law, as mandamus we command; capias you may take; affidavit he (she) has made faith to; scī-lĭcĕt to wit, that is to say, (SCI-RE to know, LĬCĔT it is lawful;) vīdē-lĭcĕt to wit, namely, (VĬDĒRĔ to see,—it is easy to see,—it may be seen;)

mittimus we send; căveat let him beware; certiorāri to have notice given.

63 *Gender*. Many English forms depend upon the variations in the originals indicative of gender. The name Maximus (*greatest*, primarily an adjective,) indicates a male, of which the feminine would be Maxi-ma, and the neuter maximum. But there are exceptions to such indications of gender. In Greek, canon is masculine, chaos and drama are neuter, and exodus is feminine; and in Latin, QVĒRCŬS (an oak) is feminine, and GĔNŬS γένος neuter.

Masculine,	*Feminine*,	*Neuter*.
Antoni-nus	Antoni-na	tympa-num
pylo-rus	hyd-ra	fulc-rum
nauti-lus	spicu-la	specu-lum
isth-mus	ac-me	chrysanthe-mum
asbes-tus	aor-ta	asphal-tum
direc-tor	direc-tr ix / ess	spec-trum

64 The Islandic adjectives of the three genders have the following forms—

Masc.	*Fem.*	*Neut.*	
glaðr	glöd	glatt	*shining*
goðr	gōd	gott	*good*
blindr	blind	blint	*blind*

AFFIXES

65 Affixes are additions to roots stems and words, serving to modify their meaning and use. They are of two kinds, *prefixes*, those at the beginning, and *suffixes*, those at the end of the word-bases to which they are affixed. Several affixes occur in long words like *in-com-pre*-hen-*s-ib-il-it-y*, which has three prefixes and five suffixes.

The term *interfix* is hardly necessary for *ad* in anim-ad-vert, or *t* inserted as a fulcrum between the vowels of ego-t-ism.

§ 66 A root is a word or part of a word without affix, sometimes having and sometimes wanting a distinctive meaning. *A* (in *arm*) is the *root* of a-ir and a-sthma; it has not the definite meaning of a noun or verb, but signifies *blow* in a general way, without being a part of speech.

67 *Eat* is, and *ed* is not a word, but both are *stems* in eat-able or ed-ible, and derived from the *root* AD,—but roots and stems cannot be distinguished in all cases. *Sta* is the root of sta-nd, sta-tion, and its cognate *sti* is the stem of con-sti-t-ut-ion.

68 *Irk*, the stem of w-*ork* and *irk*-some, is disguised in *org*-an, lit-*urg*-y, en-*erg*-y, su-*rg*-ery; and *work* is disguised under *wrigh-t*. *Beauty* (from *belle*) is equally the stem of beauti-ful and beaute-ous, for Etymology pertains to language and not to orthography.

69 Etymology takes cognisance of the relation of *proof*, *prove* (proov,) and requires the latter to have final *v*, which, with final *i*, *j*, and double *v*, *j*, *c*, *k*, are forbidden by English spelling. The English and Germans call *house* (haus) by the same name, so that each has four elements and closes with a consonant. Similarly orb-s, pea-se, cloth-es, beau-x, have the same plural element, and the last never had an etymologic letter *ex*—but in old French vertical script, the final '*s*' with the tail thrown forward resembled '*x*,' which printers used for it.—In dialects of old English, *the* was pronounced with *th* in *thin*, and spelt with the Anglosaxon letter þ, for which '*y*' was used by printers who wanted the type or mistook the letter, and this typographic error leads some to fancy that *the* was formerly pronounced with English *y*.

70 It cannot always be determined whether derivative words are compound, or formed with an affix. This doubt appears in overreach, undersecretary, magnificent. The following are compound—astro-logy, atmo-sphere, ceno-taph, demo-crat, hemo-rrhage, hydr-aulic, hydro-gen, leth-argy, lit-urgy, mel-ody, olig-arch, mon-arch, cham-o-mile, strat-agem, kal-eido-scope.

71 The force of affixes being variable and often evanescent, care must be taken to accept the definitions of them in a general sense; and when their force is known, it need not be

recalled in analysing a word, except where it seems to be strictly applicable. On account of their occasional indefiniteness, some of the affixes are left undefined, and in some cases the definition of the examples does not quite correspond with that first given.

72 The prefix un- is a variation of in- (not,) yet unsignificant means *not significant*, and insignificant means *trifling;* pertinent is *to the purpose*, impertinent *insolent;* and *not famous* would be an inaccurate definition of infamous. Compare disposition and indisposition, delicate and indelicate.

73 Although the Latin prefix SUB (SUC-, SUG-, &c.) means *under*, it also means *from* beneath, *in, at, towards, somewhat.* Thus SŪB-VĔHO means, I carry *up;* SŪG-GĔRO I put *under*, bring, annex, supply, *suggest;* CĒDO I go, SŪC-CĒDO I go under, submit, ascend, belong to, follow after, prosper, *succeed.* PRÆ-TĒNDO I stretch forward, place before, prefix, exhibit, *pretend.*

74 IN-DŪCO I lead in, clothe, exhibit, deceive (take in,) overlay, annul, put on (as shoes,) *induce.*

75 IN-FŌRMO I form, show, instruct, *inform.* DĒ-FŌRMO I form, describe, design, beautify, *disfigure.* ĬN means *in* or *on*, and SĪSTO I place, whence IN-SISTO I step towards, come, stop, pursue, press upon, (used figuratively in the English) *insist.*

76 The primary sense of 'ascribe' is *write to*, but it means *to attribute*, which is composed of *to* and *give.* The original sense of attribute is evident in tribute and contribution, whilst in retribution it has a more figurative extension.

77 Composed means *placed together*, decomposed means *separated* in regard to a previous union, and although undecomposed is a negative of decomposed, it is not quite equivalent to composed.

ĀDVĒRSŪS turned towards, fronting, adverse, hostile.

DĒJĬCĬO I throw under, expose, substitute, falsify, throw upwards, add, reply, hint, give, cast down, overthrow.

CŌNVĪNCĔRĔ (CŌNVĪNCTŬm) to conquer, disprove, prove, convict of crime, whence *convince, convict* and *cónvict.*

78 In the course of time the force of some words with an affix has become identic with that of their simple form, as sever dissever, loose unloose, sport for disport, encounter rencounter, ornament adornment, to adorn to ornament.

79 The Latin MĒNDĂ (a fault) has produced mend (to repair) by the loss of the prefixes (ab-, ex-,) of a-mend and e-mend, implying removal of the fault.

80 In add and aid the prefix ad- is all that is left of ĀD-DO and ĀD-JŬVO; cull is the prefix con- of col-lect; trance is the Latin TRĀNS-ĬTŬS (a going beyond,) reduced to its prefix; enter is the prefix ĪNTĔR, ĪNTRĂ deprived of the verbial termination observed in ĪNTRĀRĔ (to go in;)

81 Rencounter is composed of re-in-contra. Hipped is the prefix and suffix hyp——ed of hypochondriasised, with a dozen silent letters; in-super-able is composed of three affixes, dis-a(d)v-ant-age-ous-ly of six, and supr-eme and prae-tor of two, the latter being for PRÆ-Ī-TŎR a fore-go-er or leader, having lost its root I of ĪRĔ (to go.) Sur-pr-ise has lost the root hend (take) of com-pre-hend.

82 The prefix re- implies *back* or *again*, but it is used in re-mark without re-gard to the first speaker, or to the re-plying one; and something is re-ferred (borne back) to a person who re-ceives it for the first time. A nation is re-duced (led back) to subjection which had previously been free, and a man is re-duced to poverty who had never been poor.

3 Here the prefix has ceased to have a separate significa-tion. It is *verbal*, indicating that in practice, remark is a *word* independent of its constituents.

§ 84 A r e c l u s e is one *shut back* or re-tired, although RE-CLŪDO means to unclose, bring out, expose.

85 The al- of a l-c o v e is verbal, meaning nothing as a prefix, and there is a tendency to consider i n t e r-m e d i a t e as a verbal form—

Sometimes this composition is exactly *inter*mediate *between* that of the uplifting and that of the upheaved rocks.—'The Geologist,' 1859.

> I beg that you will *mediate* 'twixt my errors,
> And your stern mother's wrath.—*Thos. Heywood.* (Modern reprint.)

86 Affixes may be definitive, being used to limit the words to which they are applied, to some use to which the base-word would be equally applicable,—separating transitive from intransitive, and figurative from radical meanings, as in the following examples.

FĪGO I fix, make firm, thrust in, strike, *post up*.	DĒFĪGO I fix, plunge, plant, strike, *astonish*.
SĪGNO I mark, express, paint, seal, record, *sign*.	DĒSĪGNO I mark, denote, sketch out, *designate*.
LŪDO I play, sport, trick.	DĒLŪDO I deceive (some one.)
CĔRNO I sift, discern, decide, judge, determine.	DĒCĔRNO I separate, distinguish, determine, deliberate.
CLĀMO I shout, exclaim.	DĒCLĀMO I make set speeches.
f i l l to make full.	f u l f i l to fill a purpose.
λέγω I speak, col-lec-t, se-lec-t, choose, reckon up, tell over—(whence *catalogue*.)	κατα-λέγω I select, choose, count over, *make a list* (of names for military duty.)
Danish s k i l l e to separate, sever, put asunder, divide, *divorce*.	a d s k i l l e to separate, sever, put asunder, divide, *distinguish*.

87 In FRAVDO, DEFRAVDO (I cheat, deceive,) de- might be regarded as intensive, but it is better to consider it restrictive to verbial forms, the derivatives (as fraudulent) being formed without the prefix, on the noun basis FRAVS, genitive FRAVD-ĬS. So the adjective PRĀVŬS (crooked, perverted,) instead of having a verb *pravo* (I crook,) has DĒ-PRĀVO V. t. I vitiate, deprave.

88 In DĒLĪBĔRO (I weigh, consider,) the prefix *restricts* or *defines* the word as that derived from LĪBRĂ (a balance,)

thus distinguishing it from a different word, LĪBĔRO I make (LĪBĔR) free; and re- dissociates r e-m e m b e r from *member* to associate it with *memory*, which does not require it.

89 NŪDO, DĒNŪDO (I make bare, despoil, disclose,) have about the same meaning; and if we divide words in de- into sections according to the force of this prefix, d e-n u d e may occupy several places. It may be considered a *verbal* (§ 82) form of n u d e—an *intensive*—a *restrictive* to a particular object—and *privitive* or separative in regard to something removed, as in—

Charles I, having *denuded* himself of some of the principal attributes of sovereign power . . . *Rev. Michael Russell.*

90 Some words are never used without an affix, as the Latin CŌN-SĬLĬŪm coun-sel; ĒX-ĒMPLŪm ex-ample; CŌN-TĒM-PLŎR I con-template; and the English be-neath, neth-er, con-dign, dign-ity, in-fer, sub-sist, con-vict, con-nect, re-ject, as-sume, in-dignation, but Spanish has both *dignacion* and *indignacion*.

91 As forms like 'leviate' and 'lieve' cannot be used, they must be replaced by al-leviate and re-lieve (to lighten again.) This may render a word figurative, and cause the power of the affix to be so much enfeebled, that an auxiliary preposition might be required (independently of its use before an objective case,) in the locutions *al*-lude *to; de*-lude *with; de*-pend *from, upon; de*-scend *from, upon, into; re-, im*-pose *upon; sub*-mit *to; re-, ap*-ply *to; sup*-ply *with; ob*-ject *to; con*-fer *on, with.*

92 The sign of the infinitive mood being identic with the preposition *to*, this double use of the same vocable causes *to* to lose its force as a preposition and to be transferred to the condition of a prefix, as in several of the locutions following —*dis*posed-*to* work, *in*disposed *to*-work; *in*clined *to*-do it, *in*clined-*to* it;—which induce the forms—*a*verse-*to* such a course; *dis*inclined-*to* it, *dis*inclined *to*-do it.

What cat's *averse to* fish?—*Gray.*

To this I humbly must *dis*sent.—*Gay.*

They were naturally *averse to* the exercise of the tongue.—*W. Irving.* Charlemagne, ever *averse* . . . *to* judicial bloodshed.—*G. P. R. James.* . . . *averse to* study.—*Gibbon.* On his re-turn he made many at-tempts to *in*-troduce the foreign school WITH which he had become ACquainted *to* his countrymen.—*Prescott*, 1845. When we have *ac*quired Vertue *into* our reach, &c.—*Ferrand Spence*, 1686.

93 Attempts are sometimes made to secure the conjoint action of prefix and preposition, by forms like—*dis*inclined *from*, *a*verse *from*,—the use of which embarrasses the language by assigning to particles a greater force than the corresponding idea justifies.

And why not live and act with other men?
Because my nature was *averse from* life.—*Byron*, Manfred.

. . . ſuch a *de*teſtation *of* vice . . . ſuch an *a*verſion *from*, and *con*tempt *of* corrupt manners.—*Clarendon*, 1674. Burning for pleasure, not *averse from* strife.—*Byron.* With a mind *averse from* outer objects.—*Hazlitt.* Dryden had shown himself not *averse from* marriage . . . *Westminster Review*, 1855.

. . . it has been concluded by many that they were *averse from* public shows, . . . *Horatio Smith*, Festivals, &c. 1831.

94 *No uniform rule is adopted* in admitting foreign words into a language. Some words become naturalised, whilst others similarly formed, and equally good, or bad, are avoided, or if proposed, do not come into use. Thus English has from Latin, 'emolument' *profit*, but not 'emoliment' *trouble*—

absorb	not *obsorb.*	com-, re-, inter-,	not *a-, circum-, de-,*
convenient	" *ob-, pro-venient*	o-, per-, sub-,	" *di-, im-, super-,*
disturb	" *ob-, con-, pro-turb*	ad-, trans-mit	" *præ-, pro-mit*
exhaust	" *perhaust*	con-, e-, de-, in-,	" *ob-, per-, pro-,*
promotion	" *permotion*	circum-volve	" *sub-volve*
occasion	" *occision*	circumscribe	" *circumsede*
dispensation	" *offensation*	excite	not *sucsite*
pro-, de-tect	" *pertect*	implore	" *opplore*
pre-, sub-scribe	" *perscribe*	subterfuge	" *subterduce*
impinge	" *intinge*	concise	" *succise*
con-de-scend	" *conscend*	successive	" *successive*
coerce	" *exerce*	contractile	" *compactile*
prorogue	" *irrogue*	in-, re-voke	" *sevoke*
in-, re-quire	" *per-, ex-quire*	corroborate	" *roborate*
irritate	" *proritate*	arrogate	" *irrogate*
in-, oc-, re-, con-	" *per-, præ-, pro-, de-*	fabricate	" *perfabricate*
cur, suc-cour	*cur*	com-pete, repeat	" *ap-, ex-, im-pete*
de-, post-pone	" *oppone*	suggest	" *suggress*

in-, as-, con-, de-, per-, re-, sub-sist	not *circum-, ex-, inter-, ab-sist*	as-, con-, re-, dis-sent	not *per-, præ-, sub-sent*
ab-, dis-, re-solve	" *ex-, per-solve*	hypocrisy	" *epicrisy*
en-, epi-demic	" *apo-, meta-demic*	energy	" *aergy, periergy*

95 *Modern languages are not uniform* in the prefixes adopted with ancient words. Thus the Spanish has disformidad, disfamia, confraccion, confugio, conturbar, and (Latin DIS, ĀVDĪRĔ to hear,) desoir, not to pay attention.

96 *Many suffixes are lost* in English words of Latin origin, as masc. LĬQVĬD-ŬS, fem. LĬQVĬD-Ă, neut. LĬQVĬD-U^{m} liquid.

ĀNTĪQVŬS*	antique*	PĀLMĂ	palm
CLĀRŬS (-A, -U^{m})	clear	CRĪMĔN	crime
RĀRŬS	rare	MĂGNĬFĬCO	magnify
SĀNCTŬS	saint	RĔFŬGĬŬ^{m}	refuge
GRĂV-ĬS (-IS, -E)	grave	RĔMĔDĬŬ^{m}	remedy
SŎLLĬCĬTŪDO	solicitude	STŬDĬŬ^{m}	study
PLŪMĂ	plume	SĬMPLĔX	simple
PĔNNĂ	pen	SŌLĀTĬŬ^{m}	solace
HĔRBĂ	herb	ĂLĬMĔNTŬ^{m}	aliment

97 *There are many hĭbrid words* in English, with Greek suffixes to Latin or other stems, as flut-ist, drugg-ist, mineralogist, natur(al)ist; journal-ism, fanatic-ism, quiet-ism; but most of those in -ism are correct. In oxid-ation the stem is Greek and the suffix Latin; in ridd-ance the stem is English and the suffix Latin.

98 As compound hĭbrids are seldom used by the educated, the etymologist must not resort to two languages until he has found that one language is not sufficient. Călígŭlă, from CĂLĬGĂ (a military shoe,) must not be referred to the Greek καλὸς (handsome) and Latin GŬLĂ (neck); nor pentecost, πεντηκοστὴ the *fiftieth* (day after Easter,) to πέντε (five,) and COSTÆ (ribs.) Cosmó-polite means world-citizen, not world-polite.†

---

* Observe the identity of sound and accent between the Latin and English *i*.

† Such Etymology, and Entomology as bad, have been furnished "By Authority" to the defrauded citizens of New York; in a book on Injurious Insects, by E. Emmons M.D. Here, to cite a single example, Notióphilus (from νότιος *wet*, and φίλος *lover*,) is rendered *notion* beetle.

§ 99 *Care must be taken to determine* how much of a word constitutes the stem and affix. The prefix subter- in subter-fuge does not occur in subterrănean, where the prefix is sub- and the stem TĔRR of TĔRRĂ the earth; nor does sub- occur in subulate, from SŪBŬLĂ an awl, and this from SUO I sew.

100 Trans- is the prefix and form the stem of transform; whilst in exude and transude, the stem is SŪDĀRĔ (to sweat,) and the prefix ec'-, tran'-, with the first *s* absorbed by the second. If TRĀNSĬTŬS a *passing* over, were improperly divided, it would mean (SĬTŬS) *situated* over.

101 As re- means *back,* and retro- *backwards,* a re-traction or *drawing* back, might be converted into retr-action an *acting* backwards; and abs-tain to *hold* from, might be taken for ab-stain to *stand* from.

102 The English word angelic and Anglish angelic are far removed from each other, the latter being an-ge-líc *a-like;* and in Danish, unytte is *in-ut-*ility, as if from Latin ŪTŎR I *use;* but the prefix is u- *not,* and the stem is cognate with the German nutz *profit.* The Danish vandrende is both a *wanderer* and a *water-pipe,* in the former sense from vandre to *wander,* and in the latter from vand *water* and rende a *channel.*

103 The Latin PĪSC-ĀT-ŎR and Welsh pysg-ot-wr (fisherman) are from the cognates PĪSC-ĬS, pysg (fish,) and seem to correspond in all their parts; but AT in the Latin is participial, and Welsh -ot is for the plural sign -od of pysg-od (fish-es,) and -wr is for gwr (man,) so that the Latin word means a *fish-er,* and the Welsh a *man* (of) *fish-es.*

104 The Romans often omitted *s* after ex-, as in ĔXPĔCTO for ĔXSPĔCTO *I expect.* Hence ĔXPŎLĬO, to *polish off, scrape,* (from PŎLĬO, to polish,) may stand for ĔX-SPŎLĬO, from SPŎLĬO, to *strip, spoil.* If extinct, extirpate, exult, exile, had retained an etymologic form, they would have the forms of *exstinct, exstirpate, exsult, exsile.*

§ 105 In Greek, ἄστρον is a *star*, νόμος *law*, and ὄνομᾰ *name*, so that if astro-nomy (the *law* or science of the stars) were divided into astr-onomy, it would mean *star-naming*.

106 *The position of an affix is seldom changed* (as in *mis*-take, re*miss*) altho it may happen that a prefix in one language may be a suffix in another.* German has ab-brennen, an-halten, and Danish af-brænde, an-holde, where English has *burn off*, *hold on*. English has ful-fil and mirth-ful; an off-set and a set-off; an off-cut and a cut-off; to up-hold and hold up; to over-look and look over; an out-breaking and a breaking out.

107 *If the same affix were used* both as a prefix and suffix, the listener could not in many cases determine whether an affix between two words should belong as a suffix to the first, or a prefix to the second, as in—

> His teeth all ſhattered, *rush in*mixed with blood.—*Pope*, Odyſſey, 18: 117.

The Anglish tosettan to *set to*, was not continued in English, because the use of the infinitive sign tŏ would cause an awkward alliteration, as in tŏ-tō-set.

108 *As long as the constituent parts* of a word remain, there is no difficulty in detecting them, if the language to which they belong is known; but the case is different when the significancy of the fragments ceases to be perceived.

109 If the prefix ex- (ecs) had become extinct, the relation between the *e* of e-duce, and the *s* of s-pend could not be determined, and were there two words spend and pend (nip snip, plash splash,) of the same signification, it would be difficult to determine whether *spend* was the original and *pend* a mutilated form, or this the stem and *s* a prefix. In a

* As in the language of Georgia (or Gurgistan,) where bustani is a *garden*, and mebustani a *gardener;* marili *salt*, samarili a *saltcellar*. Hindoostanee Īmān *faith*, bē-Īmān *faithless*, be-iman-i *faithlessness*. Basque berdin *equal*, berdinxu *subequal* or *nearly equal*. But other languages differ, as Hebrew, where a vowel change distinguishes between bāqār a *herd*, and bōqēr a *herdsman;* kerem a *vineyard*, and kōrēm a *vinedresser*.

strange language a pair of words like l o n e and a l o n e would present the same difficulty.

110 In Welsh, y s (*ardency* as a noun, *exists* as a verb,) is a common intensive prefix—used also by induction in introduced words, by prefixing *y* before *s*, as in y s g o l f e i s t e r, y s g a r l a d, (schoolmaster, scarlet.) Its force appears in the following Welsh examples—

pig *a point, pike, beak*	yspig *a s-pike, s-pine*
par *a germ, a s-pear*	yspar *a s-pear, lance*
plan *a ray, a shoot*	ysplan *s-plendid*
llac *loose*	yslac *s-lack*
taen *a sprinkling*	ystaen *a s-tain*
paid *quiet*	yspaid *cessation*
porth *aid*	ysporth *sustenance*
ig *vexing*	ysig *fretting*

MARKS AND ABBREVIATIONS.

Words hyphened like met-hod, hyp-hen, to indicate their etymology, are not to be thus pronounced.

‡ Assimilation, as when ad- becomes af-, in af-fect‡.

+ Obsolete, disused, or supposed forms, as +TEMPLOR, which does not exist, but is inferred from CŌN-TĔMPLŎR I con-template.

☞ *See*, refers principally to the Vocabulary.

The grave accentual is used for long accented syllables, and the acute for short ones, as in depòse, depósit, deposítion.

⸸ Indicates that a word is not under its original form, as ⸸*shine*, which is not the original of *shone*, as ⸸CÆDO (I cut) is newer than its apparent derivative IN-CĪDO.

— The dash separates forms like "temperature—enclosure," the former being regularly deduced from Latin, and the latter not. It also separates Greek from Latin forms.

A word printed like voy-**age** is explained under **-age**.

Educed elements are represented as in number, numer-ous, where *b* is educed from *m*.

The Anglish (Anglosaxon,) Gothic, and Norse, Nordish (old Islandic,) characters for *th* in *thin* will be represented by Greek θ. English *z* is sometimes represented by ʒ, and *sh* by ʃ, and *z* in azure by ȷ. The old English character ȝ in ¶ 11, page 41, is not a *z* (a letter often improperly used for it,) but a representative, according to the dialect and place in the word, of *y*, *g*, and *gh*.

.. Indicate (with italics) lost or "silent" elements, as in counterfei..t, which has lost the *c* of counterfict; may.., mi*gh*t, &c.

A single dot (·) is sometimes used to indicate the length of a syllable by position (§ 34,) as in CA·PTUM, where the *vowel* is naturally short, whilst in MĒNSURA the E is long independently of the consonants which follow.

A few Sanscrit words quoted, are in Latin orthography, the character corresponding to English *w* being represented by V; *k* by C; and *y* by J; —*ch* in *chip* by Tʃ, and *g* corrupt in *gem* by DJ. R̥ is a kind of untrilled *r*.

with the tongue so far from the palate that the element is considered a vowel, and is long and short. 5 is used for a kind of *h* which becomes *s* in Greek and Latin.

ş and ţ are a peculiar *s* and *t* (termed cerebral,) formed by turning the tongue back. Their formation need not be attempted. PH, TH, &c. are pronounced as in *uphold, pothook.* Sanscrit short vowels are commonly unmarked. See the author's Analytic Orthography (Trevelyan Prize Essay,) Philadelphia, J. B. Lippincott & Co., 1860.

ș and ț represent Arabic săd and ta, Hebrew sadēi (which is *not* ts,) and teth. They are formed with the flat of the tongue. Q is used for Arabic qaf and Hebrew quph, a deeper sound than *k.*

Ss. *Sanscrit;* G. or Ger. *German;* D. or Dan. *Danish;* Isl. *Islandic;* B. Belgic, the language of Holland (commonly called Dutch) including Flemish; Go. *Gothic* (i.e. Mœso-gothic;) W. *Welsh;* Ir. *Irish;* It. *Italian;* Sp. *Spanish;* Port. *Portuguese;* Fr. *French;* Gr. *Greek;* L. or Lat. *Latin,* but these are seldom used, the Latin being in LATIN or capital letters, and Greek characters are well known.

Heb. *Hebrew,* generally given in *Latin* letters, so that J is English *y,* V English *w,* &c. In a few cases it was convenient to represent Hebrew and other languages in Greek typography. Ohg. old high German.

Ang. *Anglish* (Anglosaxon;) Sax. *Saxon* (or Plattdeutsch,) a living language. It is a grave error to use the term *Saxon* for *Anglosaxon.*

Pronounce Anglish *c, g, v* as in Latin, *y* like Danish *y,* French u, Gr. *υ;* and æ as in *fat.* (Compare cirnel *kernel,* brocen *broken,* vul *wool,* vægn *wagon.*) ð is *th* in *then,* þ *th* in *thin,* but *θ* is used for this, and the Latin v for its Anglish form ƿ.

v. *verb;* adv. *adverb;* n. *noun* (or s. *substantive;*) m. *masculine;* f. *feminine;* neut. *neuter;* pl. *plural;* a. (or adj.) *adjective;* dim. *diminutival.*

In headings like A- AB, the hyphen is omitted when the prefix can be used as a separate word, like the prepositions. Latin prefixes are printed like ABS-, Greek like *SYN,* and all others, including true English forms, and modifications of Latin, like **be-**, **-ness**. -N-oUS shows that *o* does not belong to the Latin form, which is -N-US.

Silent letters are often in a different type, and in some cases they have no etymologic value, as the *e* in apocalyps*e* compared with that in apocope.

Words which form exceptions are frequently in italics.

In the definition of "abs-tract (TRĂHO) to draw from," &c., "to draw" belongs to -tract and TRAHO, and "from" to the prefix abs-. Many of the words with Latin prefixes occur in Latin, so that *abs-tract* might have been referred to ABS-TRAHO; *abstain* to ABS-TINEO, &c.

As TRAHO means strictly, *I draw;* and TRĂHĔRĔ *to draw,* a word and its definition are separated by a comma point when they do not quite correspond, thus TRAHO, *to draw.*

Old English was pronounced mostly like the European languages, with *e* in *they,* &c. as in Chaucer's bifore *before,* diocise *diocese,* gret *great,* slee *slay,* her-es *hairs,* goo *go,* stoon *stone,* hoom *home,* goot *goat,* awook *awoke,* na-tu-res *nature's,* in three syllables, accented on the second. The rhythm determines the accent and syllabication, as in the following examples—

Stomak ne con-ſci-en-ce know I noon ; . . .
And ſche agayn anſw-erd in pa-ci-ence : . . .
Compaſſi-oun, my fai-re Cana-ce, . . .
And for the foul-es that ſhe herd-e ſyng, . . .
And therfor hath this worthy wiſ-e knight . . .
Yer-es and day-es fleet this cre-a-ture . . .
And ſtraun-ge made it of hir mar-i-age.—*Chaucer.*

PREFIXES

a- *on, at, in.*

[**a-** is a fragment derived from several originals. It commonly indicates adverbs, and is applied to prepositions (a-b-ove,) adjectives (a-kin,) nouns (a-piece,) and verbs (a-rise.)]

¶ 1.

The heterogeneous nature of **a-** appears in the following examples—

a-mong Ang. onmang, āmang, on-ge-mang, Old Eng. bi-mong.
against Ang. togean, ongean, agean, āgēn.
afore, before Ang. toforan, onforan, ætforan, vıθ-foran.

> Braſtias had ſlaine a knight tofore.—'*King Arthur*,' 1634.

along Ang. onlenge, emb-long, andlang; em- *even, equal,* sometimes used for emb- *about.*

> Yclenched overthwart and endelong
> With yren tough.—*Chaucer.*

¶ 2. *in, on,* &c.

a- is partly due to the Anglish on, ān, meaning *on, in, un-;* and partly to old Frisian and Islandic ā *on, in, at.*

onbæc (Islandic ā bak) *aback;* onbedippan *to dip in;* onlēsan *to make loose* (unloose;) ānbīdan *to abide;* ānvadan *to invade;* ānvēg *away;* **adays** Ang. āndæges; on handa, old Eng. anhond, onhande, old Frisian ā hand, *on* or *in* hand; ānbūgan *to obey* (bow to;) anælan *to anneal* (ælan *to burn, bake.*)

Old English has forms like on sleepe, in slepe *asleep;* on side *aside;* on life *alive.*

> And here-againes no creature on live
> Of no degree availleth for to ſtrive.—*Chaucer.*
>
> How that they wolde on huntinge gone.—*Id.*

¶ 3. Position.

amidst (Ang. on middan,) in the middle.

aboard on board. (Nordish ā borði, Fr. à bord (¶ 9,) Ger. am (for an dem) borde, Dan. om bord. **astern** at, towards or behind the stern. **aground** on or at the ground or bottom.
atop abed ashore alee aside apeak abaft +ahorse +adoors afield ahigh

Ab-out, round the outside, Ang. emb-utan, on-butan; as in emb-long *along*. See AMBI-.

. . . between 9 and 10 a Clock,—*Dr. Thos. Short*, Hist. of the Air, London 1749.

. . . he then went out a-doors.—*Pepys*. Born 1632.

¶ 4. Condition.

asunder in a divided condition. (Ang. on sundran; old Ger. besunder.) **adrift** in a drifting condition.

aga'te, aga'd on the (Sw. gata, old Eng. gate) way, road.

abroad from home. (Nordish ābraut *forth;* braut a road, travel, region.) **agog** on the lookout. (Ger. gucken to look.)
apart afloat ablaze alive awake asleep astir agape —anew afresh—+afeared or **afraid** (¶ 13.)

Of perill why that she oughte a f e r d e to be . . . .
They were a d r a d d e of him as of the death.—*Chaucer*.
Their dam upstart out of her den e f f r a i d e, . . . *Spenser*.

¶ 5. Direction.

athwart across. (Ang. on θveorh; old Ger. in duëran.)

aback towards the back. **abreast** opposite, or towards the breast. **ahead** in advance of the head; in front.

alength (on, at,) in the direction of the length.
aslant across askance—awry afar askew—above abaft

My berd that hangeth long a d o u n.—*Chaucer*.

¶ 6. Manner.

astride in the manner (or condition) of striding.

atilt in the manner of tilting; in a tilting position.

afoot by means of the feet; on the feet.

aslug like, in the manner of a slug.

aloud in a loud manner.

¶ 7. For *off.*

adown (Ang. of dūne,) down, downwards, towards the ground.

¶ 8. For *of.*

ashamed, made the subject of shame. (Old Eng. ofchamed; English verb of-sceamian.)

anew in the new. (Old English of new.)

¶ 9. For *ad-*.

[Fr. à *at, to.* See AD-.]

agree to be on good terms. (GRĀTĬĂ favor, good terms.)

appoint, Fr. à point; Ital. a punto.

assets, old Fr. assez, Lat. SĂTĬS enough.

apiece apart alert adieu amort apropos avast aver affront avail avow ⁺agreve annoy (a n o i e, Chaucer) **abash abate abroach abandon ameliorate alarm alloy achieve**

Obs. The ad- of affront, appoint, a-scribe, a-scend, a-droit, amass, has become a- as perfectly as *on* has, in *aside,* or *at* in *ahead;* because English speech does not admit of doubled consonants.

¶ 10. For *in.*

around, Fr. en rond; Ital. in ronda.

arrange, Fr. en rang, au rang; *au* being for à le *at the.*

¶ 11. For *ge-*. See c-.

aback aright aware alike adrift among ⁺anough

The fifchers wer radi a n o u ȝ . . . . (See in Halliwell.)

. . . . bothe yliche
Honoured were.—*Chaucer.*

¶ 12. *be-*, *by*, period.

anight (Chaucer,) by night, during the night.

anights nowadays afore aforesaid aforetime

. . . afore the harveſt.—*Isaiah,* 18 : 5.

¶ 13. For *ex-*.

amend (for emend) to remove (MĒNDĂ) a fault.

award the sentence of an arbitrator. (Old Fr. esward, a right to something; eswardeur, an inspector.)

4*

afraid impressed with fear. (Fr. effrayer *to frighten.*)

Ther wol I firfte amenden and begin.—*Chaucer.*

What frayes ye, that were wont to comfort me affrayd?—*Spenser.*

I hid my felfe from it as one affeard;—*id.*

¶ 14. For *ah, oh.*

alas alack, exclamations of sorrow.

¶ 15. Verbal, or redundant.

alight awake arise arouse abide adry afar ado

Alone is composed of *all* and *one,* with the old spelling and pronunciation.*

Sire, he feide . . . the Lord ys God al one, . . . —*Robert of Gloucester,* about 1300.

A-, AB, ABS- *from.*

[Lat. Ā-, Ă B, Ā BS *from;* Sanscrit APA, AP-, AVA *far;* ἀπό, ἀπ-, ἀφ-, ἀ- *from;* Russian, Polish, Bohemian ob-; Irish as; (Aztec accidental,) Irish, Gælic a-; Welsh af- (negative,) o *from,* aw *a flow;* eb, wff *motion from* or *out;* ob *a going from,* if *that is impelled;* wy *that proceeds from.* Gothic af, abu; German ab; Anglish af-, of-, a-; English of, off. Sanscrit root AB, AMB *to go, to move.*]

abs-tract (TRĂHO) to draw or take from; an abridgment.
abs-tain (TĔNĔO) to hold from; to forbear or refrain.
abject (JĂCTŪm) thrown away; mean; worthless.
abjure (JŪRO) to swear from; to renounce on oath.
abrupt (RŪMPO, RŪPTUm) broken off.
abs-ent being away. (ĔSSĔ to be; ĔNS, gen. ĔNT-ĬS being.)
a-vert (VĔRTO) to turn aside, from, or away; to prevent.
ab-use to use improperly; to maltreat; to revile.
abs-cond (CONDO) to hide from, whence s-coundrel, with abs- reduced to *s.* **ablution** a washing off (LUO I lave.)

abbreviate and **abridge** (βραχύς BRĔVĬS brief) to shorten. **abridgment** a synopsis or compendium.

advance and **advantage, avant-,** belong here as heteronyms of the French av-ancer, av-antage, from AB, and ĂNTĔ *before.* The old English authors give the true forms.

As footh is fayd, elde* hath gret avantage; — * *Old age.*
In elde is bothe wifdom and ufage.† — † *Experience.*
Men may the old out-renne but not out-rede.‡ — ‡ *Counsel.*
Chaucer.

To ketch him at avauntage in his fnares.—*Spenser.*

Obs. 1. s-cout is from ĀVSCŪLTO I listen, AVS for ĀVRĬS the ear, and CŎLO (CŪLTŪm) to practice.

2. By the loss of *b*, abs- may become as-, as in ĀSPŌRTĀRĔ to carry off; ĀSPĔLLĔRĔ to drive away; and ab- is AV- diphthong in AVFĔRO I bear away; AVFŬGĬO I fly from.

3. It is doubtful whether ab- or ad- is the prefix in *abbreviate* and *aperient*.

apo-calypse (κἄλὐπτω I cover,) a revelation or uncovering.
apo'cope (κόπτω I cut,) a cutting off.
aph-elion a planet's most distant position from (ἥλῐος) the sun. **a-podal** footless.

A- without. See *AN-*.

a-damant or **diamond** (ἄδἄμᾶς, *α-* not, δαμάω I subdue, whence *tame*,) that (mineral) which is unconquerable.

The dore was all of athamant eterne.—*Chaucer.*

AD *to.*

[ĂD, Welsh at, idd *to;* Ss. ADHI, A *towards, at;* Fr. à; Go. at; Ang. at, oð; Isl. ad, at. Gaelic ath- *very.* (Heb. ἰθ, ἐθ-.) Ss. root AT *to move;* Welsh eth, s. what is in motion; add, s. *a laying upon;* idd *to, into;* eto *yet, also;* Gr. ἔτῐ *yet.* Akin to Ss. AT'HĬ *and;* Ang. ant, an *and;* Lat. ĀT *but;* ĔT *and;* Eng. and, at, y-et, to.]

a- ac- ad- af- ag- al- an- ap- as- at- ar-

adapt (ĀPTO) to fit to. **adhere** (HÆRĔO) to stick to.
admire (MĪRŎR) to wonder at. **adore** (ŌRO) to pray to.
accept‡ (CĂPĬO) to take to. **accede** (CĒDO) to give to.
affix‡ (FĪGO) to fix to. **affluent** (FLŬĔNS) flowing to.
aggregate‡ (s. GRĒ-X) flock together.
aggression (V. GRĂDĬŎR, S. GRĔSSŬS) a stepping towards.
agglutinate‡ (S. GLŪTĔN) glued together.

alleviate (LĔVO) to give comfort to.
alloquy‡ (v. LŎQUŎR) a speaking to.
annex (NĔCTO) to tie to.
annotation‡ (NŎTĀTĬO) a noting to.
announce (NŪNCĬO) to bring news to.
annihilate‡ to reduce to (NĬHĬL) nothing.
annul‡ (NŪLLŪ^m nothing) to make void; reduce to nothing.
apparent‡ (PĀRĔO) to be present to.
append (PĔNDĔO) to hang to.
apposition apprehend approve apply appropriate applaud approximate.
assign‡ (SĪGNO) to inscribe, commit to.
associate (SŎCĬO) to join to.
a-scend (SCĂNDŌ) to climb up.
a-scribe to attribute to (in writing.)
attract‡ (TRĂHO) to draw to.
attribute (TRĬBŬO) to ascribe to.
arrogate‡ to claim to (one's self.)
arrest (RĔSTO) to bring to a stop.
a-l-e-r-t, Fr. alerte (**a-** for **ad-,** see **a-** ¶ 9; l- for the French article la *the,*) at the e-Rec-T, on guard. (Lat. Ē-RĬG-ĔRĔ, E-RE·C-T-Ū^m, to erect, animate, take courage.)

Obs. The dental vocables ad-, ana-, ante, and, at, in, on, &c. may be regarded as akin.

al, el *the.*

[The Arabic article al (ar-, as-, ad-,) el. The Spanish article el (Ital. il, Port. o,) is different, being derived from the Latin pronoun ĬLLĔ *he.*]

alcove the vault, the arch; Arab. qubbah, Heb. qŭbāh.
ar-roba the fourth (of 100 lbs.)
alcanna the henna, a kind of plant used in dyeing red.
alcaid (qâĭd) the câdi. **alcoran** (āl qorān) the reading.
Fomalhaut (al hūt *the fish,* fam *mouth,*) the name of a star.
Aldebaran (ad dabarân.) **l-ute** a kind of guitar. **alqali**
Alpherat alchemy alcohol algebra el-ixir a-thanor a-pricot artichoke admīr-al ăs-săgay′ (-gay as in guide.)

Al-ligator, Port. o lagarto, Sp. el lagarto, *the lizard*, Lat. LĂCĔRTŬS, with *c* as *k*, which accounts for the pure *g* (gay.) Elecampane is for *Enula campana*.

ALL-

[ἄλλος; ĂLĬŬS *other, another*. ĂLĬĀS *otherwise*. ĂLĬBĪ *elsewhere*.]

all-egory ἀλλ-ηγορία a speaking differently (conveying a sense different from the natural meaning.) ἀγυρεύω I speak in public. **par-all-el, par-all-ax** see *PARA*.

alien-ate aliquot alter alternate

AMBI, *AMPHI around, on both sides.*

[Ss. ABHI; Greek 'ἀμφί˘, ἀμφίς, Aeolic αμπί; Ang. emb, embe, ymb, ymbe, imb, umb, em; Belg. om-; Dan. om; Swed. om-; old Ger. umpi, umbi, umb; Ger. um *around;* Lat. AMBI, AMB-, AM-, AN-‡, as in ĂN-QVĪRO *I seek carefully*. Ss. root ĂB, ĂMB *to move*. See AB.]

amb-i-ent sur*round*ing. (ĔO, Ī-RĔ, Ĭ-TŪ^m^, to go.)

ambitious. am-pu-tate (PŬTO) to cut round or off.

amphitheatre (θεάομαι, to see) a theatre with the view from all sides.

amphibrach a poetic foot (˘ ¯ ˘) with a (βραχὺς) short syllable on each side of a long one.

ab-out (Ang. ymb-, ymbe-, embe-, emb-utan) round the outside.

AMBO *both.*

[Ss. UBHA; Gr. ἄμφω; Lat. ĀMBŌ *both*. Ss. root ŬMBH *to heap up*. The Greek and Latin forms are confused with AMBI, ἀμφί.]

amphi-bious (βί'ος life) living in air and water.

amphis-bæna (βαί-ν-ω I go) a genus of serpents with the head and tail very much alike, and thought capable of moving in either direction.

am'-phora (φέρω I bear) a vessel with a handle on each side. **amb-iguous** (ĂGO I move) dubious, moving on both sides. **ambidexter ambi'logy ambi'loquy**

AN-, A- without. See IN-, un-.

a-byss (*ϐυσσὸς* the bottom) a bottomless pit; immensity.

a-chromatic without (*χρῶμα*) color.

a-maranth (*ἀμάραντος*) unfading.

am-brosia‡ (*ἀμβροσία*) the food of the gods; *ἀμϐρόσιος*, *ἄμβροτος*, *ἄβροτος* immortal; *ϐροτὸς* mortal. (The *m* is due to the *b*.) **a-cephalous** headless. **an-omaly** (*ἀνωμᾰλία*) irregularity, not (*ὁμαλὸς*) re-sem-bling. **an-onymous** without name. **an-odyne** (*ἄν-*) without (*ὀδῠ́νη*) pain; whence (using *νὴ-* without,) *Νωδῠνία*, n., *Νώδῠνον*, adj. whence the corrupt Latinised form **laudanum,** a medicine which relieves pain.

apetalous asymmetric an-ecdote aphyllous a-sym-ptote a-sylum a-tom azoic azote an-æsthetic anarchy atonic

an-

ann-eal to temper by means of heat. (Ang. an-ælan, for on *in*, ælan *to burn, bake.*)

ann-eal (aneal, anele, Ang. æl *oil*) to anoint.

> Cut off euen in the bloſſomes of my ſinne,
> Vnhouzzled, diſappointed, vnnaneld,—'Hamlet' Act 1, Sc. 5. 1596.

Anoint is a corrupt form of *unguent,* but Chaucer uses en-oynt (also anoynt,) as if to associate it with French en-, Latin in-.

Answer belongs to *ANTI.*

ANA back, up, again.

[Ss. ANU *on, after;* Gr. *ἀνᾰ́ back,* &c., *ἄνω upwards;* Gothic ana *up, on, in;* Ger. an; Eng. on. Ss. root ĂN to *move.*]

analysis (*λῠ́σῐς*) a loosing back, an undoing, unravelling, or explanation. **analyst analytic**

anapest (*παίω* I strike, *ἀνὰ* back) a poetic foot, like ă′năpēst, used in Greek and Latin verse.

an-eurism a disease of the arteries. (*εὐρῠ́νω* to *di*late, swell *up*, broaden *out.*)

ana′-dromous running up, said of sea fish which ascend

rivers. **anadem** a chaplet. (ἀνα-δέω to bind up or around.) **analogue** something with a *parallelism*, or correspondence with something else. **ana'logous** **ana'logy**

anamorphosis a forming *anew*, or over again.

anatreptic *over*turning, upsetting, subversive.

an-choret one who retires, goes away, goes back; from χωρέω I go, give way.

ana-tomy dissection, a cutting up, through, or apart.

anabaptist one who baptises *again*.

anachronism a *transposition* of periods of (χρόνος) time.

anagram **anastomo'sis** **ana-glyptic** **ana-lectic**

AN-O adv. *above, up.*

ano'stoma a genus of snails in which the (στόμα) mouth or aperture of the shell is turned upward.

ANTE, ANT- *before.*

[Ss. ATI *beyond*, ANTI *against;* Gr. ἄντα, ἀντί *against, before;* Lat. ĀNTĔ, ANTĬ-, Oscan ANTER *before;* Ital. ante-, anti-, anzi; Russ. ot-; Go. anda, and-; Ang. anda-, and-, æt-, et-. Sanscrit root AT or AN to *move.*]

ante-, anti-, ant-, an-, -aunt, -ance, anci-

antecedent (CĒDO I go) going before.

an-cestor for *antecessor* or *antcessor*.

antedate **antemeridian** **antediluvian** **anti-cipate**
an-ti-que **anci-ent** adv-**ance** adv**antage** av**aunt**

ANTI, ANT-, ANTH- against. See ANTE.

ant-agonist he who has (ἀγών) a contest *against* some one.

ant-arctic *opposite to* the arctic region or circle.

anth-elmintic (ἕλμινς a worm) a medicine given to expel tape-worms, &c. **anti'pathy** adverse (πά'θος) feeling.

an-swer (swear, Ang. andsvarian,) to speak in return.

a-long (Ang. andlang, ondlong,) at length, lengthwise.

antispasmodic **antibilious** **antichamber** **ant-acid**
ant-ecian **anth-em** **antidote** **anti'pod-es** **anti'thesis**

APO, AP-, APH- from. See AB-.

apogee a point in the orbit of the moon (and sun) most distant (ἀπὸ) from (γῆ) the earth.

apologue (λόγος a discourse) a fable with a moral meaning apart from the narration. **apology** vindication, excuse.

apoplexy (ἀποπληξία) a striking down. Adj. **apoplectic.**

apostrophe **apostasy** **apocalypse** **aph-elion** **aph-orism** **aph-æ'resis** **ap-agoge** **apo-stle** **apothegm** **apothe'osis**

AR-

[An obsolete Latin preposition in ĂR-BĬT-ĔR, assimilated to ag- in ex-ag-ger-ate, and present in ĂRCĔSSO (frequentative of CĬĔO *I call,*) *I summon, accuse, repeat.* Irish and Welsh ar *upon,* hence Armorica a country *on* (mor) *the sea.*]

arbiter (BĪTO I go) one who goes near; a looker on; an umpire. **arbitrator** **arbitration** **arbitrary** **arbitrate**

exaggerate to heighten by representation. (A·GGĔRO *I heap up, add;* ĔXA·GGĔRO *I heap up much, magnify.*)

AUTO- self.

autograph (αὐτὸς one's self, γρᾰφὴ a writing) a person's handwriting.

auto'maton (μᾰ'ω to feel an impulse,) a self-moving mechanism. **autocrat** (κρᾰ'τος rule) one who rules alone.

The said hero of this auto-biography or auto romance of Casanova appears to narrate it with design of exciting our admiration both of his gallantry and wit.—*Westminster Review,* 1827.

auth-entic self-authoritative; αὐθεντέω, to have authority or independent power; from the second aorist participle εἷς, gen. ἕντος, of ἵημι to be (or to put) in motion. Ellenic (Modern Greek) αὐθέντης, pronounced ἀφθένδις (with τ as English *d,*) a master of his own actions, a proprietor, whence the Turkish **effendi** *Sir*, a title of respect. **Reis effendi** *chief effendi;* Arabic râïs a chief.

Author is from ☞ ĀVGĔO.

avant *before.* See A-, AB.

avantcourier (CŬRRO I run) one who runs (ĀNTĔ) before.

B-, P-, F-, v-, w-, m-, be- *by; to make*, &c.

[Hebrew B-; Syriac, Ethiopic BA *at, by, in.* Arabic, Persian VA- (wa-) *by, with,* Pers. bi-. Go. bi; old Eng. be-, bi-, by-; old Frisian bi-, be-, b-; old Ger. bi, pi, pe, be, pa, ba; old Saxon bi-; Ger. be-; Ang. be, bi, big, b-, as in b-innan *within;* Belg. bij; Dan., Swed. be-, bi-. Sanscrit ĂBHĪ *by, on,* API *near, on.* Pers. ba, aba *with;* Gr. ἐπί, *on.* Sanscrit labial roots VĀ, VI, AB to *move.* Welsh uf *that is over* or *diffused,* aw *a flow,* af *a going forward,* ib *that runs forward,* ffy *aptness to move.* Akin to ☞ AB, OB-, AMBI-, and indicating *approach, junction.* It sometimes serves to locate the act, and sometimes intensifies.]

beset (Ang. bisettan) to set on, make an onset.
besiege to sit by, to invest with an army.
benumb (Ang. benuman) to make (cause to be) numb.
bemire to make miry, or cover with mire. § 86.
behead to deprive of the head. (Ang. biheáfdian.)
f-la..me (*φ-λέγ-μα*, F-LĀMMĂ‡) **f-licker, fu-lgid, b-leach, b-lanch, blink, blank, bleak, black, blight, blaze, please, placid, flash,** (Latin LŪCĔO, to glitter; *φ-λέγ-ω*, F-LĀGRO, to burn.)
b-lot (LĬNO, LĬTŪm,) to bedaub. **p-recation** rog-ation.
p-linth, p-late, f-lat, ☞ LĀTŬS broad.
b-rave Welsh rhab, old Ger. raw.
w-aste ἔσθω, to eat, waste.
flap, blab, lip, lobe, λεπὶς λοπὶς a scale. **break** wreck **flavous livid**

begin, old Eng. biginnen, 1250; bigan, 1280. bi gete, Rob. Gloucester. **bethought,** bithoute, 1280. **bylaw,** Ang. bilagu. **a-b-ove,** Ang. b-ufan. **a-b-aft,** Ang. beæftan.

becalm bedim bedeck bedrop become befal betray below between before beside

dep-**rive** be-reave	**plaud** laud	**flag** lag
block lock	**plump** lump	**blithe** lithe
brim rim	**frigid** rigid	**flaccid** βλάξ lax

work irk, co-erce. **b-eak, b-eac-on** see under *-N.*
m-orn ☞ ŎRĬŎR.
b-ooth W. bwth, from wth *that expands.* **f-oo-d** see D-.
m-axillary **m-ucron**ate **m-eagr**e **m-agn**ify **b-ig** **m-icro**scope
v-ex **v-oice** **v-ictim** **v-agrant** **v-icin**ity **v-igor**

Obs. 1. This prefix may be *locative,* as in **bemoan** to moan for a particular object, **behind,** in the posterior position: it may be *intensive,* as in **berate;** and *completive,* as in **become.**

Obs. 2. In Welsh names, B, P (for *ab, ap*) means *son,* as in Price (ap Rhys,) Pugh, Parry, Barry, Bevan, Bowers.

Obs. 3. In old books are found the forms biholde, bihelde, bifore (old Ger. bifora,) bigynne. Ihon Frampton 1577, uses bicause; R. of Brunne bicome, bisought, biforhand; Wiclif biholde; and Chaucer (born 1328) beblotte, begiled, berained, bimene (moan,) biwopen (weep,) bilieve.

Obs. 4. In German graben is *to dig,* begraben *to bury;* halten *to hold,* behalten *to keep,* verhalten *to retain;* klagen *to complain,* beklagen *to pity,* anklagen *to accuse;* langen *to reach* (*ng* as in singer,) verlangen *to desire,* belangen *to attain,* whence *belong.*

Obs. 5. Polish lewy *lef-t,* (*w* as English *v,*) wlewo *on the left.* An accidental resemblance occurs in the Caffre amba *to catch,* pamba *to hold fast.*

BINI *two by two.* See BIS.

bin-ocular pertaining to, or having two eyes; pertaining to a telescope or other optical instrument, adapted to vision with both eyes simultaneously.
binary **combination** **binoxid**

BIS, DIS- *in two, twice.*

[Sanscrit DVIS *twice,* DVI; *δύω;* Lat. DŬŎ *two;* BĬS, BI-, VI-, DIS, DI-; Zend BI-; Irish di-; Welsh dis-, di-. Gr. *διχῆ in two ways; δι·σσὸς* (Ionic διξος, Attic *διττὸς*) *double; διά through.* Sanscrit root DO or DVIS *to cut, separate.*]

bi-sect dis-sect (SĔCO, SĒCTŪ^m) to cut in two.
biscuit twice baked **bicornous** having two horns.
ba-lance BĬLANX (LANX a dish) a pair of scales.
biangular **bivalve** **biped** **bis-sextile**
Biology is a (*λόγος*) discourse on (*βίος*) life.

bu- augmentative.

[βοῦ, often referred to βοῦς an *ox*, but Eichhoff refers it to Sanscrit BHŪJAS *much*.]

bulimy (βουλῑμία) morbid insatiable (λιμὸς) hunger.

Bu- means *ox* in bugloss (oxtongue,) bucolic, bucentaur, bucrania.

c-, g-, y-, a- *much*, *perfectly*, *be-*.

[Gothic ga-; Ger., Ang. ge-; old Ger. ga-, gi-, ka-, ca-, ki-, gha-, cha-, ha-; old Saxon gi-; Swed., Dan. ge-; old Frisian gi-, i-, je-, ie-, e-, i-, a-; Gr. ε-, γ-, κ-, as in λήμη and γλήμη *bleαredness;* λάβω *I take,* κ-λέπ-τω *I steal.* Old Eng. i-, y-; English a-; Welsh c-, g-; Celtic h-. Akin to the Greek and Latin guttural reduplication of the perfect tense. Its intensive power is seen in the Welsh wrdd *impulse*, gwrdd *vehement;* Ss. RĀr (as if *rash*) to *ring*, CRŬr to *resound.* As intensives and restrictives, ge- and be- are allied, and the following are Anglish examples of their use—

fyllan *to fill,*	befyllan *to fill up,*	gefyllan *to fulfil.*
healdan *to hold,*	behealdan *to behold,*	gehealdan *to preserve.*]

c-roup a disease of the throat accompanied by a peculiar cough; Belgian roepen (*oe* as in shoe) *to call;* geroep *a cry*.

a-ware (Ger. v. gewahren,) having a perception of.

g-leam (λά'μπω) to shine much.

ch-lor-ine a gas of a greenish color. (χλορὸς green; λειρ-ὸς pale, (whence *lily;*) LŪR-ĬD-ŬS lur-id.)

in-**c-line**, as if in-**ge-lean**, κλί'νω I bend.

q-uake, **q-uag**-mire, wag. **g-uile**, wile. **c-reep** RĒPO.

a-mong Ang. gemang, mæng-an (*ng* as in singer) *to mix*. **a-back** Ang. gebæc. e-**nough** Ang. genóh. **y-ore** Ang. geára, ær, or *time*. **y-ond-er** Ang. geond. **c-lammy** loam, lime. **cloud** Ang. hlidan *to cover*. **c-lump** lump. **c-rumple** rumple. **ga-llop** **c**-lip leap. **c-liff** λεπὰς a rock.

c-rib, **g-rab**, **g-ripe**, rob. **g-rumble** **g-lance** **g-lobe** **c-rude** **a-like** **a-right** **a-wake** **a-long** **a-weary** **a-go** **+agon** **y-cleped** **+ygon** **+ydon** **jeo-pardy** **aready**, **aredy**, Gothic garaids.

And ſawe his barge yſailing in the ſe.—*Chaucer*.

. . . . it ought ynough ſuffiſe
Five houres for to ſlepe upon a night.—*id.*

I know you well inough.—'King Arthur,' 1634.

CATA, CAT- CATH- against, down.

cataplasm (πλάσσω I smear) a medicinal plaster.

cat-echise, ἠχέω I echo, utter, κατηχέω I sound *abroad,* teach (with the voice.)

cataract a falling or dashing down.

catastrophe a turning over, or upside-down.

cat-acomb an underground structure for the repose of the dead. (κατα-κοιμίζω to set κατὰ down to sleep.)

catachresis, (χρῆσις) use (of a word, κατὰ) against its proper sense, as in calling a *camel* a 'ship.'

catalogue has the prefix *restrictive;* the word meant *according to* account or selection, having been applied to the list of persons se-lec-ted for military duty. See under § 86.

catalepsy, a disease in which sensation and motion suddenly cease: λαμβάνω, to take, *seize,* (and with κατα-) to seize *firmly,* the prefix being *intensive* and restrictive.

cath-olic pertaining to, or including (ὅλος) all; general; universal.

Catholick Affections of ſimple Bodies, namely Bulk, Shape, and Motion, or Reſt . . .—[*Boyle*, 1675.

Fiſhermen of the Catholic religion.—Asiatic Researches, 1799.

The Catholic or general epistles: viz. of James, Peter, John, and Jude.—*Dr. Adam Clarke*, 1820.

CAT-O adv. *below.*

cato'stoma, a genus of American fishes (known as suckers) in which the (στόμα) mouth is (κάτω) below.

CIRCUM *around, about.*

[Lat. CĪRCŬS, CĪRCŬLŬS a *circle;* γῦρ-ός *cur-ved, gyr-ate.* Ss. root G R̥ H to *enclose.*]

circumambulate to walk around.

circumnavigate to sail round.

circumpolar about the poles.

circumscribe -vallation -ambient -locution -flex -spect circu-itous

CIS *on this side.*

[cĭ-s, a Latin preposition formed of the indicational element C, and the adverbial suffix -s in bĭs, twi-ce.]

cisalpine on thi-s (the Roman) side of the Alps.

cisatlantic on this (the Europèan) side of the Atlantic.

C-L' continuative.

The root of ech-o (and ĭc-tŭs a blow,) gives the following—

clack (l-augh l-ick) **click** **clock** **cluck** **clang** **clink**

CO-, CON-, *SYN with, together.*

col-, com-, cor-, cu-, cur-; co-ad-, co-al-, co-ap-; co-ex-, co-ef-; co-en-, co-in-; con-de-; con-sub-; coun-.

[Gr. ξὺν (csyn) σὺν; Lat. co- cŏn-; Rhaetian cun-; Wallachian kon-. Welsh can-, gan-, cy-, cyn-, cyd-, cym-; Irish co-, comh-. Akin to c-, g-.]

concur (cŭrro I run) to agree in opinion.

congregate (grēx a flock) to assemble together.

coun-sel cōnsĭlĭŭm consultation, advice. (consŭlo, to consult, advise.)

coun-cil cōncĭlĭŭm an assembly summoned by authority. (cālo and călo I call.)

comb-ustion (☞ ūro,) *b* is educed from *m*, which is assimilated from *n* before the labial vowel.

cu-stom, Lat. COnSueTUdineM. **co-uch** COllOCo I put in place, lodge. **cur-ry** to dress leather; Ital. corredare, old Fr. conroyer *to dress or prepare.* (*H. Wedgwood.*)

qu-ash, old French esquachier *to crush;* Latin cŏ-āctŭs *a constraining.* (*Diez.*)

construct **convene** **conduce** **condign** **co-gnate** **co-operate** **coequal** **coexist** **co-st** **coun-tenance** **compose**‡ **compress** **compatriot** **commotion** **correct**‡ **correspond** **correlative** **corrode** **collapse**‡ **collect**

synchronous (χρόνος time) simultaneous.

synonymous (ὄνομă name) identity of meaning.

sy-stem (ἵστημι, to set) a setting together to form a theory.

sy-stole (στέλλω I send,) the contraction of the heart which sends the blood forward; the reverse of dia-stole.

syllable (λαμβάνω I take) a taking together (as much of a word as can be pronounced at an impulse.)

sym-ptom‡ (πίπτω, to fall) that which happens *with* something else; a concomitant sign or indication.

symmetry (μέτρον measure) regular proportion.

sympathy (πάθος feeling) fellow feeling.

sy-zygy (ζυγόω, to yoke) a joining together.

Obs. syn- becomes sy- before Greek Z because this being *sd* (in wisdom,) the n of syn- would be brought before *s*, which would not be a Greek sequent. But if Greek Z were *ds* (as some suppose) it would be possible, *nd* being a Greek sequent, as in συν-δυλεία joint-servitude; ανδρία manhood.

COM- *with.*

[In Sanscrit, the root ϛAM or SAM to *unite*, gives rise to SAM, SA, SAN-‡ SA,-‡ *with*, which are probably distinct from CON, σὺν, ξὺν. The Latin CŪM, Gr. ἅμα (FĂMĂ) *with*, we refer to the Sanscrit JAM to *hold*.]

con-com-it-ant going (CŪM) with, accompanying.

com-ity companionableness.

CONTRA *against, opposite to.*

[L. CO'NTRĂ; Oscan CONTRUD; Fr. contre.]

contra-st (STŌ) to stand against, or in opposition to.

counter-march to march in an opposite direction.

counterbalance to balance with an opposite weight.

contrary **contravene** **contradistinguish** **contradict** **contro-vert** **counter** **counteract** **-sign** **-current** **-poise**

country-dance, in which the dancers stand opposite each other. A heteronym.*

cont-rol, as if counter-roll, a check-book—its primary meaning; restraint; v. to restrain; to direct.

* That is, a form due to a second (ἕτερος different) etymology, as sparrowgrass, Jerusalem artichoke, admiral, corporal.

CONTRŌ- *against.*

[Akin to CONTRA; and probably, with INTRŌ- and RĔTRŌ-, obsolete ablatives.]

controvert (VĔRTO v. a. I turn, change, overthrow) to turn an argument against an opponent; to dispute.

C-R', G-R'

[Intensive and imitative, and commonly indicative of noise. See C-L'.]

croak (CRŌC-ĬO, ⊥κρώζω,) to cry as a raven.

crack the noise of striking or breaking. (κρέκω, to strike, to sound from striking.) **cricket** a noisy insect.

creak s-creech crash craunch or **crunch crake grackle grunt groan grin grumble grate s-cratch s-crape scrub**

D-, T-, L-, N- intensive, frequentative.

[Greek intensive δα-, ζα-, (Bohemian do-,) as in *δά-σκῐος very shady,* (compare du-sk-y;) *ζα-πλοῦτος very rich; δ-ρέπ-ω I reap; τ-ρίβ-ω I rub; δ-ρύπ-τω I tear; θ-ρύπ-τω I break.* *ἀκοὴ a sound, the ear; ἠχὴ clamor; ἠχὼ echo; Λ-άκω, to sound like breaking;* Λ-έγω, to speak. Lat. L-ŌCŪSTĂ *a grasshopper* (a noisy insect;) L-ŎQVŎR *I speak,* FLĀGĬTO *I demand;* D-ĪCO *I say;* D-ŎCĔO *I t-each;* R-OGO *I ask;* LA-R-YNX *the seat of the voice.* Welsh frequentative dy-, as in yw *that exists,* b-wy *to live,* b-wy-d *f-oo-d,* bwyta *to eat,* dy-fwyta *to be eating often;* Irish d-lìghe *law.*]

d-ictate diction doctor or **teach**er—**l-ogic** dia**l-ogue** dia**lect apology—locution loquacity locust c-l-ack c-l-ang f-l-ag-iti-ous-ness—d-rum t-rumpet** rumble rumor st-rep-erous—**t-ake,** δέχομαι [☞ TĀNGO] **tangib**le **touch tact technical dignity d-ecens** in**d-ic**ate **d-extrous** pan**d-ect dactyl th-ing—l-ick** a blow, Lat. ĪCTŪS; ĪCO *I strike;* N-ĔCO *I kill.* **t-rib**ulation dia**tribe t-rouble th-rob d-rub,** (τ-ρῖπ-τὴρ a pestle.) **d-rive** p**l-ague kn-ock n-udge** k**n-uckle—n-oxious** i**nn-ocent n-ight**

d-windle wane **d-arn** (Welsh *a patch,* from arn *a fragment.*)

d-eep, W. wf a flow, a glide, that is liquid; dwfn *origin,* the *deep.*

t-wirl whirl **t-roll t-rill trip tramp tripe trap**

de, d- *of.* See DE.

[French de, d' *of.*]

dandelion Fr. dent de lion *lion's tooth.*

daffodil Fr. fleur d'asphodèle *asphodel flower*.

diaper figured linen (d'Ypres) *of Ypres* in Flanders. (In the language of Holland and Flanders, *y* or *ij* has the power of English *y* in by.) **louis d'or** **moidore**

(**d-** *duck.*)

d-rake the male of the (ĂNĂS, gen. Ă'NĂTIS, Ital. anaTRa, Ger. enTĕ, Dan. anD,) duck. (Ger. ent-r-ich, Dan. an**d-r-ik** a *drake*.) In old English, *drake* is also a form of *dragon*, as in *fire drake* a meteor.

de-coy a lure or snare (originally, to take ducks;) v. t. to lead into danger. (Flemish eend *a duck*, kooi *a cabin*, een**dekooi** a locality contrived for taking wild-ducks.)

decoyman he who decoys wild fowl. (Flemish kooiman, the *oo* as in *floor*.) The *e* of *decoy* is to be sought in the plural *eenden*, rather than in *eende* the dative singular,

DE-

[Lat. DĒ. Sp. de-; Ital. de-, di; Fr. dé- *from*. Irish di-, dith *want of*. Akin to DIS-, and SE-. Ss. roots DI to *decrease*; SE to *finish*.]

¶ 1. *down, downward.*

depend (PĒNDĔO) to hang *down from*.

depose (☞ PŌNO) to put *down*, *from*, *aside*, *off*, *away*.

deponent **deposit** **deposition** **depot** **depository**

dejected (JĂCĬO) cast down; disheartened; discouraged.

despise, despite (☞ SPĔCĬO) to look down on.

destitute (STĂTŬO) placed or fixed down; forsaken.

decoction (☞ CŎQVO; DĒCŎQVO to boil *down* or away.)

degenerate grown *worse*, or *from* its kind. ¶ 2.

decurrent running downward.

decadence, deciduous (CĂDO) a falling down, or from.

debate (Fr. battre) to beat down (with argument.)

depress **degrade** **debase** **decrease** **deteriorate** **depreciate** **decline** **declivity** **descend** **devolve** **decumbent** **detrude** **demulcent** **defluxion** **demersion** **devexity** **demise** +**demit**

Obs. As *he* shortens into *his, him*, so de- is mostly dĭ- in pronunciation, whence the spelling forms **di-**(for de-)**minutive** and **di-stil**; and Chaucer's distructĭōn.

Dec-ussate (DĔCĔm *ten,*) having cross lines in the direction of those of the numeral sign X.

Den-ārius (DĒNI *ten by ten,*) a silver coin equal to ten ases. See Matthew 20 :2, 22 :19, etc. where it is wrongly translated penny. It was worth about eight pence English.

¶ 2. *from, away, aside.*

detain (TĔNĔO) to hold *from* or *back;* to hinder.
despair (☞ SPĒRO I hope,) removal from hope.
deduce (☞ DŪCO) to draw from; infer. (DĒDŪCO I draw or bring down, from, out, with, in, back.)
deflect to bend aside.
deviate to go *aside, from,* or *out of* the (VĬĂ) way.
deambulate to walk abroad.
decease to die. (DĒCĒDO I go away, depart, subside.)
deliquesce to *dis*solve, *se*parate by liquefaction.
debar to shut *out,* keep *from.*
defend to fence *out* or *in,* ward *off,* keep *away, re*pel.
deport to carry away. **-ment** carriage; behavior.
detriment (☞ TĔRO, to rub, wear,) damage by use.
detri'tus material worn away, particularly from rocks.
defray to remove or discharge (Fr. frai*s*) expenses.
detraction a drawing away. **detergent** cleansing away.
devoid void by taking something away.
destitute poor, in want of, (as food, virtue, &c.) DĒSTĬTŬO I fix or fasten *down,* abandon, run *away from,* desert.
de-gen-erate removed from its ancestral kin-d. ¶ 1.

decamp debark depart deter (**desert, dehort,** ¶ 4) **detain deduct desist defraud deforce defalcate deprive deceive decide derogate des'ultory** (**decay** ¶ 1) **detach detail deter depurate deputation dethrone detruncate decollate defile** n. **delight delectable delicious detort detour detract derive decree** +**decern devest** or **divest**

Quickſilver . . . deveſted of its external Sulphur, . . . —*Boyle* 1675.

Deb-ility is from DĒBĬLĬS feeble; δέω, to need.
Decent, DĔCĔT it is fit.

¶ 3. Privative.

Separative of an object, and based mostly on nouns.

decorticate to deprive of, *remove*, or *separate* the (CŌRTĔX) bark. **deodorise** to deprive of odor.

desulphurate to deprive of (SŪLFŬR) sulphur.

depilatory a preparation for removing (PĬLŬS) pile or hair.

demented deprived of mind.

decarbonise depopulate decapitate demoralise denaturalise demercurialise desquamation despumation

Defame probably belongs to dis-, Lat. DIF-FĀMO, to speak evil of.

I ſhall diffame him.—*Chaucer.*

¶ 4. Negative, oppositive.

Reversive of, or oppositive to an act, and based on verbs. The *negative* of composed is uncomposed, but its *oppositive* is decomposed.

de'suetude want of practice; disuse; *not* (SVĒSCO, SVĒTŪm,) in the habit of.

destruction (STRŬO I build, construct,) the act of pulling down, *un*fixing, *dis*arranging; the *reverse* or *opposite* of *con*struction, as **develop** is the reverse of *en*velop.

devaporation the changing of vapor into water.

demolish (MŌLĬŎR, to build,) to *un*build; pull down.

dehort to advise to the contrary; to dissuade.

deform to unform; to deprive of form; to disfigure.

deplete (CŌMPLĔO I fill up, make full,) to render less full.

. . . depleting measures would have killed the patient.—*T. J. Bowen.*

detect (TĔGO, TE·CTŪm to cover,) to *un*cover, *dis*cover, expose. **decrease** to grow less.

de'sert an uncultivated waste. (SĔRO, SĂTŪm, to sow, plant; DĒSĔRO to cease to sow; to leave uncultivated.)

dese'rt to abandon in contravention to a compact. (SĔRO, SE·RTŪm, εἴρω, to bind, join.)

decompose to separate what was composed; to decay.

defective, deficient not fully or *per*fectly made; having a part *un*made.

defeat to undo; to overthrow; to frustrate.

> The incantation backwards ſhe repeats,
> Inverts the rod, and what ſhe did defeats.—*Garth*, 1669.

di-shevel to have or put the hair in disorder. (Fr. décheveler; from cheveu *hair.*)

Demerit may be placed here, but in Latin it would belong to ¶ 5.

desecrate **defeasible** **defection** **derogate** **detach**

Obs. Some words in de- are spelt with di-, and Chaucer has forms like discend, dispise, dispoiled.

¶ 5. Intensive.

Much, entirely. Based upon verbs, and perficient, conclusive, or completive.

detonate to burn with a sudden explosion; TŎNO to sound, to thunder; DĒTŎNO to thunder; to finish thundering.

deflagrate to burn violently.

depredate, despoil to plunder much.

devastate to lay waste much, or entirely.

decide (CAEDO) to cut short; to determine.

declare to make very clear, to maintain.

dehiscent gaping wide. **deputise, delegate** to give in special charge, to intrust with a particular business. ¶ 7.

decrepitate to split with continued crackling, or to the utmost, as salts in the fire. (DĒCRĔPĬTŬS *past* making noise.)

decrepit completely shattered.

desolate entirely (SŌLŬS) alone.

dereliction an entire re-linq-uishment.

desiccate to make thoroughly (SĬCCŬS) dry.

defunct (FŪNGŎR to perform,) entirely done, performed, or gone through with.

depasture **depauperate** **devour** **desiderate** **desire** **debullition** **indefatigable** **despond**

☞ SPŌNDĔO I promise, pledge, give a hope; DĒ-SPŌNDĔO I promise, pledge, *despond*,—which may be a *negative* of SPONDEO in its sense of giving a hope; it may be an *intensive;* and by associating the prefix with de- of *deject, despair,* it may in this place have the sense of *down* or *from*. Similarly, *dethrone* may mean to *de*pose, ¶ 1; to drive *from*, ¶ 2, or deprive of a throne, ¶ 3; and to *un*throne, as the opposite of *en*throne, ¶ 4. These examples show that in some cases the same word may be placed under different heads according to the shades of meaning with which it is associated. See §§ 86–89.

¶ 6. Causative.

deprave to make or cause to be (PRĀVŬS) crooked or perverse. **depraved** vitiated; distorted. **depravity** perversity.

destine to cause to stand; to appoint, assign, determine.

determine to fix a (TĔRMĬNŬS) limit; establish; adjust.

¶ 7. Locative.

dedicate to *in*scribe or *as*sign to a *particular* person or purpose. **devote** (**devout**,) to consecrate *to* a special use. (VŎVĔO I vow.) **deride** (RĪDĔO, RĪSŬ^m) to laugh at a particular object. **deplore** to lament, etc. **delinquency** a leaving or departure *from* a duty; an omission.

depict to paint or draw from an object.

demonstrate to point *out*, *ex*plain something.

deprecate to pray (earnestly, ¶ 5,) *against* something.

detestation (TĔSTŎR, to aver,) imprecation against.

denunciation a threatening announcement; a declaration against.

delineate describe define determine designate denote denominate delude delirious default defalcation demand demur deny ¶ 5, 8.

¶ 8. Verbal.

deliberate demean deplore ¶ 7 **deprave** ¶ 6 **declare** ¶ 5 **declaim demand deserve debate deny defraud decease**

¶ 9. For DI-, DIS-.

Defer, is *differ* accented on the second syllable. *Defy*, Ital. dis-fidare, to break faith. *Delay*, for *dilay*, DĪLĀTĬO a putting off. *Deluge*, Lat. DI-LUvIUM. *Device*, *devise*, are from the root of *divide*. *Device, devise*, are from the root of *divide*.

Obs. Spelling and etymology have but little connexion, and an English word may or may not follow a French original. The deceptive form 'phthisic' is supposed to be as much Greek as *thesis*, although the pronunciation and the form indicate the contrary, the Greek word being φθίσις (phthĭsĭs,) French phthisie, Italian tisica, and Spanish tisica. Bishop Wilkins wrote 'tissick' in 1668, and Milton 'tizzic' about the same time, 'phthisic' being apparently a later form, whereas, *dropsy* and *quinsy* are regularly derived from 'hydropisy' and 'squinancy,' which had preceded them.

The following are examples of variation between French and English words.

adresse	*address*	manuel	*manual*
caractère	*character*	mariage	*marriage*
désordre	*disorder*	messager	*messenger*
discorde	*discord*	préambule	*preamble*
discours	*discourse*	pretention	*pretension*
extorsion	*extortion*	propriété	*property*
frise	*frieze*	restauration	*restoration*
hysope	*hyssop*	rapport	*report*
jaunisse	*jaundice*	symétrique	*symmetric*
losange	*lozenge*	zèle	*zeal*

demi- *half.*

[DŬO *two;* DĬMĬDĬŪm, Fr. demi *a half.* See BIS-.]

demigod demiquaver demilune demigorge demitint

Demiurge a subordinate creator; δημιουργός a maker, a chief Dorian magistrate; δήμιος public; ἔργον a work, a business.

des- separative; intensive.

[French dés-, a form of DIS-, confused with DE.]

des-cry (DĒ-CĔRNO,) to perceive distinctly; to discover.

des-cant DĒ-CĂNTĀRĔ to sing or repeat often.

despatch, Sp. despachar, to do or send immediately.

dis-, des-habille (Fr. dés*h*abillé) an informal dress.

desse'rt the last course of a repast.

DIA through. See BIS.

diameter (δῐᾰ̀ μέτρον) measure through.

di-æresis (αἱρέω I take,) a taking *apart* (the two elements of a diphthong, as in saying claw-y for *cloy*.)

diatribe a continuous discourse (δια-τ-ρῐβή a rubb-ing, a lecture, a dispute.) **diadem** (δῐᾰ-δέω I bind around.)

dialogue (λόγος) discourse *between* (several persons.)

dea-con διάκονος an attendant; (κόνις dust; κονέω I run rapidly, raise dust, be active, serve.)

diaphanous **diagonal** **diagram** **diatonic** **de-vil** **+divel**

Or hellifh feend rayfd up through divelifh science.—*Spenser.*

DI-, DIS- *apart, un-.*

[Separative. DĬS-, DĪ; It. di-, dis-, s-; Sp. di-, dis-, de-, des-; Fr. di-, dis-, dé-, des-. See BIS.]

¶ 1.

diverge (VĔRGO) to incline apart.

dislocate to put out of (LŎCŬS) place.

disquisition (QVÆRO I seek) inquiry into part-iculars, or separate parts. **digress** (☞ GRĂDĬŎR) to step aside.

discuss (QVĂTĬO, QVĀSSUm, to shake, beat, *quash*, *concuss*,) to shake apart;—used in its primary sense in surgery, as, to discuss pimples. Compare *debate*, DE, ¶ 1.

Peny-royal and Nep difcufs and fhake off the cold in Ague.—*Holland's Plinie*, 1635.

dispel to drive apart. **distract** to dra-w apart.

disjoin to unjoin, place apart, separate.

diminish to lessen by separation of a part.

discourse a passing from one thing to another.

disperse (☞ SPĀRGO) to scatter widely.

di-stant stand-ing apart. **direct** to regulate, arrange.

dispose (☞ PŌNO) to distribute, arrange, adjust.

dis-cern **dis-tinguish** **discriminate** **dissolve** **dispose** **dif-fer** **diffuse** **display, splay** **disport, sport** **dilate** **dilapidate** **dilute** **digest** **deluge** **divide, devise, device**

¶ 2.

Dis- has a separative and negative or reversing force, as in **disagree** not to agree. **dishonest** not honest. **difficult** un-fac-ile, not easy. **dishearten** to deprive of heart or cour-age. **defame** (DIFFĀMO,) to spread an evil report of.

I erryd in hurtyng and dyffamyng his book in dyverce places.—*Caxton*, about 1481.

disable disabuse displease disclaim disinter disclose dispossess disparage disarrange discoloration diffident

¶ 3.

In **difficult discolor discomfort disease discord disaster** the *idea* of dis- is allied to that of *δῠς- ill, badly.*

Obs. 1. *Disease* is based on *ease* like Bohem. *neduh* (sickness) on *ne* (not) and *duh* (to thrive.)

Obs. 2. The *dis* in disc-iple (DĪSCO I learn,) and disc-oidal form part of the root. In di-shevel, *s* belongs to the next syllable. See DE-, ¶ 4.

Obs. 3. Dis- is used for de- (or the two are confused) in disguise, disdain, distress, disarm (DĒ-ĀRMĀRĔ,) dishonor (DĒ-HŎNŌRĀRĔ, Fr. dés-, Sp. des-,) dissever. Gosson (1579) uses *discifer* (decipher;) and Chaucer *discent* (descent,) and *dispise.*

Obs. 4. Although DĒFĔRO (I carry, offer,) is a Latin word, *defer* and *differ* are from (dis-) DĪFFĔRO I spread, scatter. Defy, defame (¶ 2; DE, ¶ 3,) derange, deform (Fr. difformer,) may be placed here also.

DUO, DU- *two*. See BIS.

duel duet dual duplicate double duo-decimo (DŬŎDĔCĪM twelve) **do-deca-hedron deu-ce twi-ce twe-lve dou-bt**

DYS- bad, badly.

[δῠς-; Ss. DUS̱, DUR *bad, badly*, as in DURMANANAS, Gr. *δυσμενής ill*-MINDED, *hostile; δῠ΄η misfortune;* Russ. dúrno *badly.* Ss. root DŪ, DŬS̱ to *harm.* Gọthic tuз- and Irish do- (implying *difficulty*) probably belong here.]

dyspepsy *δυσπεψία* bad digestion. (*πέπτω* to cook, digest.) **dysopsy** dimness of sight. (*ὦψ* eye, look.) **dysentery** **dyspnœa** difficulty of breathing. (*πνοὴ* air, breath.) **dysphagy** difficulty in swallowing. (*φᾰγεῖν* to eat.)

e-

[Go. and, anda-; Ang. and-, on-; Ohg. and-, ant-, unt-, int-, en-, in-; old Fris. and, ande, anda, ende, end *in, at, on.*]

e-lope Belg. ont-loopen, Ger. ent-laufen, to run away, escape; loopen, laufen *to run.*

e- prosthetic.

[This e- is without meaning. In Spanish, initial S is not followed by certain consonants, as *cay* and *p;* but as esc-, esp-, &c. are initial combinations, there is a feeling that initial S in forms like sc-, sp- ought to make a distinct syllable, a feeling which is realised by prefixing e-, which caused SCŌRPĬŌN-ĬS and SPĔÇĬĒS to become *escorpion* and *especie.* French has this feature to a less extent.—*Hald.* Analytic Orthography § 219–20.]

e-squire or **squire** SCŪTĬGĔR (SCŪTŪ^{m} a shield, GĔRO I bear,) the armor-bearer of a knight; one legally entitled to use armorial ensigns; a justice of the peace.

epaulette escalade escutcheon eschew espalier espy etiquette

EN in.

[ἐν *in, on, very;* ἐγ-‡, ἐλ-‡, ἐμ-‡, etc. See IN.]

engrave (γράφω) to write or cut in. **enaliosaurian** pertaining to a (σαῦρα) lizard living (ἐν) in the (ἅλς) sea.

en *in.*

[The French form of ☞ IN, em-‡, am-,‡ an-.]

enclose to close in. **am-bush, am-busc-ade,** old Eng. emboyssement, abuchyment, Ital. imboscata, Fr. embûche, (as if) in-bush-ed, in the bushes.

embrace‡ (BRĀCHĬŪ^{m} the arm,) to clasp in the arms.

encircle enfold entitle endure entail entice enmity embody‡ empower emperor embalm embellish engine

Obs. En- is preferable to in-, inasmuch as it has a uniform meaning, whilst in- means both *in* and *not.*

Their wicked engins they against it bent;—*Spenser.*

ENDO-, ENTO-, INDI-, IND- within.

[Lat. INDŬ; ἔνδον *within;* ἄντρον, ĀNTRŪm *a cave.* See IN, INTER.]

endocarp (καρπὸς fruit,) the hard lining or stone of fruit like the peach or cherry.

endo'genous, endogenes plants growing within the trunk, and not by external layers like the exogenes.

indi-genous produced within; native to a country.

ind-igent in want. (ĔGĔO I want, need; ĔGENS needy.)

entozoa (ζῶον an animal, pl. ζῶα) animals (worms) living in other animals.

enter- See INTER

enterprise an undertaking. **entertainment entersole**

EPI over, on. See B-.

[ἐπὶ, ἐπ-, ἐφ-, often intensive or determinative.]

epide'rmis the cuticle or outer skin, that (ἐπὶ) *on* or *over* the true (δέρμα) skin.

epi-scop-al having the super-vision of a bi-shop.

epitaph an inscription on a (τά'φος) tomb.

epi'phany (ἐπιφάνία,) a festival commemorative of the appearance of our Lord; ἐπι-φαίνω (see -N- intensive,) to shine upon, to come forth (on an occasion.)

epi-stle ἐπιστολὴ (στέλλω I send,) something *sent*, as intelligence, a despatch, or a letter (by a messenger.)

eph-emeral pertaining to (ἡμέρα) a day.

ep-e'n-thesis the (θέσις) placing of an element or syllable (ἐπὶ, ἐν,) in a word, as in saying Ta*r*tar for Tâtar.

equi- *equal.*

equi-val-ent of equal val-ue. **equinox** the period when the (NŌX) night is (ÆQVŬS, gen. ÆQVĪ) equal to the day.

equilibrium (LĪBRĂ a balance,) of equal weight.

equidistant equiangular equity equ-animity equality

EU, EV-, well, good.

[*εὖ well, very;* Ss. sŭ *forcibly, well;* Ss. root sŭ to *produce; σεύω I throw, drive.*]

euphony (*φωνή* voice,) good or agreeable enunciation.

eulogy a formal (*λόγος*) discourse speaking *well* of some one.

ev-angel-ist an announcer of good; *ἄγγελος* a messenger; *αγγέλλω* (*ἀνα·γγέλλω*) I report. **eucharist** **euphemism**

EX, EC-, E- *out, out of, from.*

[Lat. Ē-, ĒX-; Ital. e-, ex-, es-, s-, eg-; *ἐξ-, ἐκ-*; Ss. VAHIS; Pers. aз; Gaelic as; Welsh es- and the noun ych *that is out*, and preps. o, oc, odd *from, out of.*]

except ☞ CĂPĬO, to take out.

exclaim ☞ CLĀMO, to call out.

eclogue (*λέγω*) a culling out. **excentric** out of the centre.

effigy‡ FĬNGO, to fashion out.

ec-lipse, el-lipsis (*λείπω* to leave,) a leaving out.

efflux‡ ☞ FLŬO, to flow out. **educe** ☞ DŪCO, to lead out. **elect** LĔGO, to cull out; to select by vote.

e-normous out of, or beyond (NŌRMĂ) rule.

e-radicate (☞ RĀDĪX a root,) to root out.

expostulate to urge, demand as a right, complain earnestly. (PŌSTŬLO, to demand, require, arraign.)

explode to drive out, condemn (as a false theory;) to burst with noise. (‡PLAVDO, to applaud with clappings; EXPLŌDO, to drive off by clapping and hissing; to condemn.)

. . . water refulting from the explofure of hydrogen and common air, . . .—*Prieftly.*

extenuate (TĔNŬĬS thin,) to thin out, mitigate, excuse.

extirpate (STĪRPS a stem, a race.)

exterminate **express** **expire** **extant** **exhale** **exit** **explain** **expose** **extend** **extract** **egress** **elude** **emanate** **emit** **educe**

s-trange is formed from ĔXTRĀNĔŬS (foreign) by eliding *ec* and converting E (through J) to English *j*.

iss-ue v. to proceed, pass out; n. progeny, result. (ĒX-ĪRĔ to go out; old Fr. iss-ir, participle masc. issu, fem. issue.)

The prefix is ec- or eg- in execute (for ex-secute,) exult, execrate, expire, expect.

s-camper (CĂMPŬS a field,) to hurry away through fear.

s-carce, the same as **ex-cerpt,** from CĂRPO I select.

s-poil **s-trip** (drape) **es-cape** **example** and **sample** **expand** and **span** **ex**(or **dis**)**pend** and **spend**

Ex- is intensive in **exalt** **exaggerate** **extenuate** **exhilarate** **es-tablish** **es-planade** **s-pecial**

Elegy is from the exclamation ἒ *alas* and λέγω I speak.

Obs. Astonish, stun, astound, are usually referred to AD (AT-TŎNO, &c.) but Fiedler refers them to EX.

> But in the taverne all dispendeth
> The winning whiche that God 'hem sendeth.
> *Chaucer*, Romaunt of the Rose, l. 5684.

EX-O adv. *outward.*

ex-o-t-ic (T participial) ἐξωτικὸς coming from abroad.

exo-skeleton a skeleton (ἔξω) on the outside, as in insects.

exogen a plant whose stem grows by means of external layers. ☞ GĔNŬS, *ENDO*genous.

EXTRA *beyond.*

[Lat. ĒXTRĀ, Oscan EHTRAD. ĒX gives the adj. m. ĒXTĔR or ĒXTĔRŬS, f. ĒXTĔRĂ *external*, whence the fem. ablative case ĒXTRĀ, used as a preposition and an adverb. Similarly formed are ĪNTRĀ, INTRŌ, SŬPRĀ, ŪLTRĀ.]

extravagant (VĂGĀNS) wandering beyond; wasteful.

str-ange (ĒXTRĀNĔŬS) extraneous, foreign, surprising.

The positive form ĒXTĔRŬS gives the comparative ĒXTĔRĬŎR, and the superlative ĒXTRĒMŬS extreme, utmost.

f- prosthetic.

f-lannel or **f-lannen** (Welsh gwlanen) a loosely woven woollen fabric. Lat. LĀNĂ, W. gwlan *wool*, o wlan *of wool.*

F-L' *motion.*

[Composed of F- and L-; φ, λ; and of F- preceding L of the root. See under B-, D-.]

fly fleet flow flush flutter flurry flicker flagrant flare flame flirt flash flaunt flinch fling flippant flagitious flounce flounder flaccid flagellate in**flict** in**flect**

Obs. **blow blast** belong here, but **bl- pl-** are much rarer in this sense than **fl-**, which is preferred on account of the greater continuousness of **f.** It is sometimes intensive.

for- *be, from, against, entirely.* See PER.

[Ang. for-, as in for-loren; Ger. (*v* as *f*) verloren, Dan. forloren, Sw. förlörad *for-lor-n, los-t.* Go. fair-, faur-, fra-; Ohg. far-, fer-, fir-, for-, fur-.]

forbid (Go. faur-biudan; Ang. for-beódan; Ger. verbieten;) to bid against. **foredo** to ruin; Lat. DO *I give, put, do;* PER-DO (old Eng. for-do,) *I ruin, destroy, waste,* i.e. put through, whence perdition. **fore-go** (furgo, 1250.) **forefend**

This is the very extafie of love,
Whose violent property fordoes itfelf.—*Shakſp.* Hamlet.

I fee no more but that I am fordo.—*Chaucer.*

And if thou tell it man thou art forlore.—*id.*

And their forwafted kingdom to repayre: . . .
Forwafted all their land . . .
Ye all forwearied be . . . .—*Spenser.*

forsake seek. **forgive,** Go. fragiban, Ang. forgifan. **forswear forbear forget foreshorten foredo forelay**

fore- *before.* See PRO.

[Ang. fore-, for-, foran; as in forecuman *to come forth;* foreheafod the *forehead.* Go. faura, faur-; Dan. fore; Sw. före; Belg. voor; Ger. vŏr.]

foretell forewarn foreknow foresight forward Ang. foreveard, forveard. **foregoing foreland foreman forehead**

Gay girlonds from the fun their forheads fayr to fhade . . . —*Spenser.*

fore- *out.*

[Lat. FŎRĀS, Gr. θύραζε *out of doors;* FŎRĬS a *door, gate;* θύ'ρα, Doric φόρα; Ger. *th*ūr, Ang. dūr, Eng. door. Akin to PĔR.]

foreclose (CLŪDO,) to shut out. (Old Fr. foreclore, to forbid entrance.) **forfeit**

F-R'. See B-, R-.

frigid **freeze** **fracture** **frequent** **friction** **freckle** **fritter** **fry** **fray**

Fright has the *fr* of *fear.*

fro- *from.*

froward refractory, going from (the proper direction.)

gain- *against.*

[Ang. gēăn, on-ge-gen; Ger. gēgen, Dan. gjen- *against.*]

gainsay to say against, contradict, controvert, deny.

G-R' intensive or imitative. See C-R'.

crake, grackle imitative names of noisy birds; from the root of *ech-o.*

HEMI half. See SEMI-.

hemi-sphere half a (σφαίρῐον) sphere.

HETERO- other, different.

[Ϝέτερος *other, different, strange;* CĒTĔR-ŬS, -A, ŪM.]

heterogeneous of a different (GĔNŬS) kind.

HOLO-, SOL-.

[Ϝόλος, Eng. whole, all; Lat. +SŌLLŬS *all.* Ss. ALA, *much,* AL to *occupy, fill.*]

holocaust a burnt offering the *whole* of which was consumed.

holograph a writing of which the whole (the body as well as the signature) is written by its author.

soli-citude SŎLLĬ-CĬTŪDO *great* anxiety; (CĬĔO to move, excite,) whence also **solicit** to put in motion, tempt, urge.

sol-emn ceremonial; sacred; reverential. (SŎLLĒMNĬS celebrated every (ĂNNŬS) year.—*Kaltschmidt.*)

HOM-, SIM- *like*. See COM-.

[Ϝομὸς, ὅμοιος; SĬMĬLĬS *like*, the *sam-e; ἅμα* (CUᵐ) *with;* SĬMŬL *together.*]

homogeneous of a like, or of the same (GĔNŬS) kind.

simul-taneous occurring at the same time.

homonym **homologous** **homeo-pathic** **similar** **same**

HYPER beyond, over. See SUPER.

hypercritical beyond, or exceeding (just) criticism; over-critical. **hyperbol-e** a carrying (of speech) beyond strict truth. (*βάλλω* I throw, cast.)

hyperborean far (*βορέᾶς*) north.

HYPO under. See SUB.

hypogene (*γένω*, to produce,) produced beneath, as certain rocks.

hypothesis (*θέσῐς* a laying down,) that which underlies an argument; a *sup*position.

hypothecate (ib.) to deposit under a pledge.

hyph-en (*ὑφὲν, ὑπὸ ἕν* under-one,) a mark uniting the letters of a written word into one group.

HYPSI- high.

[Ϝύψῐ *above*, *ὕψος height*, *ὑψηλὸς high.* See OB.]

hypsometry the art of measuring heights. (*μέτρον* a measure.)

Hypsiprymnus a genus of kangaroos with the (*πρύμνᾰ*) rump elevated.

IN-, **un-** *not, without.*

[Ss., Zend, AN-, A; ἀν-, ἀ-. Welsh an-; Gaelic ana; Irish an-, ain-. Ger. ohn-, ohne *without.* (Coptic an; Heb., Arab., אַיִן (▹AJIN) *nothing, not,* have a doubtful place here.) Bohem., Russ. ne-; Pol. nie-. Gothic, Saxon, German ūn-; Swed. o-; Dan. u-; Belg. on-; Ang. un-, on-, an-, in-; Eng. un-, in- *not.* ἄνευ (to which Scheller refers SĬNĔ,) *ἀν, ἀ- without.* Hindoo un-, ụ- (pronounced with *u* in *up,*) ni-, nā-, nā *no, not.* Lat. ĬN-; Fr. in-, im-; (and by accident, Aztec a-, an-.) Ss. root ŪN to diminish. In- is used with adjectives, adverbs, participles and nouns.]

un- or **in-constant** *not* constant; *without* or *wanting* constancy. **un-crowned** *adj.* not crowned, without a crown; (part.) deprived of a crown.

un-(or **in-**)**conceivable** **-conclusive** **-constant** **-compact** **-proper**

immense‡ (MENSŬS; ☞ MĒTĬŎR to measure,) not measurable. **uncolored** not colored; without color.

i-gnoble not *g*noble. (NŌBĬLĬS, †GNŌBĬLĬS; GNŌSCO I know.)

en-emy ĬNĬMĪCŬS unfriendly. (ĂMĪCŬS a friend.)

i-gnominy **i-gno-r-ant** **immodest‡** **illegal‡** **irreverence‡**

> Some lead a life unblamable and juſt,
> Their own dear virtue their unſhaken truſt . . . —*Cowper*, 1737–1800.

Obs. 1. The un- is intensive in unloose (Ang. onlesen, on- meaning *into, to,*) unremorseless, until.

Obs. 2. In some words un- has displaced the Latin in-, as in unambitious, ungenial, unhumbled, unnumbered, unfortunate. In- is used where assimilation is required, as un- is never assimilated.

Obs. 3. "There can be little doubt that *in, on, un, αντι,* are all from one stock."—*Webster.*

Obs. 4. Un- is the preferable form, used almost exclusively in Anglish, as in untemed *untamed.* Latin has a bad feature in the use of IN-, not only for *into* (as in ĪNDŪCO to lead *in,*) but negatively, as in ĪNCŌNSTĀNS *not* constant; INVŎCĀTUS called upon, and *not* called upon; IMMŪTĀTUS changed and unchanged;—and intensively, as in ĬNÆQVO, to make level; ĬNÆSTĬMĀBĬLĬS *very* estimable; INGĔMO, to groan; INFŪSCO, to sully.

Altho the definite Germanic ūn- is naturalised in the English ŭn-, there is a tendency to retain the indefinite in-, which leads to the use of discrepancies like *unequal* and *inequality; unfailing* and *infallible;*—causes the toleration of forms like *invaluable,* apparently used by Bp. Taylor for *not valuable,* or *not able to be valued;* and (as if ironically) by quacks in describing their nostrums;—and it obscures the spoken language, as in asserting that—

The chriftian doctrine . . . . makes our greateft happinefs here to lie *in dependence* of God's providence and contentment in our conditions.—*Stillingfleet.*

In offensive operations, the points which it is desirable thus to occupy, reduce themselves to, . . . &c.—Westminster Review.

Already the Richmond papers indulge *in offensive* criminations . . . —Philadelphia "Press," Feb. 1862.

In a word, all good and every ill are *in common* among them, and all work together *in harmonious* union for the good and defence of the whole.—*Mrs. A. H. Dorsey.*

Sinners seek for delights only *in sensible* things.—*id.*

It is written throughout with great power and *in harmonious* language . . . . —Penny Cyc. 3, 431.

A Chriftian's wit is *inoffenfive* light,
A beam that aids but never grieves the fight.—*Cowper*, born 1731.

The contents of the sheath are composed of a series of globules, arranged very regularly, their convexities causing the sheath to project *in definite* lines.—*Wyman*, Lectures on Comparative Physiology, 1849.

Pollen . . . cohering *in definite* or *indefinite* waxy masses.—*Lindley*, Botany 1830.

I could scarcely realize the terrible event, and *in voluntarily* addressing the corpse, I muttered, 'Are you really dead, Kozengo?'—*Andersson's* Okavanga River.

. . . the astonished spectators begin to believe that it has been trained to dance *in correct* time.—Illustrated Magazine of Art, 1853.

The entire machine was now *in action*, every separate wheel was revolving . . . . —*Rev. William Kirby.*

IN *in; upon; very.*

[Ss. ĀN, Ā *at;* NI, Pers. ni- *in;* ἐν, ἐνί; Lat. ĬN *in;* Irish in-, an- *in, very;* Welsh en (intensive) yn n. *a state of being in,* prep. *in.* Ang. an, on, in *in;* Go., Ger., Eng., Belg., in. Dan. i, ind, inde; Sw. i, in. Fr. en, em-, in-. Russ., Pol., Bohem. na-. Ss. root AN to *move.* Akin to *ANA.*]

include IN-CLŪDO to shut *in;* to contain; to comprehend.

il-lumine‡ to throw (LŪMEN) light *upon.* **illumination**

incite to rouse *up, on, against.* (CĬĔO, CĬTŪm, to call, incite.)

emphasis‡ (ἐν, φἄ'σῐς assertion,) stress of voice on particular words in sentences.

energy active vigor. (ἔργον work.) **engrave,** see *EN.*

The prefix is intensive in infringe, infraction, inflame, ensign.

infuse **infer** **inculcate** **induce** **ir-ruption**‡ **irritate** **il-lude**‡ **im-bibe**‡ **impel** **improve** **embalm** **em-** or **im-body** **in-** or **en-gulf** **-close** **-quire** **-sure** **-dorse** **-dite** **-sue**

IND-, INDI- *within.* See *ENDO-.*

INFRA *below.*

[Lat. INFRĀ adv. from INFĔRŬS, Ă-, ŬM; adj. compar. INFĔRĬŎR.]

infraorbital below the orbit (of the eye.)
infer-nal pertaining to the lower regions.

INTER *between.*

[Lat. I'NTĔR; Ss. ĂNTĂR; Zend (Anc. Pers.) antare; Pers. ender, enderūn; Gaelic eader; Go. undar; Ger. ŭntĕr; Ohg. untar, intar, undar, under, undir; Eng. under, inner. Gr. ἐντός, ἐντ-, ἐνδ-, *within.* See IN.]

interpose (PONO,) to place between. **interposition** **intermix** **-line** **-pose** **-rupt** **-cept** **-sect** **-vene** **-lude** **-marry** **-jection** **inter-ior** **inter-nal** **entertain** **enterprise** **entr-ails** ἔντερα internal parts, (influenced by -ĀL-IA.)

INTRA *within, inwards.*

[Lat. adv. I'NTRĀ *on the inside,* See I'NTĔR.]

intravert to turn inwards. **intramarginal** inside of the margin. **intramural** within walls; inside of a city.

INTRO *within.*

[ĪNTRŌ adv. *into a place, within.* See I'NTĔR, ĔXTRĀ.]

introduce to lead in. **introversion** a turning inwards.
introit (ĔO, ĪTŪM to go,) an entering (psalm.)

is- *in.*

is-agogic εἰσ-ἀγωγικός elementary, introductory to a science or art. (ἀγωγή a leading, a method or system.)
eso-te'ric more inward; abstruse or secret. (ἐσώ-τερος, the comparative degree of ἔσω, εἴσω *within.*) **ep-is-ode.**

JUXTA *near, next.*

[JŪXTĀ, from JŪNGO *I join.*]

juxtaposition contiguity of position.

l- *the.*

[French article masc. le, fem. la *the;* Lat. pronouns ĪLLĔ *he,* ĪLLĂ *she.*]

a-l-e-rt = at-*the*-erect. See under AD.

l-oover or **l-ouvre** (French l'ouvert the opening,) a kind of steeple or ventilator for the exit of smoke.

l-one is for al-one, all one.

M-. See B-.

[Welsh my (*y* as in myrrh,) *that is, that is in agency;* ma *what is produced;* mw *that is forward* or *about.*]

mash (commonly spelt 'mesh,') W. masg (my-as-g) *that is interwoven, lattice work, an interstice of a net.* From as *a particle,* asg *a splinter;* whence also b-asg *a plaiting of splinters,* basged *a basket;* and fflasg, fflasged *a wicker vessel,* whence fl-ask, fl-asket.

W. ma *what is produced,* ma-g *the act of rearing,* magi *a principle of generation,* magïod, (a collective plural,) **ma-gg-ots.** W. ma-d *what proceeds,* madr adj. *become pus,* madredd *putrefactive ma-tter.* W. mus (from mw *that is forward,* and ws *that is impulsive,*) *that starts out, an effluvium,* hence **mu-s-k** and **mu-s-tard,** tardd *issue.*

ma *my.*

[Lat. masc. pron. MĔ-ŬS, fem. MĔĂ, neut. MĔŬm; Fr. fem. ma.]

madam and **madonna** my (DŎMĬNĂ, Ital. donna, Fr. dame) lady.

(MAL-, MALE *bad, badly.*)

[Lat. MĂLĔ *badly;* MĂLŬS *bad.*]

malaria bad (Ital. aria) air; poisonous air of marshes.

malady (APTŬS seized, adapted,) dis-ease; indisposition.

mal-a-pro-po-*s* Fr. (Lat. MĂL-, ĂD, PRŌ, PŎSĬTŬm *placed,*) put forward badly, or at the wrong time or place.

malĕ-diction malĕ-factor mal-ad-ministration malformation malcontent maltreat malice mala-pert mau-gre

META with, beyond, after.

[Gr. *μετἄ̀*, *μετ-*, *μεθ-*; Ss. MIT'HAS; Lat. ĂPŬD; Go. *miθ*, mid; Ger. mĭt; Ang. mid; Dan. med (ved *by*,) *with;* English with. Ss. root MID *to fit.*]

metaphrase (*φράσις* an explanation,) a version with each word translated.

metaphor, *φορὰ* a carrying, *φέρων* carrying (a word *beyond* its meaning.)

metacarpus the bones *beyond* or after (CĂRPŬS) the wrist.

meta'-thesis a *change* in words by the *trans*position of parts, as LeaF compared with FoiL, or cURdle with cRUddle.

met-em-psych-o-sis the passing of the (*ψῡχὴ*) breath or soul (em-) into another body *after* death, a doctrine taught by Pythagoras.

metamo'rphosis a changing to a different (*μορφὴ*) form, or beyond the proper form.

method (*ὁδὸς* a way, an art,) a mode constructed with skill, or *according to* rule; order; systematic arrangement.

within inside of. **withal** with the rest. **without** outside of. See under **with-**.

mis- *wrongly, ill.*

[Go. missa-, miss-, *evil, different;* old Nordish â mis *alternately* (Grimm, Diefenbach 2,75;) old high Ger. missa-, missi-, miss-, mis-; Ger. miss- or misz-; Sw., Isl. miss-; old Frisian, Ang., Belg., Dan., Eng., mis-; Eng. to miss. Ital. mis-; Fr. mes-, me-. Gr. *μῖσος*, *μισ-* *hatred;* Ir. meis *bad;* Welsh mêth a *failure;* Ss. MIT'HJĀ *falsely* Ss. root MAT'H to *move.* There are probably two distinct roots here.]

misdeed a deed done wrongly; an evil deed. (Go. missa-deds, Ger. misse-that.) **misreading** a false reading.

misguide -call -inform -fortune -apply -judge -print -co'nduct -demeanor -govern -adventure -understanding

Obs. 1. The Greek *μῖσος* (hatred) appears in **mis-anthropy** hatred of (*ἄνθροπος*) man. **miso-gyny** hatred of (*γῠνὴ*) woman. **miso'-gamy** hatred of (*γἄ'μος*) marriage.

Obs. 2. The prefix mis- has become confused with the French més-, mé-, Ital. mis- (as in misfatto) which according to Fiedler, is from the Latin

MĬNŬS less. **misprision,** old Fr mesprision; Fr. mépris (contempt, despising, undervaluing,) Lat. PRĔHĔNSĬO, PRĒNSIO (a taking;) a crime near, but *below* or *less than* a capital offense. **mischance,** old Fr. meschéance. **mischief,** old Fr. meschief.

Nay, quod the fox, but God yeve him mefchance
That is so indifcrete of governance.—*Chaucer.*

Chaucer uses mis (ill, amiss,—misse being *to fail,*) as in mifchefe (misfortune,) mif-de-port (to distribute wrongly,) mifefe (un-eas-iness,) mifgie (to misguí-de,) mifgied or mifgyed (misguid-ed,) mifborn (misbehaved,) mifgo miflede miffaye miftake, &c.

To fclander you is no thing min entent,
But to correcten that is mis I ment.—*Chaucer.*

MON-, MONO-, UNI- *one.*

[Gr. μόνος, ŪNŬS, *one.* W. môn *an individual.* Ir. man *solitariness.*]

monopetalous having a single petal.
mon-arch the (ἀρχή) rule, of one person.
monotony **monologue** **monad** **monochromatic** **monk**
uniliteral of one letter. **unicornous** having one horn.
uniformity **univalve** **universe** **one-eyed** **oneness**

MULTI-, *POLY- many.*

multiform **mult-angular** **multifarious** **multivalvular**
polysyllable **polypetalous** **polygon** **polytheism** **polypus**

n- *an.*

[An otosis (error of the ear,) as in saying *a neg* for *an egg.*]

n-ewt an eft; a salamander or lizard.

N-, NE, NEC, NEG-, NO, NON *not.*

[Ss. NA *not;* Lat. NĒ, NI-, NEC, NEG- *not;* NEQVE *and not,* (QVE, καὶ *and,*) N-ŪLLŬS *not any;* νε-, νη-, ν- *not;* NŌN *not, no.* Ital. ne-, ni-; Russ., Bohem. ne-, Pol. nie-; Persian ni-, n-; Welsh na, ni *not.* Akin to IN-.]

ne-uter not (ŬTĔR) either. **ne-ut-r-al-ity** **neutralise**
ne-cessary that cannot be (CĒDO, CĒSSŪ^m^,) ceded, given away, or dispensed with.
neg-otiate (ŌTĬŪ^m^ ease, NĔG-ŌTĬŪ^m^ business,) to traffic.

nu-bi-lous cloudy. Ss. na-bhas, νέ-φος NŪBĒS a cloud; that which does not (bhā) shine.

nefarious not to be (FĀRĪ) uttered; wicked.

deny, (NĔGO, NE not, ĀJO I say.—*Kaltschmidt.*)

negative negation nay nonessential nonentity n-ullity an-n-ul n-ever n-one n-aught n-either no n-or no-thing

No-t (**n-aught**) is the German nicht, (n-ichts nothing,) the stem of which is akin to the German ăchtĕn to regard, to value; ĕcht genuine, real, (Ss. IC̮S to see,) as if *something seen.* (Chaucer uses not for ne wot *know not.*)

The prefix of neg-lect, (LĔGO to lay together, pick up,) is considered by Prof. Key as identic with the German nach (after, at, by,) as in nach-lassen (to leave behind.)

(NUN-)

an-nun-ci-ation, an-noun-ce-ment the delivery of a message. (NŪN-CĬ-ŬS a messenger, from NŎVŪM new, and CĬĔO I call.)

nun-cup-at-ive (NŌMĔN name, CĂP-ĬO I take,) mentioning by name; pertaining to a verbal declaration.

OB *against, upon.*

[Lat. OB; Oscan OP, ŬP. Gr. επι' *upon,* ὕψι *high.* Eng. up, above; Dan., Belg. op; Sw. upp; Go. ufar *over;* Ger. ob *above,* auf *on.* Welsh wp a state of being *out* or *up.* Russ. po *along, beyond.* Ss. API *towards,* UPA *by, near;* Ss. root UB'H to *heap up.*]

obje'ct (☞ JĂCĬO,) to throw or place *against.*

obstinate (☞ STO, STĀNS) standing against, or (OBS-TĬNO,) holding against. **ob-ey** (☞ AVDĬO,) to give ear *to.*

oblige (☞ LĬGO,) to bind *upon;* to constrain; to favor.

obliterate (LĪTTĔRĂ a pen mark,) to blot *out;* efface.

obvious in the (☞ VĬĂ) way; easily seen; distinct.

obconic *inversely* conic. **o-mit** not (☞ MĬTTO,) to send.

oc-casion‡ (☞ CĂDO, CĀSŪm,) a falling upon; a happening. **offer**‡ (☞ FĔRO,) to bring before; to present.

officious (☞ FĂCĬO I make,) acting against, or contrary; intermeddling. **oppress**‡ (PRĔMO,) to press upon.

oppose (PŌNO,) to place against.

os-tentation (☞ TĔNDO, to stretch,) a showing out.

upright (Ang. upriht) **upturn** **upstart** **upland** **upo'n** **upward** **uproot** **upset** **uphold** **uplift** **uphill** **upright**

Obs. The s in obs-cene is from OBS-.

off *from.*

[Go. af; Ger. ab. See A-, AB.]

offshoot a shoot from. **offspring** **offset** **offhand** **offal**

on *upon, forward.*

[Ss. ANU; Gr. ἄνω *up.* Go. ana, at; Ger. ān; Ang. on; Belg. aan. Russ., Pol., Bohem. na. See AD, *ANA-*.]

onset **onslaught** **onward—away** **along** See **a-** ¶ 1.

OMNI- *all.*

omniscient all-knowing. (☞ SCĬO I know.) **omnific** **omnipotence** **omnipresent** **omnivorous** **omnibus**

or- for **over**

or-lop a kind of deck, or an additional deck. (Belg. loop a walk, a run.)

(OR-, ORI-.)

[See under ŎRĬŎR, OR-T-US, *to rise.*] **orient** **ori-gin** **ab-ort-ive**

out See EX.

[Ss., Angl., Isl., Sw., old Frisian UT; Dan. ud; Gothic us, ut. Russ., Pol. ot; Bohem. od. Ger. aus; Eng. out. In Angl. ut is *out,* and oð- *from, out of,* as in oðberstan *to burst out;* oðhȳdan *to hide from;* oðstandan *to stand out.* Ss. UT, UD *above, out.*]

outburst a bursting *from,* or from within.

outside the *exterior* side.

outcast one cast *off* or *away.* **outlandish** foreign.

ou'twork n. **outer** **utter** **uttermost** **utmost** **outmost**

out- *beyond.* See ULTRA.

out-bid to bid beyond. **outlive** **outdrink** **outlast** **outr-age**

OS-

[For OBS-. See under OB.]

os-tentation a showing off. (O·STĒNTO I present to view, make a show of.)

PARA *beyond, beside.* See PER.

par-allel *by, beside,* or *near* one-another; equidistant. (πăρă' beside, ἀλλήλων one-another, reduplication of ἄλλος *other.*)

parallax change of position from being viewed from different points. (ἀλλάσσω I change, ἀλλάξω I will change.)

parasite Greek priests who collected grain for the sacrifices; afterwards, a hanger on. (παρὰ *by,* σῖτος grain.)

paraphrase a version beyond the text.

parody (ᾠδή an ode,) an altered version.

paradox a (collateral or) *false* opinion.

parhelion a mock sun. (παρὰ near, ἥλῐος the sun.)

pa-lsy (for **paralysis,**) loss of voluntary motion.

pray (PRĔCŎR,) παρ- and ευχή a prayer, as in παρ-ηχ-έω, to imitate a sound; παρ-ηγορέω to exhort, soothe, relieve; whence **paregoric**, a medicine which relieves pain.

para-, par-

[French, from Latin PĂRĀRĔ *to contrive, pre-pare,* &c. Ital. parare *to parry.*]

para-sol a defense from the (SŌL) sun.

parachute a defense from a (Fr. chute) fall.

parapet a protecting wall as high as the (Ital. petto, Lat. PĔCTŬS) breast.

r-am-**par-**t (re-, in-) a parrying or defensive wall.

Par-affine is from the Latin adv. PĂR-Ūm but little, and A·FFĪNĬS allied. Par-ity ☞ PĀR equal.

PALIN again, backwards.

palin-drome (*παλιν-δρομία* a running back,) a word or sentence which may be read backwards without variation, as—

"snug & raw was I ere I saw war & guns"
name no one man

palim-psest‡ (*ψάω*, to rub,) a parchment from which the first writing has been (nearly) obliterated, and replaced by a second. The remains of the earlier writing often afford valuable literary material, and some of the productions of Cicero have been recovered by a careful study of palimpsests.

PAS, PAN, PANT- all.

[Greek masc. *πᾶς* (gen. *πάντος*,) fem. *πᾶσα*, neut. *πᾶν* (pl. *πάντα*,) *all, every.*]

pasigraphy universal (*γρᾰφὴ*) writing.

panto-logy universal (*λόγος*) science.

pantheist one who believes creation to be (*θεὸς*) God.

pantheon (*πάνθεον*) an ancient temple devoted to all the heathen deities. **dia-pas-on** see -*ON*, 3.

panace'a (*ἀκέομαι*, to heal,) a universal remedy.

Panax a genus of plants, all-heal, ginseng.

panorama panegyric pandæmonium panoply pantagraph

PEN- *almost.*

peninsula (PÆNĔ) almost (ĪNSŬLĂ) an island.

penultimate next to the last. **penumbra**

PER *through.*

[Ss. PĂRĀ *across, against;* PĂRĂ,; *πᾰρᾰ̀*, *πέρα* *beyond*, *πέρ-* *very.* Lat. PĔR; Bohem. pro *through;* Span. por, Fr. pour *for.* Old high Ger. far-, for-, fer-, fir-, furi-, Ger. vĕr- (*v* as *f;*) Eng. for-, far, fr-om, forth, frith or firth, to fare. Gr. *πείρω* *to pierce;* *περᾰ́ω*, *to traverse, penetrate.* Lat. FŎRO, *to bore.* Ss. root PUR *to advance.*]

per-for-ate (FŎRO,) to bore through.

perfect (☞ FĂCĬO to make,) finished, thoroughly made.

peroration the close of a speech.

perish (☞ ĔO, ĪRĔ) to go, through its course.

perennial (ĂNNŬS the year,) lasting.

perjure (JURO,) to swear, *beyond* the truth.

perfidious past (FĬDĒS) faith.

per-p-lex (PLĔCTO,) to involve, *much.*

pervert v. tr. to turn aside.

perspicuous (SPĔCĬO to see,) very evident.

pil-grim a wanderer abroad, or through the (ĂGĔR field, or) country. **pellucid**‡ shining through, transparent.

pur-sue (Fr. poursuivre) and **persecute.** (PE·RSĔQVŎR, PE·RSĔCŪTŬS to follow *up* or *after.*)

par-don (DŌNO,) to give (forgive) *entirely;* but the Romans used CONDŌNO I present, remit.

para-mount (Fr. monte*r*) to rise *above;* superior.

Per- is intensive in **peracute** very sharp; **permute** to change entirely; **persuade** to exhort much.

For- is intensive in **forbid forlorn forgive**

For- is negative in **forbear** (to bear fr-om,) **forget forswear forsake** (seek,) as in the German kaufen to buy, verkaufen to sell.

Obs. 1. *l* and *r* are akin and subject to interchange, as in pilgrim for *peregrine,* and French co-lonel, pronounced *curnl* in English.

Obs. 2. Although *per* and *very* agree in their elements, the latter belongs to ☞ VĒRŬS true.

Per agrees with *for* in the phrase PĔR MĒ LĬCĔT for me it is lawful.

PERI around.

[Gr. περί; Ss. PARI *around,* as in AP to *hold,* PĂRJĀPTĂ5, περιάπτός, Lat. PĔRĀPTŬS *adapted.* See PER.]

pericardium the membrane around the (καρδία) heart.

period (ὁδός a way,) a circuit; the year of a planet, &c.

perihelion the point where a heavenly body passes round (and nearest to) the sun.

periphery and **periphrase** from the Greek, correspond with *circumference* and *circumlocution* from the Latin.

POLY- *many.*

[Gr. πολύ'ς. Akin to ☞ PLŪS *more*, ☞ PLĒNŬS *full*, and probably to MŬLTŬS *many*. Ss. PUL to *augment*.]

polytechnic (τέχνη art,) pertaining to many arts.

Polynesia polygon polyglot polysyllable polygamous polyp

POR- *before.* See PRO-.

[Lat. PŌRRŌ, πόῤῥω, Eng. far, be-for-e.]

por-rect (PŌR-RĬGO, -RĒCTU^{m},) st-retch-ing or reaching before **por-tend, -tent,** a showing before, a foreboding.

For por-trait see pur- and PRO. Chaucer uses pourtraie, pourtraiture, purtraye, purtreiture, purveye, parfit (perfect,) parfourme (perform,) etc.

POS- See B-.

[Lat. in PŌS-SĬDĔO, POS-SESSŪ^{m}, *to have, own, enjoy.* Russ. po *by, near, on.*]

pos-sess to own. (Ang. besitten, Ger. besitzen. SĔDĔO, SE·SSŪ^{m}, *to sit, stay, dwell.*)

possession that one owns, as land which one has acquired the right to *settle on.*

Po-mer-ania a country *by* or *along* (Russ. more, Lat. MĂRĔ, Fr. mer) the sea.*

P-russia (formerly a Slavonic country,) along Russia.

Pos-sible is from PO·SSŪ^{m} I am able, for PŎTĬS able, SŪ^{m} I am.

POST *after.*

[Lat. PŌST, allied to PŌNO (PŎSĬTŪ^{m},) *to place.* Persian πες *after.*]

postpone to put after; defer. **postscript** written after.

pu-ny, Fr. puis né, Lat. POST NĀTŬS after-born; inferior.

Obs. The Romans often reduced POST to PO-, as in POST- or PŌ-MĔRĪDĬĀNŬS, after (MĔDĬŬS, μέσος) mid- (DĬĒS) day.

---

* Ar-mor-ica is similarly formed on an Irish basis, with ar *at, upon.*

PRE-, PRÆ *before.*

[Lat. PRÆ, PRĔ-; Ital., Sp. pre-, pri-; Fr. pré-, pre-, pri-. See PRO-.]

precede (PRÆ-CĒDO) to go before. **prejudice** judgment beforehand. **premise** **prætor** or **pretor** ☞ ĔO.

prison, PRĔHĒNSĬO a taking. See -ION.

provost ☞ PŌNO.

The Latin PRÆ- becomes pre- in English, as in **predestine** **prefix** **preside** **prevail** **prevent** **prejudice** **preclude** **preface** **preamble** **precipitate** **precocious** **predict** **prefer** **prea..ch**

PRÆTER *before, past.* See PRÆ.

preter-it (☞ ĔO, ĬTŪ[m] to go,) a past tense implying an action finished; the perfect tense.

preternatural beyond nature.

preterperfect a past tense.

PRO- *before.* See PER.

[Ss. PURA, PRA; Zend FRA; Gr. πρό (Eolic πραί, Lat. PRÆ;) Russ. pred-, Bohem. před; Go. faur, *before.* προί *early,* πρῶτος *fir-st.* Lat. PRŌ, PRĔ, PRI-, PRÆ, PRĬŬS *before;* PRÆTĔR *beyond;* PRĪMŬS *first;* PRI-ST-ĪNŬS, Ss. PRATANA5 *ancient.* Gælic roi; Ger. vōr *before.* Eng. ☞ for-, ☞ fore-, for-mer, for-ward. Welsh noun masc. pri *origin.* See PER.]

promote (MŎVĔO, MŌTU[m]) to move, forward.

proceed (CĒDO) to go forward. **provident** (VĬDĔO) to see or look, before. **provoke** (VŏCO) to call forth.

pro-d-igal (ĂGO to act,) squandering away.

procrastinate (CRĀS tomorrow) to defer.

procure (CŪRĂ a care) to get in advance; to have in care *for* (some one.)

pro-ph-et (φά'ω I tell) he who foretells.

prostyle a colonnade in front.

prologue **protract** and **portrait** **prior** **pri-me** ☞ **-me,** PRĪMŬS

☞ **fore-** **forward** **forth** **far** **farthest** **first**

Pro- means *instead of* in **pronoun,** **proconsul.**

The prefixes are intensive in **procure** **prolix** (LĀXŬS loose,) **pre-**

cinct (CĬNGO, to bind, surround,) as in the Latin PRÆPŎTĒNS very powerful. NŪPĔR newly, lately, PRŌNŪPĔR very lately; PRÆCLĀRŬS very clear.

Obs. PROD-, RED-, SED- may have been the original form of PRO-, RE-, SE; or the D may be akin to the Oscan and archaic Latin ablative case ending, and preserved in Latin between vowels, where it would act as a fulcrum. The Oscan forms of CONTRA, EXTRA were contrud, ehtrad. Compare the Russian pered *before.*

PROS

[Gr. πρὸς *to, upon, in addition, towards, near,* etc. See PER.]

proselyte one who (comes towards or) adopts some view or system. (ἐλεύθω I draw near, approach.)

prosody προσῳδία, (ᾠδη a song, an ode,) the laws of versification, over and above those of prose.

pros'-thesis an addition to the beginning of a word, (the reverse of aphæresis,) as 'espy' for *spy* (see under **e-**,) 'squench' for *quench*—

Rivers ſquench'd their thirſt.—*Ferrand Spence*, Miscellanea, 1686, p. 74.

PROTO- first. See PRO-.

prototype the first or earliest type or model.

prot-oxid the first or lowest degree of oxidation.

proto-martyr (St. Stephen.) **protho-notary**

pur- See PRO-.

[Fr. pour, Sp. por *for,* para. Lat. PRŌ *before,* confused with PĔR *through.*]

purpose (PRŌ-PŎSĬTŪ^{m},) to set before; to intend.

purvey to supply; to procure. (A form of pro-vide.)

pursue, Fr. poursuivre, Lat. PRŌSĔQVŎR or PERSĔQVŎR (PE·RSĔCŪTŬS,) to follow after.

purchase (PER-,) Fr. pourchasser to follow ardently, as a deer or an employment,—from CĀPTĀRĔ to catch at, strive to obtain; through the false form CApTJare, whence *chase* and *catch.*

> And here I ride about my pourchafing
> To wote wher men wol give me any thing:
> My pourchas is th' effect of all my rent,
> Loke how thou rideft for the same entent.—*Chaucer.*
>
> So was it fhewed in that purtreiture.—*id.*

R- intensive.

[Akin to S, and transmutable with L. Gaelic ro *very;* Lat. R-ĀRŬS, Gr. ἀραιός *rare, thin.* W. rha *that forces onward;* rhe *a swift motion, active;* rhy *excess, very.*]

r-ogation supplication. **ar-r-ogate** to make undue claims. (RŎGO I ask. See under D- and C-R'.) **r-ec-ent**

im-p-r-ec-ate to invoke evil on any one. (PRĔCŎR I p-r-ay.)

r-asher, W. rhasg a slice; from rhy, and asg a piece sliced off.

c-r-ow, r-ook, c-r-eak, break, are partly imitative.

RE-, RED- *back, again, down.*

[Lat. R-, RĔ-, RĔD-; Sp. RE-; Ital. RI-, -RE; Fr. ré-, re, r-; Irish a-. Ss. root R̥ to *go,* to *reach.*]

ra-m-; re-ab-; re-ad- (-af-, -an-, -ap-, -ar-, -as-;) re-con- (-com-, -co-, -col-;) re-de-; red-in; re-dis-; re-e-, re-ex-; re-en- (-em-, -in-, -inter-, -intro-;) re-n-; -re-re-; re-sur-; re-sus-.

re-sur-rec-tion a rising again. (RĔ-, SŬB, RĔGO; ☞ SŬRGO.) **recede** (☞ CĒDO,) to go *back.* **recline** (C-LĪNO,) to lean back. **red-eem** (RĔDĬMO; ☞ ĔMO,) to buy back.

repeat to mention *again.* **revolve** to turn over.

red-ound (☞ ŬNDO,) to run over. **recall** to call back.

red-undant running over. **ra-m-par-t**,‡ see **para-**.

re-pose a lying *down.* **remote** moved *away.*

repel to drive back or *off.* **redraft** n. a second draft.

re-col-lect re-ad-apt renovate or **renew refuge re-duce red-olent un-re-con-cil-ed un-re-pre-sent-ed respect revise residuum resign reprobate reside re-st refer ra-gout**

Obs. The Latin RĔD-DO, RĔDDĔRĔ to give back, gives **render** and **rent** (with *n* educed from *d*,) which are essentially formed from the prefix. Spence (1686) writes *riflex, riflection.*

Alexandria, which beeing rafed and deftroied by the Barbarians, *Antiochus* the fon of *Seleucus* re-edified.—*Holland's* Plinie, 1635.

RĒTRŌ *backwards, back, again.* See RE-, RED-.

retrospect (SPĔCĬO,) to look backwards.

retrocession (CĒDO I cede,) a ceding back.

arrear AD RE'TRŌ. **retrograde** **retrogression** **retropulsive**

The -tro, of INTRO, RETRO means -wards.

S- *much, very.*

[An intensive prefix in various languages.* Bohem. pál-iti *to burn*, s-pál-iti *to burn up.* Gr. σ-μῖλαξ and μῖλαξ *bindweed;* σ-μῑκρὸς and μικρὸς *small;* σ-τρωφάω and τρωπάω *I turn*, whence **s-trophe** and **trope**; σ-τερ-εός, DŪR-ŬS *firm, solid;* σ-τέγω, TĔGO *I cover;* ĂGO, to *move, drive*, S-ĔQV-ŎR to *follow;* S-ERVO, *to guard, prevent*, **s-erve**, ἐρῡ΄-ομαι, *to ward off, protect, ransom;* γρᾰ΄φω, S-CRĪBO, to *write*, Eng. **s-cribe**, **s-cribble**; μειδᾰ΄ω *I* **s-mile** (*d* to *l*, or *l* frequentative;) κίδ-νημι and σ-κεδ-άω to s-catt-er. W. ys *that is, that issues, that is active.*]

s-pade, **s-pud**, **s-patula**, (πέτᾰλον) petal, paddle.

s-pace, (PĂTĔO,) to extend. ☞ PĂNDO.

s-kul-k, CĒLO I cover, hide; W. cel shelter, cel-c conceal-ment; Ir. ceal con-ceal-ing, ceal-g treachery, a cceilg in ambush.

shad a fish like a herring, which swims in herds. W. cad a reach or spread out, cadw a herd, ysgadan herrings.

smelt *v.* μέλδω melt	**spread** broad	**slender** lean
spare *v.* PĀRCĔRĔ	**splash** plash	**scroll** curl
spunge FŪNGŬS	**scrutiny** critic	**stolid** dull
splice ply	**scold** call	**snap** nab
surge irk	**skiff** cup	**snip** nip
swirl whirl	**slat** lath	**scourge** correct
scratch grate	**smoke** See M-	**spike** peg

* S- in Ancient Egyptian, is the sign of causative action. "It is the sign through the agency of which *being* becomes *action*, or an action is converted into the cause of an action, the stimulus, as it were, to the activity of the predicate."—*Bunsen.*

spigot peg	**storm** TŪRBO	**swing** wing
spur bur, Ir. bior *a spit*	**squeak** quack	**spit** *v.* pit-uitous.
spar bar	**swab** wipe	**scintillate** kindle
scald CĂLĬDŬS	**smash** mash	**scoop** cup
sparrow PĀRŬS	**spine** pin	**sway** wag
slime LĪMŬS	**stun** din	**stin-gy** ten-acious
slab lap, lobe	**smut** mote (Webster.)	**squench** quench
slack lax	**slight** light	**stir** tur-n

sneeze, snore, snarl, nose. **squash,** quash. **stick** v. **swash** **swell** **scarce** **slough** **strew** **sprig** **skirmish** **shadow** **scrape** **scud** **small** **squeeze** **spank** **scow** **snipe** **snare** **snow**

Obs. S-ombre belongs to SUB-; s-corch (ex-cortic-ate) s-creen, to ☞ EX; and s-coundrel to ABS-.

The following are Welsh examples—

aeth a prickle,	saeth a dart.
enyd time,	senyd, ysenyd a while.
yff a tendency out,	syfag what spreads out.
iâd the side of the head,	siad the top of the skull.

sans *without.* See SINE.

sansculotte (Fr. culotte breeches,) a ragged fellow; a radical republican. First applied to the poorest class of the people but assumed as a title of honor by the adherents of the French constitution of 1793. (*Gattel,* 1803.)

Their arena of *Sansculottism* was the most original arena opened to man for above a thousand years; . . . —Westminster Review, 1837.

The spirit of modern *sansculotte*-ism . . . —Democratic Review, 1838.

S-C', sq-, sh-

[Indicative of action, sound, and intensity.]

sc-ratch rake ratchet. **sc-raw..l** (RĒPO I creep.)

scream a shrill outcry. (Old Eng. reme, Ang. hreman.)

squeak (VĀGĬO,) voc-ative, q-uack, of which **sq-ual..l,** **sq-uea..l** (cater-)wau..l are frequentatives, with the guttural elided. **sh-red** a piece torn off. (RĀDO I sc-rape, rub.)

sc-rub **scrabble** **scamble** **scribe** **screw** **scream** **screech** or **shriek** **shrill** **scramble** **scranch** **shrivel** rivel, ruffle. **shrink** wrink-le **squabble** **squib** **squirt** **squash**

SE- *aside, apart.*

[Lat. SĒ-, SĔD-, SŎ-. Sanscrit root SĔ to *finish.*]

seclude (↓CLAVDO,) to shut apart. **select** (LĔGO,) to gather apart. **segregate** (GREX a flock,) to se-parate.
secern s-creen (CĒRNO, κρίνω I sift, separate)
so-lve (SŌ-LŬO,) to wash apart; to remove difficulties.
s-ober, (ĒBRĬŬS drunk.) **secede sever separable**

Obs. *Se-cure,* without (CŪRĂ) care, may have SE- from SĬNĔ *without.* *Sedition* is commonly referred to SE-, with *d* (see T) connective and ☞ ĔO, but Prof. Key thinks it may be connected with DĬTĬO power.

SEMI-, *HEMI- half, somewhat.*

[Ss. SĀMI; Lat. SĒMĬ; ἡμι half. Ang. sam- *half,* samod *together.* Sanscrit root SĀM to *place together.*]

semiannual half yearly. **semilunar** half-moon shaped.
semifluid somewhat fluid. **semi-vitreous** somewhat vitrified. **sin-ciput** (SĒMĬCĂPŬT) the front of the head.
semitone or **hemitone** a half a tone.
semi-bituminous hemicycle megrim (for hemicranium.)

SESQU-, SESQUI *one and a half.*

sesquichlorid a compound of three parts of chlorine and two of a base.

SINE *without.*

[Lat. SĬNĔ; SĪ *if,* NĔ *not.* Sp. sin; Ital. senza; old Fr. sens; Fr. sans.]

sinecure (an office) without care.
sin-cere without mixture. (κεράω I mix.)—*Kaltschmidt.*

S-L' intensity.

sling slug slack sleight slight slap

S-P' motion, intensity.

sp-ic-ule (ĂC-EO to be sharp,) a small sp-ike.
sp-rink-le ir-rig-ate **sp-eak** ech-o

sp-lice (PLĬCO I fold, LĬGO I tie.)

spirt sprout spray spill split splash spit sputter spew speed spray sprey spring sprig spruce spark

Obs. The same -irt occurs in sp-irt, bl-urt, fl-irt, squ-irt; but s-tart is akin to s-tir, tur-n.

S-T' *much, very.*

st-roll roll. **stretch, streak** reach. **strip** rob, rip. **straight** or **strict** right, rect-ify. **strand,** Ger. rand (a margin.) **str-ike, st-ick, st-ing** (ĪCTŬS a blow.) **st-alk** v. στείχ-ω (I go, stalk.) **struggle** wriggle. **stake stick string strong strive street stream streperous**

SUB, *HYPO under, somewhat, after.*

[Sanscrit UPA; 'ὑπό; Lat. SŬB; Go. uf *under.* See OB.]

submarine *under* the sea. **subacid** *somewhat* acid. **subangular** *nearly* angular. **subrotund** somewhat round. **suffix** to place *after* or under. **re-sur-rec-tion.** See RE-. **subscribe** to write a signature after or under a document. **succor** Fr. secourir to aid. (Lat. CŬRRĔRĔ to run, SUB- or SUCCURRĔRE to go near, hasten to.)

s-care to startle with fright. (SU·CCŬTĔRĔ (QVĂTĬO I shake,) Fr. secouer to shake violently.)

s-lip to slide on a surface. (SUBLĀBŎR to go to ruin, glide away, as 'relapse' to slide back.)

sub-di-vide (FĪNDO, to split,) to divide *farther*, or again. **supplicate**‡ (PLĪCO, to fold,) to kneel down; to pray earnestly. **sur-rep-titious** in a sneaking, dishonest manner. (RĒPO I cr-eep.) **s-ombre** under (ŪMBRĂ) shade.

subjugate succeed succinct sufficient suffer suggest* sum-mon‡ ('mon' as in ad-mon-ish.) **suppress surrogate**‡

Sub- is much used in natural history for *somewhat*, as in

* Sug- of *suggest* is for sub- before pure Latin *gay*, the change of which involves the former. English has its laws of assimilation as well as Latin, and these forbid a union like *g-j*, so that *gay* is as improper in sŭ'gest and exă'gerate as it would be in cudgel (from cog,) according to the laws of *speech*, which are seldom consulted by the orthoepists.

"black, subrugulose, subsulcated, sides convex, angles sub-acute."

Sub- is verbal, or it has lost its force in **so-journ**, and **sup-ple** (PLĬCO to fold or bend,) often pronounced *soople* in accordance with its French original *souple.*

The adverb SU·BTĔR is used in **subterfuge** (evasion,) and SU·BTŬS (Fr. sous,) is observed in **subs-traction.**

Su-rrender is the French 'se rendre' to render one's self; Ital. rendere, with *n* educed from the *d* of Latin RĔDDĔRĔ.

SUPER *above, beyond.*

[Ss. UPARI; 'ὑπὲρ; Lat. SŬPĔR; Ital. sopra-. Go. ufar; Ger. über; old Fris. ova, bova, ovir, ur; Eng. over, upper; Ohg. oba, ope, ob, op; Eng. up, Ger. auf. Persian зeber *above;* aber, ber *upon.* Lat. SŪRSŪ^m^, SUS-upwards; Fr. sur, sus-. Etymologically -ER is an adjective suffix, as in EXTRA. See OB, SUB.]

superpose (☞ PŌNO,) to place *above* or *over.*
supernatural *beyond* nature; spiritual.
super-ab-undant super-in-cumb-ent -fine -scribe -sede
super-ior super-b — hypercritical hypochondria hypocrite
sove-re*ign* supreme. (Ital. sovrano; Lat. SŬPĔRNŬS.)
over-flow -shadow -reach -act -arch -plus -load -whelm

sur *over, beyond.* See SUPER.

surmise (MĪTTO, MĪSSŪ^m^ to send,) to pass over (mentally.)
survey to look over; inspect. (VĪDĔRĔ to see, *to view.*)
survive to live beyond (some event or contingency.)
surbase the part above the base.
surname or **sirname** a name besides the personal name; a man's real name, or that with which he is born.
surpass to pass beyond. **surplus** overplus.
sur-pr-ise surtout surface surfeit surmount

Obs. Sur-reptitious and sur-rogate belong to sub-; and sur-geon is composed of χεὶρν *hand,* ἔργο *work.*

SUS- SU- *up, above.* See SUPER.

sus-pend (PĒNDĔO,) to hang up; to interrupt; to delay.

sus-ceptible taking up; readily subject to an influence or affection. (CĂPĬO, CA·PTŪ^{m}, to take.)

re-sus-ci-t-ate (T intensive,) SUS-CĬTO to rouse, raise up, cause to rise (again.)

sustain (TĔNEO,) to hold, up.

su-spic-ion, su-spic-ious looking upwards, or with mistrust; distrustful.

Obs. Sus-picion may be from *sub-*, under the form *subs-*, as in *abs* for *ab.*

SY-, SYL-, SYN, SYM- with. See CON.

quin**sy** or **s**quin**a**ncy a disease of the throat;—corrupted forms of συνάγχη, from ἄγχω to suffocate.

T- intensive. See D-.

t-rite worn out. (Lat. T-RĪT-ŬS bruised, rubbed; RĀDO I shave, RŌDO I gnaw. Compare ir-rit-ate.)

t-rachyte a rough lava. (τρᾰχῠ'ς, rough, ῥᾰ'γος, ῥᾰ'κος a rag, wrinkle.)

t-wink wink **t-winge** wince

Obs. Compare Irish baladh *a scent,* do-bhaladh *a rank scent;* dealbh *the countenance,* doi-dhealbhach *ill-featured;* faghail *to procure,* do-fhaghala *rare, hard to be found;* blasda *savory,* do-mblasda *insipid.*

t- repetitive.

[Anglish ed-, oð-, æd-, æt- *again, re-,* as in edgifan *to give again,* edcoelnes *a recooling.* Gothic id-, as in idreigon *to re-form, convert;* Ohg. lōn *wages,* itlon *re-payment;* old Saxon idur *again.* Irish ath-, aith-, as in cogadh *war,* athchogadh *re-bellion;* beòdhaim *to enliven,* aithbhéodhaim *to re-vive.* Welsh ad-, at-, dy-, as in byw *alive,* adfyw *re-vived;* bod *to be,* atfod *to re-exist;* cre *a cry,* dychre *a cawing.* Lat. ĔO (ĬTŪ^{m},) *to go,* ĬTĔRO *I repeat.* Ss. root Ĭ, ĬṬ *to go,* JAT *going.*]

t-wit to reproach by citing faults. (Ang. edvītan to reproach, vītan to blame.)

And evermore ſhe did him ſharpely twight
For breach of faith to her, which he had firmely plight.
Spenser, Faerie Queene Bk 5, canto 6.

T-awdry, Saint Awdry (Ethelred,) from a fair bearing his name.

T- *this.*

[The indicative dental consonant of *th*e, *th*is, *th*ere Ger. da *there, here;* Greek neuter article *τὸ*; Ger. plur. and fem. sing. die *the.*]

t-auto-logy repetition in speaking. (*αὐτὸ it, τ-αυτὸ the very same*, *λέγω* I speak.) See *AUTO-*.

to separative.

[Gothic dis- (differing from Latin DIS-, according to Diefenbach 2,629;) Ohg. zar-; German zer-, with a separative and destructive force (as in Ger. reissen *to tear,* zerreissen *to tear to pieces,*) but confused with **to-** *at* &c. Gothic du-, as in duginnan *to begin;* [2]dugann iaisus[1] qiθan[3] *Jesus began to-say.—Matt.* 11 :7; dugannun . . . . raupjan ahsa *they-began to-pluck ears.—Marc* 2 :23.]

Common in old English, and not restricted to the infinitive, as in to-torn *torn apart;* to-broke (Ger. zerbrochen) *broken to pieces;* to-hewen *hew to pieces;* to-bete *beat much;* to-shrede *cut to pieces.*

The helmes they to-hewen and to-ſhrede . . . .
For which Almachius did him to-bete
With whip of led.—*Chaucer.*

So they ran together that Sir Griflets ſpere all to ſhevered.—'King Arthur.' 1634.

And a certain woman caſt a piece of a millſtone upon Abimelech's head, and all to brake his ſkull.—*Judges* 11 :53.

to- *at.*

[Gothic du, *to, at, by, be-;* old Saxon te; Ang. tō; Ohg. za, ze, te, ti; Ger. zu *to, at, at the.*]

tomorrow, Go. du maurgina; old high Ger. in morgan, te (ti, zi, ze) morgane; Islandic ā morgun; Ang. to morgen, on morgen. **tonight**, Ang. to-niht. **today**, Ang. to-dæg.

together, Ang. to-gedore. **against**, Ang. to-genes. Ang. to-middes in the midst. +**tofore**, here**tofore** formerly.

In parts of England toyear (to-yere of Chaucer,) is used for *this year*, and Halliwell has to-month, to-medis (in the midst,) to-whils (whilst.)

to supinal. See **to** *at*.

[The preposition 'to' indicating a supine, as in 'to go.' Ger. zu haben, Danish at have, Swedish att hafva *to have;* Gaelic do bheith *to be;* Cornish tha vewa, Armorican da veva *to live.* In Spanish, de *of* is used, as in de ver *to see;* and in Albanian me *with*, as in me passune *to have.*]

T-R' **dr- thr-** motion.

[Composed of T- or D- preceding R- or r. W. rholyn *a roll*, trolyn *a roller;* rhef and dref *a bundle.*]

tr-emble (τρέω, τρέμω.) **dream** **trepidation** **tramp** **trape** **travel** **tread** **trot** **trip** **intrude** **thr-ust** **trend** **trundle** **trudge** **trill** **troll** **drive** **thrive** **throw** **throb** **strike**

TRANS *beyond*.

[Lat. TRANS, TRAN-, TRA-, as in TRĀNSLĀTŬS or TRĀLĀTŬS; TRĀNSMĪTTO or TRĀMĪTT ; TRĀNSSŬO or TRĀNSŬO *I sew through.* Welsh tra *over.* Sanscrit TĪR to *traverse.*]

transmit (☞ MĪTTO,) to send beyond, or forward.

tra-vesty (VĔSTĬO,) to dress beyond; to disguise (Fr. travestir, as a man in female attire;) to make a ridiculous translation. **transmontane** beyond the mountains, north of the Alps, unItalian.

transfer **trans-it** **tran-scend** **tran-scribe** **tres-pass** **tra-ject** **tra-duce** **tra-dition** **tra-verse** (**tra-vail** or **travel**) **tur-moil**

ULTRA *beyond*.

[Lat. adj. masc. ŪLTĔR, fem. (adv.) ŪLTRĀ *of that side;* comparative ŪLTĔRĬŎR *farther:* superlative ŪLTĬMŬS *farthest.* Fr. outre; Eng. out- *beyond.*]

ult-, ulter-, ultra-, ut-, outr-.

ultramontane beyond the mountains, south of the Alps, Italian. **ultraist** one who goes to extremes.

ult-imate extreme. **ult-imo** the (month) preceding.

Ut-recht (ŪLTRĀ-TRĀJĔCTŬS.)

outr-age (ĂGĔRĔ) to act beyond (propriety,) old French oultrager, (and also ostraige.)

un- *not; without; -less.* See IN-.

unfit *not* fit, without fitness; v. t. to deprive of fitness.

unfruitful not producing fruit; fruitless; unproductive.

Christina, though uncrowned [having relinquished her crown,] demurred on some points of court etiquette.—*Mrs. Jameson.*

Burke's phrase, nevertheless, must be allowed to be infinitely more unphilosophical, immoral, irreligious, uncivil, impolitic, inhuman, and insolent than either.—*John Adams,* Works, 6,413.

Young (Night 7, London 1776,) uses — **un-absurd unask'd unavoidable unbelief unbelieving unborn unbounded unbrewed uncaus'd unconfin'd unconfounded unconscious undebaucht undesign'd undrawn undrew un-embittered unexpected unfading unfaithful unfashion'd unfear'd unfeign'd unfelt unintelligent unlock unmade unmann'd unmarr'd unmerciful unmixt unpaid unportion'd unprecedented unquench't unrefunding unrequested unresolveable unriddle unripen'd unroll'd unsound unstretcht unsubdu'd untaught untie untill'd un-tormented unwilling unwisely unwish't unwrought**

Th' illuftrious mafter of a name *unknown;*
Whofe worth unrivall'd, and unwitnefs'd loves,—*Young*, Nt. 8.

Unpeopled, unmannurd, unprovd, unprayfd ;—*Spenser.*

All mourn the minstrel's harp unstrung,
Their name unknown, their praise unsung.—*Scott.*

un-

[Gothic und- *to, unto, against;* old Frisian ont, und *till.*]

until to a certain time. (Old Frisian ont, und *till, to;* Swedish till *to, till, at, by;* Danish til *to, towards, in,* as in tildeels *in part;* tilforn *before, formerly;* ind *in,* as in indhegne *to hedge in;* indfrossen *frozen up;* indtil *until.*)

un-

[Anglish on- *into, to,* as in onlesan *to unloose.*]

unloose to make loose; to loosen. **unrip** **unstrip**

unto to, implying motion towards, or onwards. (*To*, without un-, expresses various relations.)

+**an hungered** hungry; the subject of hunger.

Obs. Old English has anhonged *hung up,* anhytte *hit,* anlifen *livelihood,* anondyr *under,* and others.

UNI- *one.* See *MONO.*

unity oneness. **unite** to join into one. **disunitedly**
union **unicorn** **uniform** **universal** **un-animous** **unit** **unique** **triune** **unison** **univalve** **univalvular**

under *beneath, less than.* See INTER.

underrate to rate at less than the true value.

underling an inferior agent. **underhand** clandestine.

undercurrent **-clerk** **-sell** **-growth** **-wood** **-value** **-neath**
Used figuratively in underhand, undergo, understand.

up See OB.

uphold **upset** **upstart** **upland** **upright** **uproar** **uproot**

VE-

[A Latin intensive (Ss. AVA, VI *of, to;* Pers. BI;) perhaps akin to B-. Ss. VĪ to *pass.*]

ve-st-ige a footstep; στ-είχ-ω I go, st-alk. **in-ve-st-ig-ate.**

ve-stibule an antichamber. (STĂBŬLŪ^m^ a standing place.)

VE-, wi- *without.*

[Ss., Zend vĭ, Pers. BI- *without.* Latin, as in VĒCŌRS *without* (heart or) *mind.* Russian, Polish, Bohemian bez *without.*]

veh-e-ment, Lat. VEMENS (and VĔHĔMĒNS vehement, inconsiderate.—*Eichhoff.*) Ss. VĬ; and MAN to think, whence also *man* and *mind.*

wi-do*w*, Lat. VĬDŬĂ; Sansc. VIDHAVĀ, from DHĂVĂ5 a husband, (root DHŪ to move, direct.)

vice *instead of.*

[Lat, vĭcĭs a *turn* or *change;* vĭcĕ, its ablative case, a dissyllable pronounced as a monosyllable in English.]

viceroy one who governs in the name of (old Fr. roy) a king.
vicegerent (GĔRĒNS ruling,) exercising delegate power.
vic-ar a substitute. **vis-count** one next in rank to a count.
viciss-itude regular change.

Obs. This prefix ought to be pronounced vĭs- to prevent confusion with vice (a fault,) Lat. vĭtĭŭm; and vice or vise (a screw-press,) Fr. vis a screw. Vicinity, vĭcĭnŭs near. Vicennial, vicenary, vĭcēnī twenty.

with- *from.*

[Ss. root VIDH *to separate.* Goth. viθra; Ang. viðer-, við-; Ger. wider *against;* widrig *contrary;* widerlich *repugnant.* Dan. mod; Sw. mot *against,* mota *to hinder.*]

withdraw to retire, recall. **withhold** to hold back.
withstand to stand against. **notwithstanding**
whitwitch (in Devonshire,) one employed to counteract witchcraft.
To **weather** a storm, Ang. viðrian *to resist.*

with *with.*

[Ang. við, old Eng. mid, Ger. mit; *μετὰ with.* Ss. root MĔT'H to *adapt, unite;* Lat. MŪT-UUS *mut-ual, reciprocal.* See *META.*]

within, Ang. viðinnan. **without**, Ang. viðutan.

Obs. The Ang. við *with* and *against;* and probably the Greek *μετὰ with* and *beyond,* include this and the preceding prefix.

y- See **c-**.

z-

The reprehensible exclamatory oath zounds (and oons) is for by-his-wounds (woonds,) in allusion to the sufferings of our blessed Savior.

LIST OF THE PREFIXES

a- *at on*
a-fore ☞ **be-**
a-like ☞ **c-**
an- *in*
a-shamed *of*
a-round *in*
a-pricot **al**
a-vow ☞ AD
a-way *on*
a-ward ☞ EX
A- ☞ *AN*
A-
AB } *from*
ABS-
ab-out ☞ AMBI
ac-cept ☞ AD
AD *to*
adv-ance ☞ AB
af-fect ☞ AD
ag-gressive ☞ AD
al-loquy ☞ AD
al *the*
ALL- other
am-bush ☞ **en**
am-brosia ☞ *AN-*
AM-
AMB- } *around*
AMBI
AMB-iguous
AMBO } *both*
AM-phora
AMPHI ☞ AMBI
an-oint ☞ **en-**
an-eal *on*

an-nex ☞ AD
an-swer ☞ *ANTI*
AN- without
ANA- again
anci-ent ☞ *ANTI*
ANO up
ANT-
ANTH- } *against*
ANTI
AP-
APH- } *from*
APO
ap-pend ☞ AD
Ar-morica ☞ POS-
ar-rest ☞ AD
as-sume ☞ AD
as-sagài ☞ **al**
at-tract ☞ AD
AUTH-
AUTO- } *self*
+**av-**antage ☞ AB
avant *before*

ba-lance ☞ BIS
B-
be- } *by*
bi-
BI ☞ BIS
bi-shop ☞ *EPI*
BIN
BINI } *two by two*
BIS *twice*
bu- *much*
by-law ☞ B-

c- *much*
CAT-
CATA } *against, down*
CATH-
CIRCU- } *round-about*
CIRCUM
CIS *on this side*
CL' continuative
CO-
COL- } ☞ CON-
COM-
COMB-
COM- *with*
CON *with*
CONTRA
CONTRO- } *against*
cont-rol
COR-rode } ☞ CON
c-ouch
counter } *against*
country-
CR'
cu-stom } ☞ CON
cur-ry

D- *very*
d- } *of*
de
DE *from*
dea-con ☞ *DIA*
dec-ussate ☞ DE, Obs.
de-vil ☞ *DIA*
de-fame ☞ *DI-* ¶ 3
demi- *half*
den-ârius ☞ DE, Obs.
des separative
deu-ce ☞ DUO
DI- ☞ BIS
di-stil ☞ DE
DIA through
DIS- ☞ BIS
DIS- ☞ DI-
dif-fer ☞ DIS-

do- } *two*
dou-ble
dr- ☞ TR'
DU- } *two*
DUO
DYS badly

e-lope
e- prosthetic
e-nough ☞ C-
e-
ec- } ☞ EX
ef-
ef-fendi ☞ *AUTO-*
el-ixir ☞ **al**
el-lipsis ☞ EX
EM- ☞ IN
EM- ☞ *EN*
EN in
en *in*
ENDO- within
en-emy ☞ IN- *not*
enter-tain ☞ INTER
ENTO- ☞ *ENDO-*
entr-ails ☞ INTER
EP-
EPH- } *on*
EPI
EQU-, EQUI- *equal*
ESO-teric ☞ **is-**
EU, EV well
EX *from*
EXO outward
EXTRA *beyond*

F- ☞ B-
f- prosthetic
FL'-
fl-ask ☞ M-
for-, fore ☞ PER
fore- *out*
fore *before*
FR'-
fro- *from*

g- ☞ **c-**
gain- *against*
GR'- ☞ CR'- intensive

HEMI half
HETERO- different
HOLO whole
HOM-, **homeo** *like*
HYPER beyond
HYPO- under
HYPSI- up, above

i-gnorant }
il-legal } ☞ IN- *not*
il-lude ☞ IN *in*
im-mature ☞ IN- *not*
im-bibe ☞ IN *in*
IN- *not*
IN *in*
IND-, INDI- ☞ *ENDO-*
INFER }
INFRA } *below*
INTER }
INTEL- } *between*
INTRA *within*
INTRO- *within*
ir-regular ☞ IN-
ir-ruption ☞ IN
is- *in*
iss-ue ☞ EX

jeo-pardy ☞ **c-**
JUXTA *near*

k- ☞ **c-**

L- ☞ D-
lau-danum ☞ *AN-*
l-ute ☞ **al**
l- *the*, &c.

M- ☞ B-
m-ash, **m-**esh ☞ M-
ma *my*
ma-tter ☞ M-
MAL- }
mala-pert }
MALE }
mau-gre } *badly*
me-grim ☞ SEMI-
MET- }
META }
METH- } *after*
mis- *wrongly*
mis-chance ☞ **mis-** Obs.
m-iss ☞ **ma** *my*
MON-, MONO- one
MULT-, MULTI- many
mu-s-tard ☞ M-

n- *an*
N- ☞ D
N- }
NE- }
NEC }
NEG- }
no }
NON }
NU- } *not*
NUN- *new*
NUN- *name*

o-mit }
OB }
OBS }
oc-cur }
of-fer } *against, up*
off *from*
OMNI *all*
on *forward*
op-press ☞ OB
or- *over*
OR-, ORI- *begin*
OS- ☞ OB
out- beyond
out EX
outr-age ☞ ULTRA
over ☞ SUPER

P- ☞ B-
P-russia ☞ POS-
PALIN, PALIM-† *again*
pa-lsy ☞ *PARA*
PAN, PANT ☞ *PAS all*
PAR- PARA beyond
par- para- *protection*
par-affine ☞ **para,** Obs.
par-don
para-mount } ☞ PER
PAS, PASI- all
PEL-lucid ☞ PER
PEN- almost
PER *through*
PERI around
pil-grim ☞ PER
pol-lute ☞ PER
POLY many
Po-merania ☞ POS-
POR- *before*
POS- *by, near*
POST *after*
PRÆ
PRE-
prea-ch } *before*
PRÆTER
preter } *beyond*
PRI-
PRO
PROD- } *before*
PROS near, &c.
PROTO-
protho- } *first*
pu-ny ☞ POST
qu-ash ☞ CO-
ra-m-part
RE-
RED- } *back*
RETRO *backwards*
sans ☞ SINE
s-trange ☞ EX
S- *much, very*
s-ombre ☞ SUB
s-coundrel ☞ ABS

s-ober ☞ SE
sove-reign ☞ SUPER
SC'- action, &c.
SE *aside*
SEMI *half*
SESQUI *one and a half*
sh- ☞ SC'-
SIM
SIMUL } ☞ *HOM-*
SIM-ple
SINE } *without*
so-journ ☞ SUB
so-lve ☞ SE
SOL- ☞ *HOLO-*
s-care ☞ SUB
s-port ☞ DIS-
sp- motion, &c.
sq- ☞ SC'-
ST- *much*
str-ange ☞ EXTRA
SU-, SUS- *above*
SUB *under*
subs-
SUBTER } ☞ SUB
SUC-cor
SUF-fer
SUG-gest
sum-mon } ☞ SUB
SUPER *above*
SUP-plicate
SUR-rogate } ☞ SUB
sur-pass ☞ SUPER
su-rrender *self* (☞ SUB).
SY-
SYL-
SYM-
SYN } *with*

T-, T-AUTO- this
T-, **th-** intensive
t- repetitive
thr- ☞ TR'-
to- *at*
to

TR'- motion
TRA-, TRAN-, TRANS, **tres**-pass, **tur**-moil — *beyond*
twe-lve, **twi**-ce — ☞ DUO

ULT- **Ut**-recht, ULTRA — *beyond*
un- ☞ IN- *not*
under
UN-, UNI- — *one*
up ☞ OB
ut-ter ☞ **out**

v- ☞ B-
VE *very*
VE- without
vic-, **vice**, **vis**- — *instead of*

w- ☞ B-
weath-er v. ☞ **with**-
wi-dow ☞ BIS a.
whit-witch, **with**- — *from*
with *with*

y- ☞ **c**-

z-

SUFFIXES

-A adverbial.

[Latin in ĒXTRĀ, I'NFRĀ, I'NTRĀ, JUXTĀ, SŬPRĀ. Formed on the ablative case of feminine adjectives in -Ă.]

-A, -E, n. *that which.*

[Gr. -α,[a] -η;[b] Lat. -Ă, rarely -E. Sanscrit -Ā, -A5; Bohem. -a. Nouns, mostly feminine. PŎĒTĂ *poet* is masculine; PĀRRĬCĪDĂ *parricide* is common.]

idea that which is seen or known mentally. (ἰδεῖν to see, to know.) **plethora** fulness, repletion. (See -*TH*-.)
asth-ma (see -*TH*-) **cassia** **dogma** (see -*MA*) **hye-na** **man-ia** **naphtha** **nausea** **trachea** **scoria** **sphere** (σφαῖρα)—**ac-me** **zone** (ζώνη) **strophe** **epi'tome** **diatribe** (see *DIA*) **hyperbole**

Obs. 1. This suffix is sometimes omitted, as in axiom-a poem-a sophism-a stratagem-a epigram-ma epoch (ἐποχή.) epoch-a crown (CŎRŌNĂ,) aunt (ĂMĬTĂ,) ruin-a picture (PĬCTŪRA,) fame (FĀMA.)

Obs. 2. Many of these words being anglicised (as epítomĕ rather than epitomèe,) it is equally proper to give them an English plural form, as epitomes and areas, rather than epitomai and areæ; and as singularity is to be avoided, it is better to say dogmas, tsarinas, and saharas, than dogmata, tsaritsa, saharats, and zemindarân, with the original plurals.

Latin—**alga** (pl. algæ) **amphŏra** **animal** **area** **arena** **argilla**ceous **caesura** **calumnia**te **camera** **catena**ry **corolla** **causa**tive **cera**te **Claudia** **Cornelia** **creta**ceous **crusta**ceous **corona**l **culpa**ble **epistola**ry **fibula** **Flavia** **forma**l **formula** **fortuna**te **herba**ceous **ira**te **Janua**ry **Julia** **lamina** **linea**r **luna**r **larva** **lyra**te **materia**l **mola**r **nebula** **palma**te **pecunia**ry **peninsula** **penumbra** **rota**te **salīva** **scapula** **silva**n **Silvia** **spat-ula** **stella**r **tabula**r **testa**ceous **tibia** **terra**queous **Tullia** **villa**—**conclave** (CŌNCLĀVĒ.)
banana **quota** **savanna** **sofa** **sultana** (Arabic sooltāna, with ā in *arm.*) **tarantula** **tsarina** **umbrella** **lava** **vista** **Nĭă'gără**
jerboa is Arabic, with German *j* or English *y*, and from the difficulty of pronouncing the Arabic final, it should be suppressed.

-a, -ah, n.

[Hebrew and Arabic nouns in -h.]

masora (māsōrāh) tradition. **cabala** (qabbalah) **ephah** **mishna** —Arabic **he'gira** (flight) with *eg* as in *edge* or *idge*.—(It is better to say hedge-ra, omitting the *i*.) **Sāhăra** a desert, (with ā in *arm*.)

-A, -I-A, -T-A, n. pl.

[*-α, -ια, -τα*; Lat. -A, -IA. Pol., Bohem., Gothic -a. Plural nouns, mostly neuter.]

phenomena **prolegomena** **exanthemata** **apocrypha** **arcana** **paraphernalia** **synonyma** **credenda** (see -AND) **data** **regalia** **effluvia** **strata** **errata** **genera** **lustra** **militia** **stamina**

-able, -uble, -ible, a. See -ble.

In some badly formed modern words, -able has the power of *full*, as veritable *truthful;* forcible *forceful;* charitable *full of charity;* sociable *companionly;* profitable *full of profit.* Capable, instead of being applicable to an object that *may* (or is worthy to) *be taken*, means one having the power of taking. Although honorable, favorable, sensible, have Latin originals, they are not used quite in their original sense, for the first means—*that procures honor;* the second—*in favor, popular;* and the third—*perceptible by the senses.*

-AC, -IC, adj., n. *having; pertaining to.*

[Gr. *-ακός, -ικός, -αχος*; Lat. -AC-US, -ŪC-US, -IC-US, ĪQVUS, -EC-. Fr. -aque, -ique. Welsh -awg, -og, -ig; Irish, Gaelic -ach. Norse -ag-r, -ög, -ag-t. Sanscrit -CA5 (preceded by a vowel,) and nouns in -CA, -CI. Gr. *ἔχ-ειν*; Goth. aig-an *to have;* Ger. eig-en *own.* Ss. ⫰īr to *possess.*]

demoniac *having, pertaining to*, or *possessed by* a (*δαίμων*) demon.

maniac *affected by* (*μήνη*) the moon; one moon-struck.

didactic *employed in, qualified for*, or *adapted to* (*δίδαξις*) instruction.

humectate made moist. (HŪM-ĒC-TO, to make (HŪM-ĬDŬS) moist.)

elegiac **paralytic** **arctic** **ascetic** **stom-ach** **mon-ach-ism**

prismatic dramatic athletic typic angelic conic cad-uc-ous prosaic public economic generic concentric fabric Gallic antique unique op-aque zodiac (see *-D-*) **music logic mathematics physic cler-k clerical vern-acular or-acular medical lettuce** LĂCTŪCĂ **loricate tunicate vesication urtication**

Obs. 1. *Music* &c. (MŪSĬCĂ, adj. and noun fem.) stood originally for the music *art* or *science*.

Obs. 2. The suffix of *pacific, specific, horrific,* is FĂCĔRĔ to make.

-ace, n.

[Lat. -ĀT-ĬŪM,[a] as in PĂLĀTĬŪ[m] a *palace;* -ĀT-ĬO,[b] -ĀT-ĬĂ.[c]]

preface[b] (FĀRĪ to speak,) something said (PRÆ) before; a preliminary discourse.

solace[a] condòlence. (SŌLŎR I condole.)

And I wol tel you verament
Of mirthe and of folas.—*Chaucer.*

menace a threatening. (MĬN-ŎR[b] I threaten.)

bullace ('bolas' in Chaucer,) a sort of plum or sloe.

terrace (written 'terras' by Sir Wm. Temple, Lat. TĔRRĂ the earth, Fr. terrasse, Ital. terrazo, Sp. terrado.) **palace** ('paleis' in Chaucer.) **space**[a] **grace**[c] **sur-plice** ('surplis' in Chaucer.)

Populace, see Obs. under -AC-eous. Furnace, FŪRNŬS, FŎRNĀX, see -AX. **pinnace,** see **-ass.**

AC-eous, AC-ious, adj. *of, like, having.*

[Lat. -ĀC-ĔŬS,[a] -ĬC-ĔŬS,[b] -IC-ĬŬS,[c] (-IT-IUS.) -ĀX,[d] -ŌX,[e] -ĒX,[f] ĪX;[g] Gr. -αξ. Russ. -ok. Ital. -acoo, -ace. Fr. -ace, -acé, -oce. Ss. -CA5 (,-ſA5) as in AD-ACA5 (Lat. ĔD-ĀX) *voracious;* SUTſACA5 (Lat. SĂGĀX) *sagacious.* Ss. root ĭr to *have.* See -AC, -AX. Commonly, words in -ĀCEUS (-aceous) are from nouns, and those in ĀX, -acious from verbs.]

arenaceous[a] *of, like,* or *having* (ĂRĒNĂ) sand.

crustaceous *having* a crust; crust-like.

advent-itious[c] (-ĪCIUS) coming by chance.

capacious[d] (CĂPĀX, from ☞ CĂPĬO, to take,) having capacity. **ar-gill-ac-eous** *composed of* clay; clayey.

pugnacious[d] *prone to* (PŪGNĂ) strife.

pertinacious[d] **fallacious**[d] **vivacious**[d] **efficacious**[d] **tenacious**[d] **audacious**[d] (AVDĔO I dare.) **loquacious**[d] (☞ LŎQVŎR.) **rapacious**[d] **voracious**[d] **mendacious**[d] **atrocious**[e] **ferocious**[e] and **fierce** (FĔROX, Fr. féroce.) **vertex**[f] **nutritious** (-ĪCIUS) **propitious** (-ĬTIUS) **coriaceous**[a] and **cuirass** (CŎRĬŪm leather.) **feli-c-ity**[g] **radical**[g] **fugacious** **rosaceous**[a] **capricious**[c] **cetaceous** **setaceous** **cretaceous** **liliaceous** **alliaceous** **predaceous**

Obs. To -aceous belong *embarrass, populace,* (Ital. popolaccio;) and to -ICEUm the nouns *lodge, hash, lattice,* (Fiedler,) and *pelisse.*

-AC-I-Ty -IC-I-Ty -OC-I-Ty. See -AC-eous.

audacity **pertinacity** **veracity** **mendacity** **voracity** **rapacity** **capacity** **pugnacity** **loquacity** **sagacity**—**felicity** **simplicity** **duplicity** **electricity**—**atrocity** **ferocity** **velocity**

-acle, **-icle**, n. *agent; place.*

[Latin nouns in -ACŬLUM,[a] (Ital. -acolo,) -ĬCŬLŬM,[b] -CŬLŬM,[c] (CRŪm, -BŬLŪm, -ŬLŪm, -TRŪm, -STRŪm,) are derived chiefly from verbs, and indicate the ag-ent, implement, or place, of the ac-tion of the verb. See -AC, and -L ¶ 3.]

or-acle[a] (ŌRO I speak, pray,) the person who announces; a prophetic announcement; and the place whence made.

spiracle[a] a breathing aperture.

cubicle[b] a place in which (CŬBO,) to lie down.

miracle[a] something at which (MĪRŎR) to wonder, or which causes wonder.

spectacle[a] something (SPĔCĬO,) to see.

ob-st-acle and **st-able** (ST-O I stand.)

peril (PĔRĬCŬLŪm) a trial, ex-peri-ment.

oper-culum[c] (ŎPĔRĬO I cover.)

receptacle[a] **curriculum** **curricle** **vehicle**[b]

Obs. **pinnacle**[a] may be an aug-mentative of PĔNNĂ a feather, PĬNNĂ a fin, or PĬNŬS a pine; or it may be named from some resemblance to them. **manacle** (MĂNĬCĂ,) a chain for (MĂNŬS) the hand. PĔRTĬCĂ a per-ch, pole, has the same -ICA. See **-ch.**

-AC-UL-AR

or-ac-ul-ar pertaining to (ŌRĂCŬLŬ[m]) an oracle. See **-acle, -cle**, -L. ¶ 3.

vernacular (VERNA a home-born slave,) home-born, indigenous; a vernacular language, that spoken at home.

-AC-y, n. *state of being; -ing; -tion.*

[Gr. *-ακ-εία* or *ακ-ία*;[a] -ĀC-ĬA;[b] *-αξ*. See ACeous.]

con-tum-acy[b] (TŬMĔO, to swell,) a *state of being* puffed up; a swell*ing* up or infla*tion*.

fallacy (FĀLLO I fail,) a deception.

pharmacy[a] the application or preparation of (*φάρμἄκον*) a remedy.

-ac-y, n.

[-ĀT-ŬS[a] n., -ĀT-ĬO[b] n.; *-ατ-εία*,[c] *-ιτ-εία*.[d] -T- participial followed by *i* and a vowel, the *i* taking the power of *s*, through the influence of elided *t*.]

ob-stin-acy[b] a (STĀNS) standing (ob-) against.

demo-cracy[c] (*κρἄ'τος*) rule, by the (*δῆμος*) people.

theocracy (*Θεὸς* God,) divine rule.

aristocracy (*ἄ'ρῐστος* best, bravest.)

celibacy[a] the state of being (CÆLĒBS) an unmarried person.

piracy[c] **policy, police** and **polity**[d] **accuracy**[b] **conspiracy**[b] **magistracy**[a] (Fr. magistrature.)

Obs. This suffix is mostly taken from the French, as in suprematie supremacy; intimité intimacy; legitimité legitimacy; episcopat episcopacy; célibat celibacy. The following are not French nor classical Latin forms:—intricacy, lunacy, secrecy, privacy (or privity) degeneracy,[b] legacy (LĒGĀTŬ[m],) delicacy, confederacy.[b]

Apostasy and *extasy* belong to *-σῐς*; and *fancy, fantasia, fantasy*, to *σία*. See *-SIS*.

-*AD*, **-ade**, -*ID*, n. *relating to.*

[Greek adjectives and nouns with a base in -δ- (-τ-, -θ-.) Nom. -ας, gen. -αδ-ος (-ατ-ος and -αντ-ος;) -ις, gen. -ιδ-ος; Lat. -AS, gen. -AD-IS. But χά'ρις *grace,* ὄρνῑς *bird,* and ἕλμινς *worm,* have χάρῐτ-ος, ὄρνιθ-ος and ἕλμινθ-ος in the genitive.]

dryad (δρῠὰς, gen. δρυάδος,) pertaining to forests. (δρῦς an oak, a tree, whence *tree.*)

decade pertaining to (δεκὰ'ς, gen. δεκά'δος,) the number ten. **sporad**ic (σπορ-ὰς, gen. σποραδος dispersed,) applied to scattered cases of disease.

Iliad (a poem) pertaining to (ĪLĬĂS, -ĂDĬS,) Troy.

Nere'ïdĕs (νηρηΐ'δες, pl. of νηρεΐς,) nymphs of the sea and daughters of (νηρεὺς) Ne-reus. (νηρὸς wet; νέω I swim; Nērĭtă a genus of sea snails.)

drom-ed-ary (DRŎMĂS, gen. -ĂDĬS;) δρομὰς (-ά'δος) running, δρέμω I run, perfect middle δέ-δρομα.

pleiad (πλειὰ'ς, pl. πλειά'δες.) **Pleiădes Hyădĕs** "ῦάδες **Aeneid Naiad monad triad myriad chiliad hebdomad**al **Jeremiad pyramid caro'tid paro'tid hĭ'brid ped**agogue **ornitho**logy **helmintho**logy **charity**

nit κόνις, gen. κόνῐδος. iris, pl. **irid**es. lepas, pl. **lepad**es. chrysalis, pl. **chrysalid**es, adj. -id, -idan.

> A HAMADRYAD flourifh'd in thofe days,
> Her name Pomona, ... —*Garth*, 1669.
>
> The Pleiads, Hyads, Lefs and Greater Bear.—*Dryden's Ovid*, 1680.

-Æ, -AE, n. plural.

[The Latin plural of nouns in -A is an added -E, which was originally -I. Greek μοῦσα *muse,* μοῦσα-ι *muses,* Latin MŪSA, pl. MŪSAE or MŪSÆ. Accidental in Hebrew גוֹב GŌB *locust,* גֹּבַי GOBÆ *locusts.*]

striae more than one stria or streak.

larvae tracheae areae or **areas vertebrae antennae**
Cornucopiæ (horn *of* plenty,) is a genitive case singular.

-ade, -ado, -ada, -ata, n.

[Lat. adj. masc. ĀT-ŬS, fem. -ĀT-Ă, neut. -ĀT-Ŭm. Sp. -ādo, -ada; Ital. -āto, -āta; Fr. -ade. Welsh -od, -ad, -ed, -id, -aidd. Ger. -et, -t;

Eng. -ate, -ed, -t. ¶ Primarily past participles and adjectives in Latin, but used also as nouns, and in English as adjectives, nouns, and verbs. See -ATe.]

brocade something (as silk or lace,) ornamented by means of a (brocca *Ital.*) wooden needle. Whence also **brocket** (or **pricket**) a young deer with tapering unbranched horns; also called a 'spitter' for the same reason.

arcade something (ĀRCŪ-ĀTŬS -ĀTĂ -ĀTŪm) arcuate or arched. **colonnade** a columned (way;) a row of columns.

parade a prepared show. (PĀRĀTŬS apparatus, equipage, PĂRO I prepare.)

lemonade (as if LIMONIATUS) lemoned, endued with the quality of lemons; water and lemon-juice sweetened.

esplanade something (ĒXPLĀNĀTŬS) spread out; (another form of ex-plain-ed.) A term in fortification.

armada an armed (fleet.) **pintado** a painted (fowl.)

barricade **blockade** **stockade** **palisade** **crusade** **brigade** **cavalcade** **promenade** **ambuscade** **cannonade** **maskerade** **serenade** **cascade** **tirade** **gasconade** **rodomontade** **bravado** **tornado** **panado** or **panada** **bastinado** **desperado** **cantata** **sonata**

Cockade is for the French cocarde.

-age, n. collective.

[Lat. -ĀT-ĬC-ŬS,[a] -ĀT-ĬC-ŪM,[b] (-ĀTĬO,[c]) Ital. -aggio,[d] -eggio; old Fr. -adge; Fr. -age; Sp. -age. The suffix -age has been confounded with the heterogeneous terminations of VĒSTĪGĬŪm *vestige*, CŌLLĒGĬŪm *college*, PRĪVĬLĒGĬŪm *privilege*.]

> Redy to wenden on my pilgrimage
> To Canterbury with devoute corage.—*Chaucer.*

voyage a traveling (by sea.) Lat. VĬĀTĬCŪm provision for a journey. (Port. viatge, Sp. viage.)

umbrage, Lat. ŪMBRĀTĬCŬS in the shade, retired; ŪMBRĀTĬO a shading; ŪMBRĀCŬLŪm a shady place, a retreat.

savage wild, uncultivated. (Lat. SĬLVĀTĬCŬS, from SĬLVĂ, a forest.)

mileage traveling expenses allowed according to the distance traversed.

wharfage charge for the use of a wharf.

cellarage available space in a cellar.

leverage the power of a lever.

parentage the condition of a parent.

verbiage mere wordiness. **plumage** feathers collectively.

foliage leaves collectively. (FŎLĬĀTĬO foliation.)

courage[d] constitutional bravery, or that which depends upon (CŌR) the heart, mind, or temperament.

forage[d] **herbage**[d] **visage**[d] **personage**[d] **language**[d] **beverage**[d] **assemblage** **vicinage** **coinage** **tonnage** **bandage** **bondage** **cordage** **lineage** **usage** **badinage** **carnage** **damage** **homage** **message** **advantage** (see A-) **marriage** **hostage** **manage** v.

Obs. 1. *Outrage* (ŪLTRĀ beyond,) *advantage* (ĂB ĀNTĔ,) and *disparage*, may be enforced by ĂGĔRĔ to act. *Nonage* means *not* of *age*. *Privilege* (LEX law.) *Suffrage* (SŬB, FRĂNGO I break.) *Présage* (SĀGĬO I perceive.) *Hemorrhage* (ἅῖμᾰ blood, ῥήγνῡμῐ to burst.) *Cartridge*, Fr. cartouche. *Appendage* is akin to *appendix*.

Obs. 2. Image, mucilage, and cartilage belong to -AGO. *Cottage* may have been produced from cot, cottier, cot'ger, cottager, cottage.

A pore wydow, fomdel* ftope in age
Was whilom duellyng in a pore c o t a g e,—*Chaucer*.

* *Somewhat*.

-age, n.

[Ital. -iccia, Sp. -icha, Fr. -isse. Lat. -ĬTĬĒS, -ĬTĬĂ. See **-ice.**]

sausage (-idge) meat minced and seasoned. (Ital. salsiccia, Fr. saucisse, from SĂLSŬS salted, savory; SĂL salt, whence also *salad*, and *sauce*.)

-AGO, -UGO, -IGO, n. resemblance.

[L. -ĀGO, gen. -Ā-GĬN-ĬS; -ŪGO, gen. -ŪGĬNĬS; -ĪGO, gen. -ĪGĬNĬS. Perhaps akin to -C-.]

plumbago a mineral *like* or *resembling* (PLŬMBŬ[m]) lead.

Solidago golden-rod, a plant like the (SŌL, gen. SŌLĬS) sun.

plantain PLĂNTĀGO a weed like a (PLĂNTĂ) young plant.

Tussilago TŬSSĬ-L-ĀGO a plant as if for (TŬSSĬS) a cough.

serpigo a serp-ent-like tetter.

lumbago rheumatism of the (LŪMBŬS) loin.

vertigo* a sensation of turning.

lentigo a lens-like freckly eruption.

Ustilago a genus of parasitic fungi infesting maize.

albugo an eye disease. (ĀLBŬS white.) **image**, as if from IM of im-it-ate, s-im-ilar. **origin**, (ŎRĬŎR to arise.) **mucilage** (MŪCŬS.) **virago** (VĬR a man.) **farrago** a mixture (FĀR wheat.) **cerago**

Obs. 1. *Indigo* is Spanish, for ĪNDĬCŬS Indian, *color* being understood. Fustigate see -IG-.

Obs. 2. The corresponding adjectives are formed on the genitive case, as plumbaginous, plantaginous, lentiginous, ferruginous, rubiginous, aeruginous, cartilaginous, -gin- being the base, or crude form.

-AL, adj. *relating to, like, capable of being —.*

[Lat. adj. m., f. -ĀL-ĬS[a] (neut. -ĀLĔ,) -ĒL-ĬS,[b] -ĬL-ĬS[c] (neut. -IL-Ĕ.) Gr. -λις, -λός. Ital. -ale. Fr. -al, -ale, -el, -elle. Gaelic -ail. Welsh -awl. Old Eng. -all, -ell, -eil. Words in -AL are derived from nouns or adjectives, and verbs. Akin to -OL-, -UL-, -UR-, -ER-, -AR-IS, -AT-US, -ID-US, -AN-US.]

-al, -al-ic, -el, -eel, -il, -l-e, -l-ian, -l-ity, -l-ism, -l-ist, -l-ist-ic, -l-ity, -l-ness, -l-ty.

austral *relating to* or *pertaining to* (ĀVSTĔR) the south.

liberal having the *quality of* one (LĪBĔR) free.

social *like* (SŎCĬŬS) a companion; companion*able; adapted to* companionship.

fluvial pertaining to (FLŬVĬŬS) a river.

in-imical not like (ĂMĪCŬS) a friend; like an en-emy.

tractile[c] that may be (or capable of being) drawn out.

cruel[b] (CRŪDĒLĬS; CRŪDŬS rough,) inhuman.

docile[c] *that may be* instructed; easily taught.

From nouns and adjectives—**dual** **punctual** **gradual** **vocal** or **vowel** **juvenile** **infantile** **hostile** **civil**[c] **gentile**, **gentle** and

* Vértĭgo, léntĭgo, sérpĭgo, as English words,—wer-tēe-go, &c. as Latin. Incongruous hĭbrids like vert-eye-go are neither Latin nor English.

genteel **carnal** and **charnel** **fidel**ity[b] **annual** **annal**ist **lateral** **celest-i-al** **mart-i-al** **judicial** **ether-e-al** **triumphal** **natural** **naval** **humil**ity **util**ity

From verbs—**utensil** **fertile** **vers-at-il**ity **s-erv-il**ity **noble**[c] **facil**ity **fossil** **April** **fragile** or **frail** **superficial** **potential**

Inſtitutions, . . . Practicall, Ethycall, Œcumenicall, and Politicall.—*Quarles*, 1641.

Obs. 1. This suffix has been extended to a few Latin and many English nouns, as in L. ĂNĬMĂL having (ĂNĬMĂ) breath; CĂNDĒLĂ a candle, from CĂNDĔO, to shine; CĂPĬTAL a covering for (CĂPŬT) the head.

capital the head of a column; principal; chief.

ratio-n-âlĕ[a] n. the reason or explanation of a phenomenon. (NĀV-ĀLĔ a ship-yard, CŬB-ĪLĔ a couch.)

hospital and **hotel** **general** **cardinal** **mortal** **signal** **canal** and **channel** **cathedral** — **apocryphal** **choral** — **vassal** **trial** **reprisal** **proposal** **reversal** **denial** **renewal** **burial** **nonpareil**

Obs. 2. Entrail-s, victual-s, reprisal-s, are formed by the adjective collective plural -AL-IA.

Obs. 3. Corporal, n. is a heteronym of Fr. caporal, Ital. caporale.

-AL-IA, n. pl.

regalia ornaments pertaining to a (RĒX) king.

penetralia the inmost parts (of a temple, &c.)

paraphernalia **Bacchanalia** **Cerealia** **Ferealia**

-AL-ITy, -IL-ITy, n.

brutality the quality of being (-al) like a brute.

legality **formality** **frugality** **principality** **plurality** **facility** **docility** **agility** **humility** **servility** **ductility**

-AN, -IAN, -EN,

-ain, -ane, -ean, -en, -ene, -ine, -une, -ne, -on.

adj. *of, like, pertaining to;* n. *one who,* &c.

[Ss. -ANA5, -ĪNA, -IN, -T-ANA5. Gr. -ᾱνός, -ηνός, -ῑνός, -ίνης; -τ-ινος, -σι-νος. L. -ĀN-ŬS (-Ă, -Ŭm,) ĒN-ŬS, ŌNŬS, -ŪNŬS, -INŬS, -T-INŬS, -NŬS. Welsh

-ain. Ss. JAM (yam) to *tie, hold,* JĀMINA5, Lat. GĔMĬNŬS *joined, twin.* Ss. PALĀLĪ *straw,* PALĀLINA *full of straw.* But (see **-en**) -ῐνός, -ĪNŬS, with ĭ means *made of.*]

African *of* Africa. **Protean** *like* Proteus.

Alexandrine (ἀλεξανδρῖνος) *pertaining to* Alexandria.

veteran *one who* has become (VĔTŬS, gen. VĔTĔR-ĬS) old.

opportune convenient to an occasion. (PŌRTŬS a harbor, an asylum.) **alien** of (ĂLĬ-ŬS) another (place.)

pristine most ancient. (*t* educed from *s* of PRĬŬS *before,* the adverb of PRŌ.)

kitchen (CŎQVĪNĂ) a place for cooking. (CŎQVO I cook; CŎQVĪNŬS pertaining to cooking.)

fluorine an element found in fluor spar.

dams-on and **damasc-ene** the Damascus plum.

foreign (Fr. forain, foraine,) exterior; alien; irrelevant. (FŎRĀS out of doors.)

> Which that thofe knights likewife mote underftand,
> And witneffe forth aright in forrain land,—*Spenfer,* born 1510.

If any *Englifh* man fhould now write or fpeak as our forefathers did about fix or feven hundred years paft, we fhould as little underftand him as if he were a foreiner;—*Bp. Wilkins,* Real Character p. 6, 1668.

sylvan (SĪLVĀNŬS) **human** and **humane** **urban** and **urbane** **christian** **benig-n** **ger-m-ane** (GĔRO I bear) **meridian** **terrene** **serene** **corona**l **colo'n**ial **tribune** **divine** **serpentine** **feline** **canine** **marine** **peregrine** or **pilgrim**

The following are from Latin feminine nouns in -ĀNĂ, -ĪNĂ, &c.

fortune pertaining to (FŌRS) luck.

saline (SĂLĪNŬS salty, SĂLĪNĂ a salt work.)

CŎL-ŌNŬS a farmer, from CŎLO to cultivate, whence **colony** **colonist**. VĔN-ĒNŬ^{m} (a neuter noun,) whence **venom**.

etesian (ἔτος year,) periodical (winds.)

medicine **discipline** **doctrine** **columbine** **membrane** **rapine** **resin** **ruin** **quartan** **captain** or **chieftain** **citiz-en** (CĪVĬTĀS a city.) **certain** **chaplain** **barbarian** **historian** are formed from supposable adjectives in **-anus**; **quatrain** **curtain** **train** (TRĂHĔRĔ to draw,) **jacobin** from **-inus**; and **mountain** **fountain** from others in **-aneus**.

cou-s-in is the adjective and noun forms COnSobrIN-us, -a, or without the prefix con-, the nouns SŌBRĪN-ŬS, -Ă. **shagreen** is probably from an adjective form CĂRCHĂRĪNŬS of CĂRCHĂRŬS (whence) *shark*, from χάρχἄρος rough, snappish.

Obs. 1. MŪSĬCŬS means both *musical* and *musician* (see -AC, Obs. 2,) so that -ian in 'physician' is an adaptation of the Latin -ianus, formed from the genitive case of a noun or adjective, with -anus added, as in PHȲSĬCŬS, gen. PHȲSĬCĪ, physici-an-us, musici-an-us, politician-us, rhetorician-us, magician-us, &c. which are not Latin words.

Gangrene, γάϝγραινα, from γράω and γραί-ν-ω I gnaw.

Profan-e not sacred. (FĀNŬm a temple.) *Anodyne*, see *AN*-.

In Persian geographical names, -an is part of -stān (country, region,) as Bagistân the place of vines; Daghestân (*gh* guttural) land of mountains; Hindustân country of Hindoos.

In Hebrew there are nouns in -an, &c. as qŏrbān (an offering, Mark 7 :11;) leviathan (Job 41.)

-ANA, n. pl. *sayings*, &c. *of*. See -AN.

Of our English *Ana*, by far the most celebrated is the Walpoliana, being a collection of the conversational remarks of Horace Walpole, together with a good many fragments copied from his papers.—Penny Cyclopædia, 1833.

-ance, -ancy, -ence, -ency, n.
quality of (being —;) the act of; the result of; an —ing.

[Lat. ĀNT-ĬĂ,[a] -ENT-ĬĂ;[b] Ital. -anza, -enza (*z* as *ts*;) Sp. -ancia, -anza, -encio, -encia; Fr. -ance, -ence. Formed from present participles by adding the fem. noun termination (☞ -A) to the genitive case, as in PRŌ-VĬDĔO I foresee, pro-vide; PROVIDENS (genitive PRŌVĬDĔNTĬS) provident; PRŌVĬDĔNTĬĂ providence or prudence.]

providence the *quality* or the *act of* foreseeing, or *of being* prudent; a foresee*ing*.

abundance the quality of abounding; an abounding.

defiance the act of defying.

elegance, elegancy the quality of being elegant.

silence (SĬLĔNTĬŬm) the result (consequence, effect,) of being silent.

continence **countenance**[b] (CŎNTĬNĔNTIA) **obedience** and **obeisance**[b] **semblance** (DĪS-SĬMŬLANTIA) **observance** **difference** **albescence** **efflorescence** **audience** **impatience** **science**

experience indulgence constancy significancy repugnancy decency fulgency refulgence clemency potency urgency

Hindrance is a heteronym of the Belgian hindernis, see **-ness.**

-AND, -ANDUM n., a. something *to be —ed.*

[Lat. -ĂND-ŭS (-Ă, -ŭm;) ĔND-ŭS (-Ă, -ŭm;) the future participle of the passive voice of the verb, used as nouns in English. Ital. -ondo, -anda, -enda. Obs. 1. The neuter forms in the genitive, accusative, and ablative cases, constitute the gerund, which are sometimes used as English nouns. Obs. 2. The N is that of the present participle (see -ANT,) and the D corresponds with the past participles and adjectives in -TUS. See **-ate.**]

multiplic-and something to be multiplied.

memorandum something to be remembered.

deodand to be given (DĔŬS, dative case DĔŌ) to God.

reverend one to be revered; worthy of reverence.

legend something to be read.

prebend an allowance, (PRÆBEO, to allow.) "Provende or rent, or dignite."—*Chaucer,* who uses 'provendre' for a prebendary.

second SĔCŪNDŬS adj. following. (See SĔQVŎR.)

viand (VĪVĔNDŬS; VĪVO I live,) an agreeable article of food.

mori-b-und adj., n. MŎRĬBŪNDŬS adj. about to (MŎRĬ-ŎR) die.

round RŎTŪNDŬS a., as if 'rotandus' *to be rolled;* RŎTO I roll, RŎTĂ a wheel. **innuendo** by hinting; the ablative case of the gerund of ĬN-NŬO I nod, hint.

Obs. 3. The meanings of 'prebend' and 'dividend' have been changed.

Obs. 4. 'Tremendous' and 'stupendous' are adjectives formed like the participle HŎRRĔNDŬS horrible.

-and participial.

[The old English present participle. See under **-ing.**]

Eftfoones himfelfe in glitterand armes he dight, . . .—*Spenser.*

-ANDA, -ENDA, n. pl.

[The plural of -ĂND-Um, -ĔND-Um. See -AND.]

memoranda things to be remembered.

corrigenda things to be corrected.

-ANeous, a. See -AN, -ous.

cutaneous pertaining to (CŬTĬS) the skin.

subterraneous **spontaneous** **extraneous** or **strange**

-AN-ITy, -EN-ITy, -IN-ITy

urbanity the quality of one (-an) pertaining to (URB-S) a city; the politeness of a city.

-ANT, -ENT, a. *quality of —ing;* n. *that which, one who.*

[Latin present participle, -ĀNS, -ĒNS (gen. -ĀNT-ĬS, -ĒNT-ĬS;) Gr. -ων,* gen. -οντος. Ital. -ante, -ente; Wallachian -nd. Welsh -iad. Lat. infinitive ESSĔ *to be,* ĒNS, Gr. ὢν *being, existing.* Ss. pres. part. -AT (-ANT;) Zend -ans; Lithuanian -ans; Go. -ands; Ger. -end. Welsh noun en *a living principle, a spirit;* ener *an intelligence;* Gr. 'ἀνὴρ (gen. ἀνδρὸς,) *a man.* Ss. B'HARAT *bearing;* φέρων, Lat. FĔRĒNS and PĂRĬĒNS; Fr. portant (from PŌRTO I carry,) Eng. im-portant.]

-ntable, -ntlike, -ntless, -ntly, -ntiation, -ntial-ly.

provident and **prudent** having the quality of foreseeing; the being or existing of foresight.

absorbent a. having the quality of absorbing; n. that which absorbs. **assailant** one who assails.

servant and **serjeant** one (SĔRVĬĒNS) serving.

merchant one selling. **student** one that studies.

fiend, Gothic participle present fiands, from fian, fijan *to hate.*

president **tenant** (for tenent) **oppo'nent** **inhabitant** **assistant** **vagrant** **infant** **quadrant** **alb-esc-ent** **ar-rogant** **urgent** **innocent** **defiant** **elegant** **ruminant** a., n. **consonant** **expectant** **observant** **absent** **abstinent** **excellent** **resident** a., n. **adherent** **sufficient** **vol-unt**ary **authent**ic (see *AUTO-*.)

vi-ol-ent **pest-il-ent** **op-ul-ent** **truc-ul-ent** **fraud-ul-ent**

---

* As in βουλεύω I advise, consult; βουλεύ-ων (gen. -οντος,) advising; βουλευ-θ-είς (gen. -θ-εντυς,) being advised; βούλευ-σις (see *-S-IS*) the *act* of consultation; βούλευ-μα (see *-MA*,) the *result* of deliberation; βουλ-εία (see -y ¶ 1,) the *function* of a counsellor. σπάω I draw, pull; σπάσ-μα that which has been drawn, (as a sword,) convulsion; σπάσις the *act* of pulling, tension.

(see -ul-ent.) **valiant** **grand** **stand** **blind** **blunt** **splint** **squint** **pageant** **truant** **serpent** **brigand** **craven**

Obs. 1. The genitive case of some Latin nouns in -ns, -s, gives English nouns in -nt, -nd, as SĔXTĀNS (gen. SĔXTĀNTĬS,) the sixth part; octant; quadrant (equally derivable from a verb,) MĒNS (gen. MĒNTĬS,) mind.

Obs. 2. *Tyrant* is a heteronym, Fr. tyran, Lat. TȲRĀNNŬS, Gr. τῠ'ρāννος a ruler.

-*ANT*, n. *that which.*

[Greek nouns in -ᾱς, gen. -ᾱντος; Latin -AS, gen. -ANTIS. See -*AS*.]

giant GĬGĀS γῐ'γᾱς, a large man fabled to have sprung from (γῆ) the earth.

gigantic **elephant** -ine, -íasis. **adamant** and **diam-ond** see *A-*. **Atlantic** see -*AS*.

Hierophant and *sycophant* are from φαίνω I show, with N intensive, and T of -της, T-ER.

-*AR*, n.

[Greek, as in νέκτᾰρ *nectar*, ἐσχᾰ'ρα a *hearth*, an *eschar*.]

sugar is from an East Indian original, but as a Europèan word it is from the Arabic sukkar (sookkar,) and with the article as-sukkar, whence the Spanish azúcar. (Greek σάκχᾰρ, σάκχᾰρῐ; Latin SĂCCHĂRŪm; Ellenic ζάχαρη; Albanian and Turkish sheker.)

jaggary a coarse unrefined (Tamil jakarai, Malay jagara) sugar; also sugar from palm juice.

. . . . . the sugar itself [of the sap of the cocoa-nut palm] is separated under the name of Jagery.—*Lindley*, Botany, 1830.

saccharine **nectary** **nectarine** **ĕschar** **scar** **tiara**

The juice nectareous, and the balmy dew; . .
Pope, Essay on Man, I :136, 1733.

-**ar**, n.

A false spelling of -er, in **friar** **beggar** **liar** **vinegar** ('vinegre,' 'vineger,' *Holland*, 1635) **dollar** **pillar** ('piler,' *Chaucer*, 'piller,' *Holland*, 'pillour,' *Spenser*.)

With baleful beggery or foul disgrace; . . .
A stately pallace . . . without morter laid,—*Spenser*.

In *poplar* (Fr. peuplier) -ar means *tree,* as French amande an almond gives amandier an almond tree; prune a plum, prunier a plum tree.

-AR, -ARI-, ARy, a., n. *relating to.*

[Lat. adj. m. and f. -ĀR-ĬS, neut. -ĀR-Ĕ; akin to -ĀL-ĬS, and used chiefly to avoid the repetition of L.]

military pertaining to (MĪL-ĔS, gen. -ĬTĬS,) a soldier.
auxiliary affording (ĀVXĬLĬŪm) aid.
regular according to a (RĒG-ŬLĂ) rule.
salutary conducing to (SĂL-ŪS, gen. ŪTĬS,) safety or health.
collar (CŌLLĀRĔ) a band for (CŌLLŪm) the neck.
tabular **famili-ar**ity **simil-ar**ly **perpendicular** **joc-ul-ar** **par-t-ic-ul-ar** **circular** **polar** **solar** **lunar** **sublunar**y **stellar** **consular** **globular** **popular** **angular** **scholar** **columnar**

-AR-, -OR-. See -R- formative, and -ARy.

vicar (VĬCĀRĬŬS) one supplying the place of another.
cellar (CĒLLĀRĬŪm) an underground apartment.

-ARy, -ARI-, -ORy, -ORI-, a., n. *relating to.*

[Lat. adj. -ĀR-ĬŬS, (fem. -ĬĂ, neut. -ĬŬM,) ŌR-ĬŬS. Ital. -ario, -orio. Fr. -aire, -oir. See -R- formative, and I formative.]

-ari-ous, -ari-ly, -ari-ness, -ari-ed, -ari-ty, -ori-ness.

military soldier-like. **auxiliary** affording aid.
gregarious living in (GRĔX, pl. GRĔGĒS) flocks.
honorary conferring honor. **consolatory** affording consolation. **illusory** tending to, or promoting illusion.
anniversary **arbitrary** **hereditary** **testamentary** **voluntary** **tributary** **legionary** **contemporary** **judiciary** **primary** **secondary** **salary**
transitory **dilatory** **censorious** **meritorious** **territory**

Latin adjectives in -ARIUS -ORIUS were sometimes used as nouns, as in ĀDVĒRSĀRĬŬS *opposite,* and an *adversary;* STĂTŪĀRĬŬS, ĀCTŪĀRĬŬS, MĒRCĒNĀRĬŬS, NŎTĀRĬŬS, ĂQVĀRĬŬS, CŌMMĒNTĀRĬŬS and CŌMMĒNTĀRĬŬM.

antiquary he who studies antiquities.

dromedary (adj. δρομὰς running, see *-AD*, genitive δρομά'δος,) a running (camel;) one swift of foot.

statuary n. he who makes statues; a. fit for statues, as 'statuary marble.'

sorc-er-er (with a double suffix,) old Fr. sorcier, SŌRTĬ-ĀR-ĬŬS, he who practises divination by (SŌRS, pl. SŌRTĒS) lots.

January **February** **anniversary** **premier** and **primmer** **contemporary** **secretary** **stationary** **commentary**

The suffix of cutler (courtier, cavalier,) may be considered as from -arius, as if 'cultellarius,' from CŬLTĔLLŬS a small (CŬLTĔR) knife.

To this head belong vicar, mountaineer, engineer, grenadier, treasurer, bursar or purser, equerry, cordwainer; and perhaps archer and tinner (STĀNNĀRĬŬS,) but not weaver, drinker, &c.

-ARy, -ERy, -ORy, n. *of place; that which.*

[Gr. -ήριον,[a] -όριον;[b] -ĀR-ĬŬM,[c] ĒRĬŬM,[d] -ŌRĬŬM,[e] -ĀRĔ.[f] Ital., Sp. -ar, -ario, -eria, -orio; Fr. -oir, -oire. Dan. -rie; Ger. -erei, -elei. Hindoostanee -ar, as in lon *salt*, lon-ar *a salt pit.* See -AR- formative, and I formative.]

cemetery[a] κοιμητήρῐον a sleeping place. (κοιμά'ω I put to sleep, I calm; κᾰτᾰ-κοιμά'ω, to set (κατὰ) down to sleep; whence **catacomb**. See *CATA-*.)

emporium[b, e] a place of deposit. (πορεύω I transport.)

mystery[a, d] something kept concealed; μύ'ω to shut up; μυέω, (future μυήσω,) to instruct in hidden knowledge; μυστὴρ (see -TOR) a mystic. **cautery**[a] see *-S-*.

aviary,[c] a place for (ĂVĬS, pl. ĂVĒS) birds.

magistery and **ma..stery**[d] the place or power of a master; but ĪMPĔRĬŬ[m] makes **empire**.

altar,[f] L. noun ĀLTĀRĔ, agreeing with a neuter adjective form; from ĀLTŬS high. (See **collar**, under -AR, a., n.)

herbarium **aquarium** **calend-ar**[c] **library** **apiary** **granary** and **grange** **dormitory** **dispensary** **almonry** and **ambry** **réfectory** **confectionary** **dictionary** **glossary** **itinerary** **diary** **estuary** **promontory** **armory**[c] **laver**[c] **vestry**[c] **frontier** **reserv-oir** **parl-or** **orat-orio** **auditorium** **columbarium**

Obs. Its use is extended to nursery, brewery, colliery, dower, refinery, chafery, foundry, smithery or smithy, fishery, scullery, buttery, pillory, lottery, hostelry, quarry, &c.

Caravansary is a heteronym of the Persian and Arabic 'cārwān' a traveling body, and 'sura' a house. *Ivory*, Lat. ĔBŬR, gen. ĔBŎRĬ-S.

-ard, n. *one who; that which.*

[Ital. -ardo; Sp. -arde, -arte, -ardo; Port. -art, -arde; Fr. -ard, -arde. Ger. (-hart,) -art, -ert; Belg. -aard. Ger. art, Belg. aard *a kind;* akin to Latin ĀRS (gen. ĀRTĬS,) *art, faculty, quality.* Old high Ger. adj. hart *hard;* adv. harto, harte, *much, very, vehemently;* as in the proper names Adelhart (or -hard) one who is very noble; Erhart, one with much honor; Reginhart, whence Reinhart and reynard, from regin *counsel.* The masculine suffix -er, as in hunt-er, has been confounded with -art and -hart, as in (the German reich *rich,* whence the names) Reicher, Reichert, Reichhard; or in stand-ard (for stand-er) as distinguished from standard *a banner,* derived from *extend.* Similarly, Belgian -er, -aar, an *inhabitant,* has taken -d in Spanjaard *a native of Spain;* English lanyard, Fr. lanière *a long strap.*]

drunkard one who has the habit of being drunk.

placard, πλάξ a plate, Belg. plakken to stick up, plakkaat a proclamation. **halliard**, from 'haul.'

gurnard, as if horn-ard, from the bony head. (Welsh pengernyn *horn-head.*)

billiards a play with balls. (Fr. bille an ivory ball; Flemish 'bikkel' a small bone, or die, used in the play of 'cockles.')

coward, (L. CAVDĂ, Ital. coda, Fr. queue *a tail;*) first applied to timorous dogs, which indicate fear by drawing in the tail. **hazard**, old Fr. hazart a dicer.

cockade (Fr. cocarde) an ornament originally like a cock's comb.

lubbard or **lubber**, Belg. looper a runner, a vagabond; hence landlubber, a contemptuous term for a landsman.

dullard standard dotard sluggard niggard wizard buzzard braggart haggard mallard pilchard rampart pollard scabbard poniard bayard lanyard halyard

Exceptions: bustard mustard orchard lizard leopard spikenard steward.

Halbert or *halberd*, Fr. hallebarde, Ger. hellebarde, Ital., Sp. labarda, Rhaetian halumbard, from the German helm *a handle*, and barte *a broad-ax.*

Obs. 1. *Mustard* is commonly referred to MUSTU^m ARDENS, but see M-.*

Obs. 2. In old high German, the name hart is a woody mountain (whence Hartz; Harz *resin*,) as in Lindhart *linden-wood;* Spehteshart, Ger. Spessart *woodpecker-forest;* Eng. +speight a woodpecker.

-AS, -IS, n.

[Gr. -ας, -ις. Irish -as, -se. See *-AD.*]

Boreas (βορέᾱς, gen. -οῦ,) the north wind.

Dipsas (διψὰς gen. -άδος,) a genus of serpents.

pancreas (gen. -ᾰτος) **Atlas** (gen. -αντος)

erysipelas (gen. -ατος) **canvas** (κάννᾰβις hemp.)

These give the adjective forms **pancreat**ic, **Atlant**ic, and **erysipelat**ous.

Xiphias (ξῐφῐ'ᾱς) the generic name of the sword-fish. (ξῐ'φος a sword, ξέω, ξύω to scrape.)

> Huge ziffius, whom mariners eſchew . . .
> And greedy roſmarines† with viſages deforme:
>
> *Spenser*, bk. 2, canto 12, :24.

Copperas, for copperose. See **-ous**.

Bias is probably from oBLIQvUS oblique.—*J. Thomson.*

> Reaſon the byas turns from good to ill,
> And Nero reigns a Titus, if he will.—*Pope.*

Alias (otherwise,) a Latin adverb.

Capias (you may take,) a Latin verb of the second person singular number, used as an English noun.

-ass, n.

[Italian augmentative and deteriorative -accio, -accia; Fr. -as, -asse. Akin to -AC-EUS.]

---

* Welsh ta *that extends*, tar *a pervading principle*, tardd *issue*, bas *shallow*, *base*, basdardd *what is of base growth.*

† Sea-horses. The glossary does not explain ziffius and rosmarine, but Richardson quotes the latter line in illustration of the plant rosemary.

cutlass, Italian coltellaccio (a large or bad knife,) from the Latin CŬLTĔLLŬS a small (CŬLTĔR) knife or 'coulter.'

crevasse (Fr.) a large break. (CRĔPO, to break, burst; Ital. crepaccio (-accia) a large break or opening.)

matrass a chemical vessel shaped like (MATARA) a Gallic javelin. **cuirass** see -ACeous and Obs.

pinnace, Fr. pinasse, Ital. pinaccia, Sp. pinaza, from PĪNŬS a fir tree, a ship.—*Diez.*

mattress **morass** **embarrass** **calabash** (Fr. calebasse.)
Carcass is an exception.

-ASM, n. See *-ISM.*

spasm an abnormal contraction of the muscles. (*σπάω* I draw, pull.)

-AS-T, n. *-AS-T-IC*, *-S-T-IC*, a.

[See *-S-* inflectional, -T-ER, Obs. 1, *-IS-M*, *-IS-T.*]

en-comi-ast he who gives (ἐϜκώμιον) praise, or commends.

el-astic springing back. (ἐλαύνω to move, extend.)

cau-stic see *-S-*. **my-stic** see *-S-*.

enthusiastic see -IC.

dom-estic pertaining to (DŎMŬS δόμος) a house or a home.

iconoclastic **periphrastic** **ecclesiastic** **sarcastic** **plastic** **pleonastic** **fantastic** **gymnastic** **pro-gno-stic** **cabalistic**

-AT- See *-AS*, *-AT-IC*, *-MA.*

-ATe, -AT-, a. *quality of; like;* n. *the person* or *thing that;* v. *to make*, &c.

[Latin adjectives, past participles, and supines. -ĀT-ŬS,[a] (-Ă, -Ūm,) -ĒT-ŬS,[b] -ĪT-ŬS,[c] -ŌT-US,[d] ŪT-US,[e] -T-US,[f] -S-US;[g] Ital. -to, -ta. Wallachian -at, -ut, -it; Fr. -at-, -ate, -ite, -té, -tée. Gothic -θs. Islandic -dur, -tur. Welsh -t, -d, -aid, -aidd; Irish -ta, -te, -th, -the, -dha, -de, -t. English -ade, -ate, -et, -ete, -ite, -at, -ute, -ed, -id, -d, -t, -te, -ty. See ¶ under **-ade.**]

The Sanscrit forms of -TUS are -TA5, -TA5 (with the original vowel,) -DHA5, as in

DĀ to *give,*	DĂTTĂ5 *given,*	Lat. DĂTŬS whence *date.*
TĂP to *heat,*	TĂPTĂ5 *heated,*	" TĔPĬDŬS *tepid.*
LŎTr to *appear,*	LOTrITA5 *lucid,*	" LŪCĬDŬS *lucid.*
STABH to *fix,*	STUBDHA5 *stiff, dull,*	" STŬPĬDŬS *stupid.*]

advocate[a] calle*d* (ĂD) to; one called to plead a cause.

plicate plie-*d* or fold-*ed;* v. to make folds or plications.

laureat, **-ate**[a] decked with laurel, as if laurel'd.

fac-t[a] anything (FA·CTŪ^{m}) done. **se-lec-t** chosen (SĒ-) apart. **fate** what is spoken (by the gods.)

vote[f] (that which is vow'd;) choice by suffrage.

armed, Fr. armé. **army**, Fr, armée, an armed (force.)

Used as adjectives—**associate duplicate ornate striate innate roseate ovate cordate discrete effete**[b] **complete obsolete qui-et requisite polite**[c] **remote**[d] **acute**[e] **astute minute morose**[g] **abstruse**[g] **stric-t jus-t hones-t modes-t exemp-t abrup-t erec-t abjec-t beref-t righ-t**

Souls elevate, angelic, wing'd with fire . . . —*Young.*

Used as nouns—**associate duplicate reprobate advocate date rate certificate mandate consulate légate magistrate triumvirate aggregate cerate veg-et**ate **site ducat dig-it gran-ite**[a] **trib-ute statute deposit** and **depo***t* **verdict relict conflict sect insect district assignee**[a] **fusee**[g] Fr. fusée **jett-y** Fr. jetée **guarantee** and **warranty**

Used as verbs—**associate duplicate reprobate advocate date rate medicate consolidate confiscate regulate elucidate gyrate tabulate circulate stagnate veg-et**ate **complete inflec-t lif-t**

Holland's Plinie, 1635, has inueterat immoderat appropriat sophisticat senat infinit opposit, and the verbs intoxicat expectorat incorporat mitigat

Chocolate is the Mexican chocollatl.

Termite n. Lat. TĔRMĔS (pl. TĔRMĪTĒS, insects vulgarly termed white ants,) is formed irregularly from the Latin plural.

Obs. 1. As the first Latin supine resembles the neuter nominative of adjectives and participles in U^{m}, words derived from any of them may be placed under the same head, as *debt,* which is equally contained in the participle DĒBĬTŬS, and the supine DĒBĬTŪ^{m}, from DĒBĔO I owe.

Obs. 2. Forms like defrauded, derided, deluded, surrounded, grounded, have induced the vulgar form drown-d-ed, whose iterative suffix is present in English, the -d of len-d being that of loan-d. Hence len-d-ed is etymologicly equivalent to loan-d-ed, compac-t-ed to compack-ed-ed, con-coc-t-ed to con-cooked-ed, deduc-t-ed to deduced-ed, protec-t-ed to pro-decked-ed, and gir-t-ed or gir-d-ed to gyr-ate-ate or gyr-ed-ed.

Dement-at-ed is in use, and eruc-t-at-ed occurs in the transactions of a learned society. Predestinate, Rom. 8 :30; predestinated, Ephes. 1 :11.

A box where ſweets compacted lie.—*Geo. Herbert*, born 1593.

And each lock faſt the wall-compac-t-ed gate.—*Pope.*

That ſoil, impregn-at-ed with nobler ſeed
Refuſed the culture of ſo rank a weed.—*Falconer.*

Which, like a bud compac-t-ed
Their purple cups contrac-t-ed.—*Southey.*

Obs. 3. The older writers were more observant of the etymologic difference between verbs and participles, as Chaucer, who uses the verbial forms corrige (to correct,) corrumpeth, corrumpable, delibere, dissimule, encorporing—but he also uses enfecte and endite as verbs.

He became ſo confuſe, he conneth not loke.—'Piers Plouhman.

I am ſo confuſe that I cannot ſay.—*Chaucer.*

Sith firſt inhabit was the lond.—*id.*

Sal tartre, alcaly, and ſalt preparat
And combuſt materes and coagulat.—*id.*

My joy is tranſlate ful far in exile.—*id.*

The wiſdom of thoſe arts . . . is degenerate into childiſh ſophiſtry.—*Bacon*, 1625.

. . . be ye lift up, ye everlaſting doors.—Psalm 24 :7.

. . . captivate with the meaneſt vanity.—*Henry Hammond*, 1764.

Well haſt thou acquit thee.—*Shakesp.*

With head uplift above the wave.—*Milton*, P. Loſt, 1 :193.

How complicate, how wonderful is man.—*Young.*

Imaged the supreme beauty uncreate.—*Coleridge.*

To glad and fertilise the subject plains.—*id.*

Their fortunes are compact with mine;—*Aytoun.*

Obs. 4. The following have been formed nearly thus; (but see Obs. 2 under **-th**.)

have (hav'd) ha	think (think't) tho't
do (do-ed) did	may (may'd) mi't
will (will-ed) wou'd	shall (shal'd) shou'd
bring (bring-ed) bro't	owe (ow'd) ō'd, awt

-AT-IC-, ET-IC, -OT-IC, -AD-IC, a., n.

[See *-AS*, *-MA*, T[a] declensional, T[b] participial, and -AC.]

pancreatic[a] pertaining to the pancreas. See *-AS*.
dramatic[a] see *-MA*. **prophetic**[b] **athletic**[b] see T-ER.
energetic[b] see T participial. **sporadic** see *-AD*.
asce'tic pertaining to (ἀσκητής see T-ER,) one who practices any exercise. (ἀσκέω to perform a work with care, to train, to practice devotion.)
narcotic producing (νάρκη) torpor.
hypnotic producing (ὕπνος) sleep.

-AT-ILe, -AT-IL-, -T-IL-, a. 1. *capable of —ing;* 2. *pertaining to.*

[-ATe and -AL; as in m., f., HĀM-ĀT-ĬL-ĬS, neut. HĀM-ĀT-ĬL-Ĕ *like* or *with a* (HĀMŬS) *hook;* HĀM-ĀT-ŬS *hooked.* VERS-ATILIS *apt to turn, that turns, turning;* VERS-ATILIS *that may be turned, capable of being turned.*]

vĭbratĭle that may (VI-BRO,) vibrate.
fluviatile pertaining to (FLŬVĬŬS, pl. FLŬVĬĪ) rivers.
contractility **ductil**e **volatil**isation **umbratil**e **versatil**e
Docile is for docible.

-au, n.

[A French spelling of *o*, often preceded by *e*, and connected with an original *l*.]

beau (BĔLLŬS) **beauty** **portmanteau** **bureau** **flam**beau

-AX, -EX, -IX, -OX-, -YX, -X, n.

[Latin and Greek nouns (sometimes diminutives) in -X, -ξ, derived from verbs, and inflecting in -C-, -G-. See -ACeous, -IX Obs. 2.]

climax	climac-teric	**calx**	calc-ĭned
apex	apic-al	**calyx**	cắlyc-ulate
index	indic-ate	**codex**	codicil
varix	varic-ose	**helix**	helical
vertex	vertic-al	**cicatrix**	cicatrice
vortex	vortic-ose	**silex**, χά'λιξ,	silic-ious

phalanx	phalanges	**onyx**	onychite
larynx	laryngal	**phlox**	phlogistic
sphin-x pl. -xes, -ges		**append-ix** pl.	-ices, -ixes

chalice **pumice** or **pounce** **larch** LĂRĪX λάριξ **thorax** θώρᾱξ **thorac**ic **moustache** or **mustash** μύσταξ MȲSTĀX **nutr-ic**ation **imbricate** **cortic**al **radic**al

Borax, from the Arabic, has been adapted to these.

Syntax, (for syntaxis) belongs to *-SIS*, and *paradox* (-ξία) to *-SIA*.

Obs. In some cases the -c is part of the root as in *paradox* (-ξία,) *equinox, equinoctial, auspice, index, indication.*

-B-, -P-, -V-, -F, -U-, (-M.)

[Ss. BHŪ *to be born, to exist;* φῡ'-ω, to *produce, have, get;* Lat. FĪ-o, to **be,** FŬ-Ī *I have been.* Welsh -p, -f, -ff, b, as in gel-i *a shooting out,* col-p (Swed. kol-f) *a dart.* Bohem. hon-iti *to hunt,* hon-ba *the chase;* sta-ti *to sta-nd,* sta-w *a stand;* kri-ti *to cover,* kr-ow *a roof;* siti *to sow,* sitba (Coptic sit) *seed.* They appear in the Latin perfect and future indicative, as ĂMĀVĪ *I have loved,* ĂMĀBo *I will love;* and in -BUS,[a] -PUS,[b] -VUS,[c] -BER,[d] -VER,[e] -BUND,[f] &c.]

mor-b-id (MŌRBŬS disease, MŎRĬŎR I die,) diseased, tending towards death.

imp (Welsh,) a shoot, a scion. (im *that is extreme.*) Welsh gwy a fluid; gwy-f that yields, draws out; gwy-f-r **wi..re**

chir-p a chirring sound. **sa..fe,** SĂLŪS n., SA·LVŬS a.

gul-f, κόλ-πος a gulf, a deep holl-ow; κοῖλ-ος hollow, deep.

gulp, CŎLLŪ[m] the neck, GŬLĂ the gull-et.

corpse,[b] CŎRPŬS a body.

curve **serv**ant **curb** **superb**[a] **acerb**[a] **garb** **garb**age **cada-ver**ous **crab**apple **herb** **na-v-ig-at-ion** **harp** **scalp** **shelf** **shelv**e **oliv**e **saliva** **lava** **Calvary** **Calvin** **calf** **helv**e **hemp** **crisp**[b] **pul-v-er-ul-ent** **plebe**ian **bulb** **bleb** **glob**e **gleb**e **grief** **help** **yelp** **rasp** **crop** **su-b**ulate **v-oca-b**ulary **vestibul**e **vibrat**e **motiv**e **captiv**e **grav**e a. **con-spic-u**ous **con-tig-u**ous **octav**e **Octavius** **effluvium** **le-f-t**handed[c]

Obs. 1. In limb (LĪMBŬS a border,) clamp, cramp, *b, p,* may be educed from *m.*

Obs. 2. From the affinity between *b* and *m*, some of the examples under *m* may belong here.

Tu-b, a vessel with two handles, is from *two* and *bear*.

-B-ER, -BR-, n.

[Lat. -BER (gen. BRI,) -BRA; -BRVM (gen. BRI.) Perhaps akin to FĔRO, Ss. BHṚ to *bear*, but more probably -B-, and -ER agential.]

-br-ious, -br-ious-ness, -br-ity, -br-ate, -br-at-ion, -br-ic-ate, -br-ic-at-ion.

salu-br-ious bringing (SĂLŪS) health.

vertebra (or **verteber**) plural **vertebræ**, the bones of the spinal column. (VĔRTĔRĔ to turn.)

fa-br-ic-ate (FĂCĔRĔ) to make, as a (FĂ..BĔR) workman.

Terēbra a genus of shells.

lugubrious **celebrity** **lucubrate** **fibre** or **fiber**

Obs. 1. September *seventh*, November *ninth*, December *tenth* (*month* being understood,) are referred by Bopp to the Sanscrit VĀRA *period*, *time;* old Nordish thris-var *thrice*. Hindoostanee (from Persian) bar, war *time*, *turn*, as in SŌMVĀR *monday*.

Obs. 2. By the inductive influence of *September*, &c. the Wallachian has the form *Octombrie*. In the name Berosus, *ber* means son.

-BIL-ITy, n. See -ble, -Ty.

-ble, -BIL-, a. 1. *that may be —ed;* 2. *worthy of;* 3. *capable of;* 4. *full of;* 5. *causing*.

[See -AL. Lat. adj. m., f. -ĀB-ĬL-ĬS[a] (neut. -ĀB-ĬL-Ĕ;) -ŪBĬLĬS;[b] -ĬBĬLĬS;[c] -BĬLĬS;[d] (ĬP-ŬLŬS[e] n.; -BŬLĂ[f] n.; BŬLŪM[g] n.; -PŬLŬM[h] n.) Sp. -able; Fr. -able; Ital. -bile, -evole. L is the adjective element, -IS the suffix for case-inflection, and gender, (see -US;) and -AB the characteristic portion, observable in HĂBĬLĬS *fit*, HĂBĔO *I have*, ŪBĔR full. Sanscrit root AP to *hold*. ¶ In some cases the *b* of -ble cannot be distinguished from -B-. Bopp refers -BILIS, -BAM, -BO, -BUS, -BUNDUS, to the Latin root FU. Words in -ble are mostly based on verbs.]

flexible[c] 1, that may be (FLĒXŬS) bent.

credible[c] 2, worthy of credit.

legible[c] (LĔGĔRĔ to read,) 3, capable of being read; that may be read.

forcible 4, full of force. **terrible**[c] 5, causing terror.

tolerable 1, that may be borne.

stable[a] 3, (STĂ-BILIS firm, STO I stand.)

stable,[g] (STO,) a standing place; a building for cattle.

notable[a] and **noble**[d] 2, worthy to be (NŌ-TŬS) known.

laudable[a] 2. **soluble**[b] 1. **risible** 5. **commendable** 2. **in-satiable** (SĂTĬS enough,) not to be satis-fied **horrible**[c] 5. **movable** 1. **miserable**[a] 2. **culpable**[a] 2. **mutable**[a] 1, 4. **venerable**[a] 2. **memorable**[a] 2. **mutable**[a] 1, 3, 4. **disciple**[c] he who is (DĬSCĔRĔ) to learn. **fable**[f] something (FĀ-RĪ) to tell.

Amiable (ĂMĀBĬLĬS,) is a false form.

Obs. 1. This suffix is reduced to B when -ly follows, as in credi-b-ly, tolera-b-ly, remarkably.

Obs. 2. The vowel which has disappeared from the unaccented syllable -ble, has been retained by the accent in flexi-bil-ity, credi-bil-ity.

Obs. 3. For ramble, crumble, &c. see -L frequentative. For double, treble, see **-ple.**

Obs. 4. Mistakable, remarkable, and others, are hĭbrids.

. . . ſutable to the acts of our own minds,—*Wilkins*, 1668.

-bor, n. See -B.

[Persian -VAR (*v* as Eng. *w;*) Hebrew (from the Persian) -BAR, as in GĬZBĀR *a treasurer;* Gr. from anc. Pers. *γάζα a treasure.* Ger., Dan., Swed. -bar. Irish caraig *a rock,* creagmhar craggy,—*mh* as English *v.*]

hulver the holly, a tree of the genus ĪLĔX. CŎLŬBĔR a genus of serpents; originally, a house snake, (CĔLLĂ a hut, a cell.)

Sulphur, cinnabar, sinoper, caliber, are doubtful, or heteronymic.

Neighbor one living nigh; Ger. nachbar, old high German nahkipuro; bur a dwelling, bau-en to build.

But inwardly he chawed his owne maw
At neibors welth, that made him ever ſad;—*Spenser.*

-BRUM, n.

[Latin, in CĔREBRŪm, which Prof. T. H. Key thinks was originally equivalent to brain-*vessel.* Ger. hir-n *the brain.* See -BER.]

candela′-brum the bearer or support of a (CĀNDĒLĂ) candle; an ornamental branched candlestick.

cerebrum the principal part of the brain as distinguished from the cerebellum.

-B-UND. See -B, -AND.

moribund about to (MŎRĬŎR) die; a dying person.

-C-, -G-, -CIN-, -*GEN*-, genetic.

producing, having.

[Gr. *γεννά ω to produce, to become; γέν-ος,* Lat. GĔN-ŬS a *kin-d.*]

rubi-c-und having (RŪB-ĪGO) redness.

vere-c-und diffident out of respect. (VĔRĔŎR to revere.)

fa-c-und eloquent. (FŎR I speak, FĀRĪ to speak.)

ludi-c-r-ous, LŪDĬCĔR or LŪDĬCRŬS (see -ER, -R, a.) producing (LŪDŬS) sport.

medio-c-re occupying (MĔDĬŪm) the middle; ablative case MĔDĬŌ in the middle.

ratio-cin-ate to produce (RĂTĬO) reason.

vati-cin-ate to perform the function of a (VĀTĒS) prophet.

vatican a celebrated palace, library, and museum at Rome.

hallu-cin-ation a mental impression (*ἄλλος,* ĂLĬŬS) *other* than the correct one. **pur-ge** to make (PŪRŬS) pure.

hydrogen producing (*ὕδωρ*) water.

oxygen producing (*ὀξύς*) sour.

nitrogen a gas produced from nitre (nitrate of potash.)

sepul-chre SĔPŪLCRŬm. **lar-ceny** LĀTRŌCĬNĬŪm.

-C- diminutive.

[See under -C-le, -ock, -k-in.]

-C- agential.

[Lat. ĂGO *I do, act;* -c-ate, and -ca-tion. See -IG-.]

ubi-c-ation the state of being somewhere. (ŬBĪ where.)

claudication the act of halting or limping.

vellication a pulling out, as hair. (VĔLLO I pluck; VĔLLĬCO I twitch, jerk out.)

fabrication **altercation** **communic**ate **varic**ose

Obs. 1. In vocation, location, plication, vacation, and others, c is part of the primitive word.

Obs. 2. Prognost-ic-ation and sophist-ic-ation have the adjective suffix -IC; and nutrication is from NŪTRĪX a nurse.

-ce, -cy, n. See -ace, -acy, -ance, -ty.

poli-ce, **poli-cy**, **poli-ty** something pertaining to (πόλῐς) a city, and (πολῑ́της) a citizen. (πολῑτεία a political society.)

fan-cy see *-S-IA*. **necromancy** see *-MAN*cy. **prophecy** προφητεία see *-ET*. **solstice** SŌLSTĬTĬŬᵐ. **potency** PŎTĔNTĬĂ. **niece** NĔPTĬS.

-ce, adverbial. See -s.

once (+ones) **twice** (twise, Stowe 1603) **thrice** (thrise, Bp. Hall) **whence** **hence** **thence** **since**

-ce, v.

The S participial of GAVDĒRĔ, GĀVĪSŬS SŬᵐ, *to be glad,* is present in Provensal jau-z-ir, and English **re-joi-ce**, but not in en-joy.

That to myn hert it was a rejoyſynge
To here thi vois?—*Chaucer*, line 17178.

-ch, n.

perch a pole for fowls. (PĔRT-ĬCA; akin to PĂRĬO, FĔRO, to *bear.*) See -AC. **larch** LĂRĪX λάριξ.

-ch, a. See -ly.

su-ch, old Eng. swilke, swiche; Ger. so-lch; Go. sva-leiks *so-like.*
whi-ch, old Eng. whilke, Scotch quilk; Go. hvi-leiks *who-like.*

-chre

sepul-chre (SĔPŪLCRŪ[m]) a place in which (SĔPĔLĬO,) to bury. See -C-R-.

-C-le, -cel, -cul-, -cule, -cil, -cile, n. dim.

[Lat. (-ŪN-)C-ŬL-ŬS,[a] -C-ŬL-US[b] (-ŬL-Ă, -ŬL-Ū[m],*) -CĒLLŬS,[c] -CĪLLŬS,[d] -CĬLĬŪM[e]. Ss. -CA, -CA5, -CU5. Pers. -ac; Hindoostanee -k, -JĀ. Polish -ik, -ek, -ka; Bohem. -ik, -ek, -ka, -ko; Russ. -ko, -ka. Swed. -unge. Welsh -ig, -og; Gaelic -ag, -ach; Irish -ag, -og, as in bille-og a small (FŎLĬ-Ū[m]) *leaf*—(caol *small.*) Gr. -ιχος, -αξ, -υϝξ, -ιϝξ, as in *θύννος a tunny, θύνναξ a little tunny; σῡ΄ρῑϝξ a pipe,* whence Syrinx, Syringa, syringe, from *σῡ΄ρω I draw;* lynx λὺϝξ, from *λάω I see.* ¶ The resemblance of the Turkish -dzhik and -dzhiq is probably accidental.]

arti-cle[b] a little (ĀRTŪS) joint; a clause; an agreement.

auricula, auricle, a small (ĀVRĬS) ear; a plant; a shell.

per..il, PĔRĪCŬLŪ[m] a trial, an ex-per-iment; danger.

mo-nkey[a] a beast shaped like a man. (HŎMŪNCŬLŬS and HŎMŪNCĬO (*c* as *k*,) a small HŎMO, gen. HŎMĬN-ĬS, man.)

carbuncle[a] a small (CĀRBO, gen. CĀRBŌN-ĬS) coal.

uncle[a], ĂVŪNCŬLŬS, from ĂVŬS† an ancestor.

domicile[e] (DŎMŬS a house,) a habitation, a place of abode.

peduncle, pedicle, and less properly **pedicel** the foot-stalk of a plant or flower. (PĔDO, gen. PĔDŌNĬS, broad-footed.)

violon-cello often called cello (tshello,) a bass viol much larger than a violin or tenor, but smaller than the violone or double bass.

particle fascicle follicle cuticle pencil[d] **codicil**[d] **damsel animalcule ranunculus reticule corpus-cule, -cle**, -CULUM. **ossicle**, -CULUM **ungui-cul-ate fennel** FŒNĬCŬLŪ[m], Ital. finocchio.

Obs. 1. Icicle, *ice*, and Ang. gicel (*c* as *k*,) Ger. kegel a (cog) tapering body, as a wedge or cone.

Obs. 2. In *male*, (Lat. MĀSCŬLŬS a. from MĀS a male,) the sense is augmentative.

---

* Prof. T. H. Key suggests that C of *-x* is diminutive in the generic names CĪMĒX *bug*, PŪLĒX *flea*, CŬLĒX *gnat*.

† This word may have had an inflexional *n*.

-C-ous, a. *quality*. See -AC.

caducous (CĂDO I fall,) having the quality of falling.
festucous like (FĒSTŪCĂ) straw. **lubricous** slippery.

-C-R-

[Lat. nouns in -C-RU^m, -C-RE; adjectives in -CER, -CRUS, -CRIS, with -C- genetic and -ER agential.]

in-volū-crum or **involucre, involucret** or **involucel**, involving flower organs like bracts.
ludicrous (LŪDĬCĔR, LŪDĬCRŬS,) causing (LŪDŬS) sport.
sepulchre **pulchritude** **mediocre** (MĔDĬŎCRĬS) **mediocrity**

-C-UL-. See **-acle**.

es-c-ul-ent fit to be eaten. (ĔD-O, ĒS-U^m, to eat; ĒS-C-Ă food.)

-C-UND, a. See -C-, -AND.

-d, **-t**, n. *that which* (is.)

[See -ATe, **-ed**, **-t**. Irish -de, as in air *over*, air-de *height;* -t, as in agaraim *to revenge*, agar-t *revenge*, agar-th-ach *vindictive*. Welsh gwy *a liquid*, gwyo *to flow*, gwae-d *blood*, gwy-th *a channel*.]

flood (**blood**) that which flows. **deed** that which is done. **seed** sow **cold** cool **gold** yell-ow **mead**(-ow) mow **third** three **lend** v. loan **cud, quid** chew **gleed** glow **gift** give* **head** Ang. heafod **weft** weave **blast** blow

bud **stud** **sound** **thread** **nod** **build** v. **wield** v. **weald** or **wald** **shield** **yield** **guild** **beard** **sward** **swarthy** **sword** **shade, shad**ow (σκιά) **tied** and **tight** **fact, counterfeit**, and **feat** **act** **pact** **cataract** **tract, treat** as**pect** pre**fect** **sect** se**cret** **duct** and **conduit** **circuit** **Pict** **raft** **craft** **loft** and **lift** **thrift** **shrift** **rift** **cleft** **theft** **tuft** **graft** **draught** **draft** **drift** **shaft** **haft** **heft** **hilt** **float** **fleet** **sheet** **slight** **bright** **plight** **flight** **fright** **might** **sight** **fight**

---

* Similarly DO (I give) produces date a *given* (point of time,) Persian dā-d a gif-t.

height wight weight freight yacht thought drought pleat plait biscuit credit deceit receipt exploit suit fruit malt cobalt felt welt bolt holt quaint saint paint taint tint joint point hart quart request mist twist post frost thirst wrist wrest toast just August locust provost host trust gust thrust rust robust bluster spout sprout salt silt start state soft spit v.

Ophicleid, a musical instrument of the (ὄφις) serpent kind, provided with (κλεὶς, plural κλεῖδες) keys.

-*D*-, diminutive.

zo-di-ac a zone in the heavens marked by certain animal constellations. (ζῴ-διον a little ζῷον animal.) See Observation under **-let**.

ophidian pertaining to serpents; a serpent. (ὀφί'διον a small ὄφις, genitive ὄφιος serpent.)

-D-, declensional.

[FRAVS *fraud,* gen. FRAVD-ĬS *of fraud.* CŎR the *core* or *hear-t,* CŌRD-ĬS of the heart. This D is part of the base or crude form. See -*AD*-.]

fraud laud lapidary **foot ped**al **custody hered**itary **cord**ial **ped**agogue, an instructor of youth. (παῖς a boy, gen. παιδ-ός; ἄγω I conduct; 2d aorist ἤγαγον.)

dar *a holder,* **dari** *jurisdiction.*

[Persian words in common use in India.]

zeminda'r a superintendent or holder of (Persian zamîn) land.

zemindari or **zemindary** the jurisdiction of a zemindar. (Pronounce *e* as in mutter, *i* in mien, *a* in arm, and *u* like *oo*.)

sūbahdār the governor of (Arab. sūbah) a province.

chokeedar terrimdar killadar duffadar turrefdar foujdar

-den, n.

burden, burthen (φορτίον fardel,) formed from 'bear' like *growth* from *grow*, with -en diminutive.

garden, a diminutive of HOR-T-US.

golden, a. -en *made of*, -d *that which is*, gol— (Lat. GĬLVŬS, Sax. gel,) *yell-ow*. (Welsh gole *splendor;* Gaelic galla *brightness;* ἥλ-ιος *the sun;* χολ-ὴ *gall*, a yellow secretion. ☞ SŌL.)

Linden is probably a plural.

-der, adv.

yonder, Goth. jains, (ἐκεῖ, εκεῖν-η, κεῖν-η,) in that place; jainar there; jaind, jaindre thither. The -d is educed from -N adverbial, and -er is that of -TER, a.

hīnder, (posterior,) is from the root of he-re, hi-ther, Ger. hīn, with -N adverbial. (Bopp regards the -n of *hin* as a petrified accusative case sign.)

-der, n.

[The participial and gerundive -AND, with the noun suffix -ER, giving a more active signification to English nouns in -and, and a few others to which this form has been extended, often by the eduction of *d* from *n*. This -der is not a Latin suffix.]

cullender an implement with which (CŌLĀRĔ) to strain.

lavender an aromatic plant used as a cosmetic (LĂVĀNDŌ) in washing.

attainder, ☞ TĬNGO, TĬNCTŪm, to stain. **detainder**, ☞ TĔNĔO, TE'NTŪm, to hold. **provender**, see vi-AND. **remainder re-joinder**, JŪNGO, JŪNCTŪm, to join. **rudder** row. **chevender** a chub. **shoulder**, akin to scal-e. **gander**, see **-m.**

murder, Ss. MR̥, Lat. MŎR-ĬŎR, Pers. mur-den* *to die;* Ger. mor-den *to murder;* Goth. maurθr, Fr. meurtre *murder;* Ss. MĀRA5, Gr. μόρος (see marasMUS,) Lat. MŌRS, Bohem. s-mrt *death.*†

Germander is a heteronym, from CHĂMÆDRȲS, a *low oak*-leaved plant, χάμαὶ *on the earth*, δρῦς *oak*.

Elder (tree,) German holder, holunder, old high German holantar *hollow tree*. For *cylinder*, see -N- intensive.

Obs. In Greek names, -ander is from ἀνὴρ a *man*, genitive ἀνδρὸς, as in Alexander, defending men. In botany it is equivalent to stamen or anther, as in 'hexander' a plant with six stamens or six anthers.

---

* In Persian -den is infinitive, as in bürden *to bear*.

† Greek βροτὸς a mort-al, μ losing its nasality, or β is educed from it, as in ἄ-μβροτος, Sanscrit A-MARA5 im-mort-al, whence a-mbrosia. See *AN-*.

-DO, -DIN-, n.

[Latin feminines in -DO, gen. -DĬN-ĬS, nom. pl. DĬN-ĒS. Ital. -dine. Akin to -T- participial, with -N declensional.]

-din-ac-e-ous, -din-ari-an, -din-ary, -din-ate, -din-ous.

tĕre\'do (τερηδὼν fem., from τερέω, to bore,) that which pierces; a boring shell-fish known as the ship-worm.

torpe\'do a fish which causes torpor or numbness in those who touch it; a contrivance for blowing up ships.

ure\'do a blight, (ŪRO, to burn, infest,) a genus of minute parasitic fungi infesting living cereal plants, and known as 'rust' Urēdo rubīgo, and 'smut' Uredo segetum.

testu\'do that which has (TĒSTĂ) a shell; a genus of land tortoises; in antiquity, a defence made by joining shields.

vale-t-ud-inary, **-ari-an** pertaining to (VĂLĒTŪDO) health, or disease. (VĂL-ĔO, to be well.)

Mucedo **testu-din-ate** **multitu-din-ous** **arun-din-ac-e-ous**

-dom, n. *domain of; condition of; act of.*

[Ang., old Frisian, Belg., Swed., Dan., -dom; Ger. -*th*ūm, old Ger. -tom. Ger. *th*ūm *judgment*, Eng. doom. Grimm refers it to Lettish nu-dōm-āt *to discriminate;* Lithuanic dumā *deliberation, opinion.* In old high German it was rarely used as a prefix, as in tomphaffo *priest-dom.*]

Christendom **kingdom** **dukedom** **martyrdom**
Wisdom is the domain of (wit) knowledge, and **freedom** of the free.
thraldom the condition of (Anglish θræl) a slave.

> Yet wifedome warns, ... —*Spenser.*
>
> . . . . monkeydom,
> Tigerdom, donkeydom, sunk into flunkeydom.—'Punch.'

-dor, -dore, -door, n.

[-dor is the Spanish form of Latin -TOR.]

corridor a covered passage way. (CŬRRĔRĔ to run.)

matador a slayer. (Sp. matar, L. MĂCTĀRĔ to slay.)

battledoor, Sp. b a t i d o r a striker.

ambassador, Spanish, from the Arabic.

stevedore he who stows a cargo; from the root of stuff, Lat. STĪPO I pack, cram.

> But glimmering through the dusky corridore,
> Another chequers o'er the shadow'd floor.—*Byron.*

-DOT-

sacer-dot-al pertaining to (SĂCE·R-DŌS) a priest. See SĂCĔR.

-E, imperative.

[Latin imperative of the second person singular, as in VĪDĒ *see;* DĒLĒ *blot out;* VĂLĒ *farewell.*]

val-e-dic-t-ory a bidding farewell; a farewell oration. (DĪCO, DĪCTŪ^m, to say.)

-e, feminine

[The French -e feminine, used for masculines, as quadrille, and feminines, as bagatelle.]

due a. owed; that should be rendered. (DĒBĒRĔ, Fr. devoir *to owe;* participle masculine dû, feminine due *owed.*)

iss-u-e v. to proceed, emit, result; n. a passing forth, result, offspring, point in dispute. (ĔX-Ī-RĔ to go out; old French iss-ir, participle issu, feminine issue, the -u being a participial remnant of the Latin -TŪM.)

> Or th' utmoſt yſſew of his own decay. . . .
> But the fiſt troupe moſt horrible of hew . . . —*Spenser.*

avenue **belle** **carte-blanche** **gauze** **jonquille** **parole** **rue** **prude** **programme** (and program) **clique** **hue** (outcry) **cue** and **queue** **value** **valve** **fibre**—**dialogue** **theatre** **lucre**

Profile is the French masculine noun profil, with *l* pronounced. *Eye* was formerly a dissyllable. *Ax* is preferable to *axe*. *Glue* is for French glu, and *pulse* is for pouls, German puls.

Obs. Written English is subject to the freaks of lipogrammatism, in forbidding certain letters to occupy their proper place. Thus 'v' must not be doubled (except latterly in *navvy*, a *navi*gation or canal workman,) nor must it occur final in spelling words like believe, cleave, heave, leave, weave, sleeve, give, live, sieve, missive, salve, solve. Final 'u' (formerly confused with 'v') is also avoided, as in true, blue, glue, pursue, argue.

-E, neuter.

[Primarily neuter adjectives in -E, with the masculine and feminine in -IS. See -AL.]

ration-al-e n. **sim-il-e** n. **facile** a. **mobile** a. **volatile** a.

-E, n. See -A.

acme syncope hyperbole apostrophe scene machine ode systole diastole Calliope Penelope—conclave Agave

-E, adv. *-ly*.

[Latin adverbial -E, as in BĔNĔ *well*, MĂLĔ *badly*.]

ben-e-volent kindly wishing; disposed to do good.
mal-e-volent mal-e-diction ben-e-factor benefit beneficiary

-E-, -I-, -y, formative.

[-Ĕ-ŬS, -Ĭ-ŬS, -Æ-ŬS, (-Ă, -Ŭm;) -Ĭ-ĒS; -N-Ĕ-ŬS. -ε-ος, -ι-ος, -ει-ος, -αι-ος, (-α, -ον,) -ε-ύς. Sp., Port. -ia; Ital. -ia, -ajo; Fr. -ie. Go. -ei (= I) as in diup-ei *depth*. Ger. -ie, -ei. Sw., Dan. -i. See **-y**, n. ¶ 3, 4.]

Europ-e'-an (EVRŌPA-E-ŬS, εὐρωπα-ῖ-ος, εὐρώπιος, εὐρωπ-ε-υς) pertaining to Europe; a native of Europe.

Athen-i-an (ἀθηνα-ῖ-ος) pertaining to Athens, or to ἀθηνᾶ Minerva. **Athen-e-um** a building devoted to literature.

Epicure'an (ἐπικούρ-ε ι-ος) pertaining to Epicurus.

master-y, MĂGI·STĔR-Ĭ-Ŭm the function or condition of a master; superior power or skill.

nausea, ναυσ-ί-α sickness from the motion of (ναῦς) a ship.

vitreous composed of (VĬTRŬm) glass; glassy.

Obs. This -I- cannot always be separated from I genitive.

museum see **-eum** **sçoria** σκωρία **mania** **trachea** **aculeate** **roseate** **eleg-y** **miser-y** **progeny** PRŌGĔN-Ĭ-ĒS **series** **congeries** **trochee** τροχαῖος **spondee** σπονδεῖος **apogee** ἀπόγειον

-ed, -d, -t, pp., a. *made; having; did; was,* &c.

[See -ATe, **-d**, **-t**. Latin -ĀTŬS; old Fr. -ad; Ang. -t, -d, -ed, -id, -od (as in lufod or gelufod *loved,* nacod *naked,* dypt *dipped.*) Old Eng. -ed, -d, -t, -te, -de, -yd, -yde, -id, -yt-, -ud. Ger. -et, -t; Dan. -de, -t. French participle past -té, -tée, -é, -ée, -i, -ie. Irish -the, -dha, as in airg-im *to spoil,* airg-the *spoiled,* airg-the-ach *a spoiler;* aer *air,* aer-dha *airy.* Welsh verb oedd *was, did exist.* Probably connected with Eng. do, (Ss. DŬ to *move,*) of which di-d may be a reduplication, and done the old German gĕdūăn (from duan *to do,*) deprived of its prefix.]

rounded made round. **bearded** having a beard.

ruined in the condition of a ruin.

prepared (PĂRĀTŪm, Welsh parod,) made ready.

watered supplied with water.

pressed was under pressure.

horned (L. CŌRNŪTŬS) whence **hart** (a deer, i.e.) a horned animal.

shod supplied with shoes. **cold**, **gelid** made cool.

mild **wild** **old** **bald** **made** **staid** **laid** **right** **just** **fit** **apt** **fast** **Celt** (pronounced *kelt*) **gilded** or **gilt** **gird**

> By me was nothyng added ne mynufhyd.—*Caxton*, about 1481.
>
> To let not others honour be defafte . . . . . .
> Through countreyes wafte, and eke well edifyde,—*Spenser.*
>
> A beam ethereal, fully'd, and abforpt!
> Tho' fully'd, and difhonour'd, ftill divine!—*Young.*

Obs. When past time is not in view, words in -en, -ed, may be regarded as adjectives, as in hidd-en faults; land-ed property; one possess-ed.— -ed is also used to indicate past time in verbs—

> And fmott and bitt, and kickt, and fcratcht and rent,—*Spenser.*
>
> Then paused, and look'd, and turn'd, and seem'd to watch.—*Byron.*

-ee, -ey, -y, n. *one who; that which.*

[See -ATe, **-ed**. French participial -é masc., -ée fem., pronounced with the true E of *they,* like the old English *ee* of Chaucer's freeltee (frailty,) femininitee (womanhood,) auctoritee. But -ée is not always feminine in French, pygmée a *dwarf* is masculine, and solidité is feminine.]

grantee one to whom something is granted.

guarantee, (Fr. participle past garanti *warrant-ed*,) the person who warrants;—sometimes used for the **warranty**.

trustee one specially trusted. **jury**, Fr. juré swor-n.

causeway a heteronym of **causey**, Fr. chaussée.

fosse (FŎDĬO, FŌSSŪm, to dig,) a ditch, especially in fortification. (Fr. fossé; but fosse (a pit or grave) is commonly given.)

. . . furrounded by a foffee half a mile in compafs.—*Pococke*, 1738.

absentee legatee refugee referee assignee patentee lessee legatee committee fricassee repartee mêlée soirée mortgagee congé resumé exposé levy dory alley volley

Journey, originally a day's work or a day's travel, (as journee in Chaucer;) Ital. giornata, Sp. jornada (*j* nearly as χ,) Fr. journée; Lat. DĪĒS *day*, DĬŪRNŬS *done by day*. The meaning being modified in English, the phrase 'a day's journey' (really—a day's day's work) is proper. Similarly, 'journeyman' has ceased to mean a worker by the day.

Fusee (of a watch,) FŪSŬS a spindle. *Fusee* (a portfire,) Fr. fusi*l*, Ital. focile, diminutive of Latin FŏCŬS a hearth, a fire.

Grandee, Sp. grande, (a dissyllable.) *Decree*, DĒCRĒTŪm. *Trochee*, *spondee*, and *apogee* belong to E formative.

Brahman-ee (BRĀHMANĪ, with *h* pronounced, *a* as in *far*,) a female brahman; brahma-n, a priest of Brahma.

But who can turn the ftream of deftinee,
Or break the chayne of ftrong neceffitee,
Which faft is tyde to Jove's eternall feat?—*Spenser.*

-eel, a. See -ILe.

genteel an unetymologic spelling of GĔNTĪLĬS (gentile, gentle, jaunty.)

-el, n. See -AL.

vowel vocal. **channel** canal.

Obs. Hebrew has proper names in -ēl, as Isrāēl (Soldier of God;) Mahalalēēl (Praise of God;) Mehetabēl (Blest of God;) Ishmael (Whom God hears.)

-EL, n. dim. See -L, ¶ 1.

kernel a small corn. **laurel** a small LAVRŬS.

-een. See **-ene.**

tureen, for terrene, (originally) an earthen vessel.

-eer, -ier, n. See -ARy, ¶.

engineer one who contrives and adapts engines, originally those of war. An engine-driver is not an engineer, for the same reason that an organ-blower is not an organist.

farrier a shoer of horses; a veterinarian. (FĔRRĀRĬŬS a. occupied with FĔRRŪ^{m} iron.)

mountaineer auctioneer muleteer musketeer privateer pamphleteer volunteer gazetteer charioteer bombardier grenadier brigadier financier cavalier or **chevalier** (French; Ital. cavalĭérĕ) **chandelier courier premier harrier tarrier** or **terrier rapier grazier glazier clothier garreteer**

Obs. This suffix is to some extent confused with -er, as in currier, furrier, terrier, courtier, collier, drov(i)er, barrier (Fr. barrière,) career (carrière,) treasurer (Lat. THĒSĀVRĀRĬŬS,) compeer (Lat. PĀRA equal.) *Chanticleer,* the clear singer. In *sold-ier* the suffix is for Welsh gwr a man. *Domineer,* see **-er,** v. infinitive.

-en, part. present. See **-ing.**

[The genuine etymologic form of the English participle present, which has been corrupted into -ing.]

barr-en, Ang. un-ber-ende (Luc 1 :7,) Gothic fem. participle un-bair-andei *unfruitful, not bearing.*

fri-end, Goth. fri-jon to love, fri-jonds loving, a friend.

> Curteis and wife, and wel doande.—*Chaucer.*
>
> He come criande.—*id.*
>
> Soone as thofe glitterand armes he did efpye,—*Spenser.*

-en, a. *made of, like.*

[-ῖνος, -εινος, -ινεος; -ĬNŬS; Sanscrit and Hindoostanee -IN. Gothic -eins; old Ger. -īn; Ger. -en, -n; Welsh -in. See -AN.]

earthen made of earth; **earthy** having the qualities of earth; **earthly** like (pertaining to, having the accidents of) earth. **crimson** (Ital. cremesino) of kermes.

golden woollen flaxen leather-n oaken hempen silken beechen oaten wheaten brazen leaden waxen wooden

Obs. 1. The nouns *linen, satin, robin* and *iron* probably belong here.

Obs. 2. The resemblance is accidental in Turkish, as in آتش (ātesh) *fire;* آتشين (ateshin) *of fire, belonging to fire,* where 'in' is the genitive case sign. See note under N adverbial.

-en, v. *to make, cause, add, use,* &c.

[Sanscrit -ĂNĂ; Hindoostanee -ànă, -na; Persian -en; Javanese -ên. Gr. (-αίνω, -ύνω,) -ειν; Doric -ην, -εν. Albanian -on. Welsh -ain. Go. -an, -jan, -on; Ohg. -an, -on, -un, -en, -jan; Ang. -an, -on, -n, -ean, -ian, -gan, -gean, -gian; Ger. -en. (The old Frisian -a, Norse -a, Sw. -a, Dan. -e have lost the n.) (Irish -im.) Old English -en, (-in, -ne and -e,) as in to wondr-en, to tell-en, to riden, to bērin, to doen, used by Chaucer, but which must not be confounded with the old verbial plural, as in the following example—

And smale foules m a k e n melodie
That ſl e p e n al the night with open yhe.—*Chaucer.*

Infinitive mood signs akin to -ANT.]

war-n to cause to be-ware; to make a-ware.

ear-n, Ang. e r i a n to plow.

dead-en to cause to become dead. (Flemish—een mensch dōoden, *to-kill a man.*)

mour-n, Lat. MŒR-ĔO. **b-ur-n**, Lat. ŪRO, COM-BŪRO. **g-lee-n** g-low, g-lea-m, λάω I see. **lear-n** (lerin *Chaucer.*) **happen listen dizen shun dawn yawn** (see **-sp**) **fawn spawn drown turn own**

And grete trefouris up to laine.—*Chaucer.*

Obs. Belgic prefers *t*, as in l a t e n, to German *ss*, as in l a s s e n, Eng. to *let;* and as *t* is often dropt in Saxon (as in m o..e r *mother*, b r a..e r *brother*,) l a t e n is l o..e n in Saxon, and these may have influenced the English forms loan, lend, the last with *d* educed from *n*.

¶ In the following, -en is used to form verbs from nouns and adjectives, but they are not strictly infinitives.

strengthen to make strong, to add strength.

bolden whiten fasten fatten madden moisten lengthen lighten frighten heighten hearten gladden threaten cheapen deepen darken reck-on (reken *Chaucer*) **beck-on**

-en, participle past.

[Anglish -en, -n; Ger. -en. Sanscrit past part. passive -NAŌ, fem. -NĀ, neut. -NĂ. Akin to -en v., -AN, -ANT. This -en is a participial suffix of Grimm's *strong* conjugation, in which the preterit is formed by a vowel change, as in *blow*, (preterit *blew*,) *blown*, where the form of the weak conjugation would be *blowed, growed, waked, cleaved*, &c.]

driven woven smitten cloven shaken taken hidden broken chosen forgotten driven fallen forsaken slai-n tor-n bee-n do-ne **go-**ne **bor-**ne **tor-n—heaven leaven**

Craven belongs to -ANT.

-en, n. diminutive.

[Lat. -INĂ; Ital. -ino, -ina. Gr. -ιον. Gaelic, Irish, -an, -in, as in dionn *a hill*, dionnan *a little hill*. Welsh -an, -en, -yn. Hindoostanee -un. Heb. -ŌN.]

kitten a young cat. **chicken** a young chick.

cabin, Welsh caban, a small (Welsh ca-b) hut.

patten garden jerken (jerkin) muffin cordon carinate **careen**, CĂRĪNĂ a keel. **burden, burthen**, see **-den.**

-EN one.

hyph-en (ὑφὲν, ὑπὸ ἓν under-one,) a mark uniting the letters of a written or printed word into one group.

-en, n. *one.*

[Welsh nouns are often collective, and are individualised by the diminutive suffixes, masc. -yn, fem. -en, neut. -an, (perhaps influenced by the numeral en *one*,) as in rhos *roses*, rhosyn *a rose;* yd *corn*, yden *a grain of corn;* ffa *beans,* ffâen *a bean.* This accounts for -en in **hoid-en**; and in **Derw-en-t**, from derw *oak trees,* dâr *a male oak*—whence *Darby,* often spelt 'Derby,' but pronounced properly. W. gwlan *wool,* gwlanen *flannel,* called **flannen** in some parts of England and the United States. For *goblin* see **-lin.**]

kil-n, W. co, cw, a rounding, a concavity, cwl what surrounds, a kiln, cylyn a single kiln..

aspen, W. aethwydden, from aeth *a point,* gwydd *trees.*

-EN -IN-, n.

pect-in-ate comb-like, as the gills of fishes. (PĔCTĔN a card or comb, πέκω to pick off wool, to card or comb; Lat. PE·C-T-O, T intensive.) **pollen** dust from the **stamens** of plants.

unguent, ŪNGVĔN and ŪNGVĔNTŪm (*t* participial) something with which (ŪNGO, ŪNGVO,) to anoint.

Latin GLŪTĔN (CŌLLĂ glue*;* γλοι-ός clammy,) whence **glut-in-ous.** The primary idea of *glue* was general, of *gluten* special, as between a *clammy* and an *adhesive* substance.

-en, -in, n. pl.

[Anglish (of the 2d declension) -an; German and old English -en. Persian -an for living objects, as peder *father,* pederân *fathers.* Welsh -on, -ion. Irish, as in ceasd *a quest-ion,* pl. ceasdan. The resemblance to Aramaic, Chaldee and Syriac -IJN, -IN, and Chippeway -an is accidental.]

ox-en plural of ox. **kine,** old English plural of Anglish cu, cy *cow.*

welkin (the clouds;) the concavity of the sky. +**eyen** +**candlen**

She found hirefelf and eke hire doughtren two.—*Chaucer.*

Targum-in, plural of targum, a jewish paraphrase or interpretation of the old Testament. A Chaldee word.

Obs. 1. Child-r-en is a surplural. The plural *childr* is sometimes heard among old people.

Obs. 2. The final -n of many English nouns cannot be distinguished from the adjective forms -an -en, participial -en, and -en diminutive.

-END, -ENDous. See -AND.

-ene, **-een**. See **-en**, -AN.

terrene pertaining to the (TĒRRĂ) earth.

tureen originally a vessel made of (TĒRRĂ) earth. Fr. terrine an earthen vessel.

Damascene a native of Damascus.

Gergesenes **Gadarenes** **Hagarenes**.

-enger, n.

[Chiefly due to -ger with *n* induced by the *d* of corrupt *g* or *dzh*, as in Sellenger for St. Leger.]

messenger the bearer of a message. (French messager.)
pass-enger (Fr. passager.) **pottinger** and potager (Fr. potager.)
scavenger +**pollenger** +**murenger** **harbinger** **wharfinger**

-ENS, participle present. See -ANT.

ut-ens-il something that may be used; an implement. (UT-OR to use; ŪT-ENS using.)

-ENSic, a. *pertaining to.*

[The Latin suffix -ĒNSĬS is confounded with others in English.]

forensic (FŎRĒNSĬS) pertaining to the FŎRŪ^m^ or court.

castrensian belonging to (CĀSTRĂ) a camp.

ĂTHĒNĬĒNSĬS, CĀRTHĀGĬNĬĒNSĬS, pertaining to Athens, to Carthage.

-E-**ous**, a. *formed by; made of; like; -y-.*

[E formative, and -ous. Based on nouns.]

chalceous of or like (χαλκὸς) brass.

igneous, ĬGNĔŪS formed by (ĬGNĬS) fire. Lava (an igneous rock) is due to igneous agency, i.e. the agency of fire.

ligneous formed of (LĬGNŪ^m^) wood; woody.

terreous of earth. **ochreous** of the nature of ochre.

cupreous flammeous membraneous vitreous aqueous cinereous osseous sulphureous tartareous gramineous

Obs. plenteous, beauteous, courteous, piteous, bounteous, &c. are false forms in -ous. *Righteous* belongs to -ways.

-er, v. frequentative.

[Heteronymic, partly akin to frequentative -L in wrangle, wriggle, gabble, gibber, (often used to prevent its repetition, as in *bewilder*, which has already an *l*, and *prattle*, which has an *r*,) and partly to **-er** infinitive. Some examples cannot be discriminated from the latter; nor from nouns in -ER used as verbs.]

wander wend	**scatter** ⊥shed	**waver** wave
batter beat	**stagger** sta*l*k	**falter** fail
patter pat	**clamber** climb	**welter** wallow
linger long	**bicker** pick	**slumber** sleep
bewilder wild	**chatter** chat	**flicker** ⊥fly

flutter whisper stammer flounder whimper simper simmer shudder twitter spatter sputter sp-l-utter slippery

Obs. In Norse, -r indicated the nominative case masculine gender of nouns and adjectives, as in dagr *day*, dalr *dale*, elgr *elk*, kalfr *calf*, rettr *right*, stormr *storm*, sœtr *sweet*, kaldr *cold*, diupr *deep*, enskr *English*, fullr *full*.

-er, v. infinitive.

[Latin infinitive sign of the 1st conjugation -Ā-RĔ; 2d -Ē-RĔ; 3d -Ĕ-RĔ; 4th -Ī-RĔ; old Fr. -ER; Fr. e*r*, -IR. Ital. -āre, -ere (mostly short,) -īre. Wallachian -are, -ere. German -īr-en.]

rend-er RĔDDĔRĔ **measure** MĒTĪRĔ **domineer** DŎMĬNĀRĔ

ponder sunder smoulder smother flatter banter hamper founder cower

Tol-er-ate, consid-er, recup-er-ate, belong to -R- formative.

-ER, -R, adjectival.

[Adjectives in -ER, -R, -R-US, -RIS, -ηρ, -ρος, -ρις. Sanscrit -RA5. Akin to -US.]

eag-er, vine**g-ar**, **ac-r-**id; Lat. ĀC-ĔR (*c* as *k*,) or ĀCRĬS sharp, keen. **meag-re** MĂCĔR **miser**able MĬSĔR a. **prosper**ous PRŌSPĔR **poo..r** PAVPĔR **aus-t-ere austerity**. See -RoUS.

tender **slender** **limber** **integer** or **enti..re** **neut-er** or **n-eith-er** **oth-er** **vesper** **asper** **celeb-r**ated **alac-r**ity **celer**ity **salubr**ity **liber**ty **equestr**ian **lud-ic-r**ous **dex-t-r-**ous **sac-r**ed —**hither** **thither** **whither**—**inner** **outer** **upper** **over** **after**

-er, -OR, -IOR, a. *more.*

[Lat. -ĬŬS, -ĬŎR. Sanscrit -ĪJAS (J as English *y.*) Ang. -er, -ere, -ar, -ære, -ir, -or, -ur, -yr; Dan. -ere; Ohg. -ōr, as in fer *far,* ferrōr *farther,* ferrōst *farthest.*]

smaller **larger** **farther** **senior** **junior** **superior** **major** **minor** **melior**ate **deterior**ation **ulterior** **+ofter** **better** **wiser**

And they the wiser, friendlier few confest
They deem'd him better than his air exprest.
Byron, Lara I. vii.

Obs. The comparative sign was originally S, as in less, least; worse, worst.

-ER-, -OR-, n., a. declensional.

[Lat. -ĔR-ĬS,[a] -ŎR-ĬS,[b] -ŪR-ĬS,[c] genitive case signs in the 3d declension. See -R declensional.]

itin-er-ary, ĬT-ĔR a going, gen. ĬTĬNĔRĬS. ☞ ĔO.
pulv-er-ul-ent,[a] PŪLVĬS dust, gen. PŪLV-ĔRĬS of dust.
in-cin-er-ate, **cin-er-**ary, **cind-er**, CĬNĬS[a] ashes.
cucumber, CŬCŬMĬS[a]. **feder**ate, FŒDŬS[a] a compact.
flower, **flo-r-**al, FLŌS.[b] **tellur**ic, TĒLLŪS[c] the earth.
femoral, FĔMŬR[b] the thigh, gen. FĔMŎRĬS or FĔMĬNĬS.

-ER, -R, -OR, -UR, -oir, -re, n. agential.

[Lat. -ER,[a] -OR,[b] -UR,[c] -ERA,[d] -ORA,[e] -ŪRA.[f] Gr. -αρ, -ωρ,- -ήρ, -υρ, -ης, -εύς; mostly passive nouns. Akin to -R- formative, and to nouns in -S. Ital. -ere, -ore; Fr. -re, -oir, -eur, -er, -ère, -erre. Go. -arja; Anglish -ere; old Eng. -er, -our; Sw. -are, -ar, -er; German and Danish -er. Polish -arz. Irish -aire. Welsh -ar, -awr, -wr, -ur, -or.]

Obs. English -er is used indifferently for *active* nouns, as defender, feeder, jailer, lover, robber; or *passive* ones, as tinder, fender, rudder, counter, hammer, beaker, pitcher, ladder, dollar, order, saucer, fodder, prisoner, widower, stranger, Hollander, member, owner, and for *utensils* when distinguished from *persons*, as ruler, scraper, roller, stamper, digger, boiler, rubber, piercer, skimmer, feeder, plunger, slider, pounder, wringer.

compiler *he who* compiles.

Even the abridger, compiler, and tranflator, though their labours cannot be ranked with thofe of the diurnal hiftoriographer, yet muft not be rafhly doomed to annihilation.
Dr. Johnson, Rambler, Auguft 6, 1751.

a-ir, **aer**ial *that which* blows. (ἄω, to blow.)

ether, αἰθήρ the bright upper sky, from its supposed quality of burning. (αἴθω, to burn.)

gore, W. gwy a liquid; gwy-ar that flows, gore.

coulter CŪLTĔR **chamb**er CĂMĔRĂ[d] **anchor** ĂNCŎRĂ (ἄγκῦρα) **pepper** (PĬPĔR πέπερι) **sulphur** (SŪLPŬR or SŪLFŬR) **copper** (CŬPRŪ[m]) **guttur**al[c] and **goitre** **fulgur**ation **in-teg-er** **vesper** **lucifer** **arbiter** **nectar** νέκταρ **martyr** μάρτυρ ex**agger**ate[a] il**liter**ate[d] **agri**culture[a] **murmur**[c] **crater** in**carcer**ate[a] **iter**ative[a] **tuber**[a] **cadaver**ous[a] **arbor**eal[b] **minister**ial[a] ex**uber**ance[a] re**verber**ate[a] **viper**[d] **figur**e[f] **lib-r**-ari-an **liberty** **gener**ic[a] and **gender** **cancer**[a] and **canker** **puer**ile **femor**al[c]—**rudder** **pitcher** **coffer** **weather** **shower** **leather** **feather** **udder** **ledger** **girder** **adder** **salamander** **conger** **ginger** **beaver** **otter** **clover** **badger** **border** **finger** **lever** **silver** **dodder** **pewter** **muster** **prayer** **slumber** **cider** **stair** **lair** **pliers** **pinchers** **wi-seac-er** **boor**

Obs. 2. The following are under false spellings—liar beggar pillar poplar manor sailor demeanor memoir goitre acre theatre theater θέᾱτρον. See **-ar**, n.

Obs. 3. Some of these are equally nouns and verbs, as plunder cumber fetter hammer slur clatter; and the frequentatives—quiver shiver &c.

Obs. 4. In Belgian -er (Ang. -ere) is masculine, and -ster (Ang. -stre) feminine, as in spinner spinster, zanger zangster. The German hŏckĕn to squat, to sit about, to take upon the back, gives the English (masculine) forms *hawker* and (feminine) *huckster;* also, to *hatch,* to sit on the (haunch-es or) hunk-ers, namely, like a huckster beside her wares; and *hunker,* one who keeps sitting in the same place; hence, in America, a politician who will not desert established principles.

Obs. 5. The Semitic languages have an analogous suffix, as in Heb. nɛrɛr, Arab. nasr, Syriac nɛrora, Ethiopic năsɛrɛ, an eagle. Arabic khandjar a large knife, whence *hanger* a kind of sword, usually but improperly referred to *hang.*

Obs. 6. This termination is commonly considered of the masculine gender when applied to persons, but it is sometimes used for both sexes, as in author, lover, and swinger (she who swings, Spectator, September 24, 1712.)

One fees in it the expoftulation of a flighted lover, the refentments of an injured woman, and the forrows of an imprifoned queen.—*Addison*, Spectator, June 5, 1712.

Larder and *ewer* belong to -ary, n.

Saucer, denier, purser, and perhaps *salver,* belong to -AR.[b]

Jasper is for iaspis.

Gander is regularly formed from χήν a goose, *d* being educed, and the masculine -er added. Or, *d* is transmuted from *s* of the German gans, Latin ĀNSĔR, Sanscrit HANSAS. See -N intensive.

Younker is the Belgian jonker, jonkheer, composed of *jong* and *heer*, equivalent to young gentleman.

-er, n. pl.

læmmergeir the vulture of the Alps. (German lamm lamb, lämmer or læmmer lambs; geier vulture.)

child-r-en, see **-en** pl., Obs. 1.

-er, n. masculine.

cat-er-waul the (sq)ueal or howl of (Belgian and German kater) a male cat.

-ern, a. *toward* or *in.*

[This suffix is essentially due to the use of both -r and -n, as observed in the Norse norðr *the north, northward;* norðan *of,* or *from the north;* Danish öst *east;* öster, adv. *eastward;* östen, adj. *eastern.* Old high German has sund, sundert, sundar, sundan, *the south, south,* sundrōni *the south wind;* sundirīn (Anglish suðern) *southern.*]

eastern western northern southern

-ERN, n.

[Latin n., a. -ER-NUS,[a] fem. -ERNA;[b] Greek -ερν.]

cav-ern[b] a place (CĂVŬS) hollow or excavated.

la(n)tern[b] sub-**altern**[a] **cistern**[b] **tavern tabernacle**[b] **modern postern slattern quartern bittern bickern**

govern v. GŬBĔRNO, κυβερνάω, (primarily) to guide a (K'YμBη) canoe.

-ERNITy, n. See UR-N.

-ery, n. See -ARy, -Ry.

[A form induced by -ARy, -ERy, n., and applied as in thievery, Ger. dieberei; lottery, Fr. loterie.]

-ES, n. singular.

con-ger-I-es, a mass formed by bringing together its component parts. (CONGĔRO I bring together.)

ser-i-es a row or line the parts of which are in connection or succession. (SĔRO I connect.) **iso-sceles**, adj. **herpes**

spec-i-es, (SPĔC-ĬO I see.) **dermestes**, see *T-ES*. **caries**

Kermes is Arabic, on a Sanscrit base.

-ES, n. plural. See -S.

apices, pl. of apex. **pleiades**, see *-AD*. **aphides**, pl. of aphis. **ephemerides**, pl. of ephemeris. **apsides**, pl. of apsis. **cantharides**, pl. of cantharis. **irides**, pl. of iris.

The following have the singular in -is. **axes fasces bases crises Pisces theses ellipses amanuenses metamorphoses analyses syntheses emphases phrases phases synopses hypotheses**

-es', n. possessive. See -'s.

ESC**e**, v. *to become*. -ESC-**ent**, a. *becoming*.
ESC-**ence**, n. *state of becoming*.

[Gr. -ασκ-, &c. Lat. -ASC-, -ESC-, -ISC-, -SC-. The force of these inceptives is seen in

LĂBO, to totter;	LĂBA·SCO, to begin to fall.
ĀLBĔO, to be white;	ALBE·SCO, to become white.
DŌRMĬO, to sleep;	DORMI·SCO, to begin to sleep.
HĬO, to gape, open;	HI·SCO, to yawn.
FLŌRĔO, to flower;	FLŌRE·SCO, to flourish.
ἀλδέω, to grow;	ἀλδέσκω, to flourish.]

deliquesce (LĬQVĒSCO) to become liquid. (LĬQVĔO to be liquid.)

deliquescence incipient liquidity; the state of becoming liquid.

coalescent **convalescence** **acquiescence** **effervesce** **incandescent** **evanescent** **intumescent** **crescent** **dehiscent** **adolescence** **juvenescence** **reminiscence** **irascible** ĪRĂ anger. **nigrescent** NĬGĔR black.

¶ 1. **feverish** having some fever. **bluish** somewhat blue. **sweetish** somewhat sweet. **modish** in the mode.

¶ 2. **foolish** like (in the manner of) a fool.

fiendish **thievish** **wolfish** **selfish** **dwarfish** **sluggish**

Obs. 1. The -ess- in FĂCĔSSO I cause, from FĂCĬO I make, seems to be a corruption of the same form.

Obs. 2. -isc has become -ish (Russ. -sky) as in Flem-ish, Scott-ish or Scot-ch, Pol-ish, Welsh, &c. Latin TEVTISCUS, Ital. ted-esc-o, Sp. tudesco, Fr. tudesque, Go. θiotisk, old high German thiudisk, Ang. θeodisc, Dan. tydsk, Belg. duitsch, Ger. deutsch, Eng. 'Dutch,' i.e. *teut-onic* or German, from diot *people*. Ang. dēnisc Danish; dēnisca a Dane.

Obs. 3. The suffix -ish (Ger. -isch) is partly due to -ic, as in HĪSPĀNĬCŬS Span-ish.

Obs. 4. In Russian geographical names, -sk indicates place, as in Krásnŏbŏrsk, from krásnŏ *red*, bŏr *forest*. Smolensk, from smŏlă' *pitch*.

-ese, a. *pertaining to;* n. *a native of.*

[Ital. -ese. Akin to -esce, Obs. 2; and to -ENSIS the Latin suffix of place.]

Maltese **Tyrolese** **Chinese** **Portuguese** **Milanese**

-esque, a., n. *manner, like.*

[The French spelling of -esc, Ital. -esco. See -esce, Obs. 2.]

moresque or **morisco** in the Moorish manner.

picturesque like a picture.

arabesque **grotesque** **burlesque** **romanesque**

-ESS, n. fem.

[Fr. -esse, -euse, -ice; Ital. -ice, -essa; Sp. -isa, -iz; Port. -iz; Welsh -es. Lat. -īx, -ĔSSĂ. Gr. -ις, -ισσα, as in πέρσης *a Persian*, περσί'ς *a Per-*

sian woman; δεσπότης *a master,* δεσπότις *a mistress;* ἥρως *a hero,* ἡρωΐσσα and ἡρωΐνη *a heroine;* Atlantis *the daughter of* Atlas. Bohem. -ssi.]

abbess princess empress laundress heiress tigress pl-aice P-LAT-ESSA a f-lat fish.

Talbot suggests that *dormouse* may be from the French la dorm-euse *the sleeper.*

-ess, -esse, -es, n. See -ice.

[Fr. -esse; It. -ezza, -izia. Lat. -ITIA,[a] -ITAS,[b] &c. It may include Bohem. -ez, -iz-na,—the *z* as in English.]

duress[a] **fortress finesse largess**[b] **prowess**[b] **distress wages riches** (+**richesse**) **promise +feblesse +humblesse +simplesse**

> To ſtondin forthe in ſoche dureſſe
> This cruilte and wickidneſſe.—*Chaucer.*
>
> Ther richis was ther old ſervife.—*id.*
>
> To fill his bags, and richeſſe to compare ;—*Spenser.*

Burgess, Ir. buirgeìseach, bruigḟis, from brug *a town.*

Obs. In mattress, buttress, trellis, the suffix is heterogeneous.

-est, a. *most.*

[Sanscrit -ISTHA5 (-Ā, -A,;) -ιστος, (-α, -ον.) English -ast, -aste, -æst, -est, -ist, -ost, -ust, -yst. The sign of the superlative degree, as in *μέγ-ιστος bigg-est,* *βέλτ-ιστος,* Go. batists, Ang. betst *be-st.* The original sign of the comparative degree being *s,* the superlative was formed by adding *t.* The *s* which afterwards fell into *r* was (English) *z* in Gothic, as in aldiza *older,* sutiza *sweeter.*]

Some of the positive, comparative, and superlative forms of 'nigh' are as follows, the English having the greatest resemblance to the North Friesian—being identic in the positive and comparative.

Old Saxon	nā	nāhor	nāhist
Anglish	neah	ne-ar	nehst
Islandic	nā	naerri	naestr
Old Frisian	ni	nīar	nest
North Friesian	nai	najer	naist
English	nigh	nig*h*er	nig*h*est
	nigh, near	ne-ar-er	nearest

From *near* comes *nigher,* because the vowel of the former is older than the diphthong of the latter. The superlative is *nearest, nighest, next,* the last from a form allied to *nigh,* with a distinct guttural. The Zend (ancient Persian) form of *nighest* is nazdista, showing the loss of the guttural as early as 1500 years before the Christian era. Chaucer uses hext for highest, showing the presence of a *cay*—

For the firſt apple and the hext
Which ygrowith unto you next.

first as if fore-est, advanced before all others. (Danish forst, Ang. fyrst, Persian firist, Gr. φέριστος and πρώτιστος. Norse fiarr *far*, firri *farther*, firstr *farthest*, naerst *nearest*.

whitest hardest fullest soonest utm-ost mo-st wor-st

The worſt and moſt dangerous thing euery way that can be in all the courſe of our liſe, is Exceſſe and Superfluity.—*Holland*, Plinie, b. 12, ch. 54, 1635.

Obs. 1. In German, *first* is ērst, from ēh *before* (with *h* silent,) ēher *formerly*, whence 'ēre' and 'erst,' but not ê'er *ever*. The German Fürst is a Prince, whence perhaps the proper name Forest may be in part derived; and Forester from Vorsteher (*h* silent, *v* as *f*, really a forestander,) a Warden.

Obs. 2. The use of -est with polysyllables is inelegant, as in fugitivest, vehementest, violentest, used by Boyle, 1675.

The ordinarieſt, courſeſt, hard-favouredſt *temptation* that they can ſee.—*John Hammond*, D.D., Works, 1764. . . . rhetoricall'ſt . . . impoſſibleſt . . . decrepiteſt . . —*id.*

Dunluce Caſtle is without any exception the grandeſt romanticeſt and awfuleſt ſea-kings caſtle in broad Europe.—*Ld. John Manners.*

-EST, a., n. See **-d, -t, -ty.**

[Lat. -ĔS-T-ŬS[a] adj.; -ĔS-T-ĀS[b] n.; -ĔS-T-ĬC-ŬS adj. T participial.]

est-ic, -ic-ally, -ic-ate, -ic-at-ion, -ic-at-or, -ic-it-y, -u-ous, -ly.

modest[a] according to (MŎDŬS) mode or propriety.
honest[a] according to (HŎNŎR, HŎNŌS,) honor.
domestic pertaining to the (DŎMŬS) house or home.

tempest[b] **honesty**[b] **majesty**[b] **(sacristy amnesty interest)**

Harvest, old Ger. herpist; καρπίζω, to collect (καρπός) fruit.—*Grimm.*

Earnest, Welsh er *an impulse forward;* ern, m. *what serves to drive on;* ern-es, f. *earnest-money.*

-ET, -ETE, -ITE, -IT, -OT, -T, n.
he who; that which.

[The agent or actor. *-ητης;*[a] -ĒTĂ, -ITĂ, -ITĀS; *-ιτης,*[b] neut. *-ιτον.* Fr. -ète. See T-OR, *-ITE,* and T participial.]

prophet[a] he who foretells. (*φᾰ΄ω* I tell.) *προφῆτῐ̆ς* a prophetess. **acrobat** a rope-dancer.

poet idiot despot athlete anchoret hermit comet[a] **planet diet** *δῐ΄αιτᾰ.* **epithet** *επῐ΄θετον.*

-et, -ette, -etto, -etta, -otte, -t, n. *small.*

[Fr. -et, -ette; Ital. -etto, -etta, -ita; Sp. -eta, -ita.]

bullet, pellet, a small ball. **pullet** a small (Fr. poule) hen. **poult**ry **turret** a small tower.

mignonette a little (Fr. mignonne) favorit (flower.)

locket casket facet mallet lancet hatchet car-t rosette violet is-l-et eye-l-et stylet egret puppet cruet crotchet lappet leveret cygnet signet cabinet coronet skillet bucket (-ket) **bouque***t* **budget gullet plummet wallet mul-et-**eer **sonn-ett-**eer **palette lunette gazette Harriet Henri-etta burletta Charl-otte stil-etto palm-etto cavetto gibbet helmet target garret minuet banquet paroquet**

et, n.

freshet a flood in a river. **cricket** a noisy insect.

musket bayonet triplet gorget brocket pricket suet ferret hornet racket russet velvet sarcenet carpet

Thicket, German dickicht, dickigt, belongs to -IC, and T participial. It is not from *thicked* as Richardson has it.

Trivet is a form of tripod.

Owlet is from Fr. *h*ulotte, which is applied to a large species.

Dulcet is from DŪLCĬS sweet, DULCĒDO sweetness.

Basket, see M-. *Gusset,* see **-t.** *Market, garnet,* T participial.

Obs. The *-t* of val-e*t* (vassal-et) and bouqu-e*t* having disappeared, the *e* alone remains as the representative of *-et.*

-ĔT-IC, a. See -AT-IC.

pro-ph-etic pertaining to one who foretells.
pathetic athletic peripatetic emetic energetic he'retic

-ĒT-UM, n. *a place for or with.*

rosetum (RŎSĒTŬ^{m}) a garden or plot for roses.
arboretum a plantation of ornamental trees.

ēum, n.

[-εῖον, -αῖον, -εον; -ÆUM. Neuter adjective forms used as nouns. See -E-, -I- formative.]

muse'um (μουσεῖον) a temple of the muses.
lyce'um (λύκειον) Aristotle's school near the temple of the Lycæan Apollo.
hypoge'-um (γῆ the earth,) the underground parts of a building. **mausole'um colise'um colosse'um**

-eur, n.

[A French form of -OR, -ER, &c.]

grandeur hauteur connaisseur amateur farceur

-FER**ous**, a. *bearing.*

[-FĔR-ŬS; φορ-ός. ☞ FĔRO I bear.]

luci-fer-ous bearing (LUX) light.
phos-phorus bearing (φῶς) light.
pestiferous metalliferous auriferous stelliferous

-FIC, a. *making, causing.*

[-FĬC-ŬS. ☞ FĂC-ĬO (FA'CTŬ^{m};) -FĬC-ĬO (FĔCTŬ^{m};) -FĬCO, *to make.* FIO, φύω *to become, to happen, to be made.* -FĬCĬŬ^{m}, n. *what is made, done,* &c.]

pacific making (PĀX) peace. **horrific** causing horror.
terrific calorific morbific unific soporific magnificent

-fice, n. *that which is made, done,* &c. See -FIC.

artifice something done with art. **artificer** a mechanic.
benefice **edifice** **office** **sacrifice** **orifice**

-ful, a. *full of.*

[PLĒ-NŬS; πλέον. Russ. polnoe. Belg. vol; Ang. -full, -ful. Ss. root PALL to *augment*.]

painful **deceitful** **fanciful** **wilful** **mirthful** **youthful**

Obs. 1. It is used as a prefix in full-toned, full-orbed, &c.
Obs. 2. In *fulsome*, 'ful' is the old form of *foul*.

(**-fy**, v. *to make*, &c. See -FIC.)

stupify to make (cause to be) stupid.
fortify to make (FŌRTĬS) strong, to strengthen.
nullify to render null. **classify** to arrange in classes.
clarify **verify** **purify** **falsify** **amplify** **versify** **ponti-ff**

-g, **-k**, **-sh**, n. See -AC.

See under M for **mash** (or mesh) **bask**et **flask** **smoke** **maggot**

-gar, *he who.*

[A Tamil termination used in India.]

cavelgar a watchman. **monigar** a surveyor, manager.

[Partly derived from I (sometimes of a genitive case, as ÆV-U^{m}, gen. ÆV-Ī, *a-ge*;) and -E and I formative.]

age **grange** **orange** **deluge** **hinge** hang. **challenge**

-geon, n.

[Commonly for -jon, a different pronunciation of -ion in *nation*. See -ION, and -N declensional.]

pigeon PIPIO, gen. PIPIONIS. **sturgeon,** Ital. storione.
gudgeon GOBIO κωβιὸς a fish with a large (CĂPŬT) head.
dungeon, Irish daingean a *fort* or *tower;* daingion *secure.*

Surgeon (chirurgeon, χεὶρ hand, ἔργον work,) a badly formed word, χείρεργον being hand-work, and χειρουργὸς hand-operator.

IN-, *pertaining to; like.* See -AGO.

[Probably allied to -*GEN*- (see -C-,) in which case FĔRRŪGO *rust* means *producing* (FĔRRŪm) *iron;* ÆRŪGO *verdigris, producing* (ÆS, gen. ÆRĬS,) *brass.*]

ferruginous like iron ore. **aeruginous** brassy.
oleaginous like an (ŎLĔĂ) olive; or giving (ŎLĔŪm) oil.
imagin-ary, -at-ive, -at-ion. **fuliginous** sooty.

For margin, virgin, see N declensional.

-glio, n.

[Italian; the silent *g* indicates that *i* has the power of English *y.*]

imbroglio (the noun of embroil,) an embroiling.
intaglio olio punctilio seraglio

-go, n.

em-bar-go (Sp.) a bar or prohibition against passing.
cargo the load or charge of a ship. (CĂRRŬS a wagon.)

Obs. Latin has -go in MĀRG-O (gen. -ĬNĬS,) a margin. See under -GIN-.

-gy, n.

clergy, Latin CLĒRĬCŬS, perverted from the plural CLĒRĬCĪ.

Obs. The *g* is radical in energy, liturgy, eulogy, effigy, prodigy, foggy.

-h

Denoting an aspiration in words from the Hebrew, as Shekīnāh, ephah, Messiah, Shiloh, Jonah (Yonah,) where it is not a mark auxiliary to the vowel. It is also used to indicate the Greek aspirates *θ th, φ ph, χ ch.*

-head, -hood, n. *condition.*

[Ang. -hād, hādĕ; old Eng. -hed, -heed, -hede, -hode, -hod, -hood. Belg. -heid; old Frisian, old Sax., Dan. -hed. Ger. -heit, -keit; upper Ger. -ĕt. Go. haidus *kind, mode;* old Ger. haid, hait, heit *person, sex, condition,* as in dhiu ander heit, *the other person.* Norse heið *people,* whence *heathen.*]

brotherhood (-hed, Chaucer.) **likelihood Godhead manhood neighborhood widowhood childhood boyhood falsehood**

> That is to fayn, trouth, honour, and knighthede
> Wifdom, humbleffe, eftat, and high kinrede.—*Chaucer.*
>
> He was of knighthode and of fredome flouer.—*id.*

Chaucer also uses wikkedhede, pensifehed *pensiveness,* lustihed *mirth,* mistihede *darkness,* fairehede *beauty,* lowlyhede *humility,* onhed, onehed *unity,* knighthode *valor,* grefhed *grief,* humblehede, chapmanhede.

Spenser has bountyhed, iollyhead, drerihedd, drowsihedd, goodlyhead *godliness,* lustyhed *vigor,* livelyhed *liveliness.*

Livelihood is a heteronym of liflade, life-lode, as if *life-leading.*

> And former liuelod faile, fhe left me quight.—*Spenser.*

-I, genitive.

[Latin genitive -I of the 2d declension, as in CŬNĔŬS *wedge,* gen. CŬNĔĪ, in cunei-form; ĂGĔR *field,* gen. ĂGRĪ, in agri-culture; SĪGNŬ^m^ *sign,* gen. SĪGNĪ, in signi-fy.]

horticulture the culture of a (HŌRT-ŬS) gard-en.
fabricate to work like (FĂBĔR) an artificer, or with artifice.
auriferous bearing (ĀVRŬ^m^) gold.

[Latin genitive -IS of the 3d declension, as in FRĀTĔR *brother,* gen. FRĀTRĬS; RĒX *king,* gen. RĒGĬS; PĀX *peace,* gen. PĀCĬS; JŪDĒX *judge,* gen. JŪDĬCĬS; ĀĔR *air,* gen. ĀĔRĬS; ĀRS *art,* gen. ĀRTĬS.]

fratricide **regi**cide **paci**fic **cordi**al **judici**al **aeri**form **arti**fice **ventri**loquist **audaci**ty **simplici**ty **feroci**ty **melli**fluous **edi**fice

-I, n. plural.

[Gr. -οι; Lat. -I; Russ., Bohem., Welsh, Ital. -i. ¶ Heb. -IJ, -AJ, as in ADŌN *a lord,* ADONAJ (lords) *The Lord.*]

gemini radii foci triumviri dentelli asckii literati

I-, diminutive.

[Akin to -I- formative, and used with -ον, -UM, for diminutives, as in βηρύλλ-ι-ον *a small* (βήρυλλος) *beryl*. Associated with *D* diminutive in ἰχθυ'δῖον a little (ἰχθύς) fish; 'ῑμᾰτῑ δῖον a small mantle.]

cymat-i-um κῡμάτιον a small (κῦμα, gen. -ατος) wave; a waved moulding of a cornice.

Ichthidion, **Imatidium**, genera of coleopterous insects.

Ceri-th-i-um a genus of mollusca. *Con-y* CŬNĪCŬLŬS.

-I-, connective. See §§ 52, 55.

-I-, formative.

[Eng. -i-ous, -i-an. Adjectives derived from nouns. See -E- formative.]

regius (RĒX king,) *pertaining to* the sovereign.

Corinth-i-an pertaining to Corinth.

-I, adverbial.

alibi ĂLĬBĪ elsewhere. **ibi**dem ĬBĪDĒ[m] in the same place.

-I-A, n. singular.

[-ια; Lat., Ital. -IA; Fr. -ie. I formative and -A n. feminine. See E, I formative. It is used for modern forms like Tasmania, named after its discoverer Tasman.]

Ethiopia the land of the Ethiop.

Australia the country which is (ĀVSTRĀLĬS) south.

Abyssinia **Boeotia** **Ionia** **Polynesia** **Tasmania** **India** **Arabia-n** **Alexandria** **Victoria** **Asia** **Austria** **Virginia**

-I-A, n. plural.

[The plural -A preceded by I formative.]

regalia **effluvia** **paraphernalia** **penetralia** **saturnalia**

-IC, a. *relating to; like; made of.* See -AC.

[-ικ-ός; -ĭc-ŭs, -īqvŭs; Ital., Sp., -ico; Fr. -ique, -ic-. Belg. -ig; Sw., Dan. -ig; German -ig, -isch, -ich, -icht, -igt. Welsh -ig. Lappish -k. Eng. -ic, -ice, -ish, -k, -y, -ick, -ique.]

-ic-abil-ity, -ic-able, -ic-able-ness, -ic-abl-y, -ic-al, -ic-al-ity, -ic-al-ness, -ic-ally, -ice, -ic-ity, -k, -cy, -gy, -y.

proph-et-ic relating to prophecy. See *-ET.*
Levit-ic-us the Book relating to the Levites or priesthood.
metallic like metal, made of metal.
despotic in the manner of a despot.
enthusiastic full of (due to, proceeding from) enthusiasm.
prósaic like (in the manner of) prose.
chronic produced by, or due to (χρόνος) time.
historic pertaining to history. (Chaucer uses historial.)
nautic pertaining to (ναῦς) a ship.
critique the act or work of a critic.
antique (ĀNTĪQVŬS) ancient; a remain of ancient art.
cler-k, **cler-gy**, for **cler-ic.** **piracy** PĪRĀTĬCĀ, a., n. **en-erg-et-ic** **pro-gno-s-t-ic** **med-ic-in-al** **civ-ic** **public** **sulphuric** **nitric**

See under **-esce** for Judaic or Jewish, Frank or French.

Such adjective forms may become nouns, as **critic** he who is able (κρίνω) to discern, **logic** (for, the *logic art*, ĀRS LŎGĬCĀ;) **rhetoric**, **arithmetic**, **panic**, **physic**, **ecliptic**, and names of sciences in the plural, as **physics** PHȲSĬCĀ, **mathematics**, **hydrostatics**, **politics**, **pneumatics**, **mnemonics**, **hydraulics**, **tactics**, **aerostatics.**

> Phyfic of Metaphyfic begs defence,
> And Metaphyfic calls for aid to fenfe:
> See Myftery to Mathematics fly!
> In vain! they gaze, turn giddy, rave, and die.
>
> *Pope*, Dunciad, 1728—42.

. . . . . mechanicks have long ago difcovered, that contrariety of equal attractions is equivalent to reft.—*Dr. Johnson*, Rambler, Sept. 3, 1751.

grassy full of grass. **glassy** like glass. **glossy** having gloss. **ashy** of the nature of ashes. Ger. asch-ig, -icht, see -y.
windy **witty** **merry** **dreary** **melancholy** **holy** **loamy**

Obs. Intrinsic is for intrinsec, from the adverb ĪNTRĪNSĔCŬS on the inside. Mere-tric-ious, see -AX, -IX. Velli-c-ation, see C agential.

Thrasybūlus . . . restored the democratical form of government.—*J. E. Worcester*, 1826.

Whilst Phœbus down the vertic circle glides.—*Falconer.*

The speeches were declaimed with considerable rhetoric effect.—London Observer, June, 1859.

The application of electricity seems to have acted as a strong mechanic shock. Philosophical Transactions, 1810.

Poetry, in the hands of a set of mechanic scribblers, had become such a tame mawkish thing, that we could endure it no longer.—*Wm. Hazlitt.*

. . . books and treatises theoretic, critical, philosophical, and didactic.—Encyc. of Music, 1854.

. . . . swallowed up in the pursuit of literary curiosities, or mathematic abstractions, or philosophic experiments.—Westminster Review, 1827.

-IC-A, n. See -AC.

ur-t-ic-aceous like (U·RTĪCĂ) a nettle. See ŬRO, to b-ur-n. **lumbrīcal** like (LUMBR-ĪC-US) a worm.

ves-ica-te ves-ica-tory

-ICal, a. -ICally, adv.

Etymologicly, -AL after -IC is superfluous, in forms like con-ic-al comic-al metr-ic-al concentr-ic-al philosoph-ic-al spher-ic-al politic-al, &c.

-ice, n. *condition; quality of being*, &c.

[-ιτεία·[a] -ĬTĬĂ,[b] -ĬTĬŬM,[c] -ĬTĬĒS.[d] Fr. -ice (masc. and fem.;) Sp. -icio, -icia; Ital. -izio, -igio, -icio, izia. Abstract nouns derived chiefly from adjectives. See -T-, **-ac-y**.]

police,[a] **policy**, **polity** (PŎLĪTĪĂ, πολῐτεία) the condition of a citizen; the pursuits of a statesman. (πόλῐς a city, a state.)

service[c] the condition of (SĒRVŬS) one who serves. (Fr. service, Ital. servizio, servigio, Sp. servicio.)

justice[b] the quality of being (JŪSTŬS) just.

militia the aggregate of the soldiery.

malice[b] the quality of being (MĂLŬS) bad; malevolence.

notice[b] **amity** ĂMĪCĬTĬĂ **avarice**[bd] **novice**[b] **solstice**[c]—

cowardice **caprice**, Ital. capriccio. **jaundice** (Fr. jaunisse, from jaune *yellow.*) **crevice**

Obs. 1. Modifications of this suffix appear in **pent-house** "originally **pentice**, from Fr. *apentiche* a sloping shutter, Ital. *pendice* the slope of a hill."—*H. Wedgwood.* **promise** **merchandise** **franchise** **finesse** **prowess** **largess** **distress** **riches** **wages**

Obs. 2. The suffixes of ĂVĀRITĬĂ or AVARITIĒS, DĪVĒRSITAS, and ELEGANTIA, (-ice, -ity, -ance are akin.)

Obs. 3. Ac-com-plice, PLĬCĀTŬS folded. *Denti-frice,* DĔNS, gen. DĔNTĬS, tooth; FRĬCĀRĔ to rub. *Edi-fice* (ÆDĒS a house,) and *Of-fice,* FĂCĬO I make. *Lico-rice,* γλῠκυ'-ῥῐζᾰ sweet-root.

Obs. 4. For lattice, pelisse, surplice, see -AC-eous, Obs. 1.

-IC-i-an, n. *he who.* See -AC, -AN.

rhetorician **musician** **mechanician** **physician** **patrician**

-IC-UL-AR, -C-UL-AR. See -C-le, -L.

reticular like, or pertaining to (RĒTĬCŬLŪ^m^) a small (RĒTĔ) net. **vermicular** like a little (VĒRMĬS) worm.
orbicular **auricular** **canicular** **carb-uncular** **vesicular** **per-pend-icular** **funicular** **mus-cular** **corpuscular** **vascular**

I-C-UL-ATe, a., v., -I-C-UL-AT-ION, n.

articulate formed of little (ĀRTŪS, n. pl.) joints or divisions; an insect or similar animal; to utter speech.
gesticulate **matriculate** **particulate** **in-osculate** **reticulate**

Obs. The *c* is part of the root in spic-ulate, calyc-ulate.

-I-C-UL-OuS, a.

ridiculous RĪDĬCŬLŬS causing laughter; worthy to be laughed at. (RĪDĔO I laugh.)

14*

-ID, a. *quality* (in a high degree.)

[-ID-US. Akin to- AT-US. See -ATe, **-ade**, **-ed**. Adjectives, mostly based upon verbs.]

acid having the quality of sharpness. (ĂCĔO, to be sour.) **solid** firm; compact; valid; (on the SŎL-Ŭ^m soil, bottom, sole.) **viscid** glutinous; like (VĪSCŬ^m) birdlime.

col-d, as if **cool-ed** or **gel-id** **pale** for **pall-id** **arid** **splendid** **livid** **humid** **valid** **tepid** **florid** **rigid** **frigid** **stupid** **lucid** **rapid** **sordid** **liquid** **timid** **placid** **turgid** **tumid** **torpid**

-ide, n. See -ID.

A modern chemic suffix, used as in **oxid**e (or better—**oxid**, like **acid**) of iron, a compound substance formed of oxygen and iron.

sulphide **iodid**e **chlorid**e **fluorid**e

-IDES, n. pl.

cantha'rides, the plural of CĀNTHĂRĬS, a blistering fly. **caryatides** statues of women, used as supports in architecture.

-IDI-**ous**

fastidious easily disgusted; minutely critical. See -T- intensive.

-ie, **-ye**, n. See **-y**.

Old English, as in **ladye**. **centaurie** an herb. (Chaucer.) **aerie** or eyry (pronounced air-y.) Scotch **lassie**, **lassick** a little lass. See **-ock**.

-IG-, v. *to make, cause, use.*

[Ss. -IJA; Lat. ĬG-O, v.; akin to ĂGO *I do, ac-t, conduct, drive;* ἄγω *I lead, conduct, bring, rule;* ἔχω *I have, hold, &c.* See -AC.]

-ge, -ig-ate, -ig-ation, -ig-ating, -ig-at-ive, -ig-at-or, -ig-at-ory.

nav-ig-ate to conduct (NĀVĬS) a ship.

lit-ig-ate to cause (LĪS, gen. LĪTĬS) strife.
fum-ig-ate to imbue with (FŪMŬS) smoke.
pur-ge to make (PŪRŬS) pure.
mitigate to make (MĪTIS) mild, tranquil.
fustigate to use a (FŪSTĬS) cudgel.
castigate to punish with (CE·STŬS) a strap, or (CÆSTŬS) a boxing glove.

Vertigo, fuliginous, indigo see -AGO. Investigate see VE-. Obligate see LĬGO.

-IG-N-, a. *acting.*

[-IG-N-ŬS. For -N-, compare EXTER and EXTERNUS. See -IG-, N-US.]

-ignancy, -ignant, -ignantly, -igner, -ignity, -ignly.

benign, **benign**ant acting (BĔNĔ) well.
malignant acting (MĂLĔ) badly.

Obs. Condign and indignant are from DĪGNŬS worthy.

-ILe-, -ILI-, -IL-, a., n. See -AL.
that may be —; quality, like.

fiss-ile that may be (FĪSSŬS) split; readily split.
missile that may be thrown.
fragile or **fra..il** easily broken; apt to break.
puerile in the manner of (PŬĔR) a boy; boyish.
infantile **mercantil**e **civil** **scurr-il**ous **aux-il**iary, see -AR.

Obs. 1. -ile may be in part derived from -ible by the loss of *b*, as the Latin has both DŎCĬBĬLĬS and DŎCĬLĬS (neut. -Ĕ, docible, docile,) easily taught.

Obs. 2. The nouns *kennel*, (CĂNĬS a dog,) and *fusil* or *fusee* (FŎCŬS a hearth, a fire, dim. FŎCŬLŬS,) are false forms.

Obs. 3. In *domicile* (DŎMŬS house,) the -cil- of DŎMĬCĬLĬŬm may belong to -CLe. In *council* and *exile*, *il* is part of the root.

Obs. 4. *Brittle* or *brickle* may be referred to *fragile*.

-ILL-ATe, v., -ILL-AT-ION, n. See -L, ¶ 1.

scintillate to sparkle. (S-CĪNT-ĪLLĂ a spark, CĂND-ĔO I shine, burn.) **scintillation** a sparkling.

-im, **-ime**, **-imo**, -IM-US, -IM-A, -IM-UM, a. *most.*

[Superlative adjective forms. -ŪMŬS, -ĒMŬS, -ĬM-ŬS (fem. -Ă; neut. -Ūm; neut. pl. -A;) ablative sing. -IMO. Sanscrit -MA5, -T-ĂMĂ5 (fem. -T-AMĀ, neut. -T-AMA.) Lappish -umus. Lat. E·XTĬMŬS, Ss. UTTAMA5 *extreme, utmost.* M is the superlative element.]

-im, -im-acy, -im-al, -im-ari-ly, -im-ary, -im-ate, -im-ate-ly, -im-at-ing, -im-at-ion, -im-ate-ness, -im-at-ive, -ime, -im-er, -im-ism, -im-ist, -im-it-ive, -im-ity, -im-o.

maxim a principle or saying esteemed to be of the greatest authority. (☞ MA·GNUS great, MAXĬMUS greatest.)

maximum the greatest amount in a given case.

optim-ism the doctrine that every thing happens for (ŌPTĬMŬS) the best. **ultim**ate final, farthest.

pen-ultima the (syllable) next to the final one.

prime most pri-or. Lat. PRŌ before, PRĬŎR previous; PRĪMŬS, fem. PRĪMĂ, Sanscrit PRAT'HAMA5 (PRĂ, Lat. PRŌ before,) Lithuanic PIRMAS, Coordish ber *first.* The MA of PRĪMĂ may be present in *ma*gnify, *mu*ch, *mo*re, *mo*st.

mari-t-ime (-T- participial) at or on the very (MĂRĔ, genitive MĂRĬS,) sea.

minim minimum proximate proximo ultimo Maximus primate primary premier primer primordial prince

-IM, adv.

[Latin adverbs, sometimes preceded by participial or declensional T.]

verbatim word for word. **seriatim** in regular series.

punctuatim literatim ibidem quondam interim item

-im, n.

pilgrim is for peregrine, **painim** for pagan, and **megrim** for hemicrania. For maxim see **-im**, a.

-īm, n. pl.

[Hebrew plural masculine, pronounced -eem.]

tĕrāphīm household gods. **rodanim** Rhodians.

seraphim **cherubim** **Dodanim** **Philistim** **shittim**

Sanhedrim is a hebraised form of συνεδρίον (an assembly,) from συν together, and ἕδρα a seat, a sitting.

Mizraim (Egypt) is not a plural but a dual.

-IN-

[Latin, as in ŏPĪNŏR *I have an opinion;* VĔNĬO *I come,* as if akin to VĬĂ *a way.* See -N- intensive.]

op-in-ion ŏPĪNĬO what each holds (mentally;) judgment; belief. (Perhaps akin to ἕπω to take care of; ōPS, genitive ŏPĬS, wealth, power.)

It-in-erary is from the genitive case ĬTĬNĔRĬS, of ĬTĔR a journey.

Dest-ine—STANS standing (from ☞ STO,) seems to be used in DE-ST-ĬN-O I (cause to stand,) destine.

Pro-cra-s-t-in-ate to defer till (CRĀS) tomorrow. (CRĀSTĬNŬS of tomorrow. See -S adverbial, -T- participial, and -N-US.)

-IN, n.

[Crude forms of certain nouns, as MĀRGO *margin,* gen. MĀRGĬN-ĬS; PĔCTĔN *comb,* gen. PĔCTĬN-ĬS.]

origin **virgin** **ordin**al **cardin**al **tendin**ous **pectin**ate

-ĬNA, -in, -ine, *small.* See -en, dim.

RĒTĬNĂ a small (RĒTE) net or curtain (of the eye.)

LĀMĬNĂ a thin plate. **violin** a small viol.

tamborine a small (Fr. tambour) drum.

nubbin (knob) a small ear of maize.

bulletin **basin** **curtain** **coralline**

-INÆ, n. pl. See N-US.

falconinæ the subfamily of the falcons.

-INe, a. *pertaining to*, &c. See **-en**, a.

turpentine τερεβίνθ-ινος TĔRĔBĪNTHĬNŬS pertaining to the τερέβινθος TĔRĔBĪNTHŬS terebinth tree.

fluorine an element obtained from fluor spar.

Eleusinian pertaining to (ἔλευσις or ἐλευσὶν, genitive ἐλευσῖνος,) Eleusis. For *doctrine* DŌCTRĪNĂ, (with long I) see -AN.

-INe, n. fem.

[-ιννα, -ηνη, -ινη, -αινα. Lat., Ital. -INA; Fr. -inne. Ger. -in; Anglish, Teutonic -en, -in; Hindoostanee -in; Welsh -en.]

landgravine the wife of a landgrave.

qu-een, Belg. koning-in a female king.

carlin a female carl or churl; (but the Norse form is kerlings.) **vixen** a female fox. **heroine** HĒRŌĪNĂ ἡρωΐνη.

Czarina is an error for Tsarítsa.

-ing, n. *that which; act of; state of; -tion.*

[Ohg. -ŭnga, -ŭnc, -ĭnc; Ger., Angl. -ŭng; Old Eng. -unge, -inge, -yng (1307) -ynge; Belg. -ĭng; Swiss -ig;—as in Ohg. rechanunga; German rechnung; Danish regning; Belg. reekening; English *a reckoning.* Anglish feorm-an *to form*, noun fem. feormung and feorming *a forming.*]

reckoning *that which* is reckon*ed;* a calcula*tion;* the *act* or *result of* calculation. **clothing** clothes in the aggregate.

meaning the *act* or *state of* the mind; that which is meant.

bagging material for bags.

feeling **binding** **pudding** **stabling** **clearing** **morning** **evening** **with-y** **kin-g**, Anglish (c as *k*) cyning, cing, cinge.

Obs. In Anglish, this suffix is also used for *origin* and *nativity,* hence **Fleming** a native of Flanders.

-ing, participle.

[Present participle, -ων, -ον. Islandic -andi; Danish -nde; Anglish -ende; Ger. -end; Gothic -nds. Latin -ĒNS, gen. -ENTIS. Lithuanic -ant, -anti. Wallachian -nd. Sanscrit -AN, -AT. See **-en**, participial.]

having continuing to have.
making **giving** **going** **saying** **living** **working** **eating**

Syngynge he was, or flowtynge, al the day;—*Chaucer.*

. . . . . after five minutes' tugging, propping, slipping, and splashing, the boulder gradually tips over.—*Charles Kingsley*, Glaucus.

I fought for it like a tiger, wrestling, hugging, tugging, kicking, pushing, striking right and left.—*Th. Hood*, Whimsicalities.

Obs. 1. The sense of -ing is not limited to time present, as may be observed in—*was, is,* or *will be go-ing; hav-ing gone; about to be go-ing.*

Obs. 2. The departure from the original form may have arisen from a *confusion of idea,* in distinguishing the participle from the noun; and a *confusion of speech,* in saying 'feelin' for the noun *feeling,* and 'hav-in' for a form of the Anglish participle habbende, German habend *having.*

Obs. 3. Norman French entered England in the 11th century, and the participial -ing, -yng, occurs in Old English of the 13th century, (and -ande in the 15th.) The ignorance of each nation, of the language of the other, and the confusion which both may have made between the English -ng and the French nasal vowels, would be sufficient to produce or confirm the error. The following English and French forms may be compared, the final 't' of the latter being silent.

during duran*t* **pending** penden*t* **regarding** regardan*t* **willing** voulan*t*.

Obs. 4. Angl. sægen a sayen'; green (grow-en',) brown (burn, brand,) and own, are participial in form, except when used as infinitives.

Obs. 5. Participial forms are used in the following nouns—

ticken (for ticking) **heaven** **leaven** **dawn** **burden**

-ing, n. dim.

[Akin to -ing, n. German and Anglish -ing.]

farth-ing a fourth part (of a penny.)
penny, Ohg. pfennink, Ger. pfennig, Ang. pening.

-inge, *-INX*, n.

syringe (σῦ́ριγξ) a pipe for throwing water.
syrinx a shepherd's pipe. See *-YNX*.

-ION, n. *act of; state of being; that which; -ing.*

[-ĭo, -ĭūm, -T-ĭo (gen. -TĬŌN-ĭs,) -sĭo, -xĭo. Italian -iōne; Sp. -iōn, -c-iōn; Port. -ão, -ç-ão; Fr. -tioⁿ (*t* as *s*,) -sioⁿ. -τις, -*s-is*. Sanscrit -TĬ5. -t-ion, s-ion have T participial, S mutational and inflectional, I formative, -O nominative, and N declensional. -ION indicates the action of the root verb.]

vision (S mutational,) the *act* or *power of* see*ing*. (☞ VĬDĔO I see.)

exhibition the act of showing; the state of being shown; a showing; that which is shown. (ĒXHĬBĔO I show.)

question the act of inquiring.

potion and **poison** that which is (to be) drunk. (PŌTO *I drink.*) **menace** MĬNĀTĬO.

pris-on a place of confinement. (PRĔHĒNSĬO or PRĒNSĬO, gen. PRĒNSĬŌNĬS, a taking.)

venis-on VĒNĀTIO the *chase*; 2. the *game*; 3. *venison*.

¶ 1. Active nouns.

contagion multiplication expulsion explosion revision extension correction deflexion invasion collision fusion

¶ 2. Passive nouns.

oblivion reg-ion dominion commun-ion complexion repletion connexion mansion vision emulsion session

-ion-er, n.

parish-ion-er one who belongs to a parish. (French

paroissien m., paroissienne fem., from paroisse *parish.* The -ion is for -ian of musician, with -er added.)

-is, n.

[French -is (*s* silent.) See under **-ess**, **-ice.**]

abatis débris glacis

-*IS*, n.

[Greek and Latin nouns, as πόλῐς (gen. πόλεος) *city;* δελφῖ΄ς (gen. δελφῖνος) *dolphin;* τι΄γρῐς (gen. τίγριδος) *tiger.* Sanscrit AGA5 or AHI5, ἔχῐς, Latin ĂNGVĬS *a serpent.* Sanscrit ACSA5 *a wheel, a centre;* Latin ĂXĬS. See -*AS*, -*AD.*]

Cle′-ma-t-is κλημᾰτῐς (T declensional,) a genus of winding plants. (κλῆμα, gen. -ᾰτος, a twig, a vine branch; κλάω I break, break off, prune.)

metropolis chrysalis epidermis ephemeris ba-sis gene-*SIS* **phthi-***SIS* **phloc-s** (**-x**) **æg-is iris pro-bosc-is pelvis** PĔLVĬS **pest** PĔSTĬS **vest** VĔSTĬS **ni-ece** NĔPTĬS **worm** VĔRMĬS **orb** ŎRBĬS **corn-ice, corn-ish, corn-iche,** κορωνὶς a top, a peak. *Trellis* TRĬCHĬLĂ a bower, with -L, ¶ 3.

-IS, genitive.

[Latin -ĭs, genitive singular of the 3d declension, as in JŪS *right, authority,* genitive JŪR-ĬS.]

jurisdiction legal authority. (DĪCO, DĪCTŪm, to say, affirm, determine.)

Gratis (GRĀTĪS without recompense,) is an ablative plural of GRĀTŪm a favor. For satis-fy see -S adverbial.

-is-ation, n. See **-ise**, v.

civilisation demoralisation naturalisation authorisation organisation crystallisation symbolisation canonisation

-ise, **-ize**, v. *to make; give; practice*, &c.

[The following are allied, as far as *s*, *r*, and Belg. (Eng.) *z* are concerned. Fr. -īse*r*, Ital. -izzare, Sp. -izar, Port. -izar. Belg. -iezen; Ger. īren. Lat. -ĪRĔ. Gr. -ίζω (-izdo,) Doric -ιΣδω.]

apologise to make or give an apology.
sermonise to give in the manner of a sermon.
tў̆rannise to practice tў̆ranny; to act as a tyrant.
crystalise to become a crystal; to take the crystalline form.

He is fcandalized at youth for being lively, and at childhood for being playful.—*Addison*, Spectator, Sept. 26, 1712.

The invisible world with thee hath sympathi**s**ed;
Be thy affections raised and solemni**z**ed.—*Wordsworth.*

criticise organise harmonise methodise monopolise catechise baptise symbolise economise eulogise—civilise realise revolutionise naturalise immortalise authorise legalise signalise patronise humanise advertise lionise

Obs. 1. This suffix is probably regarded as Greek by those who write '-ize,' although -ise and -ism have the same sibilant in English, so that '-ize' should require '-izm.' The *d* part of ζ (*zd*) was lost in Greek derivatives, as in βᾶπτίζω (baptizdo) I baptise; βαπτι·σμός baptism; and as ungreek words like moralise, brutalise, sensualise(-ist, -ism,) are used, the spelling '-ize' need not be retained.

Obs. 2. The Westminster Review for July, 1831, has recogni**s**ed (p. 210,) and recogni**z**ed (p. 242.) "It is a pity men are most inclined to satiri**s**e that of which they know the most." id. ib. The Illustrated London News uses -ise, as in individualise, &c. "Sardinia cannot be held blameless for her dreams of ambition and aggrandisement." July 18, 1859.

Extemporize, tantalize (Th. Hood.) Conchologizing (Kingsley.) Ethymologise (Chaucer.) Sermonising (Brit. Q. Rev.) Volatilized (Geologist.) Analyse, sympathise, moralise, monopolising (Sir T. N. Talfourd.) Individualise, civilisation, equalisation (Mrs. Jameson.)

Exercise ĔXĔRCĬTO. Supervise, ☞ VĬDĔO. Com-pro-mise, sur-mise, ☞ MĬTTO.

-ise, n. See **-ice**, Obs. 1.

treatise is formed from tract-ate. **val-ise**, Sp. bal-ija, Ital. valigia.

How mortgaging their lives to Covetife,
Through waftfull pride and wanton riotife,
Herfelfe had ronne into that hazardize; . . . —*Spenser.*

S mutational appears in concise, enterprise, surprise, demise, promĭse.

-ish, v. *to make, give*, &c. See **-ise**, v.

[Latin Infinitive, chiefly -ĪRĔ, as in FĪNĪRĔ, Fr. finīr, Eng. fin-ish, but modified by *ss* of the French participle finissant *finishing*, and other inflections. In Chaucer the verb *embellish* is embelise, and the same *s* remains in *rejoice*. See **-ce**, v.]

establish STĂBĬLĪRĔ to make stable.

diminish to make less. **admonish** to give warning.

nourish, **nurse**, Fr. nourrir, Lat. NŪTRĪRĔ. **cherish** **replenish** **famish** **tarnish** **banish** **flourish** **furnish** **publish** **punish** **garnish** **abolish** **demolish** **polish** **furbish** **finish** **rush** **languish** **vanquish** **extinguish**

She crampiſh-eth her limmis crokidly.—*Chaucer.*

Obs. 1. The *r* is preserved in (DŎMĬNĀRĔ to) domineer; and lost in ally, sally, rally, dally, tally.

Obs. 2. The final -sh, -r, -s, in relish, sever, offer, caress, belong to the stem.

-ish, a. *somewhat; like.*

[-ĪSC-. Ang. -isc; old Eng. -issche; Ger. -isch. Bohem. -ský, as in nebe *heaven*, nebeský, Pol. niebieski *heavenly*. Go. barn *a child;* barnisks *childish;* barniski *childhood;* barniskei *childishness*. See -ESCe.]

whitish somewhat white. **latish** somewhat late.

thievish given to thieving. **foolish** senseless, unwise.

clownish like (in the manner of) a clown; rude, ill-bred.

Obs. -ish occurs in a few nouns, as gibberish, blemish, parish, relish.

-ISK, n. dim. *small.*

[-ίσκος, ίσκη, -ισκιον; -ĪSC-ŬS. Polish -ysko.]

asterisk a little (ĂSTĔR) star.

obelisk a little (ὀβελὸς) spit.

meniscus a little (μήνη) moon; a concavo-convex lens.

basilisk a small (βασιλεὺς) king; the Regulus or gold crested wren; a kind of lizard.

discus, **disk**, **dish**, **desk**, +δίκω I throw.

-IS-M, n. *condition; act; idiom; doctrine.*

[*-ασ-μ-ος, -ασμα; -ισμος, -ισμα.* -ASMUS, -ASMA; -ISMUS, -ISMA; Ital. Sp. Port. -ismo; Fr. -isme. See *-S*, **-m**, -M.]

barbarism the *condition* (also the *act* and *idiom*) of a barbarian. **gallicism** an idiom of (GĀLLĬĂ) France.

catholicism the doctrine of catholics.

fantasm *φἄ'ντᾰσμᾰ* **paroxysm** *πᾰροξῠσμὸς* **enthusiasm** **prism** see **-m.** **chasm** see **-m.** **schism** **sophism** **despotism** **heroism** **asterism** **syllogism** **aphorism** **solecism** **Latinism** **Judaism**

Hĭbrids—paganism witticism deism fanaticism nepotism attorneyism (Carlyle) favoritism

-IS-T, n. an agent; *one who.*

[*-ιστης*; -ISTA; Ital., Sp. -ista, Fr. -iste. The *t* is that of -TER, -TOR following *z* or *s* of a verb, as in dramat-ise, dramat-ist. See *-AS-T*, T-ER, Obs. 1, *-S-* inflectional, and *-ET.*]

monopolist he who monopolises.

anatomist **epitomist** **catechist** **sophist** **organist—florist** **annalist** **linguist** **pugilist** **plagiarist** **magazinist** **pianist**

-ist-er, n.

-is-terial, -is-tering, -is-tr-ar, -is-trar-y, -is-tra-tion, -is-try.

re-gi-s-t-er, (S mutat., T particip.) low Latin registrum for RĔGE·STŪ^m^, from RĔ-GĔRO I carry back, transcribe.

chorister **palmister** **barrister** **sophister** **canister** see -S-TER **minister** see T-ER

-IS-T-IC, a.

sophistic *pertaining to one who is* (seemingly *σοφὸς*) wise.

antagonistic **characteristic** **euphemistic — linguistic**

-IT-, -T-, -S-, *often, much.*

[ĬT-ĔRO *I repeat;* ĬTĔR *a going;* ĔO, ĪRĔ, ĬTŪ^m^ *to go.* Ss. root ĬT *to go, to move.* See under **t-** repetitive. Iteratives or frequentatives, as in JĂC-ĔRĔ *to throw;* JAC-T-ĀRĔ *to throw about;* JAC-T-ĬT-ĀRĔ *to continue to throw.* CĂNĔRĔ *to sing;* CA'NTĀRĔ *to sing forcibly;* CA'NTĬTĀRĔ *to sing repeatedly.* FĂC-ĬO *I make;* FĂC-ĔSSO *I do eagerly.*]

palpitate to throb. (PĀLPO I touch; PĀLPĬTO *I throb.*)
po-t-able drinkable. (πόω I drink; PŌTO I drink, tipple.)
agitate, ĂGO I do; ĂGĬTO, *I do often.*

calcitrate, CĀLCO I tread under the (CALX) heel; CĀLCĬTRO I kick, calcitrate.

visit **felicit**ate **hesit**ate **cogit**ate **dict**ate **dubit**ative **slaugh-t-er** **ince-ss-ant**, ĬNCĔSSO I attack; ĬNCĒDO I go, I fall upon.

Obs. T and S participial occur in consul-t abrup-t sec-t-ary cur-s-ory ver-s-atile and perhaps in dic-t-ate. Fug-it-ive (FŬGĬO, FŬG-ĬT-Ū^m^ to flee,) may be equally referred to T participial, and to this T iterative in FŬG-ĬT-O, to flee often.

-IT, n. See *-ET.*

orbit ŌRBĬTĂ the track of a heavenly body; originally the track of (ŌRBĬS) a wheel. **summit** the top or highest point.

-IT, verbial.

audit to examine accounts officially. (☞ AVD-ĬT he hears; AVDITĔ hear ye.)

plaudit an action indicating applause. (Lat. he applauds; PLAVDĬTĔ applaud ye.)

deficit (Lat. it fails,) deficiency in an account or an income. **caret** (Lat. it is wanting.)

-ITE, -IT, n. *he who; that which.* See *-ET.*

hypocrite **anchorite** **eremite** **levite** **aconite** **cenobitic**
Parasite, see *PARA.* The suffix in Shunamm-ite indicates a Hebrew (ית., -IJΘ,) noun feminine, of which the masculine form is ꞅUNAMMĬJ.
For -ite in names of minerals, see -oid.

-ITe, -IT-, a. See -ATe.

requisite **requis-it-ion** **polite** **recondite — elite**

-IT-ial, **-ici-ous**, a. See **-ice**, n.

solst-itial **mal-icious**-ly, -ness

-ITIous, a. -ITIously, adv. ITIate, n. See -IT-

flagitious pertaining to (FLĀGĬTĬŪ^{m}) a base action.
nutritious (NŪTRĪTĬŬS) affording nutriment.
factitious **fictitious** **novitiate** **ambitious** **seditious**
Adventitious belongs to -AC-eous.

-ITIS, n. *disease.*

[I formative, T participial, and *-IS.* See *-IS*, *-SIS.* Originally feminine adjective forms agreeing with the feminine noun *νόσος disease*, expressed or understood. Often (and correctly) pronounced *arthreetis*, &c.]

arthritis ἀρθρῖτῐ́ς disease in (ἄρθρον) a joint; gout.
phrenitis φρενῖτῐ́ς disease of (φρὴν) the mind; delirium; inflammation of the brain.
nephritis νεφρῖτῐ́ς inflammation of (νεφρὸς) the kidney.

-ito, n. dim.

musquito, Sp. mosq*u*ito, a small (MŪSCĂ) fly.

-IVe, -IV-, a. *having the quality of;* n. *that which.*

[-īv-ŭs (-Ă, -ūm,) -v-ŭs, -ŭ-ŭs, active forms (-ile being passive.) Sanscrit -V-A5 (-Ā, -N,.) ϝ-ος (-α, -ον.) It. -ivo; Fr. -if (masc.,) -ive (fem.,) Ger. -iv. Derived in nearly every case from participles, and therefore preceded by participial -S, -T. Sanscrit -VI, as in dȷāgr̥ *awake*, dȷāgr̥vi *wakeful.* See -B-.]

-iv-able, -iv-al, -iv-ate, -iv-at-ion, -iv-at-ing, -iv-at-or, -ive-ly, -ive-ness, -iv-ity.

delusive having the *quality* of deluding; *tending* (having the *power*) to delude.
expansive having the power of expansibility.

prim-it-ive having the quality of being or going (PRĪMŬS) first.

cer-v-ine pertaining to (CĔR-V-ŬS, gen. CER-VI,) a deer or har-t.

active **decisiv**e **massiv**e **progressiv**e **expensiv**e **passiv**e **nutr-it-iv**e **sens-it-iv**e **affirm-at-iv**e

captive or **cait-iff** (CA·PTĪVŬS) he who is taken.

fug-it-ive he who, or that which (FŬGĬT) flies.

locomotive a steam car.

motive **missiv**e **dissuasiv**e **prerogativ**e **relativ**e **adjectiv**e **lang-u-age** **statue** STĂTŬĂ **resid-u-um—hast-y** **tard-y** **test-y**

Testyf they were, and lusty for to pleye;—*Chaucer*, l. 4002.

-IV-AL.

fest-iv-al, formed from fest-iv' and fest-al; FĔSTĪVŬS pertaining to a feast or solemnity.

adjectival pertaining to adjectives. **estival** of summer.

-IX, n. fem. See -AX, **-ess**.

[-IX with cay lost in *-ισσα*, but present in the feminine ἀ'λώπηξ *fox*, and absent from the Latin feminine form VŪLPĒS. Compare English *fox* and Belg. *vos*.]

directrix she who directs.

executrix **testatrix** **mediatrix** **administratrix** **matrix**

Obs. 1. The feminines cicatrix, calyx, appendix, ilex, may belong to this head.

Obs. 2. -X is sometimes an abbreviation (see under -ACeous,) as in vōx voice, in Sanscrit ⍭VATΓAS; Greek σύζῦΓοΣ and σύζυΞ yoked together.

-izo.

Spanish **mest-izo** a person of (MĪXTŬS) *mixed* Europèan and American Indian race. (Also *mustee* or *mestee*.)

K, C, G, χ. See -IG-, -C-.

[Cay is the element indicative of breaking, making, augmenting, agency, action, beginning, (Κύω, κυέω, to hold, gestate; Γενέα birth, race; γέα, γῆ the earth;) kind, production, frui(c)t, likeness. It appears in -ago, -gen, -cin-, -kin, -cr-, -ac-, -ig. Cay is intensive in (φῶς light,) φόσκω to shine; and in (hear) hear-k-en.]

Hearken to the ſentence of the wife.—*Chaucer.*

-k, n.

[Among several powers, this -k forms verbs and adjectives. In lan-k it may be diminutive (see **-ock**, **-C**-le,) and in star-k augmentative. See -AC, -IC, **-g**. Lat. FĔR-O *I bear*, FŬR-CĂ *a for-k*. Polish, Russ. wid *vis-ion* (with English *v*,) widok *the thing seen*, (Russ. *the seer*.) Hindoostanee PÆR-NA *to swim*, PÆR-ĀC *a swimmer*.]

s-cul-k, CĒLO, con-ceal; Dan. skiule to hide, abscond.

wal-k, **wal-tz**, Ger. wall-en, to move irregularly, ramble.

ca-g a small hooped vessel. (Welsh caw-g a bowl, caw a band.)

yol-k yell-ow, see **-den**.

talk tale, tell.

bulk boll.

crook cur-ve.

smir-ch smear.

quirk queer.

lank lean.

lark laver-ock (dim.)

chark char.

star-k, **star-ch**, στερ-εός firm.

hark hear.

chirk (**chir-p**, **chir-m**) chirr.

husk "Dutch *huysken*, a little house." *H. Wedgwood.*

-k-et, n.

bris-ket the breas-t of an animal. Dan. brusk, bryske, the breast-gristle.

bu-cket (**pi-tcher**, **ba-sin**,) πίνω I drink, perfect πέ-πωκα.

-key, n. dim.

donkey a small animal of a dun color.

k-in, n. dim.

[Persian -kin; Belgian -ken; German -chen (as in kätz-chen *kitten*, mäd-chen *maiden*.) Gaelic -ach-an, -ag-an, as in sguab *a broom*, *a swab*, dim. sguabachan. Lat. -CIO, -ŪNCŬLŬS. A surdiminutive. See **-C**-le.]

napkin a small (Fr. nappe) tablecloth.

pumpkin a small pompion.

pipkin pipe **firkin** four **mannikin** **lambkin** **bodkin** **doitkin** **kilderkin** **muskin** **gherkin** **Simpkin** **Watkins**

L, **-le**, n. v.

[1. -ŬL-ŬS (-Ă, -Ū^m,) -ĪLL-ŬS, -ĒLL-ŬS, -ĒLLĂ, -ĒLĂ, -LĔŬS, -OL-U^m. Ital. -illo, -olo, -ola, -ello, -ella, -rello; Sp. -illo, -illa, -uelo, -uela. -υλλις, -υλλα, -ιλλα, -αλις, -υλος, -ιλος, &c. Go. -ula, -ilo, -ila; German -el. Ss. -ILA5, -IRA5. 2. -ŬL-O, -UL-US. 3. -λα, -λη, -άλη, -αλλα, -αλον, -αλιον, -ύλλ-ιον, &c. See **er**, n., -AL, Obs. 1.]

-ail, -al, -el, -ellum, -il, -ile, -illa, -illo, -l, -le, -ol, -ul, -ule, -yl,—alis, -ilate, -iloid, -leus, -ular, -ulary, -ulation, -uline, -ulum.

¶ 1. Diminutive.

idyl εἰδύλλιον a small picture or poem; εἶδος a figure.

nautilus ναύτιλος a little (ναῦς) ship; a shellfish fabled to sail. **kernel** a small corn. **nucleus** a small (NŪX) nut.

squirrel a small SCĬŪRŬS. **satchel** a small sack.

pistil, **pestle**, PĪSTĪLLŪ^m; PĪNSO, PĪSTŪ^m to pound.

flail FLĂGĔLLŪ^m. **spile** a spicula or small (SPĪCĂ) spike.

vea-l VĬTŬLŬS 'ἰταλός, Sanscrit VĂTSĂLĂ5 a calf.

nozzle a small nose or projecting snout.

formula **bottl**e **spangl**e **rippl**e **rundl**e **hurdl**e **gravel** **thistl**e **jug-ul-ar** **fiddl**e **fabl**e **libel** **kettl**e **tile** **titl**e **circl**e **radicl**e **cudgel** cog **swivel** **pommel** **sandal** **rowel** **castl**e **citadel** **hovel** **seal** **cowl** **rill** **snail** **nail** **buckl**e **acul**eate **ocul**ar **arm-ad-illo** **peccadillo** **flotilla** **cuppel** **trowel** **asphodel** **bagatelle** **chapt-er** (for -el) **calc-ul**-us, -ate **patella** **uvula** **cereb-ellum** **hi-ll** **grill** v. **quadrille** **freckl**e

Jonquille (JŪNC-ŬS a rush, FŎLĬŪm a leaf,) the rush-leaved daffodil.

Dishabille (French noun masc. déshabillé,) a negligent or informal dress of a woman.

¶ 2. Frequentative.

nibble to nip little or often.

ramble to roam often, or continuously.

querulous habitually complaining.

shuffle to continue to shove.

post-ulate, PŌSCO I ask for; PŌSTŬLO I demand.

ul-ulation **gratulate** **trifl**e **tussl**e **puzzl**e **frizzl**e **dawdl**e **baffl**e **travel** **drivel** **tickl**e **trickl**e track **hustl**e **rustl**e **bustl**e **toddl**e **gambl**e **grappl**e **prattl**e **tittle-tattl**e **battl**e **trammel** **bubbl**e **trail** or **draggl**e **jostl**e **struggl**e **straggl**e stray **gobbl**e **wabbl**e wave **hobbl**e **tippl**e **toppl**e **whittl**e **whistl**e **whirl** **drawl** **sprawl** **scrawl** **crawl** **squall** **kneel** **smile** **fondl**e **dwindl**e **throttl**e **strangl**e **startl**e **stumbl**e **rumbl**e **fumbl**e **crumbl**e **nestl**e **wrestl**e **dazzl**e **chuckl**e **grovel**

¶ 3. Agent, subject, implement.

style (*στῦλος* a column, &c., *στύ'ω* I erect,) that which is erected. **sty-let**, **sti-l-etto**. **chyme**, (*χύω* I pour, see **-m**.)

cymbal a kind of musical instrument. (*κύμβαλον*, from *κύμβη* a hollow vessel.)

tu-t-el-ar pertaining to (TŪ-T-ĒLĂ) a safeguard. (TŬĔŎR, to take care of; T participial.) **beetl**e a beater.

spindle an implement for spinning. **thimbl**e thumb.

sorrel that (plant) which is sour.

handle **stoppl**e **ladl**e **funnel** **saddl**e **gabl**e **muscl**e **morsel** **stapl**e **girdl**e **beetl**e **shovel** **shuttl**e **scuttl**e **bundl**e **fardl**e **needl**e **nettl**e **sickl**e **chisel** **aw-l** **rail** **angl**e **ankl**e **scalpel** **cupel** **idol** (see *-OID*) **pedal** **treddl**e **poodl**e **teasel** **towel** **epistl**e **apostl**e **speculum** **chrysalis** — **shekel** **camel**

Welsh rha that forces onward, gra what shoots, graid heat, greidell a g-r-idd-le.

Obs. The frequentative L is akin to -er, as in *wander*, Ger. wandeln; *sputter*, from spit, &c.

-ledge, n.

[Wedgwood refers it to *like*. See **-ly**.]

knowledge that which is definitely known.
a-cknow-ledge **freelage**

Obs. In old English knowleche was used for the verb *acknowledge*, and knowleching, knowelageyng, &c. for the noun *knowledge*.

. . . knowlechinge ful lowely here [their] ſynnes . . . He is well worthy to have pardoun and forgevenes of his ſynne, that excuſith not his ſynne, but knowlecheth and repentith him, axinge indulgence. . . . Oure ſwete Lord God of heven that no man wol [*] periſche, but wol that we comen alle to the knowleche of him, and to the bliſſul lif that is perdurable, . . . —*Chaucer.*

. . . to teche ſondrie knowlechynges.—*Gower.*

. . . Perception is the firſt Operation of all our intellectual Faculties, and the Inlet of all Knowledg into our Minds.—*Locke*, Eſſay, (2d ed.) 1722, Bk. ii, Ch. 9.

-L-ENT, a. See -UL-ENT.

fraudulent **corpulent** **virulent** **esculent** **violent**

less, a. *without.*

[Old Frisian -las; Belg., Ger. -lōs; Dan., Swed. lös; Anglish -los, læs, -leas; Go. -laus; Isl. -laus. Old English -les, -less, -lesse; English -less, (less-ly, -less-ness,) loose, lose, loss. Go. lius-an *to lose;* perf. indic. laus.]

worthless **merciless** **senseless** **careless** **heedless** **helpless** **bloodless** **useless** **meaningless** **nameless** **artless** **nevertheless**

Byron uses breathless deathless dauntless echoless fearless helmless swordless sheathless lifeless manless sailorless timeless tideless hopeless guiltless roofless rayless cloudless seasonless heartless soul-less sleepless quenchless stingless successless tombless fleshless treeless thankless faithless shapeless countless heedless friendless careless lawless useless matchless shaftless senseless comfortless ceaseless motionless childless sonless parentless spouseless wordless answerless hapless houseless.

Talfourd uses stainless smokeless passionless objectless rippleless waveless joyless. Sir Francis Head (Paris in 1851,) mentions "one blindless shutterless window."

Bulwer uses bloomless breadless breathless (dead,) careless childless

* The true reading seems to require this *wol* before the previous *that.*

endless fatherless friendless frontless (impudent,) fruitless restless rayless guiltless headless lifeless penniless powerless reckless relentless ruthless senseless shoreless sleepless smileless stainless thankless worthless.

> He feemed breathleffe, hartleffe, faint, and wan;—*Spenser.*
>
> And bootleffe make the breathleffe hufwife churne.—*Shakespeare.*
>
> Ah! how unjuft to nature, and himfelf,
> Is thoughtlefs, thanklefs, inconfiftent man!—*Young*, Nt. 2.

-let, n. dim.

[A double or surdiminutive.]

rivulet a small stream. (RĪVŬS a stream, RĪVŬLŬS.)

flageolet, for **flutelet**. (Low Latin *flauteolus* a small flute. FLŌ, FLĀTŬm, to blow; FLĀTŎR a piper.)

driblet, **droplet** a small drop. **samlet** a young salmon.

bracelet, a band or ornament for the wrist or arm. (Ital. bracciale, braccialetto. Gr. βρᾰχίων the arm. Irish braccaile, a sleeve or bracelet; brac *arm*, cal *covering*.)

streamlet martlet hamlet frontlet gauntlet chaplet cutlet ringlet circlet eyelet goblet driblet corselet rundlet — †**popillot**, †**popelote**, †**popelot**, †**popelet** a puppet.

Coch-ineal, a surdiminutive in N and L, Lat. cŏccŭs a kind of scarlet insect.

Armlet, a ring worn above the elbow, an ĀRMĪLLĂ; adj. ĀRMĪLLĀTŬS wearing an armilla.

Coverlet has -let for LĔCTŬS a bed, and as the word will not be accepted as a diminutive, it has to some extent become the heteronym *coverlid*.

Amulet is from the Arabic.

Obs. Diminutives are frequently represented by dentals as in στηθῡ'-Νιον, στηθῑ'Διον a small (στῆθος) breast; zodiac see *-D-*, ham**let**, kitte**n**, radicle.

-lic, n.

[Turkish -lic, -lÿq, as in ĒJĪ *good*, ĒJĪLIC *goodness;* sagh *safe*, sāgh-lÿq *safety;* صو ȿū *water*, ȿūsïə (waterless) *thirsty*, ȿūsïəlÿq *thirst*, ȿUSMĂQ *to be thirsty*, ȿùlămăq *to water, give to drink*, ȿùlănmăq *to be watered, to leak.*]

pashawlic (pāʃālÿq) the jurisdiction of a (پاشا) pashaw.

Frolic see **-ly**. Garlic see **-lock**.

-lin, n. dim.

[Ohg. -līn, -leen; Ger. -lein. Perhaps a surdiminutive (-L, -en,) influenced by the adj. k-leen, ch-līn, k-lein *little*. The Turkish diminutive suffix -lin has an accidental resemblance.]

dunlin a small snipe of a brownish color.

javelin a small gaff. (Gaelic gabhla a spear, gabhlam to shoot out.)

goblin, Welsh cw a quick motion, côb a thump, coblyn (n. dim.) a thumper, *rapper*, fiend.

> . . . . bugs and hobgoblings.—*Holland*, Plinie, 1635.

Obs. -lin has been confounded with -ling by perverting -ing to -in (as in saying 'feelins' for *feelings*,) and (in restoring the proper sound) making a new perversion of -in to -ing, as in saying 'capting' for *captain*. See **-ing**. It is probable therefore that a diminutive form like *gosling* is for *goslin*.

> The *Goſſelin* Endeavour'd to do That too;—*L'Eſtrange*, Fable CCXXII, 1692.

-ling, n. *a person or thing that.*

[Ger., Belg., Angl. -l-ing (as in Ang. irθling *a farmer*.) Danish -l-ing, -n-ing. Ohg. -ling, -linc, -linch. A double suffix akin to -ing, n.]

underling a person under the authority of another.

witling one who imitates a wit. **fopling** a petty fop.

scantling a narrow piece of timber.

gosling, Dan. gæsling, a young goose.

darling, Ang. deórling, one that is dear.

nestling **groundling** **sterling** **fatling** **bantling** **firstling**

Obs. 1. German has forms like 'kämmerling' a chamberlain; 'hauptling' a chieftain; 'fremdling' a foreigner; and 'flüchtling' a fugitive.

Obs. 2. As a person *found* or *nursed* is more likely to be a child than an adult, *foundling, nursling* (and some others) have acquired a diminutival sense. *Sapling*, a tree with much sap-wood, acquires the secondary meaning of a young tree.

> Thoſe ſpoylefull Picts, and ſwarming Eaſterlings,
> . . . . and forrein ſcatterlings—*Spenser*.

. . . . . complete series of frogs, from the full-grown froggy . . . down to that minute frogling—a tadpole.—*Th. Hood*.

16

-lion, n.

posti'lion, French postillon. **pavi'lion,** French pavillon.

-lock, n. *a plant.*

[λα'χ-ανον *pot-herbs;* LĔG-ŪMĔN *peas, beans, &c.;* LĀC-TŪCĂ *le-ttuce.* Belg. look, Eng. leek.]

char-lock a plant which is (Welsh chwerw) bitter. Called also **kedlock, kedlack,** Welsh ceden what sticks together, shaggy hair; ceddw mustard; cedys faggots, bundles, whence *cadis, caddis* or *caddice.*

hemlock a plant or weed of the genus CŌNĪŪM.

gar-lic, as if spear-leek, Irish carr a spear.

> Wel loved he garleek, oynouns, and ek leekes,—*Chaucer.*

Wedlock, Ang. -lac an offering.—*Klipstein.*
Hump-l-ock a small hump or heap.

(LOGy, n. *a discourse; science.*)

herpetology the science of rep-tiles, as serp-ents and lizards. (*ἑρπετ-ὁς* creeping; *ἕρπω,* SĔRPO, RĒPO, to c-reep.)

-L-ous, a., n.

[Lat. a., n. -L-ŬS (-Ă, Ŭm;) -λ-ος (-α, -ον.) Sanscrit L-Ă5 (-Ā, -Ă.) See -L-US, -L, -UL-oUS.]

glandulous pertaining to glands.

credulous prone or ready (CRĒDĔRĔ) to believe.

angulous stylus, see -L, ¶ 3. **sedulous tremulous nubilous pendulous scrofulous frivolous sciolous fou-l** *φαῦλος*

-L-US, m., -L-A, f., -L-UM, neut.

[Sanscrit -L-A5 (-Ā, -Ā;) Greek -λ-ος (-α, -ον.)]

nautilus, see -L, ¶ 1. **calculus stimulus regulus Tantalus ranunculus—formula nebula fecula—pendulum speculum**

-ly, a. *like;* adv. *manner.*

[-λικ-ος (-η, -ον.) -LĬC-ŬS (-Ă, -Ŭm.) Sansc. LACS *like.* Gothic ga-leiks *like,* ga-leik-on *to compare,* ga-leik-a *similarity.* Ang. -lic, -lice, -li, ge-lic; Ohg. -lih; German -lich, g-leich; Isl. lik, lig, alik, glik; Sw. lik; Dan. lig; Belg. -lÿk, ge-lijk; old Eng. -lik, -lick, -lich, -lych, -liche, -lie, -li; Eng. like *similar,* -lic (in fro-lic,) -ly, -li-, -ch (in su-ch, whi-ch.) Ss. root LIG to *approach, join.*]

friendly like (in the manner of) a friend.

heartily in a hearty manner; with the heart engaged.

masterly verily truly homely elderly freely openly richly advisedly boldly northerly duly love-li-ly sur-li-ly

And ſodenliche vpon me renneth.—*Gower*, died 1402.

. . . clerelye, frelye, ſyngulerlye and hooly . . . —*Fabyan*, died 1512.

Others conceive that thoſe Countries did not at firſt perfectly receive the *Latin* from the *Romans*, but did onely make uſe of the moſt principal *radical words;*—*Wilkins*, 1668.

I am not writing insolently, but as shortly and clearly as I can.—*Ruskin*, born 1819.

Obs. 1. In daily, yearly, &c. -ly is frequentative.

Obs. 2. In admirably, forcibly, &c. the suffix is -ble and -y.

Obs. 3. In nobly, the suffix is not -ly, but -y attached to -il of NŌBĬLĬS.

Obs. 4. -ly may be partly due to Danish -ledes, as in ligeledes *likewise;* saa *so,* saaledes *thus.*

Obs. 5. Chaucer uses costlewe (costly,) and dronkelew (given to drink.)

-M, intensive.

tremble, τρέω and τρέ-μ-ω. **therm**al, θέρ-ω, to warm; θέρ-μ-ομαι to become warm.

drea-m, **dorm**ant, DŌR-MĬO I sleep; Ss. root DRĀI to *sleep.*

-M-, participial.

[Sanscrit participle -MĀN-Ă5 (Ā, -Ă.) -όμεν-ος (-α, -ον.) This perfect passive and participial -M- indicates the action of the verb. It is also followed by the participle present -ων,[b] used substantively.]

pheno-m-enon an appearing. (☞ φαίνω, to appear.)

gno-m-on[b] that which enables one (+γνόω,) to k-now.

ichneumon[b] an animal which (ἰχνεύ-ω,) tracks.

demon[b] one that ($\delta\alpha\acute{\iota}$-$\omega$,) allots; destiny; a good or bad spirit.

eleemosynary, see -*SYNE*. **cremation** **al-um-nus** **autumn** **column**, see -MIN.

Obs. M (like T, N, SK,) is a strengthening element, as in cla-m-or-ous; CLĀMO I shout, from CĂLO, κᾰλέω I call; perfect passive κέκλημαι. φά'ω, to shine, φηΜι' to bring to light; to say, whence **eu-phe-m-ism** (φάΣΚω to assert. See **-esce**.)

-M-, superlative.

See **prime**, under **-im** *most;* and **-mer**, Obs. 2.

-m, **-me**, -*MA*, -*ME*, -MEN, -MIN-, -MON, **-ment**, n. *that which, that which is.*

[-μα[a] (gen. -ματ-ος; Lat. -MA, gen. -MAT-IS,) -μη,[b] -μος,[c] -μις,[d] -μην,[e] -μων,[f] -μον,[g] -μονη. Latin -MĔN[h] (gen. -MĬN-ĬS,) -MENTUM[i] (*t* educed,) -MO[k] (gen. -MŌN-ĬS,) (see -MŌN-ĬŪM -ĬĂ,) -IMA.[l] Pol., Bohem. -ma. Sansc. -MA, -MAN, -MA,. They indicate the result, effect, or object of the verb. See the footnote at -ANT; and -M- participial.]

bloom that which blows. **gleam** that which glows.

worm that which (VĔR-TO,) turns; a contorting animal.

stem that which (ST-O,) stands. **sham** show, deception.

brim ⟂ brow **seam** sow **team** tug **qualm** quail **s-cream** cry

palm the inside of the hand. (Welsh pa *what forms a continuity;* pal *a flat body, a spade;* palm *a spread, a flag;* palf *a blade, paw, palm.* See -B-. Latin PĀLĂ a spade.)

blossom **boom** **beam** **foam** **fathom** **claim** **gloom** **loom**ing **loam** **flam** **lime** **slime** **blame** **flame** **spume**

prism πρῖ'σμα something sawn; a prism. (πρῖ'ω I saw; perfect passive πέ-πρισμαι I have been sawn.)

chasm an abyss. (⁺χάω, to stand open; χά'-ζω, to clear a place; perfect passive κέ-κασμ-αι; perfect middle κε-καvδ-α. χαί-ν-ω, to open, gape, utter; χανδὸς (δ educed from ν,) gaping wide; χήν a gan-der; κε-χηνοτές gapers, fools; whence **ca-chinn-ation** *a fool's laugh.*)

psalm ψαλμός. (Perfect passive ἔψαλμαι, of ψάλλω, to play a stringed instrument.)

plume something with which to (πλέω, πλόω, πλῶμι,) sail.

fame a speaking of. (FĀRĪ to speak.)

har-m-ony ἁρμονία. (ἁρμόζω to join, to tune; ἅρμα union; +ἄρω, to adjust.)

hie-m-al pertaining to winter. (χέω, χύω, to pour; perfect passive κέ-χυμαι; χειμὼν stormy rainy weather. See M participial, -ων,[b] -*ON*, ¶ 2. χεῖμα, HĬE·MS winter weather; Sanscrit HIMA,—whence also **chy-me, chy-le, gu-sh.**)

foramen an aperture; the result or effect of boring. (FŎRO I bore.)

panorama a view on all sides. (πᾶν all; ὁράω I see; perfect passive ἑώρᾱμαι.)

drama-t-ic that which is acted. (δράω to do, act; perfect passive δέδρᾱμαι.)

dog-ma-t-ic that which seems true. (δοκ-έω, to think, seem; perfect passive δέ-δογ-μαι.)

dram, δραχμή a certain coin; a handful. (δραγμὶς a pinch; δράσσομαι, to grasp; perfect passive δέδραγμαι.)

diadem[a] (δέω, to tie; perfect passive δέδεμαι; διά across.)

stratagem[a] (στρᾰτὸς an army; ἡγέομαι I lead.)

axiom ἀξίωμα an admitted or established principle. ☞ ἀξιόω. **idiom** ἰδίωμα something, as a form of expression (ἴδιος) peculiar.

dilemma **diploma** **enigma**[ac] **stigma** **aroma** **miasma** **asthma** **comma**[a] **numismatic**[a] **theme**[a] **scheme**[a] **rheum**[a] **schism**[a(bc)] **phlegm** (φλεγμονή) **term**[at] **alum**[h] **at-mosphere** **an-imosity** **diagram**[a] **symptom**[a] **phantasm**[a] **problem**[a] **poem**[a] **emblem**[a] **acme**[b] **spasmodic**[c] **epidermis**[d] **gnomon**[f] **ichneumon**[f] see -M-. **pneumon**ia **etymon**[g] **thy-me**[cg] **cal-amus** **clematis** see -*IS*.

na-me no-min-al	Lat. NŌ-MĔN	Sansc. NAMAN
term ter-min-ate	" TĔRMĔN	" TARMAN
straw stramin-eous	" STRĀMĔN	" STARIMAN *litter.*

tegument[hi] that which covers,—is made to cover; the means of covering. (☞ TĔGO, to cover.)

germ[h] a bud. (GĔR-O, to bear.)

volume[h] something rolled up, as an ancient book; a modern book; a mass of smoke, &c. (VOLV-O, to roll.)

regimen, ☞ RĔGO I regulate. **charm** CĂRMĔN a song.

acu'men, ĂCŬO I sharpen. **examen** **examin**e **specimen** **abdōmen** **bitūmen** **albūmen** **legumin**ous[h] **discrimin**ate[h] **germin**ate[h] **semin**ary[h] **document**[i] **testament** **nutriment** **ornament** **monument** **movement** **moment** **aliment**, ☞ ĂLO. **judgment** **torment** **testimony** **victim**[l]

salmon[k] a fish of (ἅλς) the sea. (SĂL-ĬO, ἅλλομαι, to spring up, rush, throb; Hebrew sālāh to raise up.)

Atom ἄ-τομ-ος indivisible. (τέμνω I cut.)

Sermon, pulmon-ary. See -N declensional. *Simoom,* Coptic ϧmom.

Obs. 1. The -od- in spasm-od-ic may be due to the adverbial form σπασμώδης. See **-oid**.

Obs. 2. A part removed is indicated in 'segment' from SĔCO I cut; 'fragment' the part brok-en off; 'cement' (from CÆDO I cut,) primarily, building-stone; 2d, rubbish for filling spaces; 3d, clay, mortar.

Obs. 3. Cinnamon κίνναμον is from the Hebrew qĭnnāmōn, from qānēh cane.

-m, dative.

[An old singular and plural dative case sign. See **-mer**, **-om**, adv.]

Obs. The obsolete dative occurs in the expression "I gave him food," as compared with the objective "I gave him away."

him **whom** **them** **seldom** +**whilom**

-M, accusative.

rĕ'quĭem repose. (An accusative of the 5th declension.)

-m, n. diminutive.

film a thin fell (PĔLL-ĬS) or skin.

culm coal in small fragments.

-M, adverbial. See -IM.

idem IDĒM the same. **ibidem** ĬBĪDĒM in the same place. (ĬBĪ there.) **item** (ĬTĒM,) is a noun in English.

(-*MAN*cy, n. *divination.*)

[μαν-τ-εία divination; *μαίνομαι, to rave; μάν-τ-ις a diviner; μăν-ί'α madness.* Not properly a suffix.]

cheiromancy palmistry; divination from the (χείρ) hand.
Mantis a genus of insects of singular appearance.
necromancy divination by questioning the (νεκρὸς) dead.

With all the *necromantics* of their art,—*Young*, Nt. 8.

-*MA-T-*, -*MA-T-IC*, -*MA-T*e. See -*MA*, T declensional.

cli-mate **pris-matic** **dra-ma-t-ic**, see **-m.**

Obs. For rhythmic a New York journal uses rhythmatic(-ally,) which cannot be formed from ῥυθμὸς rhythm.

-M-ATe, a.

[The superlative -IM-US, with -ATe.]

prox-im-ate **ultimate** **intimate** **primate**

-me, **-mo**, a. *most.* See -IMUS.

supreme, (SŬPĔR over, SŬPĔRĬŎR higher,) SU·PRĒMŬS uppermost. **extreme** most external.

-MEN, **-ment**, n. See **-m.**

-mer, a. *more;* **-most**, *most.* See **-er**, **-est**.

[Sw. as in närmare *nearer*, närmast *nearest;* English (-mer wanting) -mest, -most. The *m* is due to the old dative case singular, as in

	Gothic	*Nordish*	*German*	*Anglish*
Nom.	god-s	gōð-r	gut-er	god *good.*
Gen.	god-is	goð-s	gut-es	god-es *of good.*
Dat.	god-amma	goð-um	gut-em	god-um *to, for, with good.*
Accus.	god-ana	goð-an	gut-en	god-ne *good.*

From Anglish ut *out* we may infer utum *to the out,* ytemest ut-m-ost *out* (to the) *most;* but the Gothic ūtana *beyond, outmost;* innana *within;* aftana *from behind,* simulate the accusative, or a different form of the dative.]

inmost farthest in. (Go. innuma; Ang. innema, innemest.)
aftermost (Go. aftuma, aftumists; Ang. aftema, æftemest.)
for-m-er **fore-m-ost** **far-th-er-more** **farthermost**

The formift was alway behinde.—*Chaucer.*

Obs. 1. Although the suffix -most has been confused with *most* from *much,* the two are usually distinguished in pronunciation.

Obs. 2. *Former* may be due to *pri-me-er,* or to *foremost,* and this to the superlatives Gothic fruma and frumists, Sansc. PRATHAMA5, Lat. PRĪMŬS, fem. PRĪMĂ first, equivalent to *primest* or *fore-m-est.* See **-im,** a.

Obs. 3. In Swedish, ut *out,* and om *over,* form utom *beyond, without.*

-MIN, -MN. See *-MA.*

[-MĬN-ŬS, fem. -MĬN-Ă; -MN-ŬS, fem. -MN-Ă. -M- and -N- participial.]

alumnus, fem. **alumna**, one who is (☞ ĂLO, ĂLĬTŪm,) cherished. **autumn** the season of (ĀVC-T-ŬS) increase.
column CŎLŪMNĂ, from CŎLŬMĔN a prop, CŎL-ŬS a staff.
terminus TĒRMĬNŬS a boundary; a limit; an end.

-MONy, -MONI-.

[-MŌN-ĬĂ,[a] -MŌN-ĬŪM.[b] Akin to -MEN; and -MO, gen. -MON-IS. See **-m.**]

moni-al, -moni-al-ly, -monious, -moniously, -moniousness.

acrimony[a] that which is imbued with the quality of austerity or harshness. (ĀCĔR sharp, gen. ĀCRĬS.)
sancti-mony[a] **-monious** **ceremony**[a] **-monial** **testimony**[b] **patrimony**[b] **alimony**[b] **matrimony**[b] **parsimoniousness**

-M-UL-

sti-m-ul-us that which goads (stick-s) or urges.
cumulate (ἀμ-άομαι) to heap together.

-M-US, -M-A, -M-UM, n.

[-MŬS, (fem. -MA, neut. -MUᵐ;) Sansc. -MA5, (-MĀ, -MĂ;) -μος (-μη, -μον.) The noun suffix -ŭs preceded by -M-. See *-MA.*]

hippo-potamus the river horse. (ἵππος horse, ποτἄμὸς river, freshwater stream; πόω I drink; πότημᾰ a drink; πότιμος pot-able.)

isthmus a neck of land. (εἶμῐ I go; infinitive ἰέσθαι.)

marasmus a kind of consumption. (μᾰραίνω I wither; Attic perfect tense με-μάρασ-μαι.)

ani-mus **ani-mos-ity** **chrys-anthe-mum** (-μον) golden flowered. **calamus** CĂLĂMŪS κᾰ'λᾰμος, Ss. CĂLĂMĂ5 a reed; κᾰλάμη straw, whence **halm**, **shawm**, **calumet**. **mesembryanthemum** ☞ MĔDĬŪS.

Didymus a twin. **tenesmus** **strabismus** **balsam** βαλσαμον

-mus, n.

[Latin verbs of the 1st person plural, present tense; used as nouns in English.]

mittimus we send. **mandamus** we command.
ignoramus we know not.

-N-, intensive.

[A strengthening element, as in αὔξω and αὐξᾰ'Νω, to *increase, augment.* Akin to the adjective suffix *-N-ος*, -N-US, and participle present -ωN, -ANs. See -ANT.]

do-n-ate to give, present. (DO I give, grant; DŌNŪᵐ the thing give-n; DO-N-O I give, bestow.) RĔGO I reg-ulate, RE·G-N-O I reig-n.

diaphanous to give light (δῐᾰ̀) through. (φᾰ́ω, to make clear, appear; ☞ φαίνω.)

epiphany appearance. See *EPI.*

tunny a kind of fish. (θύννος, fem. θύννη; θύω, to rush; θύων rushing; θῦνω to rush furiously.)

cylinder, κύλινδρος a roller. (κυλίω, κυλίνδω, to roll; δ educed from ν.)

Stephen στέφᾰνος a crown. (στέφω I wreathe, encircle.)

spurn (σπείρω I drive, SPERNO I disdain.)

yaw-n, ga-n-der, cachi-nn-ate. See **-m**, *CHAINO.*

hieropha-n-t sycophant pha-n-tom fantastic tympanum **machin**e **technic stagnat**e **pro-cra-s-t-in-at**e **con-tam-in-ate sign run contem***n* **constern**ation

Obs. 1. *n* is part of the stem in *stain, explain, stun, remain,* and others. *Gangre-n-e,* see -AN.

Obs. 2. *Ordain* ŌRDĬNO, from the genitive case of ŌRD-O (-ĬNĬS,) a rank, an order.

-N, n. declensional.

[The sign of the base, or crude form of Latin nouns (of the third declension,) as in SĂNGVĬS *blood,* gen. SANGVĬN-ĬS *of blood;* SĔRMO a speech, SĔRMŌN-ĬS *of a speech;* PŪLMO *the lungs,* gen. PŪLMŌN-ĬS; TĔNDO (gen. TĔNDĬN-ĬS,) *a tendon;* CĂRO *flesh,* gen. CA'RN-ĬS; TŪRBO *a top,* gen. TŪRBĬN-ĬS. Greek nominative -ων, as in σίφων (gen. σίφωνος,) *a siphon;* Latin SĪPHŌ, gen. SĪPHŌN-ĬS. Greek κτείς *a comb,* gen. κτενός; μέλᾱς *black,* gen. μέλᾰνος.]

sangui-nary **sermo-n pulmon**ary **tendon turbin**ate **carn**age **margin carbon session option motion origin su-spicion virgin legion gudgeon pigeon falcon ratio-n-**al **option**al **cardin**al **Ciceron**ian **centurion ordi-n-**al **onion occasion**al **provision**al—**siphon icon ctenoid mela-n-choly**

Obs. 1. **dolphin** is both δελφῖν and δελφῖς, gen. δελφῖνος.

Obs. 2. **human**e has both this -N, and that of **-nous.**

Obs. 3. *Famine* (FĂMĒS, gen. FĂMĬS,) and *order* (ŌRDO, gen. ŌRDĬNĬS,) are false forms.

Obs. 4. *Cupid* (CŬPĪDO,) and *soap* (SĀPO,) have lost the case termination.

-n, infinitive. See **-en**, v.

-n, diminutive. See **-en**, n.

lamper-n a small lamprey. **citter-n** a small guitar.

-N, adverbial.

[Anglish -an, -on, motion *from a place,* as norðan *from the north;* feorran *from far;* Ger. fer-n *far.* Danish adverbial and prepositional suffix -en, as in ud *out,* uden *without* (deprived of;) ned *down,* neden *below.* Bohemian podoba *likeness,* podobný *similar.* Welsh gwaith *turn, time;* weith-on *this time, now.* Greek dubitative particle ἄν. Latin ĒN *behold;* DĔĪN *then;* interrogative particle ĂN *whether?;* CON-, σὺν *with.* Gr. νυν, νυ, (Ger. nun) *now;* μὴν *truly, yes;* οὖν *then;* μᾱκ-ρ-ᾱ`ν *far;* πέραν *beyond;* πρωΐ *early,* πρὶν *before,* πρώην *formerly.* Ss. SAMA *a year,* SAMĪNA *annually.**]

when then hence be-hind even often than yon soon again non- souther-n even +beforen +beforn +withouten

Obs. 1. The stem of **whe**-n-ce appears in πῇ thither; πῆ how; ποῖ whither; ποῦ, πόθῐ where; πώς somehow; πόθεN whence; πότε when; πόσος how much, (Ionic κόσος, see Obs. 3;) Latin qVO whither, qVI who; qVAndŏ, Ger. wann, Eng. when. Ger. wo where, wie how. Eng. who, we, why, wha-t, &c.

Obs. 2. The stem of **the**-n-ce appears in Eng. the, thee, thou, thy, thus, this, those, them, there, that. Ger. die the; da here, there; dann the-n. Gr. τὶ any, τί what?; neuter article το the, this. Latin TŪm then; sīc thus (Eng. so.) Ss. TAT that.

Obs. 3. The stem of **he**-n-ce appears in Eng. he, how, he-re; in the Gr. masc. article ὁ, fem. ἡ the; ὥς how; ᾗ, οὗ where; ὧδε, ἧδε, Latin HIc, Ger. hie *he-re.*

Obs. 4. *When* and *Then* have no corresponding form for *Hen-ce,* but it appears in the Danish hen thither, and German hin toward, along; English be-hin-d, hinder, with *d* educed.

-*N* n. masculine.

pæan a song of deliverance. (*Παιὰν* Apollo as the god of physic; a deliverer from sickness or danger; a hymn to Apollo; a triumphal song. παύω I restrain, cause to cease, relieve.) **pæon peon-y**

---

* Accidental resemblances appear in Jakutisch (Yacootish) kÿn *day,* kÿn-yn *daily;* Tatar munda *here,* mundan *from here;* Turkish orda *there,* ordan *from there;* a word which is thus analysed by Dr. F. L. O. Rœhrig:—o *that,* jer (with Latin J,) *place,* den *from;* but in putting these together the vowels must be harmonised according to a peculiar law, making o jar dan, from which the *j* must be excluded (oardan) and ar transposed (oradan,) whence ordan *thence.* Baba *a father,* babadan *from a father;* babaler *fathers,* babalerdan *from fathers.* Turkish is without native *pre*positions in the English sense, postpositions being used instead, and it is supposed that the Greek and Latin case-signs are the remnants of such postpositions. The objectionable terms *preposition* and *postposition* might be replaced with *perithesis.*

-N-, participial. See -N-US.

-*N*, n.

[-να, -νη, -ῆνη, &c. -νος, -νον, -ανον, -ανος, -ν. See -EN, n.]

sel-en-ite a shining mineral. (σελήνη the moon. See -*OID.*)

org-an, ὄργ-ανον. (ἔργ-ον a w-ork.) **resin,** ῥητί'νη. (ῥέω, to flow.)

fer-n, πτέριν, πτερὶς, akin to πτερὸν a plume, a wing. (πετάω, πτάω to spread, expand.) **cum-in** a kind of plant. **fran-**tic **phren-**o-logy **dolphin**

Beac-on—Welsh ig what is sharp; p-ig a pointed end, a beak; pigwn a cone, turret, beacon.

Obs. 1. In German and Danish, -en is a suffix for ordinary nouns, some of which are formed from verbs. Akin to these are **blain coffin dozen haven kitchen oven puffin raven sloven token waggon**

Obs. 2. Hebrew has proper names in -n, as LŌTĀN covering (Genesis 36 :29;) DĂRQŌN (Ezra 2 :56,) from DĀRĂQ to scatter. Leviath-an Abadd-on SĀTĀN.

-N-AL, a. *quality.*

paternal fraternal vernal infernal internal supernal

Obs. For optional, rational, &c., see -N declensional.

-ne, -n, n. See -*N,* N-US.

grain GRĀNŪ^m^ the seed of cereal plants; a particle.

prune PRŪNŪ^m^ a plum. (προῦμνος, προύνη, PRŪNŬS a plum-tree.) **throne** θρόνος a chair of state. (θράω I sit.)

doctrine DO·CTRĪNA that which is taught. ☞ DŎCĔO.

-nel, n.

grap-n-el a small anchor. (A surdiminutive, Fr. grap-in, grap-ill, Ger. krapfen a hook.)

dar-n-el an injurious weed. (Ang. derian to injure.)

char-n-el, with -N declensional.

colonel the commander of a (column or) regiment.

-ner, n.

partner one who takes part with another.
vintner one who deals in wine.

-ness, n. *quality of being; that which.*

[Ang. -nesse, -nes, -nis, -nys; old Eng. -nisse, -nesse, -nes; old high Ger. -nessi, -nissa; Belg. -nis; Ger. -niss. Gothic -assus, -in-assus, -in-being inflectional, as in ibn-assus *evenness, equity;* lekeis, (Eng. leech) *a physician,* lekinon *to cure,* lekinassus *a curing;* vans *lacking,* vanan *to lack,* van-eins *wan-t,* vaninassus *the quality of wanting;* θiuda *people,* θiudans *a king* (i.e. the *ruling,*) θiudinon *to rule,* θiudinassus *rule.*]

firmness the quality of being firm.
wilderness that (place) which is wild.
witness he who knows. (Ang. vitan to know.)
goodness meanness proneness likeness fixedness

Holland's Plinie, 1635, has—bignesse goodnesse largenesse holines kindnes sicknes.

Byron has — freshness darkness seriousness fierceness loneliness dimness smilingness wantonness forgetfulness hoariness firmness.

Talfourd uses—loveliness listlessness nobleness spotlessness massiveness entireness venerableness.

As well in Chriſtendom as in Hetheneſſe
And ever honoured for his worthineſſe.—*Chaucer.*

His noble perſone, with al gentilnes;
He is the welle of alle parfitnes,
The very Redemir of al mankinde,
Him love I beſt with herte, and ſoule, and mind.—*id.*

. . . there are many perſons, who, by a natural unchearfulneſs of heart, . . . give themſelves up a prey to grief and melancholy.—Spectator, Sept. 26, 1712.

Brilliancy and freshness may easily be pushed into rawness and crudeness; . . . transparency may easily degenerate into flimsiness . . . spirit and cleanness of touch quickly run into hardness, and softness into woolliness and want of precision.—*John Opie*, 1807.

Obs. 1. -ness forms abstract nouns, from nouns and adjectives.

Obs. 2. The Germanic -ness is used for -ty in words of Latin origin, forming hibrids like plausibleness for plausibility, corruptible—, tractible—, credible—, rabid—, torpid—; and *oddity* is used for oddness.

Obs. 3. In some geographical names, -ness (Sanscrit and Islandic nas; Ang. nese; Saxon nes; Irish -nas, -nis; Polish nos; Eng. nose,) means a cape or promontory, as in Sheerness and Stromness.

17

-N-ITy, n. See -AN-ITy.

[-N-ous;[a] -N- intensive;[b] -N declensional.[c]]

im-por-tu-n-ity[b] that which is (im-) not opportune; or which is introduced unseasonably; hence, vexatious solicitation. (-T- intensive of POR-TO I bear, carry.)

op-portunity fitness, the right moment.

vicinity[a] VĪCĪNĬTĀS nearness, neighborhood. (VĪCŬS a village, a quarter; VĪCĪNŬS similar, neighboring.)

Trinity[a] **fraternity**[a] **divinity**[a] **indemnity**[b] **consanguinity**[c]
N is part of the root in vanity, lenity.

-N-oUS, -NE-oUS, a., n. *pertaining to; quality.* See N-US.

membranous made of, or resembling membrane.

alie-n pertaining to another place. (ĂLĬŬS ἄλλος other.)

alter-n-ate, **sub-alter-n**, ĂLTĔR one of two, other.

sub-terra-neous under (TĔRRĂ) the ground.

ruinous tending to (RŬĪNĂ) destruction. (RŬO I rush or fall down, am overthrown.)

ple-ni-t-ude fulness. (PLĒNŬS full.)

reign RĒGNŪ[m]. **jour-ney** DĬŪR-NŬS. **resinous**, see *-N.*
extraneous **erroneous** **extemporaneous** **instantaneous** **spontaneous** **cutaneous** **miscellaneous** **som-n-olent** **sign**
Diaphanous, see -N intensive; ferruginous, see -AGO; selenite, see *-N.*

-N-US, m. -NA, f. -NUM, neut. n.

[Ss. -N-A5 (fem. -Ā, neut. -Ă,) -ṆA5. -ν-ός (-η, -ον;) -N-ŬS (-Ă, -Ū[m].) Gothic -eins. Adjectives, participles and nouns (mostly passive,) akin to -T-ŬS, **-ty**, and appearing in the participial -μενος (given under -M- participial) and -N- participial of -AN, -ANeous, -N-AL. -NUS the more correct form of -nous, is preserved in proper names.]

te'tanus **echi'nus** **alu-m-nus** **Africa'nus** **Luca'nus** **Silva'nus** **Sile'nus** **Neptunus** **Vulcanus** **Vulcan** **volcano** **tyrant** τύραννος **chimney** κάμινος **are'na** **fari'na** **re'tina** **alumna** **Maria'na** **Antonina** **hye'na—madona** **tympanum**, see -UM. **arcanum** (pl. **arcana**) **interregnum** **labdanum—laudanum**

-O-, adverbial.

[A Greek (-ω) and Latin adverbial signs, a in *EX-O outwards; AN-O above, up; CAT-O below;* INTRŌ *within;* RĒTRŌ *backwards;* PRĪMŌ *at first.* Gothic -o. Russian -o.]

-O-, connective.

This occurs in compounds like **serio**-comic, **cumulo**-stratus, **Syro**-chaldaic, **gloss-o**-logy, **psych-o**-logy, **ge-o**-graphy. See § 53.

-O, declensional.

Italian and Spanish have this form; or, Latin -US, -Uᵐ have receded to o, as in the following examples—

solo alto portico nuncio studio fresco virtuoso canto intaglio punctilio motto bravo negro mulatto mestizo lazaretto incognito ditto presto manifesto peccadillo agio sirocco stucco buffalo calico rotundo mezzotinto

Grotto (from crypt, κρυπτὸς hidden,) is a mistake for Italian grotta, French grotte, Old French crota, croute, crote, crot—

Trova une crote soz terre.—Roman d'Atys.
Found a grot under ground.

-O, nominative.

[A Latin and Greek nominative case sign, as in ἠχὼ ECHŌ *echo.*]

halo tiro umbo pl. **umbones torpedo ratio Erato** ἐρᾰτώ
Hero is for ἥρως HĒRŌS, *embryo* for embryon, and *eringo* for Eryngium.

-O, genitive. See § 53.

-O, ablative.

in-nu-endo an oblique hint. (IN at; NŬO I nod; NŬENDO by nodding.) **proviso** a clause *pro*-vid-ed or seen to *before*-hand. (VĬDĔO I see.)

folio, the ablative case of FŎLĬŬᵐ a leaf, stands for *in folio.*
quarto octavo duodecimo limbo in **extenso** in **situ**

-O, imperative.

memento let them remember; a memorial. (The third person plural active imperative of the second conjugation. ☞ MĔMĬNĪ, to remember.)

-ock, n. *small.* See -C-le.

hillock a small hill. **hummock** a small hump.

pinnock a small bird with a (PĒNNĂ) tuft; the titmouse.

shamr-ock, Irish seamróg a small (seamar) clover.

bullock a young ox; Irish bo *a bovine animal*, bol *a cow*, bolog *a heifer*, of which the masculine form is bolán. Halliwell says "A bullock is, properly speaking, a calf in the second year."

haddock, Irish cud-óg, from codh *head*, but probably equivalent to a small cod-fish, i.e. head-fish.

ruddock the *red*breast. **lark** or **laverock** **burrock** **bannock** **tarrock** (a gull) **whinock** **battock**

Hammock is of doubtful origin; Belg. hangemack and hangmatt (as if *hang* and *mat;*) old Swedish hama to cover; Brasilian hamacca (Marcgrave, 1648,) but probably not native.

> The merry larke hir mattins ſings aloft;
> The thruſh replyes; the mavis deſcant plays:
> The ouzell ſhrills: the ruddock warbles ſoft;—*Spenser.*

-ock, n. *large.*

girrock a large (gar) fish.

paddoc a large (Ang. pada, Belg. padde, Sw. padda) toad.

pollock a fish named from its large head or pōll.

tussock a large (Fr. tasse) tuft of grass, as tass-el (tossel) is a small tuft. **puttock** a large (BŪTĔO) hawk; the kite.

+**waddock** a large piece.—*Halliwell.*

Obs. There is much difficulty in distributing words in -ock properly. Thus *baddock* is both a fish and a bird, and as a bird (a gull,) it is larger than the *tarrock*, and smaller than several other British gulls. *Killockdoe* is a name of the black cock, the curious tail of which may have recalled *killock* (a small anchor,) but such guesses are deceptive.

-ock, n. verbal.

finnock, phinock a kind of Scottish trout from twelve to sixteen inches long, whiter than the allied kinds, and with white ventral fins. (Irish finn white.)

cammoc the herb rest-harrow. (W. cam crooked, bent.)

havoc destruction. (Welsh haf that is apt to spread; hafog a spreading about; devastation.)

hawk a bird of prey. (Welsh hebog; hof that hovers.)

mattock a kind of hoe. (Welsh matog.)

(*OD*, n.)

[Gr. ὁδὸς *a way, mode, journey;* Latin -ŏdŭs. Not properly a suffix.]

met-hod a mode or system (*μετᾰ̀*) according to rule.

synod (*σῠ̀ν* with,) a meeting. **exodus** a going (*ἐξ*)

period (*περῐ̀* around,) a complete circuit.

ep-is-ode (*ἐπῐ̀* on, *εἰς* in,) an incident added in the course of a story. (This is distinct from *ᾠδη* an *ode*, whence *mon-ody*.)

-OID, -ITE, -ITES, a., n. *somewhat like*, &c.

[-*ειδὴς, -ίτης, -ώδης, -ῶδες;* from *εἶδος form, quality;* ☞ vĭdĕo, *εἰδέω see.* Sanscrit vīdh to *distinguish.*]

deltoid shaped somewhat like the Greek letter *Δέλτα.*

belemnites a fossil shell shaped like a (*βέλεμνον*) dart.

calamites a fossil plant like a (*κᾰ́λᾰμος*) reed.

sulphite a chemical combination between sulphŭrous acid and a base, as lime, forming sulphite of lime.

pyrites (originally flint, from *πῦρ* fire,) sulphuret of iron and other minerals with a brassy lustre.

spheroid conoidal cycloid ethmoid arachnoid peltoid sigmoid varioloid typhoid ge-ode meteorite ammonite thomsonite sienite cyanite* boracite* coracite* chlorite

* Pronounce C as K.

Obs. 1. In mineralogy, -lite (λί'θος a stone,) and -ite are used indifferently, and when the stem ends with *l*, they are not distinguishable, as in apophyllite, argillite, petalite, arendalite. -lite appears in chrysolite (χρῡσὸς gold,) i.e. gold-stone; oolite (ὠὸν an egg,) from its resemblance to fish roe. litho-graphy litho-logic lith-i-um.

Obs. 2. Greek and Latin family names in -ADÆ, -IDÆ belong here, such as Dardanidæ, Romulidæ, Aeneadæ, Druidæ, Danaidæ Δᾰνᾰΐδαι children of Danaus; Greeks. Peleiides son of Peleus. Hesperides daughters of Hesperus. Oceanides daughters of ŌCĔĀNŬS.

-oir, n. See -ER, agency.

[-oir, -eur, -re, are French forms.] **memoir** **reservoir** **devoir**

-om, n.

transom, in ship-building, a strengthening timber bearing some resemblance to a bench. (TRĀNSTRŪM a bench for rowers; a cross beam. Greek θράω I sit; n. dim. θράνιστρον, of θρᾶνος a bench (the uppermost of three) for rowers;—a projecting head of a beam.)

venom VĔNĔNŪm poison, **bane**. **axiom**, **idiom**, see **-m**.

fantom, (☞ φαίνω, to appear,) French fantôme, from PHANTAS-MA; old French en**fantosm**er to bewitch.—*Diez.*

fathom a measure of six feet. (Old German fadum a thread, Sanscrit BADH, BAnDH to bind, tie.)

besom **bottom** **bosom**. *Ransom* is a form of redemption.

-om, adv.

seldom, Ang. seld *rare*, seldon *rarely;* Ger. selten (and seltsam, with -some,) old Eng. selden; dialect of Somerset seltimes, which accounts for the *m*. **whilom**, Ang. hvile *time*, dative plural hvilum *at times*.

at random, old high Ger. rand edge, extremity; old Eng. randon haste; old Fr. randir to rush on, a randon at a blow, immediately.

Men who live much by the brain have seldom the courage to be prudent, seldom the wisdom to be patient.—Blackwood's Magazine, Sept. 1860.

-OMA, n. See **-m**.

arōma ἄρωμα the flavor of spices. **glaucōma** γλαύκωμα a disease of the eye giving it a (γλαυκὸς) bluish color.

-ON, n.

[-O nominative and -N declensional. See under -ION.]

potion **carbon** **falcon** **scorpion** **histrioni**c **mucrona**te

-*ON*, n. *that which*, &c.

[¶ 1. -*ων* n.; Ss. -Ă$_{\iota}$; Lat. U^{m}. ¶ 2. -*ων* part. pres. ¶ 3. -*ῶν* gen. pl. ¶ 4. -*ον* n. ¶ 5. -*ον* neut. adj. ¶ 6. -*ων*, -*ον* adj. comp.]

¶ 1. **canon** **siphon** **cotyledon** **scorpion** **myrmidon** **lion** **gorgon** **Crangon** **chameleon** **Amphi'on** **Ixi'on** **Endymion**

¶ 2. **horizon** that which (*ὁρῐ'ζ-ω*,) bounds; the bound*ing* line separating earth and sky. **dragon** *δρᾰ'κων*; part. *δρακὼν* see*ing* (well,) of *δέρκω* I see, glance; *ἔΔρακον* I saw. **archon** a ruler. (*ἄρχω* I command.) **ichneu-m-on**, **gno-m-on**, **de-m-on**, see -M.

halcyon **architect** *ἀρχιτέκτων* **Phae-th-on** **Phlege-th-on**

> But Phlegeton is ſonne of Herebus and Night . . . —*Spenser*.

¶ 3. **diapason**, (*δῐᾰ'* through, *πᾶς* every, gen. pl. fem. *πᾱσῶν* of all,) through all, from a note to its octave. **dia-tessaron** through the fourth. **amazon** **Parthenon**

¶ 4. **colon** a member (of a sentence;) a point indicating such a member.

cinnamon **ety-m-on** **lexicon** **melon** **chorion** **pantheon** **scholion** **criterion** **ganglion** **pneumoni**a **amphiction**

¶ 5. **auto-ma-t-on** self-acting, see *AUTO-*. **skeleton** a dry (body;) the bones pertaining to a body.

catholicon **basilicon** **octahedron** **oxymoron** **asyndeton**

¶ 6. **ple-on**asm *πλεον-ασμὸς* overplus. (*πλέον*, neuter comparative of *πολὺς* many, much.)

Obs. 1. Greek neuter nouns in -*ον* usually take the Latin form, as *στέρνον* STE'RNŪM; *μυσεῖον* MŪSÆŪM; *κολχικὸν* CŌLCHĬCŪM.

Obs. 2. In many English words, -on was not the final of the originals, as in *θρόνος* throne, see **-ne**; *τόνος* TŎNŬS a *tone* or *din*.

Sexton is for sacristan. *Crimson* belongs to -INe a.

-on, n. deteriorative.

[Ital. -ogna; Fr. ogne, as in ivr-ogne *drunkard*, ivre *drunken*. Akin to -on augmentative.]

scullion a person in charge of a scullery. **cullion** **calyon** **carrion** decaying (CĂR-O) flesh. Old English caroigne, carren, &c.

> Darke, dolefull, dreary, like a greedy grave,
> That ſtill for carrion carcaſſes doth crave:—*Spenser.*

-on, **-one**, **-oon**, n. augmentative.

[Ital. -ōnĕ; Span. -on, -ona; French -o^n (compare teton, tetasse, tetin, tetine.) Gr. *-ων*, as *κεφᾰλὴ head; κεφᾰλ-ων big-headed.* Latin -ŌNŬS, -ŌNĂ. See -AN.]

button a large bud. **seton** a large (SĒTĂ bristle,) thread. **piston** a large pes-t-le. **balloon** a large ball. **saloon** a large (Fr. salle, Ital. sála) hall. **bassoon** a large instrument for the base. **trombone** a large (Ital. tromba) trumpet. **an apron**, Fr. naperon, North of Eng. nappern, a large (Fr. nappe) cloth, as *napkin* is a small one. **Bellona** the goddess of (BĔLLŬ^m) war. **galle-on** **medallion** **squadron** **gabion** **bastion** **baton** or **batoon** **cannon** **champion** **falchion** **tampion** **tampoon** **buffoon** **barracoon** **cartoon** **cardoon** **seroon** **harpoon** **doubloon** **frigatoon** **festoon** **lampoon** **spontoon** **talon** **truncheon** **million** **latten** **griffin** **patron** **matron** **Pomona** **Fortuna**

Obs. 1. Perhaps bludgeon, dudgeon, guerdon, plungeon, puncheon, stanchion, garri-son belong here.

Obs. 2. The corrupt form 'mushroom' belongs here, being a mistake for the vulgar form musheroon, of the French *mousseron*.

Baboon converts the French nasal i^n of babouin into -oon.

-on, n. diminutive.

[French diminutive O^n.]

cocoon a small (Fr. coque) shell. **flagon** a small flask.

cordon a small (Fr. corde.)

e'chalon something arranged like the steps of (échelle) a ladder.

musketoon a short musket. (A diminutive in French, and an augmentative in Italian.)

Cushion is for the French diminutive coussin.

-OR, -R, n. *quality; -ing; -ness.*

[Latin -OR, -R; Span. -or; Italian -ore; Fr. -eur. Bohem. -r, -er, -or. Gaelic (i.e. Gallic,) -air, -oir. Greek -ăρ, -ăς, -ος. Sanscrit Ă5, as in TRĂS (Lat. TĔRRĔO,) to *fear*; TRĀS-Ă5, Lat. TĔRRŎR. Sanscrit HŎMĂ5 *a liquid*, Greek χῦμός *chyme*, Lat. HŪMŎR. -OR converts Latin intransitive verbs into (passive) nouns of *things*, as -T-OR converts them into (active) nouns of persons. See -ER agential. Akin to -US.]

error the *quality* of erring, an *erring*.

favor kind*ness*. (FĂVĔO to be kind.)

odor *that which* (ὄζω,) yields scent.

valor, VĂLĔO, to be strong.

clamor tremor tumor splendor vigor rigor favor fervor candor squalor stupor torpor horror furor liquor calorific—**savor tenor mirror** MĪRĀTŌRĬŬM—**grand-eur**

Obs. 1. Some nouns in -or cannot be referred to Latin verbs, as honor, color, odor.

Obs. 2. This suffix is simulated by the genitive case, as in corp-or-eal, from CŎRPŬS a body, gen. CŎRP-ŎR-ĬS; flow-er, see -ER-, -R, declensional.

Demeanor is for demeanure. *Flavor.*

-ORI-, -ORy, a., n. *-ing*, &c. See -ARy.

[Lat. masc. -ŌRĬŬS,[a] fem. -ŌRĬĂ,[b] neut. -ORIUM.[c] See I formative.]

transitory[a] passing. **dilatory**[a] dilating (as it were) time.

victory[b] **history**[b] **promontory**[c] **consistory**[c] **no-t-ori-ous-ly**

-OS, n.

[Gr. -ος, indicating the action of the root verb. See -US.]

chaos, see **-m. pathos bathos epos asbestos -us acanthus**

-OSe, -OS-, -OuS, a. *full; like; having,* &c.

[ōs-ŭs;[a] Italian -oso; French -eux, -euse. German -os, ös. Akin to -ŭs,[b] with which it is confounded in English and French.]

villous, **villose** VĪLLŌSŬS *full of* (VĪLL-ŬS) wool or down. **globose** *like* a globe. **studious**[a] diligent in study.

malicious MĂLĬTĬŌSŬS *having* or bearing malice.

perilous full of peril. **jocose**[a] given to joking.

morose **lachrimose** **plumose** **operose** **verbose** **gibbose** **vicious** VĬTĬŌSUS **sententious** **ponderous** **laborious** **vinous** **numerous** **cavernous** **noxious**[ab] **ingenious** **prodigious** **callous** **portentous** **monstrous** **oblivious**[ab] **ambitious** **generos**ity **suspicious** **factious** **cadaverous** **tumultuous** **ominous** **luminous** **sinuous** **sumptuous** **egregious**[b] **nutritious**[b] **fictitious**[b] **testaceous**[b] **aqueous**[b] **bilious** **varicose**

Obs. The next examples are not from recognised Latin forms. **clamorous** (CLĀMŎR noise, CLĀMŌSŬS) noisy. **illustrious**, a false form of ĬLLŪSTRĬS. **vigorous** **rigorous** **cautious** **plenteous** **virtuous**

-oso.

[The Italian form of -OSe.] **virtuoso** **amoroso** **affettuoso**

-OSI-Ty. See -OSe.

verbosity the quality of being full of words; wordiness.

pomposity **dubiosity** **curiosity** **animosity** **monstrosity**

For ferocity, precocity, veracity, rapacity, voracity, &c. see -AC-eous.

-osy.

leprosy a scaly and pustulous disease of the skin. (*λέπρα*, from λεπρὸς scaly; λεπὶς a scale. A badly formed word.)

-ot, n.

fagot a bundle of sticks. (W. ffag what unites together; ffagl a blaze; ffagod a fagot.) **maggot**, see M-.

spigot, W. ig what is sharp; p-ig a point, p-ike, be-ak; yspig a spine, s-p-ike; yspigawd a spindle, a spigot.

-ot, **-otte**, n. dim.

[French -otte; Spanish -ota. Akin to **-et**, **-ette**, n. dim.]

ballot a small ball; a closed paper used in voting.
chariot a small car or chair.
calotte a kind of cap.

Clymbe to her charet all with flowers ſpred,—*Spenser.*

-ot, n. augmentative.

hakot a large hake, a voracious fish of the genus Mer-lucius or sea-pike. (German hech-t a pike; akin to *hook* and *heckle.*)
haked a large pike. (Anglish hacod.) **owlet, howlet** a large owl. (Fr. hulotte.) **sans-cul-otte**

-OT, n.

[Gr. -οτης, -ωτης, fem. -ωτις. See *-ET*, -T-ER, T participial.]

patriot πατριώτης, fem. πατριῶτις **zealot** ζηλωτής **helot** εἱλώτης **idiot** ἰδιώτης **despot** δεσπότης **escharotic** ἐσχἄρωτ-ῐκός

-OT-IC, a., n. See *-AT-IC.*

narcotic ναρκωτῐκὸς producing (νάρκη) torpor. **exotic**

-ōth, n.

A Hebrew feminine plural as in **sabaōth** (σαβαώθ) hosts or armies. **bĕhēmōth** beasts, the plural as a more dignified form being applied to the hippopótamus. **Bĕērōth** (wells,) the name of a city. Joshua 9 :17. **măzzārōth** the (signs of the) zodiac. Job 38 :32.

-ouch, **-idge**, n.

[Ital. diminutive -occio, -uccia; Fr. -ouche; Sp. -ucho.]

cartouch an architectural ornament like a label or scroll.

cartridge a small (χάρτης) paper containing a charge for a gun.

Obs. Italian has the enormous number of two hundred suffixial diminutives, including forms like car-uncula, car-unculetta, besti-uoluccia, pagli-ucolina, bott-oncellino, bern-occolino, gall-ozzoletta, luc-ignolino, cass-ettoncino, sbirr-acchiuolo, u-ccellinuccio.

-our for -OR, n.

Obs. Some pretend that -our should be used because it occurs in words got directly from the French. This rule is followed in spelling a few words for the sake of the pronunciation, as *tour, contour, amour. Neighbor* is not French but Germanic, and is spelt 'neighbore' in the English Bible of 1380, 'neghebor' by Chaucer, and 'neibor' 'neighbor,' 'neighbour,' by Spenser. But French has -eur in connaisseur, erreur, honneur, couleur, and old French has *créditeur* where French has créancier. Henry III.'s Norman French proclamation of October 18th, 1258, has honur, and Rhaetian has hanur, errur, inferiur, inspectur, industrius, cunfessur, cunfessiun, &c. -our is old English, as mirrour, minour (miner,) trechour (cheat,) vauntour (boaster,) versifiour, hasardour (gamester,) in Chaucer; and harpour, benefactour, in F. Spence, 1686. Spenser uses treachour, pillour, favour, mirrhour, rancor, labor, honor and honour, horror and horrour, humor and humour, arbor and arbour.

Those who wish to use -our etymologicly, must distinguish between words got from old French, and those taken directly from Latin, before they can spell words like splendor, rancor, squalor, torpor, stupor, vigor, &c. Richardson uses -our, but *he does not cite the old French authorities* for his etymologies, so that there is no evidence that he is accurate in his spellings of splendour, squalor, torpour, stupor, vigour and vigorous, rancour and rancorous, honour and honourable. He refers 'splendour' to 'splendeur,' and the unlatin word 'mirror' to the modern French 'miroir,' citing Piers Plouhman's 'mirour' and Gower's 'mirrour'—producing no etymologic authority for either 'splendour' or 'mirror.'

The following old French forms show that there was no uniform etymologic basis in that language.

detracteour *detractor*	**eureur** *hearer*
savour *savor*	**conteor** *he who counts*
metrour *poet*	**sauveor** *savior*
kantadour *singer*	**coulor** *color*
conquereur *conqueror*	**maester** *master*
soldurieur *soldier*	**esquier** *esquire*

Trouthe and honour, fredom and custefie.—*Chaucer.*

-oUS, a. *having; -ing.*

[-ŭs, -ĭŭs, -ŭŭs; -ος, -ής, -ιος, -αιος. Fr. -eux, f. euse. Akin to ☞ -US n., and -ER n.]

o'dorous (ŎDŌRŬS) having odor.

gibbous (GĪBBŬS and GĪBBĔR) having a convexity.

amphibious having (βίος) life (ἀμφί) both on land and in water; as toads, the tadpoles of which live under water.

indigenous pertaining to one in- (GĔNĬTŬ[m]) born; originating in the region or country.

conterminous touching at the (TĒRMĬNŬS) boundary.

strenuous arduous barbarous anxious obvious pious devious noxious innocuous ridiculous cinereous curious ambiguous argillaceous gallinaceous sonōrous deciduous superfluous conscious herbaceous—mischievous boisterous

Obs. The suffix is lost in rigid RĬGĬDŬS valid honest robust austere just right direct beatific innate compact.

-ow, n., a., v.

[A heterogeneous English spelling, partly derived from Germanic -gen.[a] Some of them are contracted diminutives.]

shallow that which is shoal.

tallow that which is (Gothic tulgus) solid. (Islandic tōlga to solidify, congeal.)

fellow, formerly **felaw**, a companion. ("Isl. felagi, from fe *money*, and lag *community*." *H. Wedgwood.* Ang. fylgean to follow. *Skinner*.)

callow without feathers. (CĀLVŬS bald.)

s-parrow, Ang. speara, Lat. PĀRŬS, Go. s-parwa, Ger. s-perling.

shadow shade **felloe**, Ger. felge **burrow** bury **hollow** (**holwe**, Chaucer) hole **barrow** bear **swallow**, Ang. svelg-an **swallow** (a bird,) Anglish svaleve, German schwalbe **bellows** (**belous**, Chaucer) **gallows**[a] (**galwes**, Chaucer) **fallow**, Anglish faleve, fealo **sorrow**[a] **morrow**[a] **follow**[a] **borrow**[a] **furrow** **minnow** **yellow** **billow** **willow** (**sallow**) **harrow** **marrow** **narrow**

A bettre felaw fchulde men nowher fynde.
. . . . God yeve thee forwe,
What aileth thee to flepen by the morwe.—*Chaucer.*

As frefh as flowres in medow greene doe grow,—*Spenser.*

P-. See -B-.

despot δεσπότης a tyrant. (*S* inflectional, T participial. Sanscrit jâpati, *Benfey*. Sanscrit dâsa a slave, *Pott.* δέω I bind, restrain.)

-PLe, **-ble**, -PLEX, a. *fold, times.*

[-PLĔX, -PLĬC-; PLĬC-O *I fold, ply.*]

double two-fold. **triple, treble** three-ply, three-fold. **quadruple** **duplicity** **tri-plic-ate** **complex** **complication**

Obs. In temple, example, *p* is educed from *m*. Disciple, see **-ble.**[e]

-POD, -PED, -PUS, n., a. *foot, feet.*

[ποῦς *foot*, gen. ποδ-ός, nom. pl. πόδα. PĒS, gen. PĔDĬS, nom. pl. PĔDĒS. Eng. pace, foot. Diminutive πόδιον, -PODIUM. Sansc. PĀDĂ5 *foot.* Bohem. pod- below.]

polypus, **polyp**, **poulp** an animal with (πολύς) many feet. **polypodium, polypody** a fern with many stems.

octo'pus a cuttlefish with (ὀκτώ) eight feet or arms.

decapoda crustacea with (δέκα) ten feet.

apoda without feet. **hexapod** with six feet, as insects. **quadruped** **biped** and **dipus** **tripod** and **trivet** **centiped** **milleped** **soliped** **palmiped** **pedal** **pedate** **cap-a-pie** **Apus**

Por-pus is for pork-fish, and the allied *gramp-us* is from γρόμφος, S-CRŌFĂ a sow, the form and motions of the small cetacea being somewhat like those of swine. French *grand poisson* a 'large fish,' is commonly given.

-P-UL. See -B-, -L, dim.

manipulate to perform small work with (MĂNŪS) the hands.

-R-, formative.

[Akin to -L-, which is also formative. Its function is perceived in the Sanscrit MI to *throw*, MĒRU *apt to throw;* ṛ̥ to *pierce*, ṛARĀRU *injurious;* BHI to *fear*, BHIRU *fearful;* ASMAN *a stone*, ASMARA *full of stones.* ἄγω, to *lead, bring;* ἀγείρω, to *assemble.* TŎLLO I raise, lift, bear; TŎL-ĔR-O I bear (in a particular manner,) endure, tol-er-ate. It occurs in -ary, -er, -OR, -R-US (-R-A, -R-UM,) -R-ous, -ry, -TRUM.]

nec-ro-logy an account of one (νεκ-ρὸς) dead.

cle-r-gy (originally) a body chosen by (κλῆρος) lot.

the-or-em θεώρημα a proposition in mathematics. (θεάω-μαι, to behold, contemplate.)

pu-re PŪ-R-ŬS, Ss. PŪ to *clean.*

pylorus, see -R-US. **gla-re** **c-lea-r**, see C-LĀ-R-ŬS. **sepulchre** SĔPŪLCRUM. **consid-er** **desi-re** **recup-er**ate **i-gno-r-ant** **fe-r-n**

Obs. The *r* of *experience* is part of the root.

R, declensional.

[A base with S in the nominative, as MĀS (gen. MĂR-ĬS[a]) *a male;* FLŌS (gen. FLŌR-ĬS[b]) *flower;* MŌS (gen. MŌR-ĬS[b]) *manner;* -ŬS, gen. -ŎR-ĬS,[c] gen. -ĔR-ĬS;[d] PŪLVĬS (gen. PŪLVĔR-ĬS[e]) *dust;* MŪS (gen. MŪR-ĬS) *mouse.* See -ER, -OR declensional.]

marry[a] **flor**al[b] **or**al[b] **mor**al[b] **tempor**al[c] **pector**al[c] **decor**ous[c] **corpor**ate[c] **frigor**ific[c] **oper**ate[d] **ulcer**[d] **funer**al[d] **gener**al[d] **later**al[d] **remuner**ate[d] **oner**ous[d] **ponder**ous[d] **veter**an[d] **sider**eal[d] **vulner**ary[d] **ciner**ary[e] **pur**ulent[f] **jur**y[f] **mur**ine[f] **rur**al[f] (**rus**tic)

Obs. ŏs a bone, gen. ŏssĭs, gives ossi-fy.

-R, permutative.

[A permutation of S, as in SPĒS *hope*, SPĒRO *I hope;* VĪS *power*, VĬR *a man.*]

injure jus-t **inspire** **virus**

-R, v. infinitive. See **-er**.

sneer veer hear steer shear jeer leer bear char roar soar—souvenir

-r, possessive. See -ER, a.

you-r their our her

-R, adv., prep.

[Gr. as in ʻὑπὲρ, Lat. SŬP-ĔR, Eng. ov-er; NŪP-ĔR *lately;* SĔMPĔR *ev-er;* TĔR *thrice.* ĪNSTĀNTĔR *instantly.* Some are transferred comparatives.]

far near under after never yonder outer where

Obs. The question *Where?* is made with a labial root, and its answer with the glottal H, when the direction is *towards* the speaker, and with the dental T, &c. when it is *from* him. This appears in the following Greek, Latin, German, and English examples—

Ποῦ	QVŌ	wo	war	where	when	whence	what	whither
Ϝή-δε	HĪ(c)	hie	hier	here	hen*	hence	hid*	hither
Τῆ	TŪM	da	dar	there	then	thence	that	thither

-re, n., a.

[See -ER agential; -C-R-; **-chre**; -T-R-UM.]

acre wiseacre massacre austere, see -R-oUS **spectre fibre** FĪBRĂ **lucre sabre centre involucre sepulchre**
Sire is for seni-or. Fire and sphere have the *r* radical.

-red, n.

hund-red, Ohg. hunt, hundert; old Frisian hunderd; Belg. honderd; old Saxon hunderod; Latin CĔNTŪM; Albanian kint; Welsh cant. Akin to hand, and com-pre-hend.

kind-red, **+kinrede** relations by birth or marriage. (The first *d* is educed from *n* of *kin*. Swedish reda order; Welsh cenedl kindred.) **hatred** ill-will, malevolence.

* Danish. See -N adv., Obs. 4.

-rel, n.

[Diminutive or depreciative -l, following the suffix -r.]

pickerel a small pike.

timbrel a kind of small (Fr. tambour) drum.

doggerel bad poetry. (German dichter a poet.)

spandrel chaptrel mandrel tendril gambrel tumbrel mackerel mongrel hoggerel cockerel costrel

Scoundrel, Italian sconderuola, one who *absconds* from the roll or muster.—*Thomson.* *Minstrel* and *poitrel* belong to -AL.

-ren, n. pl.

children (Ang. cin-r-en,) and **brethren** are double plurals formed by adding the -n of *oxen* to the old English plurals *childre* and *brothre,* Ang. brōthra.

Obs. The -r plural in *children* and the German *kinder* is probably a mutation of *s* (as in German hase, English hare,) to avoid in the plural the *s* of the genitive singular, for in Anglish, smiðas is both *smiths* and *of a smith.*

ric, n. *jurisdiction.*

[RĔG-NŬm a kingdom. Anglish ric-e, -ric; Sw. rike; German reich. English reign, rich.]

bishopric the jurisdiction of a bishop.

rit, n.

culp-ri-t, RĔĀ-TŬS n., the condition of one arraigned, for a (CŬLPĂ) fault; a criminal.—*Sullivan.*

-R-oUS, a. *quality.*

[-R-ŭs (-ă, -ŭm.) -ρ-ός. Ss. -R-Ă5. See -OR n., **-ous,** -RUS.]

au-s-t-ere having the quality of parching. (ĀVSTĒRŬS, αὐστηρὸς harsh; αὔ-ω, to parch.)

avarous ĂVĀRŬS covetous. (ĂVĔO I covet.)
sonōrous sounding. (SŎNO I sound.)
canōrous vocally melodious. (CĂNO I sing.)
odorous ŎDŌRŬS **vigorous rigorous trai-t-or-ous sec-ure** SĔCŪRŬS **dolorous clamorous timorous humorous rapturous**

Obs. These words are mostly derived from verbs, and do not include forms like *cancerous, ulcerous, murderous, onerous,* nor those in *-ferous.*

-R-US, n. m., -R-A, n. f., -R-UM, n. neut.

[-RUS is the more correct form of -rous. It is preserved chiefly in proper names. See -R-ous, -T-RUM.]

pylōrus the (*πύλη*) passage, from the stomach.
Theo-dōrus, (*δῶρον*) a gift, from God. **Apollo-dōrus Helio-dōrus hydra** an animal living in (*ὕδωρ*) water.
fulcrum something with which (FŪLC-ĬO,) to prop.
plethōra *πληθώρα* fulness, repletion. (*πλέω, πλήθω,* to fill.)

> And late the nation found, with fruitlefs fkill,
> Its former ftrength was but plethoric ill.—*Goldsmith.*

Ce'rberus Ca'ntharus He'sperus Ta'rtarus Seve'rus papyrus humerus cedar *κέδρος*—**Auro'ra Ele'ctra Chime'ra camera decōrum**
Arct-ūrus, the (*οὖρος*) tail, of the (*ἄρκτος*) bear.
Quorum of whom; the genitive plural of QVĪ who.

-Ry, -ERy, n. 1. *aggregate of;* 2. *practice of.*

[Adj. masc. -ĀRĬŬS; nom. fem. sing. and neut. pl. -ĀRĬĂ. Dan., Sw. -eri; Ger. -erei; Belg. -erij. See -ARy.]

artillery, (gen. ĀRTĬS of art,) Port. artilh *fortification;* old Fr. artilleux *artful;* artillier *to fortify,* artillerie, old Port. artilharia *throwing engines;* Ital. artiglieria, French artillerie *cannon* in the aggregate.—*Diez.*
cavalry soldiery yeomanry infantry archery bribery carpentry thievery bravery perfumery pastry imagery mercery trumpery sorcery surgery butchery broidery rivalry revelry confectionery stationery grocery foundry
Treasury θησαυρός belongs to -RUS.

-s, -es, -ce, -x, -se, n. plural.

[Ss. -ĂS; Latin -ĒS, Greek -ες in some nouns, as κόραξ, CŎRĀX *raven*, pl. κόρακες CŎRĂC-ES; πλειάς, pl. πλειάδες *Pleiads;* QVÆSTIO *question*, pl. QVÆSTĬŌNĒS; SĒRMO *a speech*, pl. SĒRMŌNĒS; CŌNSŬL *consul*, pl. CŌNSŬLĒS; HŎNŎR, pl. HŎNŌRĒS. Islandic -R. English 1st declension -as, corruptly -es; Gothic -s, -eis, -os, -jus; old English -es, -is, -ys, -us. See under -*AD* and -AX.]

questions sermons consuls honors voices obsequies orgies boxes buttresses dice pence beaux—these those

. . . therfore alle men and women hadden greet deuocion wordus; and in alle her doyngus.—*R. Brunne* (in Richardson.)

. . . ryghtys, pryuylegys and appertenaunçys to the fayde kyngedome . . . apperteynynge: . . . —*Fabyan* (in Richardson.)

> With knotty, gnarry, barren trees old
> Of ftubbes fharp and hideous to behold.—*Chaucer.*
>
> Yeres and dayes fleet this creature.—*id.*
>
> Min ben alfo the maladies colde
> The derke trefons, and the caftes olde.—*id.*

The Songs which were fung, by fome of the ancient *Greeks*, at the Time of the Vintage, in honour of *Bacchus*, were called *Tragedys* . . . —Terence, by *Thomas Cooke*, 1734. He also uses enemys, beautys, copys, crys, &c.

Obs. 1. In some cases there is a tendency to avoid a plural form, as in

> Up fpringen fperes twenty foot on highte . . .
> Er we had ridden fully five mile.—*Chaucer.*
>
> A ftately pallace built of fquared bricke,—*Spenser.*

Obs. 2. The following are both singular and plural Latin forms—**series species superficies congeries**; but **effigies progenies facies** have been naturalised under the forms *effigy, progeny, face,* in the singular number. There is a tendency to consider the adjective suffix of Portugue-se, Chine-se a plural, and Milton (Par. Lost, 3,) uses *Chineses.* Athens (ἀθῆναι) and Thebes (θῆβαι) were intended to follow their original plural form.

Obs. 3. The following, although etymologicly of the singular number, are commonly assumed to be plural, from which a singular is formed by dropping -s or -es:—belemnites, basaltes, stalactites, ammonites, &c.

Obs. 4. *Manes,* (remains of the dead, a ghost,) is of the singular number in Latin, but singular or plural in English. *Riches* (French richesse,) *alms* (ΕΛεηΜοΣύνη,) and *wages* were originally of the singular number.

Obs. 5. *Ides* is for the Latin plural ĪDŪS, which wants the singular.

Obs. 6. The drug ălŏēs is properly singular, from the French noun singular aloès, with *s* pronounced, which distinguishes it from ĂLŎĒ a genus of plants. Butler, altho a scholar, uses double plurals in—

As other grofs phenomenas, . . . —Hudibras, Pt. 2, Canto 1, l. 189.

For we are animals no lefs,
Altho' of different fpeciefes.—Pt. 1, Canto 1, l. 864.

-s, -'s, -es', -se, possessive.

[Genitives, as in γνώμη *kno-wledge*, gen. γνώμη-ς; πἄτὴρ, PĂTĔR *father*, gen. πατρὸς, PA'TR-ĭs *father's;* Ger. vaters. Old Eng. -es, -is. Anglish of the 1st decl. sing. -es. See under **-mer**.]

A **child's** obedience **men's** opinions **fishes'** scales "**Rubens's** letters" (Ruskin.) **whose** **yours** **his** **hers** **theirs** **ours**

Achilles . . . was left Vulnerable yet in the Heel, and *Paris'es* Arrow found him Out there.—*L'Eftrange*, Fable CXLVII, 1692.

Turn the world's hiftory; what find we there,
But *fortune*'s fports, or *nature*'s cruel claims,
Or *woman*'s artifice, or *man*'s revenge,
And endlefs inhumanities on man?—*Young*, Nt. 8.

Those accents, as his native mountains dear, . . .
Friends', kindreds', parents', wonted voice recall.
Byron, Lara I. 25.

Obs. 1. Locutions like—The book of Edward—The hair of the head—are no more examples of a possessive case than—Edward owns the book—The hair on the head.

Obs. 2. The apostrophe indicates the loss of a vowel* from the old English form, as in

Of quenis livis and of kingis
And many othir thingis fmale.—*Chaucer*.

Alas min hertes quene.—*id.*

Through envies fnares, or fortunes freakes unkind.—*Spenser*.

. . . far from all mens fight;—*id.*

That houfes forme—*id.*

---

* There was consequently no etymologic reason for introducing it where it could not stand for an omitted *e*, as in writing—For science' sake,—The horse's head,—The horses' saddles,—Children's toys. In Anglish, the possessive of plurals was not formed in -s.

-S, adverbial.

[-ως, -ς, as in πῆ *how*, πώς *somehow;* τρῐ`ς *thrice;* αὖ *back*, ἄψ *backwards*, (υ becoming π.) Latin -s as in ĂLĬĀS *otherwise;* MĂGĬS *rather;* QVŎTĬĒS *how often;* Sanscrit DVIS, Greek δὶς, Latin BĬS *twice;* SĂTĬS *enough;* VĪX *scarcely;* ĒX *out of;* ĀB-S *from;* ĪNTŬS *within.* Welsh ni, ni-s *not.* Gothic -s; Anglish -es, as in fæst *fast*, fæstes *firmly;* old English then-s *then-ce.* Old French envers, jamais, alors, dans, sans, ans (frōm ĀNTĔ, Sp. ante-s) whence adv-an-ce.]

else (els in Spenser) **since** (sithens in Spenser) **a..s** (als in Spenser) **perhaps** **towards** **needs** **besides** **-wards** **thus** **unawares** **whence** **+whennes** **hence** (henne, henen, hennes, hense, hens, in Chaucer) **thence** **+thens** **once** **+onis**, **+ones**, **+onse**, **+oonys** **twice** **+twise** **always** **noways** **sideways** **straightways** **lengthways** **likewise** **ye-s** yea **out-adoors** **amid-ships** **betimes** **now-adays** satisfy **ma-s-t-er** **anights** **+amornings** (Swed. i morgens.)

> That twife he reeled, readie twife to fall:
> Thrife every weeke in afhes fhee did sitt,—*Spenser.*

Obs. 1. **Forth** (from *fore*) has *th.*

Obs. 2. The similarity between adverbial -S, and the signs of the plural, and possessive singular of nouns, has caused some nouns to be transferred to the adverbs. That betime-s is not a plural is shown by the German, where māl does not take its plural -e in dreimal *three-times*, vormals *formerly.*

Obs. 3. This -s is sometimes strengthened by T, as in whilst, against, amongst, alongst, amidst (amiddes in Spenser,) lest. In vulgar discourse, *once* is used for number—"He did it (but) once;" and *once-t* (Ger. einst) for time—"Once-t upon a time;" and when governed by *at*, as in "at once-t," which may be an old objective case governed by a preposition.

> Who, whiles he livde, was called proud Sanffoy . . .
> Whyleft here thy fhield is hangd for victors hyre?—*Spenser*, 1589.

. . . vnder the mids therof. . . . in the midft of Winter.—*Holland's* Plinie, 1635.

-S-, repetitive. See -IT-.

pulsation, PĔLLO, PŪLSŪ^{m}, to drive; PŪLSO I beat, beat often.

-S- mutational.

[A mutation of D, T, N, and R, and often participial, as in -S-ION and -S-IVE. See T, D, S, participial.]

respon**d**	respon**s**e	degra**d**e	digre**s**s	scen**t**	sen**s**e
suspen**d**	suspen**s**e	provi**d**e	provi**s**o	me**t**e	men**s**urate
se**d**entary	se**s**sile	intru**d**e	intru**s**ive	rever**t**	rever**s**e
persua**d**e	persua**s**ive	delu**d**e	delu**s**ive	depo**n**ent	depo**s**ition
eli**d**e	eli**s**ion	divi**d**er	divi**s**or	adhe**r**e	adhe**s**ive
ca**d**ence	ca**s**ual	remi**t**	remi**s**s	inqui**r**y	inque**s**t

-S-, participial.

[See under -T-, -D-, -S-, participial. French -ès, -se.]

excur-s-ion **repul-s-ive** **impre-ss-ive**

In re**mis-s** per**cus-s**ion the penult *s* is a mutation of *t*.

In **congres-s** pos**ses-s** abs**ces-s** (better abces, French abcès) the penult *s* is a mutation of *d*.

And this vyſyon ſhe ſayd all in wepynge & in laughynge . . . —Legenda aurea, 1527.

-S-, inflectional.

[ὀρχέ-ομαι *I dance;* future ὀρχήΣομαι *I will dance;* 1st aorist middle ὠρχηΣάμεν *I danced;* ὀρχήΣτρα *the place of the dancers. -S-IA, -S-IS, -ISM, -S-YNE,* have this *-S.*]

cau-s-t-ic burning, corroding. (*κάω*, to burn; future *καύσω*.) **my-s-tery**, see -ARY. **spa-s-m**, **cha-s-m**, see **-m**.

A-s-ia, as if, the country of dry winds. (**αω*, to blow; *αὔω*, to dry.) **a-s-th-ma**, see *-TH-* formative.

In a-t-mō-sphere, T represents the S of As-ia.

miasm **crisis** **orchestra** **hypocrisy** **phase** **pause** **drastic** **amnesty** **extasy** **genesis** **magnetism** **Mnemosyne**, see *-S-YNE.*

-san, n. *one who;* a. *pertaining to.* See -AN.

parmesan pertaining to Parma. **partisan** a party man. **artisan** one who follows a mechanic (ĀRS, gen. ĀRTĬS,) art.

. . . this artizan Nicophanes, a famous painter in his time.—*Holland*, 1635.

. . . the meaneſt artiſan or manufacturer contributes more to the accommodation of life than the profound ſcholar and argumentative theoriſt;—*Dr. Johnson*, Rambler, Aug. 1751.

-se, v. *to make.*

cleanse, Ang. clænsian to make (clæne) clean.

mince to cut into bits; to make (Belg. min *less*, Sw. minst) smallest.

rinse, Sw. rensa, Dan. rense to make (Sw. ren) pure.

parse (PARS a part,) to resolve or analyse a sentence.

-se, n., a., v.

[-s-ŭs, akin to -T-ŭs, T-ous, -us. See -S- participial.]

cour-se CUR-SUS, (CURRO I run,) that which is run.

lapse verse pulse obtuse profuse recluse immerse terse disperse

Phrase, phase, belong to -*S-IS.*

-sel.

[Partly German -sel, -sal, due to -l with an interposed or preceding *s*, as in stöp-sel a *stopper* or *stopple;* räth-sel *something* (rat*h*-en) *to guess*, whence *riddle.* The following are diminutives.]

eisel tinsel tarsel axle vessel torsel dorsel dossil teasel

Chisel and *morsel* have -S- mutational (from D,) with -L, ¶ 3.

Damsel, see -Cle.

There was at Bourges a damoyfell whiche herde fpeke of ẏ grete renome of this holy faynt . . . —Legenda aurea, 1527.

-set, n. dim.

marmoset a small 'marmot,' a kind of monkey.

Obs. In French, marmot means a kind of *monkey*, and marmotte a *marmot.*

(-sh.)

[Mostly due to a guttural root element; also to *s* and its affinities.]

thresh, **thrash**, Go. θriskan. **flash** φ-λέγ-ω, to burn, ☞ LŪCĔO. **wish**, English viscan. **dish** disk. **push**, French pousser. **anguish**, French angoisse.

-ship, n. *aggregate of; office.*

[Ang. -scype, -scipe; old English as in frendshyppe, felaushepe, lordschip. Dan., Sw., -skap; Belg. -schap; Ohg. -scaf, (from the 10th century -scaft;) Ger. -schaft. The *s* is a prefix. Ss. JABH to *unite,* to *join.*]

lordship the aggregate of the duties, rights, and office of a lord.

sultanship (Byron) **clerkship** **censorship** **horsemanship** **fellowship** **hardship** **friendship** **township** **wor(th)ship**

Neither did I at any time soe farre forgett my selfe in my exaltation or receaved queenshipp, but that I alwayes looked for such an alteration as I now finde;— *Ann Bulen* (or *Boleyn*) 1536.

S-IC-ian, n. See -*S*-, -IC, -AN.

mu-sician, -AN one who practices, -IC, what pertains to, -*S*- that which, MU inspires. (*μάω*, to feel an impulse.)

Ma-n-t-is (a diviner; a genus of insects,) is from the same root, with -N- intensive and -T- participial,—also **auto'-ma-ton**, see *AUTO-*.

-S-IM-, ordinal.

[Latin ordinals, as in CĔNT-ĒSĬMŬS (-Ă, -Ŭm) *the hundredth.*]

quadragesima the first Sunday in Lent, and about the *fortieth* day after Easter. (QVĀDRĀGĪNTĀ forty.)

millesimal **centesimal** **septuagesimal** **infinitesimal**

-S-ION, -T-ION, n. See -ION.

[S participial, mutational, and inflectional, T participial, and N declensional.]

S-IS, -*S-IA*, -*T-IS*, n. *that which; -ing.*

[-σις,[a] -σία,[b] -τις.[c] -SUS, -SĬO, -TŬS, -TĬO. Sanscrit -T'HA5, -TU5, -TI5, as in (STHĀ ἵστημι to *place,*) STHI-T-I5 στάσις *state, position.* Go. staθs, gen.

sta-dis; Lat. STĀ-T-ŬS *state;* STĂTĬO *station.* See -ION. -*SIS* is S inflectional, and the noun suffix -*IS*. It indicates the action expressed by the verb. See foot-note under -ANT.]

genesis a be-ginn-ing, generation. (*γεννάω*, to produce; *γένεσις* the *act* of creation; *γέννημα* the *result* of creation; progeny.)

dose something (that which is) given. (*δόω* I give.)

*ph***t***h***īsis** *φθῐ́σῐς* a disease which (*φθῐ́ω*,) consumes. (**tisic**, is the same, with an adjective suffix.)

cachexy[b] a (fem. *κᾰκή*) bad (*ἕξις*) condition of body or mind. **Asia**,[b] see -*S*.

idio-syn-cra-sy[b] a peculiar temperament; *συν* with, *ἴδῐος* one's own, *κρᾶσις* a mixing.

a-mbrosia, see *AN*-. **apoplexy** *ἀποπληξία*, see *APO*.

pleurisy[c] **fantasy**, **fancy** *φαντασία* **para-noma-sia** **euthanasia** **cystitis** **ellipsis** **thesis** **phrase**[a] **phase**[a] **synopsis** **mantis** **crisis** **praxis** **basis** **syntax** **Eleusis**

> Allots the prince of his celeftial line
> An apotheofis and rites divine.—*Garth.*

-S-IVe, a.

[S participial, as in discur-s-ive; and mutational, as in delu-s-ive.]

-*SM*, n.

[See -*S*- inflectional, **-m**, and -*ISM*.]

pri-sm **cha-sm** **spa-sm** **fantasm** **schism** **sarcasm** **miasm**

-some, a. *having the quality* or *habit of; causing.*

[Ger. -sam; Belg. -zaam; Ang. -som, -sum; old Frisian -sum; Danish -som. Gothic sama *like.* Ohg. sam, sama *like,* as in—Sie lühtet sam de sonne *it lights like the sun.* Eng. same, -some. Ϝόμ-οιος, SĬM-ĬLĬS *like;* see SĒMĬ half. Ss. SĀM to *place together.*]

troublesome having the quality or habit of troubling; causing trouble.

19

meddlesome addicted to meddling.
wholesome causing (or consistent with) health.
lonesome the quality of being alone; solitary.
mettlesome having mettle. **noisome** nox-ious, hurtful.
venturesome having the habit of venturing.
loathsome (lothsom in Spenser) **quarrelsome** **toilsome** (toilsom in Spenser) **cumbersome** **burdensome** **frolicsome** **selfsame**

A *Tortoiſe* was thinking with himſelf, how Irkſom a ſort of Life it was, to ſpend All his Days in a Hole,—*L'Estrange*, Fable CCXX, 1692.

Ferrand Spence (Miscellanea, 1686,) writes *handsom, tiresom, wearisom.*

-son, n. See -ION, -T-ION.

comparison, a form of com-par-at-ion.
season (SĂTĬO a sowing or planting.)
poison **venison** **prison** **benison** **orison** **reason** **lesson**

This Humour of Mythology *may turn to a* Poyſon *inſtead of a* Nouriſhment;—*L'Estrange*, 1692.

-sp, n., v.

ga-sp to open the mouth for breath. (⁺χάω, to stand open; HĬO, to ya-wn, ga-pe.)
crisp cur-led or cur-ved, in gyr-ations or cir-cles.
grasp to hold tightly. (Akin to grapple.)

. . . the hinder limbs [of the caterpillar] act as graspers.—Illustrated London Almanac, 1860.

-ST.

robust RŌBŪSTŬS having (RŌBŬR) strength.
enthusiast, see -T-ER, Obs. 2.

-st, n.

[T participial added to a stem with S, which may be -*S*-[a] inflectional, as in σχιστός *split;* σχίζω *to split.*]

east the region of the (ἕως, Ionic ἠὼς, Doric ἀὼς) dawn. See **Asia**, under *-S-*.

west the region of **mist, moist**ure; ὑετὸς rain; German wasser *water*.

cau-st-ic burning. (καίω, to burn, future καύσω.)

thirst, **toast**, Ss. TARS; Latin TŌRRĔO, TŌSTŪ[m], to dry, parch. **post** that which is put. (☞ PŌNO.)

amne-st-y amethyst mon-st-er locust vest zest blast forest waist nest mast (acorns, &c.) **host guest Christ**[a] **schist**[a] **dynasty**[a] **ghost gust grist yeast twist hurst frost trust thrust rest** (remainder)

Re-st (repose) and *co-st* are from STO I stand.

Durst (from dare,) is partly for *durft*, Anglish θorfte.

-st, adv.

[The -t is added to intensify the adverbial force of -s; or to give it to other parts of speech, as in les-t. The old English agens, ayens, is now agains-t; the German ein-st is 'once,' often pronounced with -t; and old Suabian wilent is English whil-st. See -S adv., Obs. 2.]

-st. See -est, *most*.

And thus, the firſt and beſt employment of poetry was, to compoſe hymns in honour of the great Creator of the univerſe.—*Dryden*, Pref. to Paſtorals.

-stead, n.

[STŌ (STĂTŪ[m],) *to stand*. German statt; Anglish and Saxon stede.]

bedstead, as if, a bed stand.

homestead the place of a home. **in stead** in place of. It appears in **steady**, **stedfast**.

-ster, -str-ess, n. *the person who*.

[Originally -ster was feminine, as in Belg. voedster *she who feeds; a nurse;* whence **foster**—successively a noun, an adjective, and a verb. See **-er**.]

songster songstress spinster dabster tapster maltster punster gamester lobster youngster

Webster and **Brewster** formerly meant a female weaver and brewer. When the meaning of -ster was forgotten, forms like seam-str-ess and song-str-ess arose.

Holster is a Belgian masculine noun, akin to the Gothic neuter hulistr a hull or covering. *Bolster* is masculine and neuter in the Norse bolstr.

-S-T-ER, -S-TRI- *pertaining to.*

[The following are Latin adjective forms in -STER,[a] -STRUM,[b] -STRIS,[c] -STIS,[d]— -TRUM. The T is participial, the S various.]

equestrian[ac] pertaining to (ĔQVŬS a horse,) ĔQVĔS a horseman.

Sylvester pertaining to (SĪLVĂ) a wood. (SĪLVĪS in woods.)

fenestral pertaining to (FĔNĒSTRĂ, old French fenestr) a window.

Badister a genus of coleopterous running insects. (*βαδιστής* a pedestrian; *βαδίζω*, I walk. The *s* is inflectional.)

cœlestial[d] **terrestri**al[c] **sequester**[a] **sinister**[a] **minister**[a] **pedestri**an[c]

Obs. 1. The following are noun forms—**pilaster**,[a] a square (PĪLĂ) column. **oleaster**[a] the wild olive tree. **trans-om**,[b] see **-om**. **canister**[b] **alabaster**[ab] **plaster**[b] **monster**[b]—**cloister** **dexter**ity **dextr**ous.

Obs. 2. *Ma-s-t-er, chori-s-t-er,* &c. belong to T-ER; and roi-s-t-er, bli-s-t-er, blu-s-t-er, to -er, v. inf. Register, see **-is-ter**.

-stri-an, a., n. See -S-TER.

pedestrian going on foot. (PĒS, gen. PĔDĬS, a foot; PĔDĒSTĔR a. on foot.)

-S-URe, -T-URe, -D-URe, n. *that which is —ed.*

[-T-,[a] -D- and -S-[b] participial, -S-[c] mutational, and -UR-.]

measure,[bc] (☞ MĒTĬŎR I mete,) a meting, or estimation of quantity.

flexure[b] the act of bending. (FLĔCTO I bend.)

erasure[bc] (☞ RĀDO, RĀSŪ[m], to scrape,) a scraping out.

en-closure[c] the act of enclosing.

ver-dure the greenness of vegetation. (VĬRĔO, to grow, grow green.)

literature the results of literary labor.

texture a web, that which is woven. (TEXO I weave.)

pasture that which is browsed upon. (PĀSCOR, to feed, browse.)

capture[a] the act of taking by force. (☞ CĂPĬO I take.)

ligature that with which something is tied. (LĬGO I tie.)

pressure **fissure** **closure** **tonsure** **exposure** **fixture** **incisure**[c] **cæ-sura** **creature** **scripture** **sculpture** **fracture**

Cynosure κῠνόσυρᾰ, (κῠ ων dog, gen. κῠνός; οὐρὰ tail,) the little bear.

-S-US, n., a.

[Ss. -S-A5 (-Ā, -Ă,;) Lat. -S-ŬS (-Ă, -ŪM,) as in MŌRSŬS *a bite;* -σος (-ση, -σον,) -θος. -*S*- inflectional or participial. Akin to -T-US.]

tarsus the instep and heel. (ταρσὸς a hurdle (for *drying* fruit;) the blade of an oar; a wing; the foot between the toes and the heel. ☞ TŌRRĔO to dry up.)

narcissus (properly, with *c* as *k*,) νάρκισσος, (νάρκη numbness, stupor;) named from its supposed narcotic power.

Narcissa **abscissa** **ortho**-graphy, ☞ ŎRĬŎR. **ob-ese** **ob-e-s-ity**

-sy, n.

idio-syn-cra-sy, syn- *with*, ἴδιος a *peculiar*, κρᾶ-σῐς *temperament.* See *-S-IS.* **tansy** ἀθᾰνασία **gypsy** Egyptian.

-*S-YNE*, n. fem.

[-*S*- inflectional; -ύ'νη, akin to -AN, -ανος; -*E*, fem. sign.]

Mnemosyne μνημοσύνη remembrance. (μνάομαι, perfect *MέΜνημαι*, to remember; μνήμη memory.)

Eu-phro-s-yn-e εὐφροσύνη gaiety. (εὔφρων gay; εὖ well; φρὴν the mind.)

Sophrosyne σωφροσύνη discretion. (σώφρων of sound intellect; σῶς sa-ne; φρὴν mind.)

eleemosynary and **alms**. (ἐλεέω, passive ἐλέεμαι, to pity; ἐλεήμων merciful; ἐλεεμοσύνη mercy.)

-T-, -D-, -S-, participial. See **-t**, **-d**, **-se**, -T-ous.

[Indica**t**ing comple**t**eness; an ac**t** finishe**d**; the ac**t**or, quali**t**y (as acu**t**e or aci**d**,) fi**t**ness, attribu**t**e. It occurs in exTra, -T-ous, -Ty, -T-ive, -aTe, -eD, -T-ER, -T-IC, -T-ION, &c. Latin masc. adj. DŎMĬTŬS, fem. DŎMĬTĂ, neut. DŎMĬTŪ^m *tam-ed;* Sanscrit DAMITA5, DAMITĀ, DAMITA,; Gothic tamiθs, tamiθa, tamiθ (also tamida.) Sanscrit neut. participle future +DAMITR̥̆, Latin DŎMĬTŪR-ŬS *about to tame.*

Sanscrit (with *g* corrupt, in *gem*,) DJNĀ *to know;* DJNĂ5, dJĀNAT *instructed;* DJNĀTR̥̆ γνωστὴρ, Latin +GNOTOR *a know-er.* Sanscrit JŬCTĀ, Latin JŪNCTĂ, English yoked, joined, junct, joint.

Sanscrit CR̥ (Lat. CR-ĔO) to create; CR̥-T (Lat. CREANS,) *creant;* CR̥-T-A5 (Lat. CRĔĀTŬS) *created;* CR̥-T-IS (Lat. CRĔĀTĬO) *creation;* CAR-T-R̥ *creator.* Greek φῐλ-έω *I love;* adj. φιλητὸς *loved;* φιλήτωρ, φιλήτης *a lover.*]

en-erg-et-ic ἐν-εργ-ητ-ιχ-ὸς energetic, efficacious. (ἔργον a w-ork; ἐργά-τ-ης a worker, irk-er.)

concour-se a running (CŎN) together. (CŪRRO I run.)

frui..t FRŪCTŬS that which is enjoyed. (FRŬŎR I enjoy.)

vi-t-al **in-domi-t-able** **vin-t-ner** **fal-se** **morose** **resolute**

Obs. T may be considered the earliest of the dentals. Its easy formation by the end of the tongue, has made it the most common, important, and varied in its use, of all the consonants.

-t, **-te**, **-d**, a., n.

[Latin past participles and adjectives in -TUS; supines (verbial nouns) and nouns in -TU^m, which agrees with the Sanscrit present infinitive -TŬ,, (and nouns in -TĀ, -TI,) Russ., Bohem. -t. Lithuanic -ti; Gaelic -adh. Welsh -t, -ed, &c. See -ATe, **-ed**, **-d**.]

rent a return for borrowed property. (RĔDDO, RĔDDĬTŪ[m], to restore.) **flood**, see **-d**.

guss-et, Welsh cwysed, from cwys a furrow.

bent lent lost bereft post point weight might light sight fight sift lift belt stilt b-lo-t we-t suite flute

-T-, -D-, -*TH*-, intensive.

[Akin to T participial and S inflectional. Bohem. -ot intensive.]

dic-t-ate to say or order with authority. (DĪCO I say; DICTo I command, dictate.)

fasti-d-ious readily disgusted. (FĀSTĪDĬO I dislike, loath; FĀSTŬS disdain.) **ple-th-ora**, see -R-US.

Phlegĕ-th-on (in mythology,) a river in the infernal regions. (*φλέγω* and *φλεγέ-θ-ω*, to burn.)

in-spec-t to look at carefully. (☞ SPĔCĬO, SPĔCTŪ[m], to see; SPECTo, SPECTATU[m], to look at; SPEC-IT-O, to view often.)

-T-, repetitive. See -IT-.

T, factitive.

[Latin, as in MĔO, *to go, pass,* (whence per-me-ate,) MĬTTO I *cause* to go, I send; whence miT, miS, of *remit* and *mission*. Akin to T intensive.]

T, declensional.

[Latin crude forms or genitive case signs, with the nominative in -S,[a] as in PĀRS (gen. PĀRT-ĬS,) *part;* SĂLŪS (gen. SĂLŪT-IS,) *health.* Greek nom. in -ρ, as ἧπαρ (gen. ἥπᾰτ-ος,) *the liver;* -ς, as in χᾰ'ρῐς *grace,* gen. χάριτ-ος, whence chari-t-y; -α, as in κλῐ'μα (gen. κλιματ-ος) *climate.* See -*MA*, -*AD*, -*AS*, and -D- declensional.]

satellite a companion. (SĂTĔLLĔS, gen. SĂTĔLLĬTĬS.)

part mind mental **dent**al **mount mound front fount, font creant gent**ile[a] **gent**le **clement nepot**ism[a] **hospit**al

sort **litigate** (LĪS strife, genitive LĪTĬS.) **salute** **night** **climate** **chromate** **hepatic** **dramatic** **ped**agogue **clematis**, see *-IS*.

The Latin nominative is -ĒS and the genitive -ĬT-ĬS, in military, satellite; but quiet QVĬĒS has -ĒT-ĬS, and interpreter INTERPRĔS has -ĔT-ĬS.

-T-, connective.

es-t-eem (ÆS money, ĔMO I gain.) **ego-t-ism** (ĔGŎ I.)

Obs. The T in pro-cras-t-in-ate (CRĀS tomorrow,) and in rus-t-ic (RŪS, gen. RŪRĬS the country,) is as much participial as connective.

-*T*-, mutational.

[Akin to -T-, -D-, -S- participial.]

chao-t-ic in the condition of (χά'ος) chaos.
gene-t-ic pertaining to genesis (see *-S-IS*) or origin.
syntac-t-ic pertaining to syntax.

-t, neuter.

[Sanscrit -D, -T. Latin -D; Gothic -ta; German -s.]

Latin QVŎ-D **wha-t** ĬSTŬD **that** ĬD **it**.
Danish neuter indefinite article et *the*.

-T, adverbial.

-T was originally adverbial in the adjective **aliquot**.

-T-ARy, a.

hereditary (-D- declensional, -T- participial.) **proprietary** (-T- participial.) **military** (-T- declensional.) **cemetery**, see -ARy.

-te, n. See -T-ER, *-T-ES*.

pirate πειρᾱτής one who robs at sea. (πειράω I try, try the sea.) **athlete**, see -T-ER. **trachyte**

Climate, see -T- declensional.

-tee, n.

[T participial and **-ee**, as in **lega-t-ee, paten-t-ee.** See -ATe.]

-T-ER, -TR-, -T-OR, -S-OR, n. *he who; agency.*

[-TER,[a] -TOR,[b] -SOR,[c] (fem. -TRIX,[d] neut. -TRUM.[e]) Ital. -tore, -sore; Rhaetian -tur, -dur. Sp., Port. -dor; Fr. -teur, -tre. Ss. -TR̥, fem. T-I5. Gr. -τηρ,[f] -τωρ,[g] -τυρ,[h] τεύς, -της;[i] fem. -τειρα,[k] -τις,[l] -τρια,[m] -τρις;[n] neut. -τρον,[o] -τήριον.[p] Irish -teoir, -thoir, -doir. Wallachian -toriu. Polish -tarz; Bohem. -tař. Albanian -tár. See T part., -OR n., -*ET* n.]

sector[b] he who, or that which (see SĔCO, SE·CTŪ[m],) cuts.

monitor[b] he who (MŎNĔO, MŎNĬTŪ[m],) admonishes.

cor-sair CŪRSŎR a runner. (☞ CŪRRO I run.)

equator **agitator**[b] **auditor**[b] **minis-ter**[a] **-tr-ation** **arbiter**[a] **arbitr-**ary **magisteri**al[a] **master** **visiter** **au-thor**[b] **factor** **extorter**[b] **digester** **incisor**[c] **censor**[c] **extensor**[c] **successor**[c]

athlete,[f i] *ἀθλέω* I toil, combat.

cerastes[i] a horned viper. (*χέρας* a horn.)

mystery[f i l] **character**[f] **despot**[i] see -P- **prophet**[i] see -*ET* **martyr**[h] **patriot**[i] **hermit** or **eremit**e[i] **zealot**[i] **nectar** *νέκταρ* **crater**[f] **plaster**[o] **philter**[o] **centre**[o] **obstructor** or **obstructer** —**father** ([a]) **mother** ([a]) **brother** ([a]) **sister** **daughter**

Ancestor (antecessor, antcessor,) has both S and T.

Presbyter (whence *priest*) is from πρεσβύτερος, the comparative degree of πρέσβυς old, venerable, a senior.

Obs. 1. This suffix is -ER, -OR, preceded by T participial, as in DŎCĔO I teac-h, DO·C-T-ŬS taugh-t, DO·C-T-ŎR (as if teach't-er) a teacher. The English word 'teacher' is more abstract than 'doctor,' implying one who teaches or may teach, whilst the Latin word is associated with an adjective form, and implies a person by whom anything is taugh-t. The English word is an index of ag-ency, the Latin one an indica-t-or of perfec-t ac-t-ion. The difference is that between explorator and *explorer*, numerator *numberer*, accusator *accuser*, declamator *declaimer*, inquest *inquiry*, deduct *deduce*, (in)spection (sus)*picion.*

Obs. 2. Greek has many verbs in -ιζω (izdo,) and when -της follows one of them (the verbial ω being dropped) d (of isdtes) is absorbed by t, or zd becomes st (ist-tes,) and -ιστης (whence -ist) results, as in βαπτίζω I baptise; βαπτιστὴς bapti-st, he who baptises. This inflectional s and participial T occur in **enthusia-st caust**ic, see -*S*. **elast**ic, see -*AS-T*.

Obs. 3. Artist, florist, chimist, algebraist, &c. are inductive forms.

Obs. 4. The *t* of Arnaut or Arnaout (pronounced arn-out) belongs here. This word is from *αρβανίτης* (Albanian) and is formed by metathesis and the mutation of *ba* to *au*. *Zemindár* (with English *z*,) see **-dar**.

-ter, n.

[A Teutonic suffix formed of T repetitive, participial, (or declensional,) and **-er** frequentative, or substantive.]

slaughter slaying in the aggregate. (Ger. schlagen to slay, schlachten to slaughter.) **rafter** a roof timber.

laughter **mur-der**, MŎRĬŎR, to die.

-ter, v. frequentative.

swelter to be overcome with heat. (Middle high German swëllen to suffocate; Ang. svelan to burn.)

welter wallow **bluster** blow **glitter** glow **falter** fail

-TER, -TERIOR, **-ther**, a.

[-TĔR-ŬS, -TĔR-ĬŎR; -*τερ-ος*; Sansc. -TĂR-Ă5; Pers. -ter. A sign of the comparative degree, which has lost most of its force in English. From the Sanscrit root TṜI, to step or place *beyond*, and seemingly present in TR-ANS, ter-mination, pene-tra-te, I'N-TRĀ-RĔ, Ĭ-TĔR-Ūm *again*, CĒ-TĔR-ŬS *other* (Ϝέ-τερ-ος, CĬ-S, CĬ-TRĀ,) A'L-TĔR *other*, N-ĒV-TĔR, I'N-TĔR, PRAE-TĔR, SU'B-TĔR, ĒX-TĔR.—*Bopp*, Comparative Grammar.]

exterior farther out, on the outside. See EXTRA, ULTRA.

eso-ter-ic pertaining to that which is (*ἐσώτερος*) interior.

other, Ger. an-der; old Ger. andher; old Sax. ōdhar; Gothic an-θar; Russ. inoi; Ss. AN-JA, compar. AN-TAR-A *other*.

better, Persian bih *good*, bihter *better*, bihterīn *best*. Go. bats *good*, batiza *better*, batists *best*. Eng. better; Ang. betere; German besser; Sw. bättere; Gr. *βελ-τερὸς* and *φέρ-τερος*.

ulterior **alter-nate** **neuter** **neutral** **iterate** **whe-ther** **either** **farther** **dexter**ous **sinister—hys-ter-ic**

-ter, prepositional.

[Gothic af-ta *backward*, aftra *in the new;* old Nordish eptir, eftir *after*. Akin to T participial, and -ER adjectival.]

-*TER-ION*, n. See -T-ER.[p]

cri-t-er-ion **acro-t-er-ion** or **acroterium** **elaterium**

-TERN. See -URN.

-*T-ES*, n.

[See -T-ER, -της,[i] and T participial.]

der-m-es-t-es a genus of insects which eat skins and other animal matter. (δέρω I flay, δέρ-μα a skin, ἐσθίω I eat.)

pyri'tes πυρί'της (from πῦρ fire,) several species of mineral with a metallic lustre, and composed of sulphur and iron, copper, &c.

cerastes, see -T-ER. **pirate,** see **-te**. **prophet,** see *-ET.*

-th, -t, n. *that which is; -ness, -ing.*

[-T-AS; Ss. -TĀ, -TVA, as in PṚTHU *broad*, PṚTHU-TA or -TVA *breadth.* Gothic, as in diupiθa *depth*, gabaurθs *birth*, dauθus *death*, friaθva *joy*, and participial -θs. Sw. -de, -te, -d, -t; Dan. -de, -te; Ohg. -ida; Belg. -de, -te, as in lengte *length*, vreugde *joy*. Ger. -ath, -at, -ut, -te, -d, as in heim *home*, heimat*h* *native place;* arm *poor*, armut*h* *poverty;* breit *broad*, breite *breadth;* tod *death*. Ang. -ð, -ða, as in fiscian *to fish*, fiscoð *a fishing.* Irish geal *white*, gealadh *whiteness;* beirim *to bear*, breith *bearing*, beirt *a burden*, beirthe *birth;* bì, beo *living*, bith, bioth *life;* beit *both*. Welsh -dd, -d, -th, as in du *black*, du-edd *blackness;* pedwar *four*, pedwaredd *fourth;* galluog *strong*, galluedd *strength;* tor *a break*, toriad *a breaking.* See **-d**, -Ty.]

month	moon	**youth**	young	**health**	hale
strength	strong	**sloth**	slow	**math**	mow
dearth	dear	**breadth**	broad	**growth**	grow
mirth	merr-y	**stealth**	steal	**filth**	(de)file
fourth	four	**tilth**	till	**broth**	brew
wealth	weal	**birth**	bear	**death**	die

herd **hoard** **gar**den **h**e**arth** **e**a**rth** **girth** **lath** **sheath**

Obs. 1. Th became T to prevent the concurrence of fθ, sθ, χθ, as in the*ft*, thir*st* (see **-d**,) i*sth*mus, wei*ght*, hi*ght* (Chaucer,) or high*th* (Milton,) drou*gh*t or drou*th* (drooth,) thou*ght*, wri*ght*.* Di*phth*ong and na*phth*a cannot become di*fth*ong and na*fth*a in genuine English; and for a similar reason, old English has fift, sixt, &c. instead of 'fifth' and 'sixth.' This is a question of speech and etymology, independent of the accidents of spelling.

Obs. 2. If 'stealth' had been derived from *steal*, it would probably have been 'stilth,' as *till* makes 'tilth.' But there is no recession from the vowel I to *ε*, the Anglish stēlan or Belg. stelen (with e in they,) being the precursor both of steal and stealth. 'Width' is not from *wide* but from Ang. Vid; 'wealth' not from *weal* but Ang. Vēlă; and 'would' not from *will* but from Latin VŎLO, German wollen, old English woll, Scotch wull, &c. § 8.

Obs. 3. The ordinal sign -th, (Ang. -oðe, Gr. -τος, Ger. -te,) is also used for partitives, as in 'a fourth part,' in German vier-tel, with -l diminutive added to the ordinal form.

-*TH*-, formative.

[A future and aorist passive participle, and present in Greek inflections of the passive voice. Compare the present active infinitive βουλεύ-ειν *to advise*, passive βουλεύ-εσθαι *to be advised;* subjunctive aorist active βουλεύ-σω *I may advise*, &c. passive βουλευ-θῶ *I may be advised*, &c. of which the participle is βουλευ-θείς *being advised*.]

a-s-th-m-a a disease accompanied by difficulty of breathing. (+ἄω, ἄημι, to blow; with S inflectional, and -*MA*.)

ari-th-m-et-ic the science of numbers. (ἀρι·θμὸς number; ἄρω I adapt.)

oph-th-almic (-ic) pertaining to (ὀφθαλμὸς) the eye. (ὄπΤομαι, to see; 1st aorist indicative passive ὤφθην; 1st future indicative passive ὀφθήσομαι.)

ortho-epy right pronunciation. (ὀρθὸς erect, right; +ὄρω, to move, arise; perfect passive infinitive ὄρθαι to be raised.)

cyathiform goblet-shaped. (χύω, to contain; κύαθος and κώθων a cup; diminutive κυάθ-ι-ον a goblet.)

Phaethon a proper name. (φαέθων the shining.)

Plethora (see -R-US) is placed under T intensive, because Θ is in the intensified form.

---

* See collateral facts by Guest in the Proceed. Philol. Soc. vol. 2, 190, 199.

-*TH*-, mutational.

[Th is a mutation of S, as in ὄρνις *a bird*, gen. ὄρνῖθος.]

orni-th-o-logy the science of birds.

helminthology the science of worms. (See -*AD*.)

But T replaces Th by dissimilation in **anthelmin-t-ic** (a medicine ἀντί against worms,) to prevent the repetition of the lisp.

Obs. -th is a feminine suffix in the Hebrew Elath, &c.

-th, adverbial.

[Danish hid (Sw. hit) *hith-er*, and did (Sw. dit) *thith-er*, seem to indicate that this -th- is adverbial, with adjectival -er in English. Go. -d- in hvadre *whither;* -θ- in θaθro *thence.* Sanscrit in TA-T-RA *there;* TA-T-AS *thence.* Old English in eath, rath, sith; English in forth. See Obs. under -R adverbial.]

	Ger.	*Gothic*		*Ohg.*	*Swedish.*	
whi-th-er,	wo	hva-r	*where,*	hwarōt	hvart	*whither.*
hi-th-er,	hie	he-r	*here,*	herōt	hit	*hither.*
thi-th-er,	da	θa-r	*there,*	darōt	dit	*thither.*

-T-IC, a.

plastic that may be moulded. (πλάσσω I mould. T part.)

rustic pertaining to (RŪS, gen. RŪR-ĬS,) the country, or rural affairs. (See T connective.)

lunatic influenced by (LŪNĂ) the moon (T participial.)

prophetic, see -IC, T part. **pris-ma-t-ic**, see **-m**, T declensional.

(**-tide**, *time.*)

noontide **eventide** **whitsuntide** **shrovetide** **springtide**

-T-ILE, a. See -AT-ILE.

fer-t-ile capable of bearing. (☞ FĔRO I bear, carry.)

-T-IM-, adv.

[From nouns and verbs. See T participial, and -IM adverbial.]

-T-IM, n., a.

[T and M participial.]

vic-tim VĪCTĬMĂ an animal bound and sacrificed. (VĪNCĬO, VĪNCTŪ^m to bind.)

mari-time pertaining to (MĂRĔ, gen. MĂRĬS,) the sea.

-T-IM-, superlative.

[Adj. superl. -im, preceded by T or S participial or intensive.]

op-tim-ist **in-tim-ate** **mac-sim-um** **proc-sim-ate** (cs for x.)

-T-IN-, -T-INe.

[Sansc. -TANA5; Latin as in CRĀSTĪNUS pertaining to (CRĀS) tomorrow. T participial.]

pro-cras-tin-ate to defer until (CRĀS) tomorrow. (S adverbial.) **vespertine** pertaining to the evening.

pri-s-t-ine (S adverbial, T participial, -INe a., see PRO.)

intestine (I'NTŬS within.)

-T-ION, n.

[Latin -TĬO (gen. TĬŌNĬS;) Ital. -tione, -zione; Span. -cĭōn; Port. -çao; French -tion (pronounced sĭ-ōⁿ.) In old Eng. -tĭōn, -cioun, &c. were dissyllabic. See T participial, and -ION.]

-tion-ary, -tion-ate -ly, -tion-ate-ness, -tion-ed, -tion-er, -tion-ist.

cau-t-ion a taking care; watchfulness. (CĂVĔO, to take care, beware.)

> How had this cherl imaginatioun . . .
> Who ſhulde make a demonſtration.—*Chaucer.*
>
> And by theſe meditations refin'd,—*Donne.*

-T-IV-, -T-IVe, a.

[-T-IV-US (-Ă, -ŪM.) Sanscrit -TAVJ-A5 (-Ā, -Ă,.) -τε-ος (-α, -ον.) See T participial, -IVe.]

fur-tive **festive** **inventive** **progressive** **active—talkative**

-ton, n.

simpleton a senseless person. (Akin to the Italian augmentative semplicione a dolt.)

wanton wandering; unrestrained. (W. gwa that throws from; gwan a dividing; gwant that divides; gwanton that is apt to separate or run off; adj. fickle, *wanton.*)

> A frere ther was, a wantoun and a merye,
> A lymytour, a ful folempnè man.—*Chaucer*, l. 208.
>
> . . . our own nation have wantoned in blood,—*J. Wesley*.

-T-ous, a.

[See T participial, T declensional, and **-ous.**]

liga-men-t-ous having the quality of a ligament.

par-en-chy-ma-t-ous **momentous** **calamitous** **felicitous**

-T-R-.

[T participial and R formative. See -TRUM.]

pene-tr-ate to pierce, advance (PĔNĬTŬS) inwards.

-tre, n. See -TRUM.

[In etymologic and phonetic points of view, -tre and -ter, like -ple and -pel, are equally erroneous, the last syllable of *theatr* and *apl* being without a vowel. The analogy of thea*tre* is that of lit*tle*, and of the*ater* that of lit*ter*.]

theatre **spectre** **sceptre** **metre** **centre** **lustre** **nitre**

-T-R-IX, **-tress**, n. fem.

[-T-R-IX. W. -dres. Fr. -trice, -tresse, -treuse; Ital. -trice; Sp. -triz; Port. -triz. The fem. form of -T-OR, -T-R-UM. See -IX.]

directrix, **directress** she who directs.

-T-R-UM, -T-R-A, n. *that which;* agency.

[Neuters— -T-R-ŬM, a shortened form of -TĔR-ĬŬM; Sansc. -TRA,; Gr. -τρον, -θρον, -τήρῐον. Fem.—Ss. -TRĀ; Lat. -TRA, -TERIA, -TORIA; Gr. -τρα, -θρα, -τειρα, -τηρια, -τρια, -τρις, -τις. Masc.— -τρος. T participial and R formative. See -S-TER.]

spectrum, **spectre** something to be seen; an image. (SPĔCĬO, SPE CTŪm, to see.)

rostrum a beak; something with which (RŌDO,) to gnaw.

plectrum something with which (+πλήγω,) to strike (the strings of a lyre.)

Py'rĕthrum (πῦρ fire,) a plant named from its pungency; the plant b a r t o n.

Lestris a genus of gulls. (λῃστρὶς a female robber; λεία booty.)

orchestra ὀρχῆστρα **mystery** -ῐον **centre** -τρον **excentricity** **theatre** -τρον **canister** -τρον **alabaster** -τρος **elaterium**

-t-ry.

poultry fowls in the aggregate. (Old French p o u l e t a young fowl, a *pullet.* See **-et**, **-ry**.)

gentry (T declensional) **pantry** **peltry** **sentry** **pageantry**

-TU-AL, a.

[-T-US (T participial) and -AL.]

intellectual **effectual** **spiritual** **punctuality** **eventually**

-T-UDe, n.

[-T-ŪDO, gen. -TŪDĬN-ĬS (see -DO;) Fr. -tude; Sp. -tud; Ital. -tudine. Akin to T participial, -UD-, and -TĀS, gen. -TĀT-ĬS.]

solitude the state of being (SŌLŬS) alone; loneliness.

plenitude fulness. (PLĒNŬS full.)

amplitude inquietude similitude vicissitude turpitude mult-i-tud-in-ous longitude habitude magnitude gratitude

Obs. 1. The accusative case CONSVETUDINEM gives 'custom' and 'costume,' unless, as Diez suggests, the Italian 'costuma' may be from CŌNSVĒTŬS *accustomed*, with -udin- rejected for -ŪMEN.

Obs. 2. Although there is a word SĔRVĬTŪDO,—'servitude' may be from SĔRVĬTŪS *service*, gen. SĔRVĬTŪT-ĬS.

Obs. 3. The similarity of -TŪDO and -TAS, gen. -TĀT-ĬS, is shown by the two Latin forms TĀRDĬTĀS and TARDITUDO tardiness; Ital. quietudine and quietezza. The Welsh -tyd, -did, &c. answer to both forms.

-T-URe, *that which is to be.* See S-URe.

[The Latin future participle, as in ĂMĂ-TŪRŬS *about to love.*]

future that which is to be. (FUI I have be-en; FĪ-O, φύω, to be.) **venture** something (VĔNĬO, VE·NTU^{m}) to come.

judicature about to (JŪDĬCĀRĔ) give judgment.

-T-US, n. m. -T-A, n. f. -T-UM, n. neut.

[T particip. Ss. -TA5, -T-A5 (-Ā, -A,.) Lat. -T-ŬS (-Ă, -Ŭ^{m}.) -τος (fem. -τη, -της, neut. -τον,) -θεις. Hindoostanee -TĪ. See -ATe, -T-ous, **-ous.**]

a-sbe-s-t-us, a mineral which resists fire. (ἄσβεστος unextinguishable; +σβέω, to quench.)

Aſbeſtos, or incombuſtible cotton, is found in a quarry of limeſtone, in the county of Eſſex.—*Guthrie*, Geography, 1795.

albata an alloy resembling silver. (ĀLBŬS white.)

stra-t-um (Ss. STṚTA,) that which is spread; pl. strata.

hiatus apparatus status impetus dictum asphaltum momentum ultimatum factotum aorta—infanta

-Ty, -TI-, -ITy, n. *-ness; quality; power.*

[T participial. -τ-ης (gen. -τητ-ος;) -θος. -TĀS (gen. -TĀT-ĬS.) Sp. -dad; Port. -dade. Provensal -tat. Ger. -tät; Belg. -teit. Ital. -tà; Fr. -té. Old Eng. -te, -tee (pronounced as in French.) Welsh -did, -dawd. It is commonly preceded by I, often of a genitive case, but this becomes E when the concurrence of II is to be avoided.]

sanity SĀNĬTĀS saneness or soundness (of mind.) (SĀNŬS healthful.) **faculty** power of doing. (FĂC-ĬL-ĬS what can be (FA·C-TŪ^m) done.)

equity the quality of justice, or of being just.

security the state or condition of being secure.

polarity the state or condition of being polar.

majesty avidity timidity validity agility atrocity diversity fluidity felicity veracity rapacity pugnacity sagacity—anxiety piety verity variety sobriety—liberty poverty fatu-ity vacuity—ci..ty summit.. bounty surety

Obs. 1. -cy (for -sy) is a form of -ty, *t* having become *s*, as in polity policy, prĭvity prĭvacy.

Obs. 2. *Oddity* and probably *laity* (λᾱός the people,) are hĭbrids. For polity, dynasty, see **-y**, n. ¶ 1.

Obs. 3. *Amity* is from AMIcɪTIᴀ, Fr. amité. *Cruelty* is from CRŪDĒLĬTĀS, but it bears some resemblance to the German grauel*th*at an outrageous (*th*at) deed.

Obs. 4. -ty in twenty, thirty, &c. is for *ten.*

> Off hem I have ffull plente
> Ffor ffolke that haven volunte.—Attributed to *Lydgate.*

-T-YL.

[-T- participial, and -L ¶ 3.] **dactyl**

-U-, formative.

[Ū formative appears in -URe, -URY, -URI-ENT, -U-ITOUS, and is often fused with U of the adjectival and participial -ŬS, -ŪM.]

-UC-, -UC-ous, a. See -AC.

Festūca, fescue a genus of grasses. **festucous**

cad-uc-ous subject (CĂDĔRĔ) to fall.

-UD-, -UT-, n.

[Lat. n. -ŪS, gen. -ŪD-ĬS, ŪT-ĬS. Akin to -ας, gen. -ΑΔος. See -*AD*, and D declensional.]

pal-ud-al relating to (PĂLŪS) a marsh.
paludina a freshwater snail.
sal-ut-ary pertaining to (SĂLŪS) safety, health.

-ue, **-u**, participial.

[French participial nouns, mostly masculine in -u,[m] feminine in -ue.[f]]

revenue[m] return or income from investments or taxation. (Fr. revenu, from revenīr, Lat. RĔ-VĔNĬO, to return.)

avenue[f] **battue**[f] **due**[m] **retinue** Fr. retenue[f] **value**[f] **residue**[m] **residual** **tissue**[m] **virtue** Fr. vertu[f] **virtuous** **virtu**' Ital. virtù[f] **virtu-oso**, fem. **virtu-osa** **vendue** **venue** akin to vicin-age **issue**[f]

-ue, cacographic.

catalogue κατάλογ-ος **pedagogue** **prorogue** **league**, Fr. ligue, ☞ LĬGO I bind. **opaque** ŎPĀCŬS **grotesque** **antique** **oblique** **pique**

-UGO, -UGIN-. See -GIN-, -AGO.

albugo (ĀLBŬS white,) a speck on the eye.
lan-ugin-ous having (LĀNA) wool or down; downy.

-U-IT-ous, a. *manner*.

fortuitous by (FŌRS) chance.
gratuitous in the manner of (GRĀTŪ[m]) a favor.
pitu-it-ous like, or producing phlegm.
in-iqu-it-ous in a wicked manner.
Circu-it-ous has -it- of ĔO, ĬTŪ[m], to go.
Ubiqu-it-ous going or being everywhere.

-UL-, -OL-, -IL-, -L-, pletive. See -UL-ENT.

-UL-, -ŬL-A, -UL-UM, **-ule**, n. diminutive; implemental.

[ŬL-US n. masc., -ŬL-Ă n. fem., ŬL-UM[b] n. neut.; Gr. -αλιον. Ital. -olo, ola, -ello, -ella. See under -L, -L-US, -C-**le**, **-acle.**]

-ul-ar, -ul-ate, -ul-at-ion, -ul-at-ory, -ule, -ul-ist, -ul-os-ity, -ul-ous.

s-pat-ula (and **epa-ul-**et,) a small spade.

nebula a small (NŪBĒS) cloud. **nodule** a little knot.

r-ule and **rail**, RĒGŬLĂ, an implement with which (☞ RĔGO,) to rule.

cir-cingle[b] a band for girding; a girdle. (CĪNGŬLŬS, CĪNGŬLĂ, CĪNGŬLŪM; CĪNGO I gird.)

vinc-ulum something with which (VĪNCĬO,) to bind.

globule cellule gran-ul-ous **ocul-**ar **vitriol spherule schedule scapula uvula fibula speculum tenaculum— gondola cupola vanilla arm-ad-illo peccadillo punc-t-ilio**

-UL-AR, -UL-AR-Ly, -UL-ARI-Ty. See -IC-UL-AR.

capsular pertaining to, or like a small (CĂPSĂ) chest.

perpendicular vertical. (PERPENDĬCŬLŪ[m] a plumb-line.)

circu-l-ar-ly circu-l-ari-ty cellular regularly angularity

-UL-ENT, a. *full of.*

[-UL-, -OL-, -IL, -L-; ŬL-ĔNT-US, -ŎLENTUS; -ŬLENS, -OLENS, -ILENS. Formed from nouns. Akin to -AL, L being the significant element. See -UL-, -ANT.]

virulent full of (VĪRŬS) poison.

pestilent full of (PĔSTĬS) contagion.

violent VĬŎLĔNS and VĬŎLĔNTŬS full of (VĪS) force.

esculent adapted for (ĒSCĂ) food.

corpulent opulent truculent turbulent fraudulent succulent somnolent purulent viol-ence -ate, -ation, -ently

Obs. *In-dol-ent* is from DŎL-ĔNS paining; *red-ol-ent* from ŎLĔO, to scent of; and *male-vol-ent* from MĂLĔVŎLĔNS badly-wishing, -ol- being part of the root.

-UL-oUS, a. *inclination to.*

garrulous inclined to (GĀRRĬO,) prate.

querulous ready (QVĔRŎR,) to complain. **tremulous**

-UL-T, n. -UL-TU-oUS, a.

tumult, TŬMĒSCO, to begin (TŬMĒRĔ) to swell or ferment.

adult grown up. ĂDŎLĒSCO, ĂDU·LTŪ^m^, to grow up; ĂLO (ĂLĬTŪ^m^ and ALTU^m^,) I feed, increase, whence **co-alite**.

Result, insult, resile, are from SĂLĬO, to leap.

-UM, n. *that which.*

[Ss. -Ă,; Lat. -Ū^m^; Gr. -ον, -ιον; as in Ss. VALA,, Lat. VĀLLŪ^m^ *a wall.* Ss. MADHJA,, Lat. MĔDĬŪ^m^, Gr. μέσον the *middle.* Ss. P'HULLA,, Lat. FŎLĬŪ^m^, Gr. φύλλον *a leaf.* Neuter nouns. See *-ON,* Obs. 1.]

tym'panum the drum of the ear. (τύμπᾰνον a drum; τύπτω I strike; τύμμα a blow.)

Greek, in *-ον*—**cranium muse'um mausole'um gymnasium scholium trape'zium asy'lum elysium plectrum asphaltum**
Latin—**medium tedium** TÆDĬŪ^m^ **delirium compendium stipendium exordium addendum mod-ic-um millennium serum premium** PRÆMĬŪ^m^ **atrium sensorium equilibrium alluvium effluvium menstruum lixivium opprobrium forum. opus-cul-um gypsum album minium interval***lum* **petr-oleum spectrum rostrum—vellum venom**, see **-om.**

Obs. 1. The suffix -um is lost in monument, document, parchment.

Obs. 2. *Begum* (Turkish, *e* as in *they,* properly *begam,*) a lady of high rank, a princess. The feminine form of Beg, bey *a prince.*

-UM, genitive plural.

nostrum (of us;) a quack medicine which is claimed as a discovery known only to the maker.

quorum (of whom; QVĪ who; the first word formerly used in commissions to justices of the peace;) the number of persons necessary to transact business legally, in a board of directors or other deliberative body.

-UND, a. UND-ITy, n. See -AND.

rotund rotundity jocund-ity rubicund vagabond

-UNe, UN-ITy See -AN.

op-port-une im-port-un-ity fortune tribune jejune

-UoUS, -UI-, -UUM, a., n.

[-Ŭ-ŬS (-Ă, -ŬM,) a form of -VUS. See -IVe.]

noc-uous having the quality of injuring. (NŎCĔO, to hurt.)
contin-uous contin-ui-ty vac-ui-ty resid-uum arduous

-UR-, -URe, -URy, n.

-ing; that which is, a state of being.

[-ŪRĂ n. (Ital., Sp., Port. -ura, Fr. -ure;) commonly added to the stem of a supine, participial, or adjective form, as JŪNGO *I join;* JŪNCTŬS *joined;* JŪNCTĬO *the act of joining, junction;* JŪNCTŪRĂ *the result of joining, a juncture* or *seam.* The U is formative, and the R is that of -T-ER. See S-URe.]

-ur-able, -ur-age, -ur-al, -ur-ate, -ur-ation, -ur-ed, ur-er, -ur-esque, -ur-ious.

figure a make, shape, form; that which is the result of making. (FĪNGO, FĪCTŪm, to make, shape.)

censure a condemnatory criticism (CĒNSĔO I judge.)

tenure a holding; the condition by which a tenant holds. (TĔNĔO I hold.)

nature that which (NĀSCŎR, NĀTŬS ĒST) is born or produced. **aperture** and **overture** an opening.

su-t-ure a state of being sewn; a seam. (SŬO I sew.)

posture PŎSĬTŪRĂ **usury** ŪSŪRĂ **cæsu'ra fissure exposure lecture sepulture picture stature ges-t-ure satur**ate **tri-t-ur-at-ion structure puncture measure**, see -S-URe **mens-ur-at-ion manu-fac-t-ur-er pas-t-ur-age temperature —enclosure failure furniture seizure miniature feature**

Obs. The distinction is not always observed between -ion and -ure, as in fraction fracture; junction juncture; position posture; torsion torture; incision incisure; compression pressure; construction structure.

-ure, n.

[French -ir in plais-ir *pleas-ure*, lois-ir *leis-ure*, due to the Latin infinitive -ĒRĔ.—*Diez.*]

-ur-et, n.

[A modern suffix used chiefly in mineralogy.]

sulphuret **phosphuret** **arseniuret** **chloruret** **cyanuret**

URI-, -URy, n.

century CĔNTŪRĬĂ that contains (CĔNTŪ[m]) a hundred, commonly a hundred years.

centurion (-N declens.) the leader of a hundred men.

dec-urion the leader of (DĔC-Ē[m]) ten men.

-URI-ENT, a. *ready to.*

[Latin part. pres. of verbs in -ŬRĬO (Gr. -σείω,) formed on -ŪRŬS of the future participle active.]

esurient (participle of ĔDĔRĔ to eat,) ready to eat.

parturient ready (PĂRĬO,) to produce. **saturient**

-UR-N-.

[See under -ERN, -ER a., N-ous, and -Ty.]

noc-t-urn-al in the (NŌX, gen. NŌCT-ĬS,) night.

diurnal and **journal**, from (☞ DĬĒS,) day to day.

yesterday (HĔSTĔRNŬS a.,) the day preceding the present one.

eternity ÆTĔRNĬTĀS, as if for ÆVITERNITAS; ÆVŪ[m] duration, ÆVĬTĀS age.

taciturnity **diuturn**ity—**ex-t-er-n-al** **internal** **patern**ity

-URy, -URI-, n. See -ER, n.

penury PĒNŪRĬĂ want, scarcity. (πένεω, to be poor.)

-US, n. *that which.*

[-ŬS[a] (-Ă, -ŪM;) -IS, -ES. Gr. -ας, -ος,[b] -υς. Go. -s. Sansc. -A5, -U5, -AT. Used chiefly for masculine nouns (and adjectives,) as -A, -α are used for feminines, and -UM, -ον for neuters. They also indicate the nominative case. With -AT-, &c. they form double suffixes, as may be observed under -ate, -ade, -tous, -ary, -rous, -an, -nous, -ulous, -tous, -mus, &c. Sanscrit GARBHA5 *a form.* Latin CŌRPŬS (gen. CŌRPŎRĬS,) *a body,* whence corp-s, corp-se, corporeal. Sansc. PICA5, Lat. PĪCŬS, Eng. wood-pecker. Sansc. CALAMA5 a reed, κἄλἄμος, CĂLĂMŬS. Sanscrit JU to *combine,* gives JŪ-5, Lat. JŪ-S *broth,* Eng. juice. Sansc. VAR to *love, prefer,* VRTI5 excellence, Lat. VĪRTŬS, Eng. virtue, worth. Ss. STAMBHA5, Lat. STĪPĔS, Eng. stipe, stem, stub. Ss. NABHAS, νέφος, Lat. NŪBĒS *a cloud.* Ss. ĀVI5, Lat. ŏvĭs *a sheep.* Ss. ÇUNA5, Lat. CĂNĬS *a dog.* Ss. COCILA5, Lat. CŬCŬLŬS *a cuckoo.* Bohem. chud' *poverty,* chud'as *a pauper.*]

hiatus a ga-p or open*ing.* (HĬO I ga-pe, yaw-n. See **chas-m.**) **exodus**[b] *OD.* **discus**[b] **chorus**[b] **Eurus**[b] **urus**[a] **calamus**[b] **polyanthus**[b] **crocus**[b] **narcis-**S-US[a] **cestus**[b] **circus** **fungus,** spunge, spunk. **nuc-le-us** **calc-ul-us** **sinus** **genus**[b] **virus** **genius** **radius** **focus** **tarsus** **impetus** **incubus** **apparatus** **afflatus** **Hesperus**[b] **syllabus**[b] **acanthus**[b] **scope**[b]**—grampus**

Obs. The suffix -us is omitted in splendid florid tumid long just honest puls-e exod-e. It is replaced by -ue in vir-t-ue, Ital. virtù, Latin VI'RTŪS (U long, but not accented,) gen. VIRTŪTĬS. See **-ue** participial.

Rebus a riddle given in pictures. (Latin *by things,* the ablative plural of RĒS a thing.)

-US-T-. See -st.

ang-us-t-ate narrowed. (ἄϝχω, ĀNGO I throttle.)
robust **locust** **combustion** **august'** **Augustus**

-VER, n. See -B-.

cada-ver-ous pertaining to a (CĂDĀVĔR) dead body. (See CĂDO I fall, die.) **culver** the European wild pigeon.

-ward, *in the direction of.*

[Gothic vairθs; Lat. VĔRSŬS; Ang. -vard, -veard, -verd, -veardes; old Sax. -ward, -werd; old Nordish adj. verdr; Belg. -waards. Ss. root VṚT to *go*, to *turn*. An adverbial -s is sometimes added, and Ohg. had an adverbial -sun, as in dār *there*, darasun *thither*.]

inward forward afterward homeward southward

Then weſtward turn the ſtem, that every maſt
May ſhoreward fall, as from the veſſel caſt.
Falconer, The Shipwreck.

I give him joy that's aukward at a lye;—*Young*.

-ways, **-wise**, adv. *manner*.

[See VĬDĔO, VĪSŪ^{m}, 'ἰδεῖν *to perceive;* Ss. VIDH to *distinguish*. Dan. viis, Sw. vis, Ger. weise *manner*. See **-oid**.]

length-ways or **-wise** **cross-wise** or **-ways** **likewise** **nowise** **straightways**

Righteous (Ang. rıhtvıs) is a heteronym influenced by -ous. Chaucer uses rightwisnesse.

-XILLAry, a., n. dim.

maxillary pertaining to the (MĀXĪLLĂ) jaw. (MĀLĂ the cheek-bone, cheek; MĀNDO, to chew.)

-xt, adverbial.

betwixt between. (Akin to -s adverbial, with -t, and following *g* of Ang. tvegen *twain*.)

Ne wold nevere God betwix us tweyne . . . —l. 11068.
That is betwixe theſt and eek the weſt, . . . —l. 6829. *Chaucer*.

. . . *we muſt Diſtinguiſh betwixt Natural* and *Moral* Actions.—*L'Estrange*, Fable CCXXII.

-y, n. *condition; faculty; subject.*

[¶ 1. -ος, see -US. ¶ 2. -η, -A, -E, -ES, -IS, -ας, -ις, -ς. ¶ 3. -ία, -IA, &c., see E formative. ¶ 4. -ιον, -IU^{m}, see E formative. ¶ 5. See **-ee**. ¶ 6. Miscellaneous.]

necromancy fortune-telling by means of departed spirits. (μαντεία divination; νεκρὸς dead.)

memory MĔMŎRĬĂ the faculty or quality of remembering. (MĔMŎR mindful.)

¶ 1. **tunny**, see -N- intens. **chimney** κάμινος **treasury** θησαυρός **lethargy** λήθαργος.

¶ 2. **pigmy** πυγμή the fist, a cubit. **catastrophe** **parody** **melody** **monody**—**galaxy** -ίας **tyranny** τυραννίς **dropsy** ὕδρωψ HYDROPS **heresy** αἵρεσις HÆRĔSĬS **cachexy** -ις **phrenzy** φρενῖτις—**botany** βοτανική (βοτάνη an herb.) **Hilary** HĬLĂRĬS cheerful. **money** MŎNĒTĂ **usury** ŪSŪRĂ **progeny** PRŌGĔNĬĒS **pyrotechny** -τέχνη.

¶ 3. **tansy** a plant with durable flowers. (Low Latin tanacetum, from ἀθανασία immortal.—Eaton's Botany, 1836; Talbot's Etymologies, 1847.) **elegy** ἐλεγ-εία, ἐλεγείον **polity**, **police** πολιτεία, see **-ice** **dynasty** -εία **antipathy** ἀντιπάθεια **irony** -εία **litany** -εία **agony** ία **fantasy** -ία *APO***plexy** ἀποπληξία **astronomy** -ία **astrology** -ία **melancholy** -ία **pharmacy** -εία **idiocy** ἰδιωτεία **geography** -ία.

-ĬA. **colony** **misery** **modesty** **history** **contumely** **calumny** **repugn-ancy** **ceremony** **harmony** **scammony** **i-gnominy**

¶ 4. **mystery** μυστήριον, see -ARy. **canopy** κωνωπεῖον a gauze net for protection against gnats. (κώνωψ a gnat.) **trophy** τρόπαιον. **augury** -IUm. **larceny** LĂTRŌCĬNĬŬm, (LĂTRO a thief.) **study** STŬDĬŬm **testimony** **scrutiny**

¶ 5. See **-ee.** **lev-y** **dor-y** **all-ey** **voll-ey** **jury** **warranty** **pansy** **country** **medley** **destiny** **puny**

¶ 6. *Miscellaneous.* **penny**, Ang. pening, Ohg. pending, that which is struck. (Ss. BĀDH to strike.) **folly**, Fr. folie, W. ffolineb. **thievery**, Ger. dieberei **b-ar-l-ey**, W. ar *upon;* bàr *the top, a tuft;* lly *that extends out;* ys *that issues out;* barlys *bread corn.* **ruby**, RŬBĔŬS red. **lunacy**, LŪNĀTĬCŬS. **balcony**, Ital. balcone. **ivory** **ferry** **cherry** **sherry**

anchovy, Spanish anchova, a kind of fish usually dried. (Basque antzua, anchua *dry*.—*Mahn*, 1854.)

Normandy, Ang. normand-ige, the isle of the Normans.

-y, n. dim.

[A fragment mostly of **-lin**, n. diminutive.]

baby a little babe. Scotch **lassie** (and lassick) a little lass. **puppy** **goody** **Sally** **cranny** **pony** **ninny**

Although *valley* agrees with VĀLLĬS, it is probably formed on the diminutive VĀLLĒCŬLĂ, Fr. vallée.

-y, **-ey**, **-i-**, adj.

[Ang., Belg., Ger. -ig; Ohg. -ac, -ag, -ec, -ic; Gothic -ags, -eigs, -ahs, -ugs; old Eng. -ie. See -IC.]

bloody imbued or covered with blood. (Ang., Dan. blodig, old Fris. blodich, Ohg. blotag, Ger. blutig.)

hungry **thirsty** **rusty** **weary** **sandy** **hairy** **might-i-**ly **stormy** **shady** **lumpy** **stumpy** **many** **any** **clay-ey** **every**

She wolde her painis everich one renewe.—*Chaucer.*

But th' heedful boteman ſtrongly forth did ſtretch
His brawnie armes, and all his bodie ſtraine,—*Spenser.*

The ground may be either muddy, sandy, weedy, gravelly, stony or rocky, and the animals inhabiting each kind of ground will be found to be more or less peculiar to it.—*Stimpson*, 1859.

This suffix has arisen from the fusion of various originals, as in—
spongy SPŌNGĬŌSŬS **lazy** LĀSSŬS **murky**, Dan. mörke **savory**, Fr. savoreux **hearty**, Ger. herzlich **balmy**, Ger. balsamisch **shiny** shining, Ger. scheinend **bushy**, Ger. buschicht **watery**, Ger. wassereich, wasserig, wässericht **worthy**, Ang. vurðe, Ger. wurdig **rightly** adv. Ang. rihte, Go. raihtaba **hasty**, **testy**, **guilty**, old French, and in Chaucer—hastif, testif, giltif, from -IVe. See also -IC, -ARy, **-ee**, and **-ly**.

-y, adverbial.

[See **-ly**, the l of which is confused with that of -ble.]

abl-y in an able manner. **sociably** in a sociable way.

-y, v. See **-ish**, v.

sully soil **tally** **sally** **rally** **dally** **parley** **bray—mutiny**

-y-er, n. *he who.*

[The same as -ER and -ARy, with y interposed.]

saw-y-er **lawyer** **collier** **pavior** **courtier** **premier** **farrier—drover**

-YNX, n. See -INX, -AX.

lar′ynx λᾰ′ρυϜξ the cavity at the top of the trachea.
syrinx σῡ′ρῐϜξ a shepherd's or pandean pipe. (σῡ′ρω I draw; σῡρίσσω I pipe, whistle.)
syringa a genus of plants; lilac.
syr-inge **lynx**

-za, n.

[Italian, formed out of Latin T before I or E and a second vowel.]

piazza πλατεῖα PLĂTEA, Spanish plaza, German platz, English place.
stanza, Latin STĀNS standing.

-ze, v.

[A consonant becoming sonant to indicate a verb.]

graze grass **braze** brass **use** use **abuse** abuse—**breathe** breath **clothe** cloth

-zen, n. *one who.* See -san.

citizen one who inhabits a (CĪVĬTĀS) city. **denizen**

ANALYSIS OF WORDS.

A few examples are parsed here for the purpose of exhibiting a more minute analysis of derivative words.

fa-t-al-i-t-y

fa *speak, decree;* **-t** *fore,* as indicating pas-**t** time in an ac-**t**-ion finish-*ed* or comple-te; **fa-t** *decree-d* (as fac-t is equivalent to ma-de;) **fate** the *decree;* **-al** *relating to;* **fatal** relating or pertaining to that which is decreed; **-i** the nominative case sign of FĀTĂL-ĬS; **-t** agen-*cy, power,* a repetition of the former T participial, used in a substantive sense, **-y** being the remnant of its gender and case sign as a noun. Hence the word fatality was constructed to express *The power which has the quality of being decreed;* or, *The power relating to that which is decreed.*

To the same root belong pro-**ph**-et (see *-ET;*) and in-ef-**fa**-b-le (see IN- *not,* EX-, **-ble.**)

un-sym-path-is-ab-il-i-t-y

-ity (as before,) *the agency of;* **un-** *not;* **-ise** v. *being;* **abil** (HĂBĔO I have, use, do,) *ab-le; to* (implied in the verb suffix -ise;) **path** *feel;* **syn** (sym-‡) *with.* Or, **un-** *without;* **-ity** *the power of;* **ab** *having;* **-il** *the quality;* **path-ise** *to-feel;* **syn-** *with.* But in the actual English word, the force of -is-ab-il may be considered lost.

c-li-ma-te

Greek (infinitive λῆ-ν to desire earnestly;) κ-λί'ν-ω *I lean, in-c-line;* κλί'μᾰ (gen. κλίματος,) *that which inclines,* a region, a clime, in regard to its polar inclination; **-t** the genitive case sign of **-ma** *that which,* **c-** (as it were) *be-* **li** *le-ans,* or leans much; **climate,** that which, by its inclination towards the pole, influences the seasons.

clima-c-t-er-ic

Akin to *Climate.* See -AX, -T-ER, -IC. κλίμαξ, -ακος, a ladder; κλῖμακτὴρ the step of a ladder, *every seventh year of human life,* particularly the 63d year, which the Greeks supposed to be a critical period.

in-f-la-mma-b-le

(*mm* for *gm.*) LŪX light; φ-λέγ-ω, to blaze, burn; φλέγμᾰ, FLĀMMĂ‡ flame— **-ma** *that which is;* **in-** *very;* **b-l** *capable of;* **f-la** *b-laz-ing* or *b-urning.*

f-l-ag-iti-ous-ness

(See under D-.) ἠχὴ clamor; λ-έγω I speak; β-λ-ηχὴ a bleat, whine; Ger. fluch-en to swear; **-it** frequentative (with a connecting vowel **i**;) **f-**, with the force of be- in be-rate, or ob- in ob-loquy; FLĀGĬTO I demand often, I dun.

-ness *the quality of being;* **-ous** (for -ose) *full of;* **-iti** *frequent;* **f-l-ag** *c-l-ack.*

sup-er-e-r-og-at-or-y

r-og akin to **l-ag** in f-lag-itious; D-ĪCO I say; R-ŎG-O I ask; **e-** out of; **-y** the case termination; ĒRŎGO I intreat, pay out; **erog-at** (the thing) demand-ed, pai-d.

or-y *relating to;* **-at** *that which is;* **sup-er** *beyond;* **e-rog-** *demand.* Relating to (supererogation) over-payment.

d-ic-ta-t-or-i-all-y

The root is akin to the preceding. See under D-, and T intensive.

con-st-it-u-t-io-n-al

STŌ, ST-ĀT-Ūᵐ, to stand; (but the supine varies with a prefix, giving) CON-STO, CON-ST-ĬT-Uᵐ, to stand with; this becomes the stem of a new verb CON-ST-ĬT-Ŭ-O I dispose, settle, determine, agree upon; CON-ST-ĬT-Ū-T-ĬO (with T participial,) that which is constitute, settled, or determined, or agreed upon. The *u* is that of the supine, and the second *n* a genitive case sign.

-al *pertaining to;* **io-n** *that which is;* (ST stand, ST-IT to stand,) ST-IT-U-T- *stoo-d;* CŎN *together;* or, less strictly—*Consistent with that which has been mutually established.*

su-b-ul-ate

SUO I sew; SŪBŬLĂ an awl.

-ate *ma-de like;* **-ul** *the small;* **-b** *thing with which;* **su-** *to sew;* hence **subulate** *awl-shaped.*

adv-ant-age

adv- for ĂB *from*, confused with ĂD *to;* **ant-** (ĀNTĔ) *before;* **-age** *that* (condition or aggregate of conditions) *which* places one before, or in, adv-ance of others. See A-; and **-age**, Obs. 1.

bu-c-k-le-..-r

Welsh bw *terror*, &c.; bwg *a scare-crow;* cled *sheltering;* cledr *a flat body, a board;* bwccled *a security against danger;* bwccledr *a buckler;* c-l-ed is the prefix c-, with ll-ed *width*, compounded of lly *that extends out*, and ed *what has aptness to act*, the sense being thus made active, (not passive, as when one is protected by a rock or other immovable defense;) **-r** *that which.* **Buckler**, *a body widening out as a protection against danger.*

c-lay-more

a great sword: Gaelic and Irish mōr *great;* Gael. claidhamh, Ir. claidheamh, Welsh cledd-yf *a sword*, c-led-r *a flat body*, ll-ed breadth; Lat. ☞ LĀTŬS, π-λατ-ὺς *wide;* Irish leith-ead *breadth;* leithe *the shoulder blade.*

co-r-ac-le

A small portable fishing boat made of wicker-work and covered with leather or canvas.

Welsh co *a rounding;* or *that is outward, an edge;* co-r *a circle, close, crib;* cw-r *a periphery, a skin;* cwrwg *a round body or vessel;* cwrwgl, corwgl, Irish cwrach.

ca-r-o-l

Welsh ca *holding;* ca-r *a friend;* aw *an impulse;* aw-l *praise;* car-awl *a love song.*

groan grumble

Welsh grw *that is uttered imperfectly;* rhw *what breaks* (or grows) *out;* grwn *a groan;* grwm *a grumble.*

VOCABULARY

OF

LATIN AND GREEK ORIGINALS, OF ENGLISH DERIVATIVES AND THEIR COLLATERAL FORMS.

ĂC-ĔO, *to be sharp;* ĂC-ŬO, *to sharpen.* ac-id ac-et-ous acet-ic ac-er-b-ity cr-abbed ac-r-id acriMONy acute ache ἄχος edge acumen acme ἀκμή oxid ὀξύς oxalic oxytone oxygen par-oxysm

ÆQVŬS, gen. ÆQVĪ, *equ-al.* equity equinox equator equidistant ad-equate equilibrium equivalent equi-t-able in-iqui-ty

ÆVŪ[m], gen. ÆVĪ, *an age.* age ev-er co-eval primeval e-ternal, see -UR-N long-evity co-e-taneous

ĂGO, -ĬGO (A·CTŪ[m]) *to do,* (ἄγω) *drive, lead.* ag-ent act amb-ig-uous co-g-ent exigency outr-age nav-igate ag-it-ate — păr-ăgōge synagogue demagogue

ĂLĬŬS, ALI-, ἄλλος,[b] *other;* ĂLTĔR *the other.* alias alien *ALL*egory[b] par-all-el[b] alter-nate sub-altern

ALO, (ĂLĬTŪ[m]) *to nourish, cherish.* aluMNus coalESCe aliment alimony

ĂNĬMĂ *breath, life* (+αω, *to blow,* see under *S,*) anim-al anim-ate

ĂNĬMŬS *mind.* un-anim-ous equ-animity anim-advert

ARCH- (ἄρχω *I take the lead, govern;* ἀρχὸς, ἄρχων, Sanscrit ARHA5 *a chief,* from Sanscrit ARH *to have power.*) archon archangel archbishop anarchy monarchy architect

asg (Welsh, see M-, R-,) *a piece split off.* r-ash-er m-ash (or m-esh, of a net,) b-ask-et fl-ask-et

ĀVDĬO (ĀVDĪTU[m]) *to hear;* AVDĬT *he hears.* audible aud-it-or ob-ey ob-ed-ient

ĀVGĔO (ĀVCTŪ[m]) αὔξω, to aug-ment. auction au..-thor— auxesis

AIXOO, ἀξιόω, *to admit, take for granted.* axiom -atic

BRĔVĬS, βραχύς *short.* brief brevity abridge (*v* and *s* being silent.)

CĂDO, -CĬD- (CĀSŪ^m^) *to fall;* CĀSŬS *a falling.* cadence caducous ac-cident de-cid-uous case casual co-in-cid-e -nt occasion in-cidental cadaVERous—decay

CÆDO, -CĪD- (CÆSŪ^m^,) *to cut, kill.* concise excision incisor decide parri-cide

CĀLO, κᾰλέω, CLĀMO, *to call,* (see -M-, Obs.) clamor claim pro-, re-, ex-claim—call halloo yell yelp

CĂP-ĬO, -CĔP-, -CĬP-, -CŬP- (CA·PTŪ^m^,) *to take.* accept capt-ive capt-or capacious (see -AC-eous) oc-cup-y recipient receive concei..t ca..tch chase purchase

CĂP-ŬT (-ĬTĬS,) *the head.* cape capital chief chapter pre-cipit-ate SUSceptible chub cube cob gable—cephalic

CĂVŬS *hollow.* cave cavity concave camber cup cupel s-kiff σ-κᾰφη cymbal cove coop hoop haven coffin coffer cap cuff coif cape hoof chamber cabin chapel chimney hovel gouge cage govern-or gubernatorial

CĒDO (CĔSSŪ^m^,) *to yield, to go.* cede accede cession process proceed recede exceed concede

CĒLO, *to hide.* con-ceal cell cellar κοῖλος *hollow, deep.* calyx chalice hole hollow hell κόλπος gulf GŬL-Ă gull-et

CĔNTŪ^m^ *a hund-red.* cent century centennial centi-pede centurion

CĔRNO (CRĒTŪ^m^,) κρῑ́νω, *to sift.* dis-cer-n con-cern crisis critic crime dis-cre-te decree

CHAINO, (⁺χάω, see -m,) χαί-ν-ω, HĬO I ga-pe; cha-s-m hiatus chaos Chama gander cachinnation yawn a-che-n-ium·

CHARTES χάρτης *paper.* chart charter card cartel cart-oon

CHRONOS χρόνος *time.* chron-ic, chron-icle chronometer (☞ MĔTIOR) ana-chronism

C-LĀ-RŬS c-lea-r; λεύω, *to shine;* W. lla *what is clear;* llewer *light.* clarify (☞ LŪCĔO) glow glare

CŎQVO (CŎCTŪ^m^,) *to cook.* concoct decoction—cook coke cake kitchen

CŬBO, CŪMBO, κεῖμαι, *to lie down.* recumbent succumb in-cubation cubit kimbo coma (lethargy) incubus cower

CŪRĂ *care.* ac-curate care curate procure procurator or proctor procuracy or proxy

CŪRRO (CŪRSŪ^{m},) *to run.* course courier career concur current cursory corsair, see -T-ER

CŪRVO, *γῦρόω, to bend.* curve coronal coroner crown gyre gyration girasōl cord gird curl

CŬTĬS *a skin; σ-κῦτος a skin, a whip, leather, anything of leather; σκυλον a skin; κῦ'ω, to contain; σκῖᾰ a shadow; σκῑᾰ'ς a tent;* SCŪTŪ^{m} (dim. SCŪTŬLŪ^{m},) *a shield;* SCŬTŬLĂ *a dish.* cut-icle cut-aneous coat hide hut house hose scotch (remove bark) sky ski-n scu-m shu-ck scutiform scutellate skull scale shell shoe shield sheath shade shed shelter skulk (coal-)scuttle skillet scullery kettle cotyledon cuttle-fish (from its sucking cups.)

DĔŬS *θεὸς God.* deity deify div-ine Iu-piter (*d* lost) theology

DŌ, (DĂTŪ^{m}, -DIT-,) DŌ-N-O, *δί'δωμῐ, to give.* date edict recondite don-ate, -ation ad-, tra-, con-dit-ion-al addendum deodan-d par-don endow dower dotal antidote dose

DĔCĔ^{m}, *δέκᾰ, ten.* decad decimal decimate decennial decagon decussate, see -DE, ¶ 1. From the root of TĂNGO.

DĬĒS *a day; δαίω, to light up.* diary meri-dian (MĔDĬŬS) diURNal journal quoti-dian dial

DŎCĔO (DO·CTU^{m},) *to teach;* DĪCO (DĪCTŪ^{m},) *to say, tell.* docile doctrine doctor teacher, see -T-ER dict-ate, -ion -ary, pre-, contra-, inter-dict

DRYS δρῦς an oak. dry*AD* druid tree

DŪCO (DŪCTŪ^{m},) *to lead.* ad-, re-, in-, con-, tra-duce conduct or condui..t aqueduct duke doge tug tow

DŬO two; duo-decimo duel dou-ble deuce dou-bt twin twain twine twice twe-lve tu-b twi-lling (a double web, as dri-lling is a triple one.)

ĔMO (E·MPTŪ^{m},) *to buy.* red-eem exempt peremptory red-, ex-, pre-emption pro-mpt

ĔO (ĬTŪ^{m},) ĪRĔ *to go.* ex-it amb-i-ent circu-it in-iti-al obitu-ary trans-it-ory pre-t-or preterit it-in-er-ary perish

ERGON ἔργον work, toil; ἐργάω I work. irksome w-ork energ-y lit-erg-y ge-org-ic. *ἀρκέω I defend;* ĀRCĔO *I restrain, ward off.* co-erce ex-erc-ise. ŪRGĔO *I impel, force.* urge urgent.

ĔSSĔ *to be;* SŪ^{m} *I am;* ĒNS (ENT-,) *being.* ent-ity abs-ent pre-s-ence (*s* of SU^{m}) ess-ence ess-ent-ial inter-es-t (ESSE with T participial.)

FĂCĬO, -FEC-, -FIC- (FĂCTŪm,) *to make.* See -FIC, -fice, -fy.
fact fea..t perfect counterfei..t refit certi-fy fi-at office benefice bene-fic-ent ponti-f fashion hacienda fig-ur-at-ive feign

FĔRO *I carry.* in-, pre-, re-, de-, dif-, suf-, of-, trans-, con-fer ferry fer-T-ILE -FER-ous bear *METAphor*

FĪDĒS *trust.* con-fid-ent diffident infidel faith af-fi-ance

FLŌ *I blow;* FLĀTŬS *a blowing.* inflate flatulent flute flageolet blow blast

FLŬO (FLŪXŪm,) *to flow.* re-, con-, af-fluent afflux fluid influence superfluity fluctuate

FŎR, *φη-μί, φα-τ-ί'ζω, to speak.* af-fa-ble fa-te fa-me pre-fa-ce in-fa-nt em-pha-sis

FŌRTĬS *strong.* fort forte re-en-force ef-fort com-fort

FRĀNGO -FRĪNG-, (FRĂCTŪm,) to break, frac-ture; fraction fragile or frail infringe re-frac-t-ory—breach os-prey (ŏs *a bone*)

FŪNDO (FŪSŪm,) *to pour, to melt.* suf-, trans-, con-, in-, pro-, dif-, fus-e -ion refund foundry

GE γῆ the earth. geometry geography apogee gigantic giant

GĔL-ĪD-ŬS col-d; chilly con-geal gelid jelly

GĔN-ŬS (-ĔRĬS,) *γένος race, sort, offspring;* +*γένω*, +GĔNO, GIGNO (GĔNĬTŪm,) *to produce.* gen-uine con-gen-ial regenerate genesis homogeneous cosmogony hydrogen gender general genteel gentle jaunty gentile—kin kind

GONIA γωνία an angle. tri-, tetra-, penta-, hexa-, hepta-, octa-, nona-, deca-, poly-gon goni-o-meter

GRĂDĬŎR, *to go;* GRĔSSŬS *a going.* grade de-grad-e -ation di-, pro-gress -ion

GRAPHO γρά'φω, S-CRĪBO *I scratch, write.* en-grave dia-gra-m graphic geo-graphy grammar a-, in-, sub-, pre-, circum-, pro-, tran-, super-scribe grave groove graft grub s-crape scrap scrub scrabble scramble

HEPTA ἑπτά' SĔPTĔm, seven; heptagonal hept-archy septenary September

HEX ἕξ SĔX six; hexagon hexangular sexennial senary

HETEROS ἕτερος different. heterodox heteroclite heterogeneous

HODOS ὁδὸς a way. peri-od met-hod exodus synod ep-is-ode (ἐπί' *on*, εἰς *in.*)

HŪMĔO, *to be wet;* HŬMŬS *the ground; χάμαὶ on the ground.*

humor humid in-, ex-hume humiliate humble chame-leon camomile (as if earth-*apple* μῆλον, from its fragrance.)

HYDOR ὕδωρ, ὕδωρ water; hydrogen hydraulics (αὐλος *a pipe*) hydrometer hydrostatic hydrophobia dr-opsy hydra otter

ISO- ἴσος *equal.* isochronal isodynamic isothermal

JĂCĔO, *to lie.* adjacent circumjacent

JĂCĬO -JĔC-, (JĂCTŪ^{m}, -JECT-,) *to throw.* ab-, e-, ob-, de-, sub-, in-, pro-ject -ion conjecture projectile je..t jetson

. . . theſe are of three ſorts, either found on the ſtreame floating, and then are called Floatſon, . . . or caſt forth there [on land] by ſtorme and the water, and then are called Ietson.—*Malynes*, Lex Mercatoria, 1642.

JŬGŪ^{m} *a yoke.* subjugate conjugal yoke JŪNGO *I unite.* join joint junc-tion, -ture

JŪS (gen. JŪRĬS,) *right, law;* JŪRO *I take oath;* JŪ-DĬCO *I declare judgment.* ad-, un-just just-ice just-ify injur-e -y -ious jurisdiction ab-, con-, per-jure juror jury judge judicial adjudicate prejudice

LĂCĬO, DĒ-LĬCĬO *I entice.* de-lec-t-able delicious delightful

LĀTŬS π-λăτ-ὺς *wide;* LĂT-ŬS (-ĔRĬS) *the side.* lati-tude di-late p-late b-lade f-lat p-lot p-laice, see *-AS* p-linth f-lint p-lat p-latitude Platanus plane-tree c-loth lath leath-er equi-, col-, quadri-lateral (and from the affinity between *l* and *r*—) b-road sp-read—buckler claymore

LĀTŪ^{m}, *to carry, bear.* trans-, re-, e-, col-, pro-, ob-late dilatory prelate legis-lat-or

LĒGO (LĒGĀTŪ^{m},) *to depute, bequeath.* de-legate legation leg-acy, -atee colleague college allege

LĔGO (LĔCTŪ^{m},) -LIG-, λέγω, *to lay together, to read;* LĒX (gen. LĒGĬS,) *a law.* col-lect di-lig-ent dialect e-, se-, neg-lect intel-lect‡ intelligent col-, se-, e-lection religion legion lexicon lesson legible lecture—leg-al legis-lature legitimate illicit privi-lege sorti-lege law loyal alloy

LĬGO, (LĬGĀTŪ^{m},) *to bind.* ligature al-ligation league oblige allegiance—ally alli-ance

LĪNQVO *I leave.* de-linquent re-lic-t re-linqu-ish

LŎCO (LŎCĀTŪ^{m},) *to place.* (Akin to LĔGO.) local locat-e -ion lieu lieutenant, *liev*-tenant or *lef*-tenant, *leftenaunt* in the Bible of 1551; *lieutenant* in Shakspere (who uses u and v indiscriminately, as in *dissolue;*) and *lieftenant* in Coles's English Dictionary of 1701.

LŎQ-VŎR λέγω (☞ LĔGO,) *to speak; λόγος a word;* -logy *a discourse.* loquacity elocution obloquy loc-ust—geology eulogy prologue logic

LŪCĔO, *to shine.* lucid e-lucidate pellucid‡ look ligh-t link (a torch) b-leach b-leak b-link b-lank ph-lox Lu..na lunar

MA·GNŬS *μα·κρὸς, μέγᾰς great;* MAXĬMUS *greatest.* magisterial ma..ster mi..stress maxim maxIMUM magnify major majesty mai..n big—macro-cosm megatherium

MĂRĔ *the sea.* marine mariner mar-aud for-ay Ar-mor-ica por-beagle (a shark which hunts in packs.)

MĔDĬ-ŬS *μέσ-ος middle.* (Ital. mezzo, *pronounced meddzo.*) mid a-mid-st meddle medium mezzotint mediocrity méd-ullary inter-medi-ate meri-dian meso-thorax mes-embri-anthe-mum *mid-day-flower* (*ἡμέρα day, ἄνθος, ἄνθεμον flower.*)

MĒTĬŎR *μετρέω, to measure;* MĒNSŪRĂ a mea..s-ure. mete meter metre im-mense dimension mensuration chrono-meter

MĔMĬNĪ *μνά'ομαι,* to re-member. memento memor-y, -able, -ise, -ial-ise mention mnemonic a-mnesty. MĔNS (gen. MĔNTĬS,) the mind; mental comment

MŎNĔO (MŎNĬTŪm,) to ad-mon-ish; monitor monument summon MĬNÆ *threats* minatory menace

MICRO- μῑκρὸς little. microscope micrometer microcosm

MŎVĔO (MŌTŪm,) to mov-e; e-, com-, loco-, pro-motion motive—mob

MĬNĔO, *to project, hang over.* e-, im-, pre-, super-e-, prominent eminence

MĬNŬO (MĬNŪTŪm,) *μῐν-ύ'θω,* to di-min-ish; mĭnus minor minute com-minute min-ce

MĬTTO (MĬSSŪm,) *to send.* ad-, re-, com-, e-, o-, sub-, per-, re-ad-, inter-, trans-mit remittance emissary com-mission-er demise sur-, pre-, pro-mise re-miss

MŪN-ŬS (-ĔRĬS,) *office, duty, favor.* muni-fic-ent re-munerate immunity ex-com-mun-ic-ate commune common

MŪTO (MŪTĀTŪm,) *to move, change.* com-, im-, per-, trans-, mut-able transmutation

†NĀSCŎR, *to be* (NĀTŬS) *born.* nat-al, -iv-ity, -ure, -ion innate nascent. *Originally* GN-ASCOR, GN-ATUS, *whence* co-gn-ate im-pre-gn-ate ☞ GĔN-ŬS.

NĀVĬS *ναῦς a ship.* nausea nav-y, -al, -ig-ate nautical navvy

┼ NŌM-ĔN (-ĬNĬS,) ὄνομᾰ, a nam-e; noun nòmenclature nominal anonymous synonym i-gnom-inious co-gnom-en ☞ GĔN-ŬS.

NŎVĒm ἐννέᾰ nine; nona-gon ennea-gon

NŎVŬS νέος new; novelty innovate novice neo-phyte

ŎCTO ὀκτὼ eight; octagon octavo October octu-ple

ŎCŬLŬS eye; ocular in-ocul-ate ocell-ate ogle

ŎLĔO, *to emit a smell.* ol-id ol-factory red-olent

ŎLĔO ĂD-ŎLĒSCO (ĂDŬLTŬm,) *to grow;* from ĂLO, *to nourish, cause to grow.* ad-olesc-ent ad-ult ab-ol-ish—ali-ment coalesce

OPO ὄπω ὄπτω, *to see;* ŌPTO *I look at, wish, choose.* optics cycl-ops option adopt

ŎRĬŎR (O·RTŬS) ὄρο-μαι, *to rise;* ὀρθόω (see *-TH-*,) *to erect, make right, straighten;* ŌRD-O (-ĬNĬS) *a rank, an order.* orient ori-gin -al-ity ab-ortive or-deal ere erst early m-or-n—ortho-graphy—order ordain ordinal disordered

ŌVŬm ὠόν *an egg.* ov-al, -ate, -oid ovi-parous—ōŏ-lite oólogy

PĀNDO (PĀSSŬm,) πετάω, *to spread;* PĂTĔO, *to be open.* expansion expand s-pan pan patent patulous pet-al paddle s-pat-ula s-pathe s-pade s-pud feath-er; πέτρα *a rock;* petrify petr-oleum *rock-oil* Peter pĕtrel f-ern (see *-N.*) S-PĂT-ĬŬm *extent, interval, delay.* space spacious expatiate ré-spite

PĀCTŬm *an agreement;* PĀX (gen. PĀC-ĬS,) peace; pact cómpact paci-fy, -fic appease

PĀNGO (PĀCTŬm,) *to set,* fix. compáct impact

PĀR *equal.* par disparage pair compare peer-less impair par-ity imparisyllabic

PĂRŌ (PĂRĀTŬm,) *to provide, furnish;* I·M-PĔRO, *to order, govern.* parade apparatus prepare repair ap-parel se-parate sever em-peror empire

PĀRS (gen. PĀRTĬS,) a part; particle parcel part-y, -isan, -ial, -ner, parse portion

PĔLLO (PŬLSŬm,) *to move, drive.* expel ex-, ap-, com-, repulsion, pulse push

PĔNDĔO (PĒNSŬm,) *to hang.* pend-ant, -ent, -ulum, -ulous, pensile suspend per-pend-ic-ul-ar. PENDO (PĒNSŬm,) *to weigh, pay, consider.* expend dis-, re-com-, ex-pense pension dispensary. PŌND-ŬS (-ĔRĬS,) *weight.* ponderous pound poise

PENTE πέντε QVĪNQVĔ five; pentagon pentecost (πεντηκοστὸς

fiftieth) pingster—quinary quinquelobate fivelobed fivefold—punch (a liquor.)

ĒX-PĔRĬŎR (ĒXPĔRTŬS,) *to try, test.* expert experiment, experimenter, -al

PĔTO (PĔTĪTŪ^m,) *to beg, desire, strive, assault.* petition repeat repetition propitiate appetite compet-e -ence, -itor, compatible impetus

PHAINO φαίνω (see -N-,) *to shine, show, expose, accuse;* φά'ω, *to make clear, to appear.* pha-se (see -*S*-) em-pha-sis dia-pha-N-ous fant-asm, -astic, -asy fancy phenoMenon epiphany. φημί *to say* (☞ FOR, -M- Obs.) fame eu-phemism pro-ph-*ET* blas-pheme (βλά'πτω *I injure.*)

PHAGO φά'γω *I eat.* ichthyophagous ἰχθύ'ς *a fish.* anthropophag-y, -i, -ous

PĪNGO (PĪCTŪ^m,) to pain..t; pigment picture depict

PLĂCĔO I please; placid displeasure com-placent pleasant com-ply. PLĀCO *I appease.* implacable

PLĒNŬS πλέος full; πλήθω CŌM-PLĔO (-PLĒTŪ^m,) *to fill.* ple-n-ty, -ary replenish de-, com-, re-plete im-, sup-, com-plement ac-com-pli-sh com-, sup-ply — plethora (see -R-US) ple-*ON*-asm (πλείων *more.*) πολύ'ς *many;* polygon polysyllable. πόλις *a city;* pol-ice, -ity, -icy

PLĬC-O (-ĀTŪ^m,) *to fold;* PLE·CTO, πλέκω, *to pleat.* com-plex im-, sup-, du-, com-, ex-plic-ate, -ation suppliant pliant multi-, im-, ap-ply dis-play ac-com-pli-ce (see -PLe.)

PLŪS (PLŪRĬS) *more.* (Akin to ☞ PLĒNŬS.) over-, non-, sur-plus plu-perfect plur-ality

PŌNO (PŎSĬTŪ^m,) *to set, place.* de-, com-, de-com-, dis-, dis-com-, ex-, im-, super-im-, inter-, op-, pro-, re-, sup-, pre-sup-, trans-pose postpone deponent deposit-ory depôt post impos-t, -ition ex-, pro-, com-pound posture provost (PRÆ-PŎSĬTŬS) put

PŎPŬLŬS a multitude. people de-populate un-popular public-ation publish republic

PŌRTO *I carry.* (Akin to FĔRO.) bear com-, de-, ex-, im-, re-, sup-, trans-port porterage portfolio

PRĔCŎR *I invoke.* de-, im-precate pray

PRĔ-HĔNDO (-HĔNSŪ^m,) *to take.* ap-, com-, re-prehend sur-, com-, enter-prise prize reprisal prison

PRĔMO (PRĔSSŪ^m,) to press; com-, de-, ex-, im-, op-, re-, sup-press print‡

PRĔTĬŪm *value, reward.* ap-, de-preciate praise price precious appraise, -ment appraiser

PRĪMŬS *first;* PRĬŎR *former.* prime primer primrose primate primogeniture pristine prince prior-ity

PRŎBO *I prove.* probe proof prove prob-able, -ity probate reprob-ate, -ation

PRŎPĔ *near;* PRŌXĬMŬS *very near, nearest.* prop-inquity proxim-ate, -ity approach

PROTO-, πρῶτος *first.* prototype protoxid

PSEUDO-, *false;* ψεῦδος *falsehood.* pseudovolcanic pseudonymous

PŪLLŬS *a young animal, a bud.* pullet poult poultry foal pullulate

PŪNGO (PŪNCTŪm,) *to sting.* Welsh ig *what is sharp;* pig *a pointed end; a pike, a beak.* punct-ure, -uate, -ual-ity pungent compunction Pagurus pungar poignant point punch pike poke pick peak beak bicker peg s-pigot spicule s-pike s-poke

PŪN-ĪO (-ĪTŪm,) *to punish.* punitive pain fine (a pen-alty.)

PŬTO *I say, think;* (πείθω *I advise;* akin to FOR.) de-, dis-, im-, re-put-e, -ation compute or count

QVÆRO (QVÆSĪTŪm,) *to ask, seek, get.* query question in-, re-quest in-, re-, ac-quire in-, ac-, re-, dis-quisition exquisite acquire conquer

QVĀTŬŎR τέσσἄρες τέτρἄ- four; QVĂDRŬS s-quare; QVĀRTŬS the fourth; TĔSSĔRĂ *a square.* quaternary quadr-angle, -ant, -ate, -atic, -ature, quadru-ped, -ple quart-er-ly s-quadr-on squad square quar-antine (French quarante *for*-ty) tetragon tetrastyle tesseral tesselate

QVŎT *as many as.* quota quotient quotidian

RĂBĬĒS *madness.* rabid rave rage

RĀDĪX (-ĪCĬS,) ῥί'ζἄ root; e-radicate radical radicle rhizophagous lico-rice (γλῠκὸς *sweet.*)

RĀDO (RĀSŪm,) *to scrape.* ab-rad-e abrasion rasorial erase raze razor razee ras-p rasberry. RŌDO (RŌSŪm,) *to gnaw.* ar-, cor-, e-rod-e cor-ros-ion, -ive ros-trum rostrate sh-red

RĂPĬO (RA·PTŪm, REPT-,) *to take away, plunder, hurry.* rapine rapacious surreptitious rapture rapid rapier bereave ravage robber rover robe reap

RĔGO (RĒCTŪm,) *to set righ-t, reg-ulate.* cor-, di-, e-, in-cor-, in-di-rect rect-ify, -angle, -or reign (but not sovereign, see SŬPĔR-) reg-al, -ent, -ion ru..le bishop**ric** rich a-l-e-r.. ..t (see AD)

RŎGO (RŎGĀTŪm,) *to ask, beg.* ab-, de-, inter-rogate arrogant prorogue rogation ☞ P-RECOR.

RŎTĂ *a wheel.* rot-ate, -ary, -ation, -und -o ro..und (see -AND) rote rut route (pronounced *root*) routine rowel ro..ll ro..le ree..l

RŪMPO (RŪPTŪm,) *to break.* ab-, cor-, ir-, dis-, inter-, e-rupt, -ion, -ive incorruptible

SĂC-ĔR (-RĪ,) ἅγ-ῐος *holy.* sacer-dot-al sacr-ed con-, ex-, de-secrate sácrament sacrifice sacristan or sexton—hagiography

SĀL (gen. SĂLĬS,) ἅ·λς (gen. ἁλὸς,) sal-t; sal-ine saliferous—halo-gene salad sau..sage sauce

SĂL-ĬO, -SĬL-, (SĀLTŪm, -SULT-,) *to leap.* salient assail con-, re-, ex-, in-sult exile resilience

SĂLVŬS *sound, well.* salu-tary, -brious, -ute salvation sa..fe save salve

SĂTĬS *enough;* SĂTŬR *full.* sate satis-fy insatiate satur-ate

SCĬNDO (SCĬSSŪm,) σχῐ́ζω, *to cut, rend.* ab-, ex-, re-scind abscissa schism scissors

SCĬO *I know.* sciolist science conscious omni-scient

SCOPEO σκοπέω *I spy, observe.* scope episcopal microscope

SĔCO (SE·CTŪm,) *to cut.* sect bi-, in-, inter-, dis-sect, -ion segment saw secTOR

SĔDĔO (SĔSSŪm,) to sit; CON-SĪDO *I sit down.* assess assize assiduous sedulous siege insidious po-ssess subside subsidy re-sid-e, -uum, -ence

SĔNTĬO (SĒNSŪm,) *to feel, think.* con-, re-, dis-sent scent sens-e, -ible, -ory sentient sentence

SĔQVŎR (SECŪTŬS,) *to follow, attend.* sequ-ent, -el ob-sequi-ous consécutive second persecute (see PER-) consequence sue en-, pur-sue suit suitor suite

SĔRVĬO (SĔRVĪTŪm,) to serv-e; de-, mis-, sub-serve service servitude. SĔRVO (SĔRVĀTŪm,) *to save, keep.* pre-, con-, ob-, re-serv-e, -ation, -oir servant

SĔX ἕξ six; sexennial bis-sextile senary hexagon sixfold

SĪGNŪm *a mark, token.* sign-al, -ature, -ify, as-, con-, de-, re-, en-sign sigil *or* sea..l

SĬMĬLĬS ὁμᾶλὸς *like.* similar-ity re-, dis-semble dis-sim-ulate simile hómo-gen-eous an-omalous

SĪSTO *I place, set, stop.* as-, con-, ex-, in-, per-, re-, sub-sist, -ance, -ant

SŌL *ἥλῐος the sun, σέλᾰς lustre, σελ-ήνη the moon.* solar solstice—peri-heli-on Hel-en El-ectra—sel-eno-graphy selenite ☞ TŎRRĔO.

SŌLŬS *alone.* sole soli-tude, -tary desolate

SŌLVO (SŎLŪTŪ^{m},) *to loose, to free, to melt.* ab-, re-, dis-, solv-e, -able solu-tion

SŎNŬS *τόνος a sound, a noise.* son-ōrous, -net ab-, dis-, con-, re-sonant sound—ton-e, -ic de-tonate mono-tonous tune din thunder

SŎPŎR, SŌMNŬS, *ὕ·πνος sleep.* sopori-fic somni-fic somnolence, -ambulism—hypnotic

SPĀRGO (SPĀRSŪ^{m}, -SPĒRS-,) *to scatter.* sparse as-, dis-, intersperse

SPĔCĬO (SPĔCTŪ^{m},) *to see.* spy spec-ulum, -trum, -tacle, -tre, -imen, -ies, -ify, -ulate, -ious per-spic-uous perspective as-, circum-, ex-, in-, pro-, re-, su-spect speck despise despite spite

SPĒRO *I hope.* de-spair de-sper-ate, -ation pro-sper-ous, -ity

SPĪRO (SPĪRĀTŪ^{m},) *to breathe, blow, live.* as-, con-, in-, re-, per-, su-, tran-spir-e, -ation spirit sprite sprightly

SPŌNDĔO (SPŌNSŪ^{m},) *to speak, promise.* re-spond respons-e, -ible sponsor sponsal spouse cor-re-, de-spond

S-PŎLĬŪ^{m} *a skin, booty;* PĒLLĬS *a skin.* spoliate spoil fell pell pelt-ry pellicle pelisse. PĬLŬS *a hair;* VĒLLŬS *a fleece;* VĪLLŬS *a tuft;* VĒLŪM a veil; PĀLLĬŪM *a mantle;* pall palli-ate, -ation pile pilose villous fleece wool peel pillage

STEREOS στερεὸς firm, solid. stereo-type, -scope, -ometry

STĪNGVO, -STĪGO (STĪNCTŪ^{m},) ⊥ *στί'ζω, to mark,* sting; stick stitch stock stoker distinct instigate ex-, contra-, dis-tinguish sti..m-ulus, -ulate stig-ma-t-ise

STŌ (STĀTŪ^{m},) *στάω, ἵστημῐ, to stand, place.* stay station -ary stand state stat-ue, -ute sub-stance co-st sta-ble establish desti-ne—meta-stasis hydro-statics extasy sy-stem stamen style stadium

STRĪNGO (STRĪCTŪ^{m},) *to touch, to bind.* string stricture con-, re-, dis-trict re-, con-stringe con-, re-strai..n con-strain-t strai..t

STRŬO (STRŪCTŪ^{m},) *to build.* constru-e destroy con-, ob-, in-, de-struct-ion

SŪMO (SŪMPTŪm,) *to take, use, wear out.* as-, re-, con-, pre-sum-e presumption

SŪRGO (SŪRRE·CTŪm; SŬB and ☞ RĔGO,) *to raise, to rise.* surge re-sur-rec-tion source

TĂNGO (TACTUm,) θί'γ-ω, δέχομαι, to tak-e, touch; in-, con-tact contagion contingent in-teg-er *or* entire attai..n index in-dic-ate dexterity dactyl digitate dog (*the taker*) thing think thank dignity (DĪGNŬS *worthy*) condign deign disdai..n te..n ☞ DĔCĒm

TĀXO *I rate, value.* tax taxation taste

TĔGO (TE·CTŪm,) σ-τέγω, *to cover, hide, defend.* de-, pro-tect-ion toga toggery tegument bedeck thatch deck duck (linen) ticking ti..le—s-teganography

TĒMP-ŬS (-ŎRĬS,) time; tempor-al, -ary, -ise extemporaneous tempest tense‡

TĔN-DŌ (-SŪm, -TŪm,) τείνω, *to stretch.* tend tent at-, con-, dis-, ex-, ob-, por-, pre-, sub-ten-d, -t, -ion in-, ex-tensive. TĔNŬĬS thin; tenuity thinness attenuate—tonic peri-toneum. σ-τενὸς *nar-row.* stenography

TĔNĔO (TE·NTŪm,) *to hold.* abs-, at-, con-, de-, enter-, ob-, per-, ap-per-, re-, sus-tain dis-con-tent con-tin-ue, -ent coun-te-nance ten-ure, -ant, -or detainder

TĒRMĬNŬS τέρμα *a limit.* term conterminous determine exterminate

TĔRO (TRĪTŪm,) τείρω, *to rub.* at-, con-, de-trition detriment trite tear

TĔRRĂ *the earth.* terr-ene tur-een in-ter-ment terrace ter-rier terrestrial terraqueous subterranean territory

TĔRRĔO *I frighten.* terror terri-fy de-ter

TĒSTŎR *I witness, declare;* CON-TĒSTŎR *I call to witness;* DĒ-TĒSTŎR *I deprecate.* test, -ify, -ator, -ament intestate at-, con-, de-, pro-test

TITHEMI τί'θημί, *to place.* theme antí-, hypó-, par-én-, sýn-, prós-thesis, -thétic

TĪNGO, TĪNGVO (TĪNCTŪm,) τέγγω, *to wet, to dye.* dis-ting-uish tinct-ure attainder—tinge distain s-tain s-tencil

TŎRRĔO (TŌSTŪm,) θέρω, θέρσω, σειρέω, *to parch;* TŎRRĒNS *burning, rushing.* torrid toast tar-S-US torrent—ther-m-al ther-mó-meter—Sirius sear sere thir-st dr-y dr-ug—σείρ, ἥλιος, Lat. SŌL,

English sun; solar hel-i'acal—ξηρός (κ-σηρος) *dry*, xerodes *a dry tumor*. See yol-k yell-ow gol-den under -den

TŌRNO, *to turn* (in a lathe.) turn-er de-, con-tour tornado tourniquent

TŎRQVĔO (TŌRTŪm,) *to twist.* con-, dis-, re-, ex-tort, -ion tor-ment dossil (torsel) tor-tion, -sion, -ture tortoise (TŌRTŪS *crooked*, from its feet,) turtle (tortle) Tortugas (a Portuguese plural,) torch truss trousers

TRĂHO (TRA·CTŪm,) to draw, drag; abs-, at-, con-, de-, dis-, ex-, pro-, re-, sub-, tract, -ion, -ive at-trah-ent track trace dray dredge drudge—trudge draggle drai..l trai..l drawl portray trait treat-y treat-ise

TRECHO τρέχω, τροχάω *I run*, τρόχος *a race course*, τροχὸς *a wheel*, τροχᾰλία *a roller*. Trochus *a genus of shells with a winding spire.* Trochilus *a genus of hummingbirds, from its swiftness.* trochee trochanter trochlea-r troche trochoid truck (on wheels) truckle-bed

TRĔMO τρέμω *I tremble, fear*, trem-or, -ulous, -endous trepidation in-trep-id-ity

TRĬ- TRĒS τρεῖς τρί'ᾰ τρĭ- θρι- three; tri-ad, -angle, -dent, -foliate, -ple, -ne, -nity, -vet, trey treble trefoil trestle dri-lling

TRĪCÆ *impediments.* in-, ex-tricate in-trigue trickery treachery (But see Diez, p. 353 at *treccare.*)

TRŪDO (TRŪSŪm,) *to push.* in-, ob-, ex-, pro-trude, -trus-ion, -ive thrust tread

TŬMĔO, *to swell, be inflated.* tum-or, -id, -efy tuber, -ous, -cle contumacy tomb

TŪNDO (TŪSŪm,) *to beat.* con-, ob-, per-, re-tus-e, -ion

TŪRBĂ τύρβη σύρβη *confusion, uproar.* turb-id, -ulent dis-, per-turb trouble

ŪNDĂ *a wave;* ŪNDO, *to surge, be full.* undulate inundate ab-, red-undant ab-, red-ound

ŪR-O (ŪSTŪm,) to b-ur-n; comb-us-tion ŪRT-ĪCĂ *the nettle*, urticaceous

ŪTŎR, *to use;* ŪSŬS use; ut-ensil ut-il-it-ari-an tool ab-use usage usu-ry, -al usurp (RĂPĬO *I rob.*)

VĂCŬŬS *empty.* vac-uum, -uity, -ant, -ate, -ation, -ancy evacuate

VĂCĪLLO, *to waver.* wag vacillate fickle boggle

VĀDO (VĀSŪm,) *to go.* e-, in-, per-vade wade waddle

VĂLĔO, *to be strong.* well val-id, -or, -iant, -ue; pre-, a-, counter-vail invalid

VĂLLŬS *a palisade;* VĀLLŪ^m *a rampart;* PĀLŬS *a stake.* in-terval circumvallation wall pale palisade

VĀS a vess-el; vascular vase

VĀSTŬS *desert, immense.* waste vast devastate

VĔHO (VĔCTŪ^m,) *to carry.* in-veigh vehe-ment vehicle weight

VĔNĬO (VĒNTŪ^m,) *to come, go, happen, suit, fit.* ad-, con-, contra-, inter-, super-vene ad-, con-, circum-, e-, in-, pre-vent re-, a-venue co-venant venture inventory

VĔRTO (VĔRSŪ^m,) *to turn.* a-, ad-, con-, contro-, de-, e-, in-, intro-, ob-, per-, re-, retro-, sub-vert a-, ad-, con-, di-, in-, ob-, per-, uni-, re-vers-e, -ion di-vorce vortex vert-ex, -igo, -ical s-wer-ve t-wir-l wor-m

VĒRŬS *true.* ver-acity, -ify, -dict very aver. *Akin to* pure mere

VĬĂ *a road, passage.* way de-viat-e, -ion devious pre-, im-per-vi-ous en-, con-voy voy-age invoice envoy convey

VĬCĬS *a change;* VĬCĔ *in change, alternation.* vic-ar-ious vic-issitude vis-count vice-regent, -roy

VĬDĔO (VĪSŪ^m,) εἰδέω, *to see, to know.* wit wise vis-ible, -ual, -age, -or, -ard, -ion, -it, -ta pro-vid-ent *or* prudent *or* pur-vey(ant) e-vid-ent, -ence revise proviso sur-vey view in-vid-ious *or* en-vi-ous advise advice*—id-ea id-ol *-OID*

VĬGĬL *watchful.* vigil, -ant, -ance wake watch

VĪNCO (VĪCTŪ^m,) *to conquer, excel.* con-, e-, pro-vince e-, con-vict, -ion victory invincible vanquish

VĪVO (VĪCTŪ^m,) βιόω, *to live.* re-, sur-vive viv-id, -ify, -acity vi-and vital victuals

VŎCO (VŎCĀTŪ^m,) *to call.* vocal voice vow..el vouch voci-ferous con-, equi-, in-, re-, pro-voke

VŌLVO (VŎLŪTŪ^m,) εἰλέω εἱλέω εἰλύω εἱλύω, *to roll, wind.* volu-tion, -te, -me, -ble con-, e-, in-, re-volve re-volt valve wallow waltz weel wheel willow or sallow (SĂLIX)

VŬLGŬS, πόλχος *a crowd.* di-vulg-e pro-mulg-ate vulgar vul-gate folk flock

---

* The French equivalent "avis," is used like *Notice*—something to be looked at, or attended to.

LIST OF THE SUFFIXES

-A adv.
-A n.
-a n. Heb.
-A n. pl.
-able a.
-AC a.
-ach n. ☞ -AC
-ace n.
-AC-eous, -AC-ious a.
-AC-I-Ty
-acle n.
-AC-UL-AR
-AC-y n.
-ac-y n.
-AD n.
-ada n. ☞ **-ade**
-ade n.
-ade n. ☞ *-AD*
-AD-IC a. ☞ *AT-IC*
-ado n. ☞ **-ade**
-Æ n. plural
-ÆUM n.
-age n. collective
-age n.
-aginous a. ☞ -GIN-
-AGO n.
-ah ☞ **-a** n. Heb.
-aice ☞ **-ess** n. fem.
-ail ☞ -L
-ain ☞ -AN
-AL a., n.
-ALE n. ☞ -AL
-AL-IA n. plural
-AL-ITy n.
-als n. pl. ☞ -AL, Obs. 2.
-AN a.
-ANA n. pl.
-ance
-ancy } n.
-and participial
-ANDA n. pl.
-AND
-ANDUM } n., a.
-ane ☞ -AN
-ANeous a.
-AN-ITy n.
-ANT a., n.
-ANT n.
-aque ☞ -AC
-AR n.
-ar n.
-AR, -ARI-, -ARy a., n. (ĀR-ĬS)
-AR- ☞ -AR- formative
-ARIUS ☞ -ARy a.
-ARIUM ☞ -ARy n.
-ARy, -ARI- a., n. (ĀR-ĬŬS)
-ARy n. (ĂR-ĬŬM)
-ard n.
-AS n.
-ass n.
-AS-M n. ☞ *-IS-M*
-AS-T, *-AS-T-IC*
-asy ☞ *-S-IS*
-AT ☞ -ATe
-AT- ☞ *-AS*
-ata ☞ **-ade**
-ATe a.
-AT-IC ☞ *-AS*

-AT-ILe
-AT-IN-ous a. ☞ -AT, &c.
-au n.
-AX n.

-B-
-BER ☞ **-bor**
-BER n.
-BIL- ☞ **-ble**
-BIL-ITy ☞ **ble**
-bl- }
-ble }
-ble ☞ **-ple**
-bl-y ☞ **-ble**
-bor }
-bour } n.
-BR- }
-BRA } ☞ -BER
-BRUM n.
-B-UND
-BUS ☞ -B-

-C- genetic
-C- diminutive
-C- agential }
-CATION }
-ce n.
-ce n. pl. ☞ **-s** pl.
-ce adv.
-cel }
-cello } ☞ **-C-le**
-ch n.
-ch a.
-chre n.
-cil }
-cile } ☞ **-C-le**
-CIN- ☞ -C
-C-le n. dim.
-cle ☞ **-acle**
-C-ous
-C-R-
-cracy ☞ **-ac-y**
-C-UL- n.
-cule, **-cul-ar**, &c. ☞ **-C-le**
-CULUM ☞ **-acle**
-CUND ☞ -C-, -AND
-cy n. **-ce**

-d n.
-d ☞ **-th** n.
-*D* diminutive
-D declensional
-D- ☞ -T- intensive
-D- ☞ -T- participial
-dar n. **-dari** n.
de *of*
-de ☞ **-ed** a.
-den n., a.
-der adv.
-der n.
-DIN- }
-DO } n.
-dom n.
-dor }
-door } n.
-dore }
-DOT-
-D-URe ☞ S-URe

-E imperative
-e feminine
-E neuter
-*E* n.
-E adv.
-E- formative
-e ☞ **-ee**
-ean ☞ -AN
-EC- ☞ -AC
-ece ☞ -*IS*
-ed a.
-ee n.
-eel a.
-een n.
-eer n.
-eer ☞ **-er**, v. infinitive.
-eign, for-eign ☞ -AN, p. 113
-el }
-eil } ☞ -AL

-eme ☞ **-me**
-en part. pres.
-en part. past
-en a.
-en v.
-en n. dim.
-*EN* }
-en } *one*
-EN n. }
-*EN*, siren, σειρὴν }
-en n. plural
-EN a., n. ☞ -AN
-ence }
-ency } ☞ **-ance**
-END ☞ -AND
-ENDA ☞ -ANDA
-ENDO
-ENDous ☞ -AND
-ENDUM ☞ -AND
-ene a.
-enger n.
-EN-ITy ☞ -AN-ITy
-ENS part. pres.
-ENS-IC }
-ENS-IS } a.
-ENT ☞ -ANT
-eon ☞ **-on**
-Eous a.
-er v. frequentative
-er v. infinitive
-ER a.
-er a. comparative
-ER- declensional
-ER n. agential
-er n. plural
-er n. masculine
-ER ☞ -R- formative
-er n. ☞ -AR
-ere ☞ **-re** adv.
-ere a. ☞ **-rous**
-erial ☞ -R
-ER-N ☞ -UR-N
-ern a.
-ERN n.
-ERN-AL, -ITy ☞ -UR-N
-ery ☞ -ARy
-ERy ☞ -Ry
-ES n. sing.
-ES n. pl.
-es' ☞ **-'s**
-ESCe v. }
-ESC-ent a. }
-ESC-ence n. }
-ese a., n.
-ese a. ☞ -S-US
-esima-l ☞ -SIM ordinal
-esque a., n.
-ESS n. fem.
-es }
-ess } n.
-esse }
-est a. superlative
-EST a., n.
-ES-T-IC ☞ -EST, -*AS-T*
-esty ☞ -EST
-et ☞ -ATe
-*ET*, -*ETE he who*
-et }
-etta }
-ette } n. dim.
-etto }
-et n.
-et ☞ **-ade**
-et (caret) ☞ -IT verbial
-*ET-IC* a.
-ETUM n.
-eum n.
-eur ☞ -OR
-EX ☞ -AX
-ey- ☞ **-ee** n.
-ey ☞ **-y** a.

-F ☞ -B-
-FERous
-FIC a.
-fice n.
-ful a.
-fy v.

-G ☞ -C-, -IG-
-g n.
-gar n. *he who*
-ge n.
-*GEN* ☞ -C-
-geon
GIN-
-glio n.
-go n.
-gy n.

-h
-head n. }
-hood n. }

-I genitive
-I- diminutive
-I- connective
-I n. plural
-I- formative
I adverbial
-i- ☞ **-y** a.
-I-A n.
-I-A n. plural
-IAN ☞ -AN
-ible ☞ **-ble**
-IC a., n.
-IC-A n., IC-AT-ORy
-ICal a., -ICally adv.
-ice n. (ITIA)
-ice ☞ -AX, -AC-eous
-ice ☞ -*IS*
-ice ☞ -ESS n. fem.
-iche ☞ -*IS*
-IC-ian ☞ -AC, -AN
-ICI-ous ☞ -IT-ial, **-ice**
-IC-I-Ty ☞ -AC-I-Ty
-icle ☞ **-acle**
-ICS ☞ -IC
-IC-UL-AR
-IC-UL-ATe
-IC-UL-AT-ION
-IC-UL-OuS
-ID adj.

-*ID* ☞ -*AD*
-ide n.
-*IDES* n. plural
-idge ☞ **-ouch**
-IDI-ous
-ie n.
-ier ☞ **-eer**
-iff ☞ -IVe
-IG-, -IG-ATe
-IG-N- a.
-IGO ☞ -AGO
-IL- ☞ -UL-
-ILe, -IL-, -ILI-
-IL-ITy ☞ -AL-ITy
-ilio }
-illa } ☞ -L, -UL-
-ille }
-illo }
-ILL-ATe, -AT-ION
-im }
-ime }
-imo } a.
-IM-US, -A, -UM }
-IM adv.
-im n.
-īm n. plural
-in }
-INA } n. dim.
-ine }
-IN-
-IN-, INe ☞ -AN
-IN n.
-in ☞ **-en** n. pl.
-INÆ n. plural
-INe a.
-INe n. fem.
-ing n.
-ing n. dim.
-ing part. pres.
-inge n.
-inger ☞ **-enger** n.
-IN-ITy ☞ -AN-ITy
-*INX* ☞ **-inge**
-ION n.

-ion-er (parish-ion-er)
-IOR ☞ **-er** *more*
-ique ☞ -IC
-is n.
-IS n.
-IS genitive
-is-ation n. ☞ **-ise v.**
-isco ☞ **esque**
-ise v.
-ise n.
-ish v.
-ish a.
-ish ☞ *-IS*
-ish ☞ ESCe
-ISK n. diminutive
-IS-M n.
-isse ☞ Ac-eous
-IS-T n.
-ist-er n.
-IS-T-IC a.
-IT n.
-IT- *often*
-IT verbial (audit)
-IT, -ITE n.
-IT, -ITe ☞ -ATe
-ITE, -ITES ☞ *-OID*
-IT-ial
-ITIate }
-ITIously }
-ITIS n. *disease*
-ito n. diminutive
-ITy ☞ -Ty
-IV- } a.
-IVe } a.
-IV-AL
-IX n. feminine
-ize ☞ **-ise** v.
-izo n. (mestizo)

K
-k n.
-ket n.
-key n. diminutive
-kin n. diminutive

-L
-L n. dim. ☞ **-L**
-L- ☞ -UL-
-le ☞ -L, -AL
-ledge n. (know-ledge)
-L-ENT ☞ UL-ENT
-less a.
-let n. diminutive
-li- ☞ **-ly**
-lic n.
-lin n. diminutive
-ling n.
-lio n. ☞ **-glio**
-lion n.
-ll ☞ -L ¶ 1
-lock n. *a plant*
*LOG*y
-lot ☞ **-let**
L-US, -A, -UM
-ly *like, manner*

-M intensive
-M- participial
-M accusative
-m dative
-m diminutive
-M adverbial
-M n. ☞ -B-
-m } n.
-MA } n.
*-MAN*cy
-me } n. ☞ **-m**
-ME } n. ☞ **-m**
-me } a.
-mo } a.
-MEN ☞ **-m**
-ment ☞ **-m**
-mer a.
-MIN- ☞ **-m**
-MIN }
-MN- }
-mo ☞ **-me** a.
-MON ☞ **-m**
-MONy, -MONI- n.

-most a. ☞ **-mer**
-M-UL-
-M-US, -A, -UM n.
-mus n.
-MUS a. ☞ **-me**

-N- intensive
-N declensional
-n infin. ☞ **-en v.**
-n n. diminutive
-N adverbial
-N participial ☞ -N-US
-*N* n. masculine
-*N* neuter ☞ -*ON* ¶ 5
-n-, **-ne** ☞ -*N* n.
-N-AL a.
-ne ☞ -AN
-ne n. pl. ☞ **-en** pl.
-nel n. dim.
-NEoUS ☞ -N-oUS
-ner
-ness
-N-ITy
-nkey ☞ **C-le**
-N-oUS
-NT a. ☞ -ANT
-N-US, -A, -UM

-O- adverbial
-O- connective
-O declensional
-O nominative
-O genitive ☞ § 53
-O ablative
-O imperative
-O n., a.
-OCious ☞ -AC-eous
-OC-I-Ty ☞ -AC-I-Ty
-ock n. *small*
-ock n. *large*
-ock n. verbal
-OCR- ☞ -C-R-
-*OD* n.
-*ODE* n. (ge-ode) ☞ -*OID*
-*OID* a., n.
-oir n. ☞ -ARy n.
-oir n. ☞ -ER agency
-OL- ☞ -UL-
-ol (vitri-ol) ☞ -L
-OL-ENT ☞ -UL-ENT
-OL-IC a.
-om n.
-om adv.
-*OMA* n.
-ON n.
-*ON* n.
-on n. deteriorative
-on ☞ **-en** v.
-on ☞ **-en** n. dim.
-on ☞ -AN
-on, **-one**, **-oon** } n. augmentative
-ond a. ☞ -AND, -UND
-OR n.
-OR- ☞ -ER declensional
-OR- n. ☞ -ER- agency
-OR a. ☞ **-er** *more*
-OR- ☞ -R- formative.
-ORy, -ORI-, **-orio**, -ORIUM } ☞ -ARy n.
-*OS* n.
-OSe, -OS- a.
-OS-ITy
-OSO n., a.
-osy n. (lepr-osy)
-ot n.
-ot n. diminutive
-*OT* n.
-ōth n.
-*OT-IC* a.
-otte ☞ **-et**, **-ot**
-ouch n. diminutive
-our n.
-oUS a.
-OuS ☞ -OSe
-ouch n.

-ow n., a., v.
-OX ☞ -AX

-P ☞ -B-
-PED ☞ *-POD*
-PLe
-PLEX } a.
-POD
-P-UL
-PUS ☞ *-POD*

-R- formative
-R declensional
-R permutative
-r v. freq. ☞ **-er**
-r v. infinitive
-r possessive
-R adverbial
-R a. ☞ -ER
-R n. ☞ -OR
-R, **-re** ☞ -ER agential
-r plural ☞ **-er** plural
-re ☞ -ER
-re ☞ -R- formative
-red n.
-rel n. diminutive
-re-n n. plural
-ress ☞ -T-RIX, **-ess**
-ric n.
-ril ☞ **-rel**
-rit n.
-R-IX ☞ -T-RIX
-R-oUS a.
-R-OuS a. ☞ -OSe
-R-US, -A, -UM
-Ry

-s n. plural
's n.
-S adv.
-S- ☞ -IT-
-S- mutational
-S- inflectional
-S- ☞ -T- participial

-S-A ☞ -S-US
-sair ☞ -T-ER
-san
-SC- ☞ -ESCe
-se n. ☞ *-S-IS*
-se a. ☞ -S- participial
-se ☞ **-s**
-se ☞ **'s**
-se v.
-sel
-sh ☞ -ESC
-sh ☞ *-ISK*
-sh ☞ **-k**
-ship
-S-IA n. ☞ *-S-IS*
-S-IC-ian
-SIM- ordinal
-SIM- ☞ -T-IM- a.
-S-ION n.
-S-IS n.
-S-IVe
-SM n.
-some a.
-son n.
-S-OR ☞ T-ER
-sp n.
-ST n.
-st n.
-st a. ☞ **-est** *most*
-st adv.
-stead n,
-ster n.
-S-TER
-str-ess ☞ **-ster**
-S-TR
-S-TRI-, -AN } ☞ S-TER
-SURA
-S-URe }
-S-US
-sy
-S-YNE

-t a., n.
-T- repetitive ☞ -IT-

-T- factitive
-T- intensive
-T- declensional
T participial
-t dim. ☞ **-et**
-t neuter
-T- connective
-T ☞ -IT verbial
-*T*- mutational
-*T* ☞ -*ET* n.
-t n. ☞ **-th**
-T adverbial
-*TA* n. pl. ☞ -*A*
-T-AN-Eous ☞ T participial
-T-ARy a.
-te
-T-ee ☞ -ATe
-T-ER n.
-ter n.
-ter v. frequentative
-TER } a.
-TERIOR } a.
-ter prepositional
-*TER-ION* n.
-T-ER-N ☞ -UR-N
-*T-ES* n.
-*TH*- ☞ T intensive
-th n.
-th adverbial
-ther ☞ -TER a.
-*THO*- ☞ S-US
-thor n. ☞ -T-ER n.
-THRUM ☞ -TRUM
-TI- ☞ -Ty
-T-IC
-tide
-T-IL-, -TILe
-T-IM- adv.
-T-IM- n.
-T-IM superlative
-T-IN- }
-T-INe }
-T-ION n.
-*T-IS* ☞ -*S-IS*

-T-IV- } a.
-T-IVe } a.
-ton
-T-OR ☞ -T-ER n.
-T-ous a.
-TR- ☞ T-ER
-*T-RA* ☞ -T-R-UM n.
-tre ☞ -T-R-UM n.
-tress } n. fem.
-T-R-IX } n. fem.
-T-R-UM n.
-t-ry n.
-TU-AL a.
-T-UDe n.
-T-URe n.
-T-URe ☞ -S-URe
-T-US, -A, -UM
-Ty
-*T-YL* (dactyl)

-U- ☞ -B-
-uble ☞ **-ble**
UC- ☞ -AC
-UC-ous ☞ -AC
UD-, -UDe n. } ☞ -T-UDe
-UD-IN-ous } ☞ -T-UDe
-UDO n. ☞ -DO
-ue ☞ U participial
Ue (stat-ue) ☞ -IVe
-ue ☞ -US, Obs.
-UGIN- ☞ -UGO
-UGO n.
-UI- ☞ UoUS
-U-IT-ous
-UL- pletive
-UL-A n. dim.
-UL-AR -ITy, -UL-AR-Ly
-ule ☞ -U-LA
-UL-ENce ☞ -UL-ENT
-UL-ENT
-UL-oUS
-UL-T, -U-oUS.
-UL-UM ☞ -UL-A

-UM n.
-um n. fem. ☞ -UM n. Obs. 2
-UM genitive plural
-U-Me, -U-MEN ☞ -*MA*.
-UM-N
-UMNAL } ☞ -MN-
-UNCle
-UNC-UL-US } ☞ **C-le**
-UND
-UND-ITy } ☞ -AND
-UNe, -UN-ITy ☞ -AN
-UoUS
-UR ☞ -ER agency
-URe, -UR- n.
-URe ☞ -R-oUS
-URe a., n. ☞ T-URe.
-ure n.
-ur-et n.
-URI-
-URI-ENT
-UR-N
-URy, -URI- n.
-US n.
-US-T
-UT ☞ -UD
-UTe ☞ -ATe
-UUM ☞ UoUS

-V- ☞ -B-
-VER-
-ver ☞ **-bor**
-VI- ☞ -IVe

-ward
-ways adv.
-wise ☞ **-ways**

-X n. ☞ -AX
-x n. pl. ☞ **-s**
-XILLARy
-xt adverbial

-y ☞ **-ee** n.
-y n.
-y n. ☞ E formative
-y n. ☞ **-ing** n. dim.
-y n. dim.
-y a.
-y adv. ☞ **-ly**
-y v.
-ye ☞ **-ie**
-y-er n.
-*YNX* n.
-*YR* ☞ -ER n.
-YX ☞ -AX

-za n.
-zan ☞ **-san** n.
-ze v.
-zen n.

STEREOTYPED BY L. JOHNSON & CO.

CATALOGUE

OF

Approved School and College Text-Books.

PUBLISHED BY E. H. BUTLER & CO.,

137 South Fourth Street, Philadelphia.

Goodrich's Pictorial History of the United States.

A Pictorial History of the United States, with notices of other portions of America. By S. G. GOODRICH, author of "Peter Parley's Tales." For the use of Schools Revised and improved edition, brought down to the present time (1860). Re-written and newly illustrated. 1 vol. 12mo., embossed backs. Upwards of 450 pages.

Goodrich's American Child's Pictorial History of

the United States. An introduction to the author's "Pictorial History of the United States."

Goodrich's Pictorial History of England. A Pic-

torial History of England. By S. G. GOODRICH, author of "Pictorial History of the United States," etc.

Goodrich's Pictorial History of Rome. A Pictorial

History of Ancient Rome, with sketches of the History of Modern Italy. By S. G GOODRICH, author of "Pictorial History of the United States." For the use of Schools. Revised and improved edition.

Goodrich's Pictorial History of Greece. A Pictorial History of Greece; Ancient and Modern. By S. G. GOODRICH, author of "Pictorial History of the United States." For the use of Schools. Revised edition.

Goodrich's Pictorial History of France. A Pictorial History of France. For the use of Schools. By S. G. GOODRICH, author of "Pictorial History of the United States." Revised and improved edition, brought down to the present time.

Goodrich's Parley's Common School History of the World. A Pictorial History of the World; Ancient and Modern. For the use of Schools. By S. G. GOODRICH, author of "Pictorial History of the United States," etc. Illustrated by engravings.

Goodrich's First History. The First History. An Introduction to Parley's Common School History. Designed for beginners at Home and School. Illustrated by Maps and Engravings. By S. G. GOODRICH, author of the Pictorial Series of Histories, etc.

Goodrich's Pictorial Natural History; Embracing a View of the Mineral, Vegetable, and Animal Kingdoms. For the use of Schools. By SAMUEL G. GOODRICH. 300 engravings, 1 vol. 12mo.

Geographie Elementaire a l'Usage des Ecoles et des Familles. Illustrée par 15 cartes et 30 Gravures. Par PETER PARLEY.

Histoire des Etats Unis d'Amerique, avec Notices des autres parties du Nouveau Monde. Par SAMUEL G. GOODRICH.

Petite Histoire Universelle a l'Usage des Ecoles et des Familles. Par S. G. GOODRICH.

Mitchell's First Lessons in Geography. First Lessons in Geography; for young children. Designed as an Introduction to the author's Primary Geography. By S. AUGUSTUS MITCHELL, author of a Series of Geographical Works. Illustrated with maps and numerous engravings.

Mitchell's New Primary Geography. (The second book of the Series.) An Easy Introduction to the Study of Geography. Introductory to the New Intermediate Geography. Illustrated by nineteen colored Maps and nearly one hundred Engravings. By S. AUGUSTUS MITCHELL. 1 vol. small 4to. This is an entirely new and beautiful book.

Mitchell's New Intermediate Geography. An entirely new work. The maps are all engraved on copper, in the best manner, and brought down to the present date. It is profusely illustrated with beautiful engravings, and is the most complete quarto Geography ever issued in the world.

Mitchell's New School Geography and Atlas. Entirely new.—Text, Maps, Illustrations,—ready January 1st, 1865.

Mitchell's New Ancient Geography. An Ancient Geography, Classical and Sacred. By S. AUGUSTUS MITCHELL. An entirely new edition, drawn from the best authorities, ancient and modern. Designed for the use of Schools and Colleges. Illustrated with numerous Engravings. 12mo. muslin.

Mitchell's Primary Geography (Old Series). An Easy Introduction to the study of Geography. Designed for the instruction of children in Schools and Families. Illustrated by nearly one hundred Engravings and sixteen colored Maps. By S. AUGUSTUS MITCHELL.

Mitchell's School Geography and Atlas (Old Series). New Revised Edition. A System of Modern Gegography, comprising a description of the present state of the World, and its five great divisions, America, Europe, Asia, Africa, and Oceanica, with their several Empires, Kingdoms, States, Territories, etc. Embellished by numerous engravings. Adapted to the capacity of youth. Accompanied by an Atlas containing thirty-two maps, drawn and engraved expressly for this work. By S. AUGUSTUS MITCHELL.

Mitchell's Ancient Geography and Atlas (Old Series).

First Edition. Designed for Academies, Schools, and Families. A System of Classical and Sacred Geography, embellished with engravings of remarkable events, views of ancient cities, and various interesting antique remains. Together with an Ancient Atlas, containing maps illustrating the work. By S. AUGUSTUS MITCHELL.

Mitchell's Geographical Question Book (Old Series).

Comprising Geographical Definitions, and containing questions on all the maps of Mitchell's School Atlas; to which is added an Appendix, embracing valuable Tables in Mathematical and Physical Geography.

Mitchell's Biblical Geography. Sabbath School

Geography, designed for instruction in Sabbath School and Bible Classes, illustrated with colored maps and wood-cut engravings. By S. AUGUSTUS MITCHELL.

Hows' Primary Ladies' Reader. Primary Ladies'

Reader, a choice collection of Prose and Poetry, adapted to the capacities of young children.

Hows' Junior Ladies' Reader. A choice and varied

collection of Prose and Verse, with a synopsis of the Elementary Principles of Elocution; expressly adapted for the use of the young, and designed as an introduction to the Ladies' Reader. By JOHN W. S. HOWS, Professor of Elocution.

Hows' Ladies' Reader. Designed for the use of

Ladies' Schools and Family Reading Circles; comprising choice selections from standard authors, in Prose and Poetry, with the essential Rules of Elocution, simplified and arranged for strictly practical use. By JOHN W. S. HOWS, Professor of Elocution.

Hows' Ladies' Book of Readings and Recitations.

The Ladies' Book of Readings and Recitations: a collection of approved Extracts from Standard authors, intended for the use of Higher Classes in schools and seminaries, and for Family Reading Circles. By JOHN W. S. HOWS, author of "The Ladies' Reader," "The Junior Ladies' Reader," "The Ladies First Reader," etc., etc., etc.

www.ingramcontent.com/pod-product-compliance
Lightning Source LLC
LaVergne TN
LVHW010234110826
845151LV00004B/1287

9781425525200